Research
Concepts in
Human
Behavior

The Century Psychology Series

Kenneth MacCorquodale, Gardner Lindzey,
Kenneth E. Clark

Editors

G. C. HELMSTADTER
Arizona State University

Research
Concepts in
Human Behavior

Education, Psychology,
Sociology

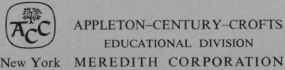
APPLETON–CENTURY–CROFTS
EDUCATIONAL DIVISION
New York   MEREDITH CORPORATION

ACKNOWLEDGMENTS

FOR FIG. 1.1, P. 13, FROM LADIES DAY by Mady. Copyright, General Features Corp.
Reprinted with permission.

FOR EXCERPT, P. 29, FROM J. Turner, *Science,* 4 Sept. 1959, **130,** 533.

FOR ONE EXCERPT, CH. 3; SIX EXCERPTS, CH. 4; FIG. 4.2, P. 107, FROM D. Campbell, & J. Stanley, *Experimental and Quasi-experimental Designs for Research,* Chicago, Rand McNally,
1963, pp. 7, 13, 15, 17, 21, 24, 25, 32, 33, 37, 43, 47, 55, 57, and Fig. 4, p. 62.

FOR TABLE 3.1, P. 84, FROM K. Schaie, "A General Model for the Study of Developmental
Problems," *Psychological Bulletin,* **64,** 1965, 93. Copyright 1965 by the American Psychological Association, and reproduced by permission.

FOR THIRTY-THREE EXCERPTS, CH. 4, FROM M. Dunnette, "Fads, Fashions and Folderol in Psychology," *American Psychologist,* **21,** 1966, 343, 344, 345, 346, 347, 348, 349, 350. Copyright 1966 by the American Psychological Association, and reproduced by permission.

FOR TABLE 4.2, P. 122, FROM E. Allen, "Why Are Research Grant Applications Disapproved,"
Science, 25 Nov. 1960, **132,** Table 1, p. 1532. Copyright 1960 by the American Association
for the Advancement of Science.

FOR FIG. 5.1, P. 137, FROM J. Becker, & R. Hayes, *Information Storage and Retrieval,* New
York, Wiley, 1964, Exhibit 1, p. 134.

FOR FIG. 5.3, P. 144, FROM C. White et al., *Sources of Information in the Social Sciences,*
Totawa, N.J., The Bedminster Press, 1964, p. 211. Reprinted by permission.

FOR FIG. 5.4, P. 146, FROM *Education Index,* 1967, **36**(4), 194. Bronx, N.Y., H. W. Wilson
Company.

FOR FIG. 5.5, P. 148. Reprinted with permission of the Macmillan Company from *Encyclopedia of Educational Research,* 3rd ed., by C. Harris, & M. Liba, p. 678. Copyright 1950 by
the American Educational Research Association.

FOR FIG. 5.6, P. 150, FROM J. Milholland, "Theory and Techniques of Assessment," *Annual
Review of Psychology,* 1964, **15,** 337. Reproduced from *Annual Review of Psychology,*
Volume 15, 1964, by permission of Annual Reviews Inc.

FOR FIG. 5.7, P. 152, FROM American Psychological Association, *Psychological Abstracts,* **41,**
1967, 881. Copyright 1967 by the American Psychological Association, and reproduced by
permission.

FOR FIG. 5.8, P. 153, FROM E. Hearst "Stress Induced Breakdown of an Appetitive Discrimination," *Journal of the Experimental Analysis of Behavior,* 1965, **8,** 139. Copyright 1965 by
the Society for the Experimental Analysis of Behavior, Inc.

FOR ADAPTATIONS STARTING WITH I, P. 158 TO END OF CH. FROM Seminar on Information Sources in the Behavioral Sciences, presented at the 75th annual convention of the American Psychological Association, Washington, D.C., 5 Sept. 1967, Exhibits 10–17.

FOR FIG. 6.11, P. 194. Reprinted by permission of Burgess Publishing Company, from *Biometric Analysis: An Introduction,* 1951, by A. Treloar. Fig. 37, p. 171.

FOR FIG. 6.13, P. 197. Reprinted by permission of Burgess Publishing Company, from *Random Sampling Distributions,* by A. Treloar, 1942. Fig. 20, p. 57.

FOR FIG. 6.14, P. 197, AND FIG. 6.15, P. 198. Reprinted by permission of Burgess Publishing Company, from *Biometric Analysis: An Introduction,* 1951, by A. Treloar. Figs. 33 and 32, p. 156.

FOR FIG. 7.1, P. 290; FIG. 7.2, P. 297; FIG. 7.3, P. 302; FIG. 7.4, P. 305; TABLE 7.1, P. 296; SIXTEEN EXCERPTS, CH. 7; AND TWO EXCERPTS, CH. 8, FROM *Principles of Psychological Measurement* by G. C. Helmstadter. Copyright © 1964 by Meredith Corporation. Reprinted by permission of Appleton-Century-Crofts. Fig. 7, p. 77; Fig. 8, p. 88; Fig. 18, p. 116; Fig. 19, p. 120; Table 8, p. 85; pp. 10, 16, 33, 45, 56, 58, 65, 70, 73, 87, 92, 96, 112, 129, 134, 156; pp. 180, 183.

FOR TABLE 7.2, P. 316, FROM D. Campbell, & D. Fiske, "Convergent and Discriminant Validation by the Multitrait Multimethod Matrix," *Psychological Bulletin,* **56,** 1959, 82. Copyright 1959 by the American Psychological Association, and reproduced by permission.

FOR FIG. 7.5, P. 322, FROM *Kuder Preference Record Occupational Form D:* Manual by G. Frederic Kuder. Copyright © 1956, 1959, by G. Frederic Kuder. Reprinted by permission of the publisher, Science Research Associates, Inc., Chicago, Illinois. Fig. 3, "Distribution of V Scores of Sixty-Two College Students Attempting to Conceal the Fact That They Were Faking," p. 14.

FOR FIG. 8.3, P. 334, FROM M. Hansen, W. Hurwitz, & W. Madow, *Sample Survey Methods and Theory,* Vol. 1, New York, Wiley, 1953.

FOR FIG. 8.4, P. 347, FROM R. Cattell, "The Three Basic Factor-Analytic Research Designs—Their Inter-relations and Derivatives," *Psychological Bulletin,* **49,** 1952, 581. Copyright 1952 by the American Psychological Association, and reproduced by permission.

FOR FIG. 8.7, P. 366, FROM *Techniques of Attitude Scale Construction* by Allen L. Edwards. Copyright © 1957, by Appleton-Century-Crofts, Inc. Adapted by permission. Fig. 2.2, p. 26.

FOR FIG. 8.9, P. 374, FROM L. Huttner, & R. Katzell, "Developing a Yardstick of Supervisory Performance," *Personnel,* **33,** items 1 and 2 from p. 373, 1957. Reprinted by permission of the American Management Association.

FOR TABLE 9.1, P. 399, FROM R. Daniel, & C. Louttit, *Professional Problems in Psychology,* Englewood Cliffs, N.J., Prentice-Hall, 1953, Table 12, p. 186. By permission of Prof. Daniel.

FOR NINE EXCERPTS, CH. 9, FROM K. Goldhammer, & S. Elam, *Dissemination and Implementation,* Third Annual Phi Delta Kappa Symposium on Educational Research, Bloomington, Indiana, Phi Delta Kappa 1962, pp. 84, 86, 88, 102, 125, 162, 180, 196.

To my students
who have convinced me of a need for this book,
and to my wife and children
who have made it possible for me to produce it.

Preface

It often becomes distressing to a teacher who is concerned with developing broad understandings to see the knowledge explosion bombard us with billions of new facts, ideas, and concepts. For, how can such information possibly be transmitted to future generations without dividing the pie into increasingly small slivers called specialties?

Yet, when one considers methodological rather than substantive knowledge, there is a glimmer of hope. Methodologically, the expansion has been as much in applying techniques developed in one specialty to other subject areas as it has been in the refinement of the approaches themselves. Thus, when methodological knowledge increases, it also becomes more general. The result is that a point has now been reached where the preparation of a single book which describes the basic logic and principles of studying human behavior, whether from an educational, a psychological, or a sociological point of view, seems both feasible and desirable. The hope in writing this volume, therefore, has been to summarize, for a wide variety of beginning students, the major approaches to studying human beings.

It was not intended that this text provide detailed instruction in the use of all the techniques which have been developed and used in each of the three major disciplines concerned with the discovery and application of molar principles of human behavior. In fact, it is not really a "how to" book at all. Rather, the main emphasis has been to (1) provide the student with a broad perusal of current methodological *ideas* which are common to all three fields, and (2) to provide some guidance as to where to look for information that is essential should one engage in research. Specific techniques and methods have been presented in detail to illustrate very general approaches that are broadly useful or to provide a knowledge basic to the reading of research results in the area.

Special care has been taken to present science not as something at odds with the rest of society, but as a straight-forward extension of older forms of inquiry—an extension which, while making use of many methods, follows a single, general, logical pattern that has been found to be highly useful. Also, because the author has found it to be of special value in teaching his own classes in research methods, the discussion of the basic logical steps of the scientific approach has been used to introduce modern concepts about the formulation of hypotheses, the nature of proof, and decision theory.

Consistent with the general approach of presenting basic ideas rather than specific procedures, the chapter on statistics emphasizes the logic of statistical reasoning rather than computation. Although some numerical examples have been included to help make the concepts more concrete, the formulas used are always presented in a form designed to facilitate the understanding of the ideas they represent rather than the actual handling of data. Similarly, the chapter on measurement suggests the major logical approaches to obtaining numerical descriptions of human behavior rather provides specific information about particular instruments or techniques. For example, the section on factor analysis describes the basic purposes of the technique, its basic assumptions, and the kind of problems for which a factor analysis approach is likely to be useful, rather than presents numerical procedures for obtaining factor analysis results.

Finally, to bring the student abreast with the modern trend in research on behavior, special emphasis has been given to controlled experimentation. In addition to the usual description of the experimental process and its advantages and disadvantages, a special section on the study of single organisms in controlled situations has been included. Similarly, the student's attention has been directed to Schaie's general model for the study of developmental problems, and considerable space has been devoted to a summary of the excellent discussion of experimental and quasi-experimental designs presented by Campbell and Stanley in the recent *Handbook of Research on Teaching*.

By thus concentrating on general methodological principles useful in all disciplines concerned with the study of molar human behavior, the present book should be helpful both as a general orientation for interested students from other areas and as a basic foundation upon which specific methodological know-how can be developed by those who later will become specialists in psychology, in education, and in sociology.

I am indebted to the Literary Executor of the late Sir Ronald A. Fisher, F.R.S., to Dr. Frank Yates, F.R.S., and to Oliver and Boyd Ltd., Edinburgh, for permission to reprint Table VII from their book *Statistical Tables for Biological, Agricultural and Medical Research*.

G.C.H.

Contents

I.

Orientation
to Research

1.

The Nature and Function of Research

RESEARCH AND ITS PLACE IN THE BEHAVIORAL SCIENCES

Research Defined

USE AND MISUSE OF THE TERM "RESEARCH" The words *science* and *research* carry an aura of respect. Their prestige is so great that almost anything to which they are applied tends to be accepted without question and, consequently, they are applied to situations far beyond the scope of their actual meaning. The extension of the term research to mean any sort of investigation, or to a verb describing the fact that some problem is being investigated, obviously serves the user by making the listener more receptive to what follows. This practice, however, does not lead to the kind of understanding that provided these words with their original prestige. It would thus seem appropriate to preface any discussion of research methods with a clear statement about the specific kind of activity referred to when the practicing scientist uses the term research.

OPERATIONAL DEFINITIONS One's first inclination, in defining a word, is to examine the word itself to see whether its component parts might suggest a true and absolute meaning. This practice is dangerous, however, for it makes two assumptions that are not always valid. First, it assumes that each component retains its literal meaning in combination; and second, it presumes that the present use of the term is the same as its original use.

3

Thus, an attempt to define research as a process of searching again does not provide very satisfactory results.

A more pragmatic approach to defining such terms as research and science usually will provide more acceptable definitions. For example, one might make a list of all those things or activities which are labeled research and describe the characteristics they have in common. But even this definition is likely to be inadequate, for it will be too inclusive. A second step is required. Starting with the preliminary definition, one also should list as many different things or activities that fit the description. To the extent that items appear on the list which are not ordinarily called research, the definition as originally formulated needs to be refined to be more specific or exclusive.

Even when this procedure is used it will not lead to an exact definition in the sense of providing a description including only those things called research and excluding only those things not called research. However, the operational approach will ordinarily lead to a definition that assures the maximum number of correct classifications of activities; and it thus results in the minimum amount of misunderstandings it is possible to achieve in language which must be imprecise because it substitutes words for actual experiences.

RESEARCH AS STRUCTURED PROBLEM SOLVING   Almost everyone who tries out the procedure described above, whether he applies his own logical judgment or whether he empirically gathers actual statements from others as to the way they use the terms, will arrive at a modern definition of research which describes it as some sort of structured problem solving. The few ambiguities which remain are those having to do with a specification as to which problem solving structures (i.e., techniques) and what kinds of problems are acceptable.

No specific list of acceptable techniques can or even should be provided for, as knowledge advances, new techniques become available and older, less useful approaches are discarded. For purposes of definition, however, it might be noted that the word *structured* refers to any one of several specific techniques that are currently accepted as adequate by scholars in the field under consideration.

To help exclude the activity involved when a student seeks an answer to a question posed by his teacher, for the purpose of having him become acquainted with known facts, the word *problem* should be restricted to a problem faced by society to which no one has yet been able to give a satisfactory answer. Once a problem has been solved and recorded, the transmission of the information to others is a matter of communication and teaching, not research. Thus, as far as this text is concerned, the activity of looking up facts and other information will not come under the heading of research (even though many lay persons use the term in this way), unless the activity also involves a reorganization or an integration of the facts in a new way to shed light on a new problem.

It is also important to note that the term research *does* include the formulation of hypotheses and the development of theories as well as the gathering of evidence to test these generalizations. The person who seeks to make projections of what is likely to happen and who is interested in tying together a set of known principles does so in the hope that new relationships will come to light and that hitherto unknown implications will be found.

In summary then, an operationally useful (though perhaps not rationally perfect) definition of research can be given: Research is the activity of solving problems which leads to new knowledge using methods of inquiry which are currently accepted as adequate by scholars in the field.

The Values of Research

THE ULTIMATE GOAL OF RESEARCH   Once research is recognized as a sophisticated approach to solving man's problems, then its value to society is immediately apparent. One need only ask where mankind would be had someone not taken the time to solve problems in a rational and realistic way. We have come a long way from trial-and-error research, but the ultimate goal of research—that of improving mankind—remains the same.

PRACTICAL BENEFITS TO SOCIETY   Even though each of us is surrounded by modern conveniences which represent the practical result of research, some people still feel that research in general, and the more basic kinds of research in particular, are a great waste of time, effort, and money. Others blame scientific investigators and their new knowledge for most, if not all, of society's current ills.

A moment's reflection, however, makes it clear that, even without any practical values, fundamental research is just as much a cultural activity as painting, sculpturing, or playing music and deserves the same kind of support as does a museum or a concert. The study of the history of science also reveals that it is the more basic studies which lead to the greatest number of practical benefits to mankind. Not every study, basic or practical, is worthwhile; but society has discovered that enough studies do pay off in the hard, practical, concrete sense to more than compensate for the cost of those that lead up blind alleys.

Those who attempt to blame some of the tensions of our times on research and the discovery of knowledge fail to recognize the essentially neutral character of problem solving. The knowledge gained from the more basic types of research can be used for good or ill; in applying research specifically toward the destruction of man, the essence of neutrality is not as clear. The power that can be used to destroy man, however, can also be used to protect him from his enemies; the efficient teaching technique which can be used to control man can just as well be used to keep him free. To do without the power or to use inefficient teaching methods will not solve the problem: both sides will still be represented. Attempts will be made to solve problems in any case, and the function of research is to see that they are solved on the basis of evidence rather than opinion, prejudice, or dogmatism. In a very real sense, then, the practical benefit of research to society is to enable man to implement more efficiently his value judgments.

BENEFITS TO THE INVESTIGATOR HIMSELF   In addition to the improvement of mankind and the practical benefits of solving one's own problems in an efficient way, research can be a rewarding personal experience. Although not everyone can find the same thrill in research as did Galileo (whose life was endangered as a result of his work), or Fechner (who nearly went blind studying visual phenomena), or the unnamed histologist (who, with a razor, removed most of the skin from his leg to study the cutaneous membrane), almost all researchers enjoy the intellectual freedom, the independence of thought, the rise above everyday humdrum that comes from participating in a creative discovery of a solution to a problem.

The possibility of self-improvement might be mentioned. This can come in many ways. For example, the more research one conducts, the less dogmatic one generally becomes. Without research, one is easily lulled into the belief that his own particular experiences and perceptions are the only ones possible, and that therefore there must be something wrong with those who see things differently. While putting one's pet ideas to the test is often discomforting (as Campbell and Stanley, 1963, have pointed out: "the ecology of our science is one in which there are available many more wrong responses than correct ones"), it forces the researcher to maintain the flexibility so essential to intellectual survival in a world where knowledge is expanding so rapidly. Doing research is also beneficial to the individual in that it requires him to think problems through in specific, operational terms rather than hiding in fuzzy generalizations, thus providing practice in accurate, clear, and concise self-expression. Finally, for the individual investigator, there is the satisfaction of making a contribution, of knowing that one's efforts will make our world a little better place in which to live.

THE SCIENTIFIC APPROACHES TO KNOWLEDGE

The Essential Characteristics of Science

Earlier, research was described as some form of structured problem solving. Although the word *science* was mentioned, no emphasis was given to the fact that in today's culture one can hardly think of the word *research* without also thinking of science. Further, somewhere in your past experience, it is likely that you have learned to visualize the methods of science as the most sophisticated approach to problem solving. It thus seems appropriate to take the time to examine this term more closely by asking, "What is this thing we so proudly hail?" and "What is the logic of its method that we so diligently follow?"

In times past, the word *science* was associated strictly with the study of specific subject matter areas. Among some lay persons, even today, the word science refers to physics, chemistry, biology, geology, and the like. As our knowledge has expanded, however, new subject matters have appeared, and the task of classifying them as scientific or nonscientific by earlier criteria has become more and more difficult. Today, we tend to speak of the physical sciences and of their fields of application as engineering sciences; of the biological sciences and of their fields of application as medical and agricultural sciences; and of the behavioral sciences and of their fields of application as the social, political, and instructional sciences.

Another way of defining science, which was used in the past and which is still found among some lay persons today, is in terms of a body of knowledge which is accurate, verifiable, and organized in a definite manner. Application of the operational check described earlier in connection with the term research soon leads one to discover that there are many things that fit this definition that by no means should be labeled science. For example, the knowledge contained in a telephone book, an airline's flight schedule, a concert program, and so forth all fit the above definition. Likewise, there are some things which we tend to classify under the rubric of science which do not meet the criteria imposed: a collection of observations not yet integrated into a framework is often considered to represent scientific information.

If science is not the study of certain specific subject matters or a body of knowledge, then what is it? Most current philosophers of science define science in terms of what they consider to be its one universal and unique feature: *method*. Since method is the essence of science, science can be thought of as a way of going about solving problems or as a body of knowledge which has been acquired through scientific logic. In psychology, sociology, and particularly in education, where scientific methods are not yet fully employed, we have some scientific facts and principles, and we have some knowledge which is not so scientific.

Some Nonscientific Ways of Obtaining Knowledge

If the scientific approach represents what today is considered the ideal way in which knowledge should be acquired, it is appropriate to ask, "What are some of the other methods man has used to obtain knowledge or facts or truth?" and "Why don't we feel that they are as appropriate as the scientific approach?" It seems well, therefore, to examine the five approaches that have been labeled the method of tenacity, the method of intuition, the method of authority, the rationalistic method, and the empirical method.

THE METHOD OF TENACITY   *Tenacity* refers to the fact that sometimes we believe something simply because we always have. An early impression leads to an opinion, which soon becomes a belief to which we later react as if it were a fact. Many of man's superstitions are thought to have been derived in this way. Perhaps, long ago, just as a hungry cave man was about to spear his quarry, a black cat scooted by and spoiled the hunting; and then, another time, as the same person was watching a black cat, he stumbled and fell into a briar patch. Forgetting, of course, all the times a black cat had been in the vicinity when nothing unusual happened, this cave man told his friends about the incidents, and they too then recalled a situation or two in which a black cat was around when some mishap befell them. Soon they acted as if it were a fact that black cats cause bad luck.

Skinner (1948) has described the way in which pigeons have acquired similar behavior. The pigeons were placed in cages in which an automatic device provided them with food at irregular intervals. Each pigeon left in such an environment seemed to develop its own ritual for obtaining nourishment. One, because on several occasions it had received food just after stretching its neck, seemed to behave as if neck stretching brought about the food—when deprived of food, it would make this response repeatedly until the reward was received. Another bird was rewarded when it started to turn in a circle, and after several rewards it would exhibit this behavior whenever sufficiently deprived of food. Similarly, each other animal developed its own "body of knowledge" about the way food was obtained.

We can imagine that as long as these birds were not able to communicate with one another each would remain convinced that he had *the* answer, *the* truth. And so it was with man. Each group developed its own set of facts and principles, its own set of truth. When one group made contact with and began to communicate with another it soon discovered that its facts and truths were in conflict. At first, disagreements arose, for each insisted that he was right and that the other was wrong. Finally, the more enlightened among them began to recognize that the difficulty was not with the other fellow but with the way each group had arrived at its knowledge. The method of tenacity led to directly conflicting facts, and thus had to be discarded. Today, we no longer base our conclusions on blind tradition.

THE METHOD OF INTUITION   Many of man's truths have come to him by intuition. Intuitive facts are thought to be self-evident. However, many propositions which at one time were held to be self-evident are now—now that our experience has been enlarged—known to be false. It is intuitively obvious that the world is flat (ask any preschool child!); and how ridiculous it must have been, in Columbus's time, to think otherwise. Obviously, it is not possible to enclose an area with two straight lines (if you follow Euclidian geometry), and everyone knows that the basic material elements of our world are air, earth, fire, and water.

All the examples cited so far have been taken from our past. Are there self-evident truths which we hold today? Walker (1960) has identified several self-evident truths in the field of education which are held by many persons. Among those described are statements that: "the smaller the institution, the better the education offered by it"; "instruction in public institutions, must . . . be inferior to that offered by private institutions"; and "that small classes are more effective than large ones." As you read each, think about it, compare it with your convictions, then go to the *Encyclopedia of Educational Research* and see to what extent these truths are and are not supported by *evidence.*

We all smile at the story about the person who said to his scientist friend, "Oh, look at all the black sheep over there," and was startled at the reply, "Oh, I don't know, they might be white on the other side." Yet this illustrates the fact that today, no matter how obvious something seems, no matter how many persons currently accept something to be intuitively true, we must insist that a fact be checked. No scientific statement ever begins with the words, "We hold these truths to be self-evident."

THE METHOD OF AUTHORITY   The method of authority is an appeal to some highly respected source of information and acceptance of the facts or truths given by that authority without further question. At one time in man's past, this was the basic way of obtaining knowledge. The story is told of a young student in the early days of universities who was dismissed because he argued with his instructor to the point of claiming that tigers had stripes. After all, who was this student to disagree with a famous Greek predecessor who had written that tigers did not have stripes. The student had only seen tigers, and one's observations could not be tolerated as a way of obtaining facts. The only truths were those stated by the authority.

There are some common examples in our life today. The most common examples are in those religions in which a sacred text or tribunal or person is vested with finality. This is not to criticize such religions, but to point out that knowledge or facts or truths which are arrived at in this manner are not to be labeled scientific knowledge or scientific facts or scientific truths. Another example may be drawn from the political-social area. In February of 1950, at a methodology conference held at the Central Statistical Administration of the Union of Soviet Socialist Republics, it was decreed that statistics based upon probability was invalid (because obviously, it conflicted with the completely planned life of dialectical materialism). No Soviet statistician had the right to disagree with this authoritative statement of fact.

By now the student is aware that there is a procedure which is inevitable and reasonable but which appears to be very much like the appeal to authority. The procedure is that of asking a specialist. Current estimates are that our knowledge is doubling about every ten years, and it seems increasingly unreasonable to expect (as was true in Newton's time) that a highly educated person can be an expert in all fields of knowledge. More and more, we will need to depend upon the opinions of experts to implement our knowledge.

The thing which differs about *an* appeal to *the* authority as a way of obtaining knowledge and *the* appeal to *an* expert is the right of the questioner to accept or reject what is said. In the method of authority, what is decreed must be accepted, while the advice of the expert may or may not be followed or challenged. The student needs to be aware that the indiscriminate rejection of the advice of experts can lead to disaster. For, while experts are sometimes wrong, they are right more often than they are wrong and they are right more often than amateurs. But, if there is good and sufficient reason to disagree with the experts, today's investigator certainly has the right to disagree.

THE RATIONALISTIC METHOD   When an attempt is made to arrive at proper truths through reasoning, it is said that the rationalistic method is being used. If the reasoning is correct, then the conclusion is accepted as being true. The classical example of this method of obtaining facts is the traditional syllogism:

> All humans die.
> You are a human.
> Therefore, you will die.

While most persons are willing to accept the conclusion reached above, we must ask if this is necessarily true. The student who has worked with syllogisms will recognize that the conclusion will hold only if the assumptions that all humans die and that you are a human are true. While it is unlikely, based on our past experience, that either of the assumptions is false, we have no guarantee that they are true. Even today some biologists are predicting that it will soon be possible to preserve the human body by deep freezing in such a way that at any future desired date the individual can be thawed out, continue to experience life as we know it, and can be refrozen and thawed out indefinitely. Further, how does anyone know except by inference that the person sitting next to him is a human being and not another organism in the disguise of a person?

The problem with the purely rationalistic approach to knowledge is that hidden assumptions—which may or may not be true—are often made.

Consider, for example, the statements:

> Two weeks ago, Team A beat Team C in football.
> Last week, Team C beat Team B in football.
> Therefore, next week Team A will beat Team B in football.

Can you depend upon the outcome? After all, the premises in this syllogism are not assumptions but descriptions of actual happenings. The answer is that while the premises are not assumptions, assumptions have been made. These are assumptions which are not apparent from a reading of the logical statements alone. Fortunately, in this specific instance, everyone recognizes from experience that the level of performance of an athletic team is not static but dynamic, and the level of performance changes (within limits) from week to week. What about the frontiers of knowledge, where our experience is not as great? How many hidden assumptions of our reasoning process are we likely to overlook when drawing conclusions?

Many of the obviously absurd answers that can be obtained from certain mathematical calculations result from a failure to note the appropriate assumptions. For example, if seven vessels can cross the ocean in 14 days, then (by dividing both values by the same number) each one can cross in 2 days. Less obviously, by using all of the principles of aerodynamics, which have enabled us to produce a rather fantastic array of successful aircraft, it can be shown that bumblebees cannot fly.

Perhaps the reader has heard of the wag who said, "There are liars, damn liars, and statisticians," or even believed that "you can prove anything with statistics." The latter is true only as far as the gullible are concerned, true only for those who know little about statistics or those who refuse to apply common sense to the interpretations involved. The trouble isn't that statistics lie, but that people can use statistics to fool you if you don't know what you are doing with statistics. If you are aware of the logic and of the assumptions made in statistical analysis and adhere to the basic principles involved, you cannot prove anything with statistics.

Reasoning is not something which we can do without, for it is absolutely essential to the scientific method. However, reasoning must never be used alone to arrive at knowledge. No matter how reasonable, we do not base scientific theory or practice on untested innovations.

THE EMPIRICAL METHOD   The empirical approach to knowledge contends that the sole criterion for judging a statement of fact or truth is whether or not it concurs with experience. If the knowledge does concur, it is accepted; if it does not, it must be rejected as knowledge.

At first, this purely empirical approach is very appealing. Before embracing this approach too closely, however, the student should become aware of some of the dangers of using empiricism alone.

First, memories are fallible. Most of the time a statement of knowledge is checked by remembering whether it coincides with our own past experience. Yet, study after study has indicated that we recall very little. Pictures of accident scenes have been shown to groups of individuals who were aware that after a minute or two of study they would be tested on the material they had been examining. The results are dramatic in showing how little is remembered even when the conditions for remembering are ideal. Imagine how much worse our memories must be when the happening occurs in a fraction of a second, when we are not aware that we will be required to recall details and when the recall is not demanded immediately, but perhaps months or even years later. Furthermore, when we forget, we do not just forget randomly. Studies suggest that we tend to forget things that are unpleasant or statements with which we disagree. Thus, the tendency is to forget those happenings which would refute our current hypothesis and remember only those things which tend to support it. Even worse, studies described by Bartlett (1932) show that our memories do not just omit but actually create. Almost all persons who were asked to reproduce a set of line drawings of miscellaneous lines some time after viewing them drew pictures of concrete objects or elaborate designs. Apparently the lines originally observed served only as a stimulus for the creation of a meaningful form and could not be remembered in and of themselves.

A second problem of the empirical approach alone is that past experience affects our present perceptions. The first weakness cannot be overcome simply by insisting that any check with experience be restricted to current experience. The classic demonstrations of this phenomenon are the trapezoidal window developed by Ames (1951) and the distorted rooms like those constructed at the Perception Laboratory in Princeton. The idea behind the distorted room demonstrations is that one's past experience with regular rooms in which the floor and ceiling are parallel, the walls are vertical, and windows and doors are rectangular and of standard size is so great that when observing a distorted room from a particular position, no distortion takes place. That is, the observer automatically sees the room as an ordinary one and thus perceives some rather peculiar happenings. For example, a ball appears to roll up hill; two friends looking in at the windows seem to have vastly different sized heads, one very large and one very small. Even when the observer is intellectually aware of what is going on, it is impossible to avoid the perceptions that past experience dictates—even with the presence of the other contradictory evidence.

Other studies have shown that our state of motivation affects what we see. Thus, McClelland and Akinson (1948) have shown that persons who have been deprived of food are more likely to see things to eat on a screen where actually only shadows are projected, and have indicated that the perceived size of a hamburger increases when one is hungry. Perhaps one of the most astonishing studies of this sort is the one described by Bruner and Goodman (1947). In this investigation, subjects were asked to adjust a spot of light on a screen so that it corresponded in diameter to various coins. The results indicated clearly that the larger the value of the coin (and this relationship holds even in the case of the nickel and dime where size and value are reversed), the greater the perceived physical size of the coin turned out to be regardless of one's personal error in making size judgments. (That is, persons who typically overestimated the size of the coins did so to an even greater extent when the coin was a valuable one, and those who typically underestimated the size of a coin came closer to its actual size or even overestimated it when the coin was worth a great deal.) Their study also showed that children from economically deprived homes tended to judge the size of the coin as much greater than children from wealthy families.

A final precaution in the use of the empirical method requires the reader to recognize that one's personal experience is very limited. This has been illustrated by the story of the seven blind men each led to a different part of an elephant. After this experience, each felt he knew what an elephant was like and proceeded to describe that part of the elephant's anatomy he had touched, assuming that all of the animal was like that portion which he personally had explored. This idea can be further demonstrated by holding a letter opener (a heavy object) and a single sheet of paper (a lighter object) at the same height above the floor and observing which hits the floor first when both are released at the same time. This observation can be verified by repeating it several times and noting the consistency with which many independent observers report the same event. The trouble is that the personal experience of all was limited. By changing things, such as crumpling the paper into a tight ball and then dropping it with the letter opener,

"Note this: The female buries the eggs with a funny sort of stick!"

FIGURE 1.1 A fallacious empirical description resulting from limited experience (*Phoenix Gazette,* 1959, copyright by General Features, Inc.)

a new idea about the relationship between weight and rate of fall is required. Failure to recognize the limitations of our experience is likely to lead us into the mistake being made by the observers from another planet seen in the cartoon of Figure 1.1.

Because our memories are fallible, our present perceptions affected by past experience, and our personal experiences quite limited, no scientist today can afford to rely alone on his impressionistic judgments to arrive at facts or truths or knowledge.

The Logic of the Formal Scientific Approach to Knowledge

The reader may have noticed that the preceding discussion of the various ways of obtaining knowledge has gradually moved along a continuum approaching more and more acceptable ways of obtaining knowledge. To complete this list of ways of obtaining knowledge only the experimental approach need be added. It is this latter approach which is the prototype of the scientific method, the ideal toward which we strive (but do not always achieve) in today's study of human behavior.

The element that is added to move from the other approaches to experimentation is control—control in manipulating, by known amounts, certain variables (i.e., characteristics or conditions which can change); and control in holding constant or accounting for the effects of other interacting variables. The other approaches are not ignored when control is added— there is a place for each. In the following discussion of the logical steps in the scientific method, special note will be made as to which of the previous ways of obtaining knowledge come into play at each point.

Since there are various ways of dividing the scientific approach into steps, the reader should not be disturbed to discover that one writer may list as many as six or seven specific steps, while another sees only three or four. The important thing is to note the sequence of thought and the basic concepts at each stage of the process. For purposes of this discussion, finding a problem will not be considered as part of obtaining its solution, and the logical steps will be viewed as: (1) setting up a hypothesis; (2) developing a method; (3) gathering the data; and (4) drawing conclusions.

SETTING UP A HYPOTHESIS   Ideally, a hypothesis represents a tentative or trial solution to the problem at hand. Most of the time these trial solutions will be implied from theory or suggested from previous investigations. However, there is no real limitation as to their source. Thus, any one of the previous methods of obtaining knowledge: tenacity, intuition, authority, rationalistic, or empirical might be utilized at this stage. To be sure, hypotheses which are developed by reasoning from theory or by making casual observations are more likely to be verified than those derived from other sources. However, there is no reason to exclude the latter entirely from consideration; and on occasion, our past traditions and intuitions have sufficient merit to be well worth testing.

While tentative solutions are relatively easy to develop when working in an area where the important variables are known and where the theory has been developed to the point of naming specific functional relationships among the variables, there are some situations in which finding a trial answer is either impossible or is so tenuous as to seem little worth the effort. Thus, the hypothesis sometimes takes the form of a list of specific questions to be answered rather than a tentative solution to the problem. This is especially true when working in a relatively new area and when the investigation involves primarily exploratory work.

Regardless of the form of the hypothesis, it is absolutely essential that it be capable of refutation; it must be posed so that more than one answer is possible, and the tentative solution must be stated in such a way that it can be either contradicted or confirmed. A hypothesis which fails to meet this requirement is said to be nontestable. To set up a nontestable hypothesis is to remove the problem from the realm of science, and any conclusion drawn under these circumstances will have to be based on faith, not science.

There are several types of nontestable hypotheses which appear so often in the study of human behavior that it is well worth the time to enumerate them and examine them closely enough that the reader will be able to avoid them in his own work. In general, nontestable hypotheses are set forth when they refer to things which cannot, in principle, be observed, when they define the conclusions, or when they include a value judgment.

A hypothesis which refers to or depends upon things which by definition cannot be observed (either directly or as a result of their effects) can never be refuted. If someone informed the reader in all seriousness that his watch was run by little invisible men, the statement must be accepted or rejected without any evidence. Since the men can never be seen, the believer can attribute to them whatever characteristics will overcome any rational objection. For example, if the reader asks what happens when the watch runs down, the response could be that the men get tired, and twisting the stem rejuvenates them; if the reader asks why does the watch stop when submerged in water or when dropped, the obvious reply is that the men have been drowned or killed, and when the jeweler opens the back to repair it all he is really doing is letting more little men inside.

While few persons today would argue about the way in which a watch runs, there are examples where the same logic has been employed. Some of the early conceptions of the unconscious as something which can never be known because it prevents you from knowing it by disguising itself are of this sort. Consider this statement: "The study of history results in implicit appreciations of our culture." It is impossible to deny this statement in any scientific sense. If the instruction changes only the inside of the student's head and has no effect which appears in any observable way at any time at any place, the scientist can only shrug his shoulders and say, "So what? What has been accomplished?" The logical positivists have pointed out in their philosophy of science that a difference, to be a difference, must make a difference; that is, to be scientifically admissible (amenable to scientific verification) the effect must be at least potentially observable.

A second form of nontestable hypothesis is a statement that defines the conclusion. There is no point in attempting to gather evidence to refute or confirm the statements, "true psychopaths never change," or "true mathematicians work intuitively, not systematically." Evidence that a person previously labeled a psychopath improved with therapy or a mathematician solved problems systematically would be rejected by a believer on the grounds that they were incorrectly diagnosed or classified in the first place. Only if the hypothesis is stated in such a way that it can be refuted by evidence is it a meaningful one as far as science is concerned.

An even more prevalent form of a nontestable hypothesis is one which sets forth a value judgment. How many times has the reader seen a hypothesis like: "Instructional Method A is better than Instructional Method B"? The scientific method cannot be used to determine whether one procedure is *better* than another, for this is a value judgment which is made by a human being. By means of the scientific method it is possible to determine what the outcomes will be if Method A is used as contrasted with Method B, but which outcomes are the most desirable is a human value judgment.

A great many of the apparent conflicts in the scientific findings of the behavioral sciences result from failure to make this distinction. For example, one investigator might conclude that teaching Method A is better than Method B because its use led to generally higher performance on a good measure of subject matter achievement; a second investigator might conclude that teaching Method B was the better because its use led to a more positive attitude toward the subject matter on the part of the students. Obviously, it is not the scientific findings which are in conflict but the value judgments of the two researchers. One investigator feels that subject matter knowledge is most desirable, while the other believes that attitude is of prime importance.

To say that science itself does not make value judgments does not mean that the scientific method cannot be used to determine what kind of value judgments humans make or to investigate the process by which value judgments are made. Neither does it imply that the scientist himself follows no value system when employing his method. Actually, the scientist, as a scientist, follows a rather specific set of values—values that sometimes bring him into conflict with other groups in our society. According to Meyers (1962) the ideal scientist holds these beliefs:

1. Truth is preferable to non-truth.
   (Truth, in this sense, means non-contradictory statements and statements which correctly predict future events.)
2. The final authority as to the truth of a statement is not a person but observations.
3. Whenever new data require it, former conclusions will be altered.
4. Each person has the right to investigate any area.
5. All scientific findings should be made available to all persons who desire them.

A scientific hypothesis, then, can be cast in the form of either a question or a tentative answer. To be admissible, a hypothesis must be capable of refutation. Statements that refer to nonobservables, define the conclusion, or make a value judgment do not meet this requirement and lie outside the field of science. They must be accepted or rejected without scientific evidence and, if accepted, must not be labeled scientific facts.

DEVELOPING A METHOD   The second major step in the logical scientific approach to obtaining knowledge is that of developing a method to test the hypothesis. This is done by specifying the observable consequences of the hypothesis. The scientist supposes that the hypothesis is true and asks, "If this is true, then what else must be true that I can observe?"

Ideally, the events specified as consequences of the hypothesis should be both necessary (the event must occur if the hypothesis is true) and sufficient (the event will not occur unless the hypothesis is true) conditions for the existence of the hypothesis. Unfortunately, in the realm of empirical science (outside of pure mathematics), this simply is not possible. Sufficient conditions do not seem to exist. Anything observed could have been the result of a phenomenon not yet even dreamed about; and many so-called necessary conditions are really only pseudonecessary in that, while high, their probability of occurrence is less than one. That is, many scientific hypotheses (especially in the behavioral sciences) are such that if they are true, it is only highly likely that certain consequences will follow—not that these events *must* happen.

Under these circumstances, the only alternative which seems open to the scientific investigator is that of listing as many pseudonecessary conditions as possible and then searching to see if he can observe them. Each time such an event is observed the scientist increases his confidence in this hypothesis; but each time he fails to observe the anticipated event the scientist will have less confidence that his hypothesis is, in fact, true. The extent to which a scientist gains or loses confidence in his hypothesis depends, in part, on the nature of the event itself. It also depends, in part, on the method used. For example, failure to find some lost document verifying a postulated historical event does not destroy one's confidence a great deal, while locating an apparently genuine relic might increase the plausibility of the hypothesis to a very great extent. On the other hand, failure to observe a predicted event in a carefully controlled laboratory situation may almost completely destroy the scientist's theory, while an observation of the expected event may be but one small chink in a wall of evidence which might ultimately be erected.

It should be apparent, then, that because empirical science lacks sufficient conditions for the existence of a hypothesis, it is never possible to accept a scientific hypothesis with complete certainty. Because of a lack of absolutely necessary conditions, it is often not even possible to reject a hypothesis with complete certainty. Not even with the scientific method is it possible to achieve ultimate proof—it is only possible to gather evidence for or against a hypothesis.

Consideration of the logic of testing hypotheses has led many philosophers of science to conclude that it is inappropriate to think of any empirical hypothesis as being true or false in an absolute sense. Rather, one should simply say that such and such holds under these conditions or within some specified limits. Not only is it unreasonable to think of a scientific theory or hypothesis as necessarily representing the truth, but such an approach tends to build in a resistance to new information which may contradict the implications of a theory and thus retard the expansion of our knowledge. It is much better to think of hypotheses and of theories not as representing truth but as being useful or not so useful. An investigator may, under appropriate conditions, behave as if the hypothesis or the theory were true because it is useful for him to do so; and under other conditions, ignore the hypothesis because he is working outside the limits within which the theory is helpful in describing or summarizing events, in making predictions, or in developing practical applications. Similarly, it is seen that it is quite reasonable for some scientists to wait for further evidence before they are willing to behave as if some theory or hypothesis is true and for others to be willing to accept lesser evidence simply because they find the conception useful within the limits of their work. To argue whether the theory is true or false is a waste of effort; rather, the time should be spent in defining or extending the limits of its usefulness by gathering additional appropriate data.

This second step in the logic of the scientific method, then, makes use of the rationalistic approach. It requires the investigator to reason deductively from the hypothesis and find specific events one should be able to observe if the hypothesis is true. When the hypothesis is in question form, the investigator must reason out what techniques will yield observations that can answer the question clearly.

GATHERING THE DATA   The third logical step of the scientific method is to use the empirical approach to gather the data that will serve as a basis for accepting or rejecting the hypothesis, or which will answer the questions raised.

There is not a great deal that needs to be said about this stage of scientific logic. The reader, however, might take special note that: (1) data gathering *alone* is not research; (2) data gathering *is* a step (without which you do not have the scientific method—only critical reflection); (3) data gathering is neither the first step nor the last. Gathering data without reference to a specific question or a particular hypothesis is generally a wasteful exercise, and to present data without drawing a conclusion or making a decision may be entertaining, but otherwise serves no purpose. Ideally, the data should be gathered under carefully controlled conditions and whenever possible (to avoid errors) recorded automatically.

DRAWING CONCLUSIONS   The final logical step of the scientific method, drawing conclusions, also requires the rationalistic approach. From the previous discussion, which indicated that sufficient conditions for the existence of a hypothesis can never be found and that often only pseudonecessary consequences can be identified, the reader should be well aware that drawing a conclusion is a complex logical process. Seldom will a simple yes or no answer be found.[1] Drawing a conclusion will, therefore, almost always require statistical inference and the application of decision theory as described in Chapter 6.

For now it is sufficient to point out that, when drawing a conclusion, the investigator is faced with both the possibility of accepting a false hypothesis and the possibility of rejecting a true hypothesis (to hold a decision in abeyance still requires him to behave, temporarily at least, as if he has either accepted or rejected the hypothesis). These two possibilities pose a dilemma. As the scientist reduces his chances of making one of these errors, he increases his chances of making the other. Every scientific conclusion will require that a value judgment be made, a judgment as to the seriousness of the consequences of making one error as contrasted with making the other error.

It is very important to be certain that any conclusions drawn are based on the evidence gathered in the investigation. While such an admonishment may appear to be unnecessary, work in the behavioral sciences seems to be so conducive to emotional attachments to preconceived ideas that this principle has been violated over and over again. All too often, conclusions (which may be perfectly acceptable on the basis of other information) do not follow, and sometimes even seem to have little relevance to the data of the study reported. The beginner especially is cautioned to examine a list of conclusions carefully, asking for each, "Which data in this study support this statement?"

---

[1] While automatic systems for accepting or rejecting a hypothesis can be set up to do the job simply once the data gathering has begun, the development of the system requires the same kind of complex reasoning required when interpreting the data by hand.

The Illogic of Scientific Practice and the
Informal Scientific Approach

The four steps of the scientific method as described above represent the logical analysis of scientific activity as provided by various philosophers of science. In actual practice all is not so monotonically ordered. In many instances the steps may blend into one another; sometimes they are carried on almost simultaneously, and often an investigator is not completely aware that he is going through them. While the experienced and competent research worker can move through the steps easily, modifying them where necessary to accomplish his overall aim of advancing knowledge, the novice seems to do best at first if he follows the steps a little more explicitly than the expert. On the other hand, lest even the novice become too rigid, it would seem worthwhile to describe here the "unformalized principles of scientific practice" as set forth by Skinner (1956) in a talk entitled, "A Case History in Scientific Method."

In this description of his own experiences, Skinner indicates that a major result of one of his early studies was that some of his rats had babies. Because observation of the newborn creatures provided some interesting suggestions for further work, Skinner arrived at his first principle: *When you run onto something interesting, drop everything else and study it.* Skinner's second principle is: *Some ways of doing research are easier than others.* This principle is important, for, because he became tired of walking to the end of a maze to retrieve a rat, and because he got tired of having to be around to provide the experimental animal with reinforcement (a reward for successful behavior), he invented an apparatus in which the animal was able to obtain the necessary reinforcement by his own actions: the now famous *Skinner Box.*

Because he was able to construct his first food magazine from a piece of discarded apparatus which had an apparently unnecessary appendage that Skinner did not bother to cut off, Skinner was led to the construction of a polygraph for recording data and then to the observation of previously unnoticed aspects of the rate of responding. Thus, a third principle: *Some people are lucky.* The fourth principle is: *Apparatuses sometimes break down.* As a result of such an occurrence, Skinner tells us, he was led to concentrate on extinction processes. Skinner admits that the final principle results partially because he applied the classical hypothetical-deductive method. While diligently following his deductions, Skinner discovered something he was not looking for. This last principle had already been given a name: *Serendipity—the art of finding one thing while looking for another.*

In summarizing, Skinner says: "I never faced a Problem which was more than the eternal problem of finding order. I never attacked a problem by constructing a Hypothesis. I never deduced Theorems or submitted them to Experimental Check. So far as I can see, I had no preconceived Model of behavior."

And, a little later: "Of course I was working on a basic Assumption— that there was order in behavior if I could only discover it—but such an assumption is not to be confused with the hypothesis of deductive theory. It is also true that I exercised a certain Selection of Facts but not because of any relevance to theory but because one fact was more orderly than another. If I engaged in Experimental Design at all, it was simply to complete or extend some evidence of order already observed."

For all his disdain of a formalized approach to science, it is essential to recognize that Skinner is advocating not less, but *more* careful thought about the general logic of the experiment; not less, but *more* careful control of the conditions in the experiment; and not fuzzy verbal qualitative descriptions but *more* rigorous operational definitions and quantitative findings. In fact, Sidman (1960) has spelled out in some detail the special characteristics of what Bachrach (1962) has labeled the "Informal Theoretical" method of research to distinguish it clearly from the "Formal Theoretical" method described in the previous section.

THE IMPORTANCE OF DATA   Those who follow the informal approach hold that the basic task of the scientist is that of gathering orderly data and finding lawful relationships among them rather than the formulation and testing of so-called scientific theories. These persons feel that the early formulation of a theory or even the development of an elaborate hypothesis to be tested should be avoided because this process tends to restrict the observational powers of the investigator and leads him to ignore highly useful data.

It follows from this view that all carefully gathered empirical data are useful and that there is no such thing as negative results. The competent investigator will simply ask meaningful questions, seek data to answer them, and ultimately judge the quality of the data in terms of their scientific importance, their reliability, and their generality.

To a certain extent, judgment of the quality of data must await the cumulative development of the science of human behavior itself. This is particularly true in the case of the criterion of scientific importance, where no impartial rules for making an evaluation seem to exist, and the only immediate basis for a judgment rests upon trust in the skill and integrity of the investigator.

When an investigator asks whether his data are reliable, he is asking to determine whether the same results will be found if the study is repeated. To answer this question, he may directly duplicate the investigation with a second group of subjects to obtain *intergroup* reliability, with other individual subjects to obtain *intersubject* reliability, or with the same subject on different occasions to obtain *intrasubject* reliability. Instead of direct replication, the research worker may evaluate the reliability of his data by means of a systematic replication in which he seeks to duplicate an earlier finding as part of a larger study which seeks to extend the boundaries of what he already knows.

The criterion of generality goes beyond mere reproducibility and requires knowledge of the important variables which lead to reproducibility. Only when those conditions under which reproducibility will and will not be found can be specified has the investigator achieved generality. Generality of the observations may refer to an extension of the findings only to other members of the same species (subject generality) or to members of other species (interspecies generality). With respect to the latter, it is especially important that the investigator seek to establish generality with regard to the variables which are relevant, the processes or interrelationships among the variables, and to the methods or techniques for achieving control of the behavior under consideration.

A HIGH DEGREE OF CONTROL   A second important feature of the informal approach to scientific investigation is the high degree of control which is required to achieve the reliability and generality of data that is described above.

In this connection, it is important to distinguish between what Sidman (1960) refers to as "control experiments" and experimental control. Control experiments are investigations in which certain observations are made to eliminate or reduce the plausibility of certain rival explanations to the contention that the results obtained are the product of the experimenter's manipulations. The basic designs for such experiments are described in some detail in Chapter 4 on the experimental method. Experimental control, on the other hand, "refers to the investigator's ability to manipulate an individual subject's behavior in a precise and reliable fashion" (Sidman, 1960, p. 342). Techniques used for accomplishing this are described in the next chapter under the heading: The Controlled Study of Single Organisms.

The emphasis on full control of the subject's behavior and other aspects of the experimental situation stems from a basic view that variability of behavior is not intrinsic to the phenomenon itself but imposed by external conditions. Those who take the informal approach to the scientific investigation of behavioral phenomena feel that it is an important task of the investigator to ferret out the sources of variability and either to eliminate variability by the manipulation of the appropriate variables or to describe explicitly its relationship with other characteristics of behavior. Among those sources of variability which are of greatest concern to the research worker who seeks to find order in data describing behavior are that which results from prior experiences of the organism, that which arises because so many different variables affect behavior, that which arises because of the "reciprocal interaction of behavior and its controlling environment" (Sidman, 1960, p. 172), and that which results from genetic differences in body morphology and physiological conditions. These latter are often lumped together under the heading of differences in capacity and are considered by some to be the primary concern of physiologists, geneticists, pharmacologists, or scientists in other biological disciplines rather than that of those who investigate the behavior of organisms.

A PREFERENCE FOR THE STUDY OF A SINGLE ORGANISM   A final important characteristic of the informal approach to the scientific study of behavior is a reliance on data from single organisms rather than large group studies. Although there are several different prototype approaches which investigators using the informal method may follow, the basic logic seems to be that of first bringing the behavior of an individual organism to a relatively consistent level (which may be either a steady state or an explicit and lawful change), then introducing the experimental variable under study, and finally carefully recording the changes which result.

Those who follow this approach generally eschew intergroup replications because such replications provide information only about the reliability of averages and other group characteristics rather than information about the reproducibility of the behavior itself. Thus, intrasubject reliability becomes of prime concern. While no one would deny the power and elegance of a study in which the behavior of a single organism is repeatedly manipulated in a quantitatively consistent fashion, it should be recognized that intrasubject replication is not possible where the conditions imposed produce truly irreversible changes inside the organism. That is, it must be assumed in many single organism studies that the effects of one treatment can be completely erased before the next treatment is applied. When this is not possible, more than one subject must be used to assess the reliability of data. However, even though several organisms are used in a single study, individual records are kept to be analyzed separately, and are seldom averaged together.

A Possible Rapprochement

At the present time, it would seem that those who are concerned with the scientific study of behavior are clustered into two great camps with respect to the appropriate logic to follow in the research enterprise—one epitomized by the approach advocated by B. F. Skinner and ably described in Sidman's *Tactics of Scientific Research,* and the other exemplified by the modern extension of the classical approach as found in the *Handbook of Multivariate Experimental Psychology* edited by R. B. Cattell. Both have their champions who would seek to exclude those in the opposite camp from the right to claim a respectable scientific approach; yet both seem to have some real strengths and weaknesses as Lyons (1965) points out in concluding his discussion of the informal approach:

It would appear that by these procedures the experimenter achieves the goal toward which any science strives—to establish precise and stable functional relations between two known influences on his part and measured results on the part of his subjects. But . . . these investigators may have bypassed a certain characteristic of the world to which the scientific enterprise is directed—what might be called the causal texture of the universe with which a science deals. In place of an exploration of the nexus of interrelations that . . . describes the natural universe, there is offered an exquisite degree of control over a set of established phenomena.

At the present time, the reader may feel he will have to make a choice between these two alternatives, as have most research workers who are currently active.

Royce (1960) has called for a synthesis of approaches, at least in the case of an integrated program of research to be carried out over a long period of time. Referring to the informal approach as a single variable experiment and to the formal approach under the label "factoral designs," and suggesting that factor theory (see Chapter 8) represents a third basic approach, Royce (p. 302) states:

The single variable experiment demands rigidly controlled conditions to which much psychological research cannot conform. The reason stems largely from ignorance of the multiplicity of sources of variation which are operative in a given domain. It has been pointed out that in such situations the experimental designs involved in factor theory are appropriate. Once the basic unities have been identified the factoral designs of Fisher can be appropriately utilized in order to extend our knowledge of the effects of one thing or another on these fundamental variables. Finally, with the clarification derived from multiple variable investigations, it may be possible to set up rigidly controlled single variable experiments which will give us quantitive empirical relationships. These may then serve as a basis for the development or/and confirmation of mathematically rationalized theories of behavior.

Whether the reader prefers the formalized or the unformalized approach to modern scientific investigation or aspires to using a combination of the two, the statement made by Geis (1964) accurately describes the situation as it stands today. "The 'scientific expert' is our contemporary medicine man. He is supposed to know the answers. He is supposed to be a living reference book. Yet, in fact, he probably knows very few answers. He is not a repository of rules, of the latest laws, of absolute answers, but rather he is engaged in applying the experimental model in order to generate questions and possibly some tentative probabilistic statements."

THE APPLICATION OF THE SCIENTIFIC METHOD TO THE STUDY OF BEHAVIOR

The Evolution of Research

The method of science has not always had the place of honor it now holds in our society, nor did it suddenly appear in full bloom as we know it now. Rather, it has slowly evolved from a crude beginning, and it has earned its prominence through competition among the ways of obtaining knowledge on quite pragmatic grounds. By experience it has been found that when the scientific method is used we are more likely to find unambiguous answers to our problems, and, as a direct result of this, our knowledge grows more rapidly, our conclusions are more lasting (both in time and across situations), and our results are more useful in terms of ultimate practical application.

While it is not necessary to go into all the details of the history of science it does seem to help in gaining a broad perspective and a keener insight into the application of the scientific method to the study of behavior if the highlights of its development are noted.

THE PERIOD OF TRIAL AND ERROR It has been speculated that in earliest times the crudest form of the scientific method was simple trial-and-error learning. While this is an agonizing and slow process, it did seem to lead to a considerable body of systematized knowledge, culminating perhaps in the ancient cultures of Egypt, Mesopotamia, and the Aegean Islands.

THE APPEAL TO REASON What has been termed the first mutation of our way of obtaining knowledge seems to have come with the appearance of the Greek civilization in the fifth, fourth, and third centuries B.C. The *Sophists* (often dated about the middle of the fifth century B.C.) solved problems by debate, and research was the process of finding proof of the statements to be made during the argument. Proof in these early times, however, did not involve gathering empirical evidence, but rather was obtained by referring to some predecessor who was deemed an authority. The person who won the debate was the one who was able to find the greatest number of quotes to back his point and whose quotes came from the most esteemed authority. It has been claimed that this argumentative approach was utilized into the early Christian era by the Goths of Germany who were said to have debated everything of importance twice: once while drunk, so their conclusions would not lack vigor; and once while sober, so their conclusions would not lack discretion.

Within the Greek civilization, however, the process of argument slowly became formalized and through the impetus of the teachings of Socrates, Plato, and Aristotle became deductive reasoning. In the later writings of

Aristotle, we find the final stage of this first change in the process we today label research: Aristotle's four steps of inquiry. These may be listed as: (1) statement of the problem; (2) analysis of the problem by a series of verbal tests or verbal "experiments"; (3) synthesis of the problem by classification; and (4) conclusion, or summing up the implications.

As the liberal scientific thinker of his time, Aristotle introduced two elements which at that time were only hints of the later stages to come in the development of the scientific method: the use of empirical facts and the rudimentary forms of inductive reasoning implied by the use of synthesis to develop a classification.

THE RETURN OF THE METHOD OF AUTHORITY   The next major identifiable step of the developmental stages in the scientific method seems to be a reversal. During the Middle Ages, with the coming of a strong religious influence on life, there was a return to debate and argument with its appeal to authority—in this case religious authority. Once again, research became a library search for proof, and proof amounted to statements made by esteemed authorities.

INDUCTIVE REASONING AND EMPIRICAL OBSERVATION   The most recent major phase of the logical evolution of the scientific method began with the Renaissance. At this time there seems to have been a shift away from interest in religious dogma and the hereafter and a renewed concern with the present and the nature of the world itself. At first this revival of learning was slow, and many writers prefer not to date the emergence of modern science until the seventeenth century. It was in this era of Sir Francis Bacon (1561–1626), Galileo (1564–1642), Kepler (1571–1630), and Newton (1642–1727) in which both empirical observation and inductive reasoning were clearly seen.

Since this time, the scientific method has been further refined and more widely used. However, there does not seem to be any clearly new logical direction which the methodology of science has taken—though perhaps those of us living in the twentieth century are too close to the situation to see a slow trend which may be occurring.

APPLYING THE SCIENTIFIC APPROACH TO THE STUDY OF BEHAVIOR   The early development of the modern scientific method described above was most closely associated with research in what we now call the natural or physical sciences. The application of the scientific method to the study of behavior did not begin until sometime later and, as a matter of fact, is still being resisted in some quarters.

With Sir Francis Galton (1822–1911) we find the first application of primitive statistical methods to research in the behavioral sciences. With James McKeen Cattell, at about the same time, we find a laboratory concerned with the problems of testing, and every beginning psychology student is aware of Wundt's first psychological laboratory at the University of Leipzig in 1879; of Thorndike's studies of 1898, and of Pavlov's works dating from 1903. Similarly, students of education will recall that the school survey was in full vogue by the turn of the century.

Shortly after this early application of the scientific method there occurred an era some have called the "great debate" during which there was much controversy as to the applicability of scientific approaches to the study of human behavior. By the late 1920's or early 1930's, however, it was generally conceded that the scientific study of behavior was here to stay. In spite of occasional calls for reevaluation and sporadic blasts at the efforts in this direction, the scientific investigation of human behavior has continued to gain in breadth of acceptance and general prestige.

Describing Research in the Behavioral Sciences

The variety of today's research in the behavioral sciences as to purpose, scope, method, level, type, and so on seems almost endless and the task of presenting an overall picture an onerous if not impossible one. Almost every author will have worked out his own unique system of classification. It will help if the reader will keep in mind the fact that taxonomies, like theories, are best thought of not as right or wrong but rather as useful or useless for different particular purposes.

The function of the classification scheme presented in the following sections is to help the student develop a feeling for the major varieties of research he may encounter in his later work and to help clarify the meaning of various descriptive labels that are attached to some research studies in reviews or other discussions of them.

It seems helpful to visualize modern research in the behavioral sciences as a three-dimensional animal—that is, to recognize that there are three relatively independent dimensions for describing research. Almost any study can be fairly well characterized if it is described in respect to these three things. The overall scheme can be seen graphically in Figure 1.2. Basically, any given study can be broadly described by placing it in one and only one category along each of the three dimensions. However, the labels used for the three dimensions and the various categories listed along them need further clarification.

BREADTH OF APPLICATION Perhaps the most frequently used dimension for distinguishing among types of research is the *breadth of application,* although it is often referred to in terms of the reason the researcher has become involved with the problem. While it may seem strange, at first, to bother with classifying studies on the basis of the motivation of the person

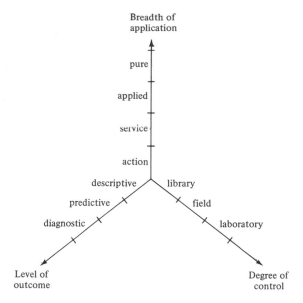

FIGURE 1.2   A taxonomy of research in the behavioral sciences

carrying out the investigation, such different kinds of outcomes occur as to make this a most useful approach.   At various choice points in research strategy, the research worker who has become involved in the effort for one reason is likely to make one decision and the investigator who has become involved for a different reason will make a different decision, so it is well worth examining types of research categorized according to purpose.[2]

The first distinction to be made along this dimension is between *pure* or *basic* or *fundamental* research and *applied* research.   In pure research, the motive is solely that of curiosity.   The investigator is interested in finding out about the world around him, with little or no thought of the immediate application or apparent use to which his findings may be put.

The results of basic research are concepts or theories, or simply a set of relationships offered as new knowledge.   A classic example of this approach is that used in the Communications and Social Science Research Department of the Bell Telephone System's Laboratory at Murrary Hill, N.J., as described by Hovland (1961) who says: "Basic research provides a fund of new knowledge to be drawn upon by those interested in its development and application.   The responsibility for potential utilization of research does not rest with the researcher.   His responsibility is that of creating new knowledge and conferring with those who see possibilities of its utilization concerning its varied and deep implications."

---

[2] A view of somewhat the same dimension seen as a research-development continuum is given by Hilgard (1964).

These basic studies may eventually lead to far more numerous applications than any applied study ever could. Among the classic examples of pure research which have ultimately found innumerable applications are Bohr's atomic theory, Mendel's studies of genetic transmission (which gathered dust in a library for fifty years as "useless findings of an impractical scientist"), the original studies of basic human individual differences (which have led to the wide use of so-called mental tests), studies of the pecking order of hens, and the study of basic structure of fibers which led to the discovery of the first synthetic cloth.

Applied research, on the other hand, is devoted to the solution of practical problems. That is, a specific use for the results is seen by the researcher and his whole attack is geared in this direction. This type of research is referred to in business and industry as developmental or product research, and obviously is the type of research which is likely to be more readily supported by those government and private agencies who must justify their expenditures to persons outside the scientific community.

An excellent example of the different research strategies which occur when an applied, as contrasted with a pure, approach is taken is to be found in a debate that took place not long ago as to how the National Institutes of Health in Bethseda, Maryland, should spend the money allotted to them by Congress for supporting research in connection with cancer. The difference was highlighted by Turner (1959) who said:

Although everyone agrees that it would be splendid if science found a cure for cancer, the problem is how should science proceed? Some investigators see great hope in testing one chemical compound after another for its effects on tumors and healthy tissue. There is a reasonable chance, these investigators believe, that a screening program will lead to the discovery of drugs that will significantly retard, cure, or prevent various kinds of cancer. Such a program requires an organized effort, a large budget, and a great number of scientists, all capable of identifying a significant effect when they see one.

Attempting to take the citadel by storm has been a respectable procedure since at least the time of Paul Ehrlich's 606 trys at finding a cure for syphilis. But other investigators hold that, although it is fine for some workers to screen compounds for possible effects on tumors, *they* have no wish to do so. In fact, these other investigators do not even set their sights on anything so specific as a cure for cancer. They are interested in seeking better understanding of how cells function. Of course, with increased understanding of how cells function may come increased understanding of what causes cancer and, consequently, of how to cure it.

As an interesting sidelight on the question of pure versus applied research, it is worth noting that in the past those research workers who preferred basic studies gravitated to the universities where there were no restrictions as to area of investigation and no need to justify research efforts in terms of practical outcomes; while those investigators who were concerned with applied problems were able to find a place in business and industrial concerns who were interested in improving their processes or products. Slowly, however, business and industry have learned the long-term value of basic research, and thus are more and more willing to underwrite this kind of effort by the scientists they employ. At the same time, the cost of doing either type research has risen so sharply that it is becoming more and more difficult for an investigator to follow his interests and carry on fundamental research without a substantial grant. Further, since granting agencies, particularly governmental agencies, are pressured to justify their expenditures to taxpayers (or donors as the case may be) in terms of concrete, foreseeable, practical outcomes, it is becoming more and more difficult to carry out pure research within some academic settings. Thus, there is a general restriction of the overall proportion of research that is of a fundamental nature and a proportional shift of basic research workers away from university settings toward laboratories within business and industry. Unfortunately, the latter is robbing university students and faculty alike of direct contact with those who are pushing back the frontiers of knowledge, and the former is tremendously reducing the benefits of science which come to society to a much greater extent from basic rather than from applied research.

The next category along the dimension of breadth of application has been labeled *service* research. Here, the initiation of the research is not generally from the researcher himself as in the first two categories, but rather comes from some administrator or practitioner who wants a study done to solve a problem with which he is personally faced. The motive of the investigator here then is to provide a service to someone; and generally speaking, the results of this kind of research are much more limited in scope than in either of the first two cases. In this instance the solution that is found is often applicable only to the particular situation at hand. This is in contrast to applied research, where, while the outcomes are foreseeable and practical, the hope is that they will be useful in a wide variety of specific situations.

The last category, *action* research, is felt by some not to deserve the name research at all. This is because the motive is not necessarily that of getting the problem solved. The motive may be as much to gain the interest and attention of certain members of the community or to bring about in-shop improvement of applied workers as it is to get an accurate answer to the question raised. Although those who advocate action research are quick to point out that there is no logical necessity for it to be so restricted, almost without exception this type of research turns out to be strictly practical and limited to a particular situation. While again this need not be the case, action research has seldom resulted in a precise answer to the initial question raised. Regardless of other desirable outcomes, from a strictly research point of view, action research produces results which are the least broadly applicable of all.

LEVEL OF OUTCOME   A second way of viewing any research study is in terms of its level of outcome. When research simply asks what something is like, it is said to be *descriptive;* when the outcome is that of anticipating the future, it is labeled *predictive;* and if it seeks to answer the more complex question of why, that is, if the outcome is a specification of a cause-and-effect relationship, then the study is frequently labeled *diagnostic.*

All three categories represent different degrees of elaboration of the same thing. Description, for example, is often considered the first step of either prediction or diagnosis, and although description alone may be the purpose of a particular investigation, it seldom represents the ultimate goal of science in any field. To test this latter statement the reader is invited to ask an investigator engaged in descriptive work why society should support him in his efforts. Seldom will the response be "for the world to enjoy." Rather, the justification is likely to be made on the grounds that ultimately the description will enable us to predict or to determine some "cause-effect" sequence.

Diagnosis can also be thought of as simply an elaborate form of prediction. Consider, for a moment, what the family physician is really saying when he makes the diagnosis that Johnny has the measles. True, the physician is telling us that the cause of Johnny's troubles is something labeled measles. But this naming process has little meaning unless it suggests to the listener a future course of events which is different than would be the case had some other diagnostic label (for example, appendicitis) been used. Thus, when a physician diagnoses measles, he is predicting the future sequence of events in Johnny's symptoms, he is predicting that certain therapies will work and certain others will not work, he is predicting something about what is likely to happen to some of Johnny's friends, and so forth. And, only in this predictive sense does the diagnosis, the specification of cause and effect, have meaning.

Even though, in the logical sense mentioned above, description, prediction, and diagnosis represent the same thing, the complexity of the study, the level of refinement of the techniques used both for measurement and for analysis of the data often differ so greatly when one of the three is seen as the outcome of the investigation rather than the other, it seems worthwhile to continue to use the separate categories of description, prediction, and diagnosis.

DEGREE OF CONTROL   Although the third continuum along which research studies in the behavioral sciences may usefully be described represents the degree of control exercised by the investigator, the broad labels most frequently applied refer to the place in which the study is carried out.   In general, when a piece of research is described as a laboratory study, it is suggested that the investigator made his observations in a highly controlled situation; when the investigation is referred to as a field study, it is implied that the only control used involved the selection of the time and place for making the observations; and, when library research is the label used to describe the study, it is inferred that the investigator sought a solution to the problem by gathering and integrating observations which were made by other individuals over which he had no control except that of choosing those which he would accept or reject as valid.

Two other sets of labels characterizing research studies in the behavioral sciences result in approximately the same grouping of investigations as that described above. One set of labels results from the fact that, although the relationship is not one of necessity, the general approach usually taken by the library worker is *historical,* the approach followed by the field worker is *descriptive,* and the laboratory worker generally uses an *experimental* approach. Similarly, the second set of labels producing essentially the same classification of studies arises because the character of the data collected seems to vary with the place the research is done. The laboratory worker seems to use quantitative data almost exclusively, the field worker much less extensively, and the library worker sometimes not at all. Regardless of whether one uses the place in which the research is largely done, the general approach taken, or the general type of data used, the studies within a category have some characteristics which are similar, and studies placed in one group differ enough from those placed in another to make the labeling of them along this third dimension worthwhile in terms of indicating what the study is like.

Doing Applied Research in Field Situations

It is impossible to ignore some of the special problems that arise when a study must be done in a field situation rather than in the library or a laboratory. In some areas of psychology, but more frequently in education and sociology, the investigator is faced with the sometimes difficult if not annoying task of gaining the cooperation of uninterested or perhaps even hostile members of the community who may serve as subjects, supervisors, or coordinators, or who are persons elected by community members to protect them from unwanted annoyances. A research worker operating in this situation must take into consideration some things which the laboratory worker can ignore.

PRELIMINARY CONSIDERATIONS   Before beginning any project that will require extensive contact with members of a community, there are several questions which an investigator should ask himself, for the answers may determine whether the objectives of the project can actually be accomplished.

First, he should ask himself whether the lack of a solution to the problem is, in fact, a real limitation either to our knowledge or to some practical operation. While this question might well be raised for every research problem, it becomes especially important when many people are going to be asked to donate their time or effort. In a laboratory or a library study, perhaps only the time of the research worker himself is wasted, but when working in a community, wasted efforts on a pseudoproblem can result in sufficient antagonism that future, deserving projects are rejected by the community.

To help ascertain whether it is appropriate to study a particular problem in a community, the worker might ask himself these questions:

1. Is the problem one which perennially causes concern? That is, is it one which appears again and again, and is recognized by not just one but several workers in the area as being of significance?
2. Can the effects of a solution to the problem be specifically enumerated? Or, are the results just something which cannot be stated in writing and are only hazily imagined by the investigator?
3. Is the problem one which can really be solved by research (by new information) or is it one which is the result of such things as a lack of funds, inadequate personalities, inappropriate attitudes of the persons in the situation, or others to which the research information can make no contribution toward changing?
4. Can the solution be obtained in some other way? Is it really necessary to do the study in the community, or could it be as easily solved with a well-conceived laboratory study?

A second major question is whether or not those who will need to be involved are aware of the problem. If the members of the community are well aware of the problem, they will probably welcome the research worker but may be a little impatient in wanting results or action immediately rather than the information which will provide the best solution in the long run. On the other hand, if some segment of those to be involved are not cognizant of the problem and its importance, the investigator will need to make certain that they can be made aware of the situation and should start making definite plans to inform them before jumping with both feet into the data gathering phase of the project.

The third major question an investigator needs to ask is whether he himself has clearly delineated the problem. While it is possible for an individual research worker who is an expert in his area to play it by ear, and perhaps partially formulate his strategy as he goes along, to alter plans in midstream when many persons are involved represents a serious imposition and can have disastrous results. To be sure, the investigator must not become so rigid that he continues to follow a planned course even if it later becomes obvious that it is unproductive. He must be flexible enough to be willing to make some compromises with rigor in order to satisfy the demands of those involved if it means the difference in completing the study or getting no information, and if the loss in accuracy is not so great as to reduce the value of the study to such an extent that it is no longer worth the time, effort, and money involved.   Nonetheless, some definite and specific plans should be made ahead of time, if for no other reason than to convince the appropriate members of the community that the study is both meaningful and feasible, and that the researcher knows what he is doing.

INVOLVING OTHERS IN FIELD STUDIES   If the answers to the three major questions outlined above are yes, then it is likely that the study is one which can be successfully carried out in the community.   The next decision with which the investigator is faced is that of whether to involve members of the community as active participant-investigators who share in the planning, gathering, and analysis of the data or to conduct the study largely as an outside agency using the community members only as subjects under study.

While there are those—the strongest advocates of what has been termed action research—who maintain that community members should always be involved completely, most modern investigators feel there is something to be said on both sides.   Admittedly, there are some real advantages to involving the entire community at every stage of the study, but there are also some situations in which it would seem best not to involve the members of the community so deeply, and sometimes not even to do a study at all.

One obvious advantage in involving the members of the community at all stages is that they are less likely to be suspicious if they are completely informed as to what is happening and why.   Second, persons who are involved from the very beginning have more time to give careful thought to the likely outcomes of the study and are more able to see for themselves the implications and values of the results.   Closely tied in with the latter is the fact that when people have themselves been involved in the planning of the study, and in the gathering, analysis, and interpretation of the data, they are more likely to accept and even carry out whatever recommendations have resulted from the investigation than they are if the recommendations come from an outside agency.   A final advantage of involving members of the community lies in the generalization which seems to occur in terms of an increased interest in further community improvement and perhaps even in both applied and pure research.

One of the situations in which it is questionable as to whether the community should be involved is that in which false pride, or perhaps the power structure (political or economic), has severely restricted the opportunity to be self-critical.   Under these circumstances, the members of the community, and especially an outsider, are not free to admit or even suggest that limitations exist—that a problem is there which needs to be solved.   Any person who does is likely to be considered uncooperative, a disturbing influence, or even disloyal to the community.   Attempts to carry out studies in such situations are likely to be met with resistance, and, even if ostensibly permitted, various administrative and other tactics may be employed which make the results meaningless. If a study must be done under these conditions, it is probably best that the investigator go about his business as quietly as possible, making necessary contacts individually and without fanfare.

A second situation in which it is probably best not to get the community involved is that in which the problem is recognized, but has become a "hot" issue. To be sure, a solution to the problem by research would probably be best, but when emotions are aroused it is wise not to have the work done by those who have a vested interest in the outcome. Even in the absence of strong emotional involvement we would all feel somewhat uneasy about the results of a study on the relationship between smoking and cancer done by cigarette companies, or a study by a manufacturer of light bulbs on the amount of light needed for reading, or of highway safety by a company which rents billboards. And few are going to accept the results—no matter how valid they are—if there is evidence of conflict of interest.

A third situation in which it is not usually advisable to involve the entire community is that in which the problem under study is a highly technical one. If the nature of the problem is such that considerable technical or professional background is necessary for an understanding of the reasons for certain procedures and approaches, any attempt to involve a great number of people is likely to be quite inefficient. Superficial explanations often arouse well-meaning but uninformed criticisms, especially from the more alert members of the community who often are the ones with the greatest influence. On the other hand, to provide thoroughgoing training for persons in the community whose time is limited and whose main interest is likely to be in other things than the research problem is obviously an arduous if not impossible task. The most effective approach when the problem under investigation is a highly technical one seems to be that of selling the key members of the community on the ability, competence, and ethics of the investigator and his team. Then the experts should proceed without involving all members of the community.

There are two other kinds of problems that may require information obtained in the field, but which make community involvement inappropriate. One having very limited applicability is typified by a case study of an individual. Here it is clearly unethical for the entire community to become involved in the gathering of information or to know the outcome of what may be a relatively private affair. The other situation is that in which knowledge of the study is likely to alter the behavior of those involved in a way which will change the outcome. In this latter situation it may be advisable to provide a complete explanation to all those affected *after* the data have been gathered, since to have involved members of the community earlier would have vitiated the results.

If none of the specific situations outlined above obtains and the investigator decides fully to involve the members of the community in the study, then there are several things which should be kept in mind when going about the process.

First, it will be to the investigator's advantage to begin the involvement early. Persons who are brought into the picture at a later time often become resentful, feeling that they are simply being used as drones to carry out the researcher's busy work, and realize that they have really had little to say about the project. At the same time, early involvement does not mean that a large community gathering should be called the minute the researcher has an idea. It is essential to think through the problem to begin with so that something specific and reasonable can be discussed at the first meeting, even though some of the plans may need to be altered considerably after this preliminary exposure.

In many instances the early meetings will be devoted to preparing the community for the project. This involves tactfully describing what the problem is, how the study will contribute to its solution, and the way in which the community can be improved by the results. It is especially important to maintain an air of honest objectivity. The attitude should always be, "Let's find out," and not, "We're going to prove," or "We're going to show that so-and-so is all wet."

Usually, when involving the community as a whole, it is worth the effort to learn something about the backgrounds and interests of as many persons as possible. This way the special talents of key persons can be used to advantage in making the project run more smoothly than would be the case if committee appointments and task assignments were made at random. When appointments are made they should be mutually agreed upon, and the tasks involved should be worked out specifically. It must be clear at all times who has the responsibility for seeing to it that each phase is completed.

Throughout the operation of the project, special effort will be needed to keep the lines of communication open. One of the greatest dangers when many persons are involved in a single research effort is that isolated groups, each concerned with its own specific task, will lose contact with each other. Progress reports, the bane of the individual researcher, become almost a necessity in a large group effort. The regular presentation of such reports before all those involved serves not only to coordinate efforts but to maintain interest and spur the more lethargic units into operation.

A final suggestion for those who deem it wise to involve the community as much as possible is that careful plans be laid for the implementation of the research results as well as for finding a solution to the problem of concern. Once an efficient organization has been set up to gather, analyze, and report the data, it can and should be used as well to see that the resulting recommendations are put into practice.

Computer Simulation

The use of computer simulation to study behavior represents the opposite of doing research in field situations.   Rather than working with real life as found in nature, the simulator seeks to produce, in the confines of the laboratory, a completely artificial but reasonable likeness of a behavioral system in which he is interested.   It is important to note, however, that the attempt is *not* that of duplicating reality, but rather that of placing important components of a real-life situation in a realistic relationship so that they can be manipulated to study the effects and implications of various ideas.

Simulation in the form of reasoning by analogy through mathematical and mechanical models has been a technique used by science for a long time. Only with the advent of the computer has such an approach become really feasible in the behavioral sciences.   For, in working with behavior, a successful analogy (i.e., a useful mathematical or mechanical model) requires the handling of a large number of variables in a dynamic rather than a static relationship.

As a feasible alternative to elaborate mathematical models, computer simulation was first used to test highly developed and sophisticated theories. However, further experience has suggested that computer simulation is even more valuable when brought into play at the beginning stages of theory and model development when the research worker is primarily concerned with the consistency of his ideas and the implications of his initial assumptions. With computer simulation, the investigator can go about the task of theory building piecemeal, developing a small part of his model, and then quickly checking this portion out with data from the computer before moving to the next component.

The computer must be highly accessible to the researcher to permit him immediate use at any time, and for an adequate amount of time, to allow a series of successive trial-and-error runs.   This essential relationship between the investigator and his computer is described by Licklider (1965):

He literally stands there, jiggling and trying to make the apparatus implement the thoughts that he has in his head. He can tell when the traces on the scope are getting better and when they are right.   Then he can look and see what structure he has produced in his analog simulation that causes the behavior he observes . . . . The idea is to represent our ideas in a way that lets them come to life when we press a button, that makes them dynamic so that we can see their implications and their behavior . . . . Always before . . . we have had to represent things in a static form on paper. When we wanted to do something with them, we had to get them back out of the static form, process them in our heads, and then put them back onto paper . . . . At last it is possible to analyze a situation by experimenting with the synthesis of relevant ideas—with the creation and modification of models—until we get them to work correctly and produce the observed data. Then we know what it might have been that gave rise to the situation under study (pp. 164–165).

The advantages of computer simulation are many. Not only can the investigator spell out the implications of a complex system involving many variables which cannot be visualized otherwise, and do it in a way which is far less costly and disruptive than working in a real-life field situation, but also he can do it without great mathematical sophistication. Further, the use of computer simulation forces him to confront his problem in explicit rather than amorphous terms and to work out relationships among variables in great detail. When computer simulation is used literally to "play around with ideas," the simulation shows up flaws in a theory before the investigator develops it too highly and becomes too emotionally involved with his creation. Finally, computer simulation permits a rapid and inexpensive testing of apparently "outlandish" conjectures where the likelihood of payoff is small but the return on a "hit" is tremendous.

The greatest danger in using computer simulation for the study of behavior is that some lay persons reading about or attempting to apply the results of the research may feel that the computer provides a precise duplication of behavioral phenomena rather than a useful analogy with which behavior might be described. But this danger is no greater in simulating behavior with a computer than it is in representing it by means of highly sophisticated mathematical or other theoretical models.

Detailed arguments for and against the use of models and analogy (and for and against computer simulation) in science can be found in Simon and Newell (1956), Nagel, Suppes, and Tarski (1962), Turner (1967), and in other discussions of the philosophy of science. Ample illustrations of the successful application of computer simulation to explore such areas of behavioral phenomena as problem solving, intelligence, learning, personality, and social behavior can be found in Newell and Simon (1961), Hovland and Hunt (1960), Loehlin (1965), and Gullahorn and Gullahorn (1963) respectively. The reader who wishes to pursue this approach to research further will find helpful general discussions of the techniques and applications of computer simulation in the behavioral sciences in such references as Hoggatt and Balderston (1963), Naylor (1966), Sackman (1967), Beshers (1965), Borko (1962), and Feigenbaum and Feldman (1963).

II.

Methods
of Research

2.

The Historical and the Case Study Approaches

THE CHARACTERISTICS OF HISTORICAL RESEARCH

The General Nature of Historical Research

Barzun and Graff (1957) have suggested that in one sense all research is historical. Since it is impossible to analyze data at precisely the same time it is gathered (even when data recording instruments feed information directly into a computer, a fraction of a second may be required for the computations), any analysis and interpretation which is made must be based on information about happenings that have occurred in the past. The student must not be misled by assuming that the only distinction between the historical approach and the others is the length of time between the occurrence of the event, the recording of the data, and the analysis and interpretation of the information gathered. There are important logical distinctions which will be described in subsequent sections.

As a truly distinctive approach, the historical method seems to fit in least well with the general scheme of the scientific method described in the previous chapter. This difficulty stems in part from the fact that historical research may be concerned with a historical problem in a special field as distinguished from a historical approach to a current problem in the field.

HISTORICAL PROBLEMS IN A SPECIAL FIELD When the main concern of the study is to produce an accurate record of what has happened in the past in the field of psychology or education or sociology, the investigator is faced with a truly historical problem. In many cases the approach used does not seem to have much resemblance to the stepwise process of the scientific method.

This is particularly true when the study is concerned with fairly recent history where, in general, the facts are available but have not yet been gathered together. Under these circumstances, for example, the research worker may simply collect the information and he may then either describe the status of the entire field at some specified period of time or describe the development of some particular aspect of the field over a period of time. In the former case, the study would be described as *cross-sectional* and in the latter as *longitudinal*. While this distinction between cross-sectional and longitudinal studies seems most often used in connection with historical research, the reader will also find it useful for describing developmental studies, where the researcher has the choice of examining a series of cross-sections of subjects at various ages or of following up a single group of subjects as they progress through the various ages. (See Chapter 3.)

On the other hand, whenever the time period studied is sufficiently long ago that records of events are not complete, the historical investigator finds a place for the steps of the scientific method. For example, a hypothesis as to what happened may be formulated on the basis of those pieces of information already at hand. Then, the investigator may say, if this happened, what else must have occurred that would leave data of some sort that could be uncovered? That is, he asks himself, if my hypothesis is true, what other kinds of data ought to be available that have not yet been found? Finally, the historical investigator seeks to verify his hypothesis by searching for this additional information.

In drawing his conclusion on the basis of whether the sought-after evidence is actually found, however, the historical investigator will generally make a different value judgment than would be the case in the typical experimental situation. This interpretation represents an important difference between the historical and the other approaches to research. When the historical investigator discovers some evidence which was suggested by his hypothesis, his confidence in the original speculation increases tremendously; but failure to find the information is often not particularly discouraging because there is a great likelihood that the appropriate material has been lost rather than never having existed. Quite to the contrary, in an experimental situation, failure to find a consequent can lead to complete rejection of the hypothesis, while verifying the existence of but one necessary condition may add relatively little confidence simply because the alternatives which could have produced the same observations are so numerous.

In spite of this difference, it is apparent that the scientific method can and should be employed even when the task is that of producing an accurate record of what has happened in the past. The reader may be surprised to note that in modern day attacks on purely historical problems, statistics is widely used. In fact, Mosteller and Wallace (1964) go so far as to use a study of the *Federalist Papers* to illustrate the use of Baysian decision theory, negative binomial distributions, correlation, regression, and other statistical approaches.

A HISTORICAL APPROACH TO CURRENT PROBLEMS IN A SPECIAL FIELD   In contrast to providing an accurate record of what has happened in the past, a second function of historical research is to help solve present problems by examining what has happened in the past.

Perhaps the most frequent application of this use of the historical approach occurs in the review of literature which may be done prior to carrying out a descriptive or experimental study. In general the review of the literature serves two main purposes. First, such a review is carried out to make certain the problem is a research one and not a teaching one. Before beginning a study the research worker needs to make certain that someone else has not already solved the problem, and that the task is not simply that of distributing the information among a wider segment of the population rather than trying to find a scientific answer. Second, the review of literature serves to suggest hypotheses. Almost always, a survey of past events provides fruitful generalizations from prior experiences which may hold for the present situation.

While there are some who might argue that the formation of the hypothesis should occur prior to the review of literature so as to prevent the limiting effects of knowing what has been said in the past, there is very little if any evidence to support this contention. In fact, some studies of the scientific problem solving process suggest that the most effective creative work is done by persons working by themselves stimulated by reviewing what has already been accomplished (Taylor, Berry, & Block, 1957). Apparently, creativity does not come from flying off into a dream world free from pressures and rational considerations, but rather from being flexible, being under a requirement to produce, and being highly self-critical (Maddi, 1965; Wallach & Kogan, 1965).

The formulation of the hypothesis is but the first step in the scientific method, and the historical method goes beyond this. The historical method can do more than merely provide suggestions on how to carry out a review of literature when one is concerned with using past events to shed light on today's problems. It can also be used to verify or refute hypotheses by means of what Chapin (1947) has termed the *ex post facto design*.

In the ex post facto design all of the steps of the scientific method as outlined previously appear. Here, when asking the question of what else must be true (if the hypothesis is) that can be observed, the research worker includes in the list of possibilities not only those events which might be observed at the present time (or in some future time in a laboratory situation which might be set up) but also those events which occurred in similar situations in the past.   In this case the element of control, so essential in modern research, is obtained by comparing the past situation with the present one, or with a second past situation which initially differed from the first only in the basic characteristic thought to produce an effect and thus under examination.   Then, by carefully describing the original conditions in the two instances, noting the differences in action, and recording accurately what happened in each case, the historical method might be used to shed light on some of today's important problems.

Before the reader becomes too taken with the historical approach as a means of answering current questions, a word of caution is in order.   As Campbell and Stanley (1963) have indicated, an ex post facto analysis has two major shortcomings.   First, no matter how many characteristics are used to match the comparison groups, there is no guarantee that they are alike in other important respects.   There will always be some initial differences between the groups beside the main variable under consideration, and there is no way of knowing which produced any observed effect.   Second, a regression phenomenon (see Chapter 4) will exaggerate any observed effects and, the more variables used for initial matching of the comparison group, the greater the exaggeration will be.

Thus, the use of an ex post facto design in an attempt to solve a current problem by means of a historical study is a poor substitute for a proper experiment.   If the historical approach is the only feasible one, it might be used in an exploratory sense to eliminate some possibilities as producers of an effect, for if no final differences between the groups appear in spite of incomplete matching and regression effects, then one can be sure that the basic characteristic under examination had no effect on other variables.

SPECIAL FEATURES OF THE HISTORICAL APPROACH   In addition to keeping the general nature of the historical approach in mind, the student should be aware of several special features of this kind of research.   Obviously, historical research depends upon observations which cannot be repeated in the same sense that a laboratory experiment or a descriptive survey can.   This in itself is an important distinction between historical research and other approaches and leads to certain special characteristics beyond those which would be anticipated if one considered all studies, even experimental, to be historical in nature.

Because the observations cannot be repeated and because they have usually not been organized or even conveniently recorded for solving a particular problem, historical research always involves intensive library usage and vast scholarly patience.   The worker who cannot tolerate the frustration of finding a crucial piece of information missing or spending the time required to sift through thousands of documents to find one meaningful statement is not likely to find much satisfaction in historical research.

A third characteristic of historical research is that, in general, each study is carried out by one individual. While there seems to be no reason why historical studies could not be done by teams of workers as is often the case with a descriptive project and, today, with laboratory studies, investigations involving the pure historical approach are only infrequently coauthored.

A fourth characteristic of the historical approach which has already been mentioned but which might be noted again is that it does not always carry a hypothesis. Closely related to this, though perhaps not so apparent, is the fact that historical research is more dependent upon inductive reasoning (or, more accurately, less dependent on deductive reasoning). In the historical approach, as compared with the experimental approach in particular but the descriptive approach as well, instances of reasoning from the specific to the general occur much more frequently than do examples of reasoning from the general to the specific cases. Both inductive and deductive reasoning are involved in almost every study, but often in the experimental study, the really important reasoning is that of deducing from the general hypothesis the specific instance which will provide the crucial test; while in the historical situation, it is the inference from the fragments of information which have been found to the general description of what actually occurred that holds the spotlight.

A final distinctive feature of historical research is the style in which the results are reported. In general, while it maintains the same objectivity, historical writing is usually much less rigid and much more narrative than is found in typical research reports of studies using other approaches. It is not, perhaps, too much an exaggeration to say that the historical investigator is generally free to present his material in the way he feels will provide not only the most accurate but also the most interesting picture of historical events possible. This does not seem to be the case with other research approaches where a fairly specific outline (as presented in Chapter 9) is often recommended or required for publication of results.

The Procedures of Historical Research

Traditionally, the basic steps of the historical method have been listed as: (1) the collection of data; (2) the criticism of data; and (3) the presentation of data. This list of only three steps probably reflects the fact noted previously that historical research does not always carry a hypothesis. While no investigator, historical or otherwise, gathers data at random, it is true that the simple question type of hypothesis serves its function of suggesting to the researcher what data to gather in such a direct and uncomplicated way that it often is not even explicitly stated and needs no further discussion. Similarly, since the presentation of data in historical research imposes no restrictions other than the objectivity and the intellectual honesty of the worker, it will not be discussed further. There are, however, some special things to note with respect to both the collection and the criticism of data in historical research.

COLLECTING THE DATA   *Types of notes*   Because a great deal of data collection in historical research involves library work, workers using this approach have developed some note-taking techniques well worth passing on to others who may find them useful in the bibliographic portion of descriptive or experimental studies as well.

First, historical investigators have found it useful to keep three types of notes.   *Bibliographical notes* are those which record facts about the article or document itself.   These are the notes which indicate the author, title, location, date, and other information which will be included in the bibliography or list of references.   *Subject notes,* on the other hand, refer to the items of information contained in the paper which may be used as evidence in the presentation of the data.   Usually, it is also necessary to indicate where the information came from.   Often this is done by means of a simple code which refers to a bibliographical note.   The final type of notes used by historical workers is called *method notes.*   In these notes the research worker jots down ideas which come to him as he is reading the material. They may include new hypotheses, new places to look for additional material, critical comments about the report under examination, and any other reactions which the reader has to the document.   In short, method notes include anything which comes from the reader himself rather than from the material.

A second suggestion based on extensive experience in note taking by historical investigators is to keep the notes on cards rather than on notepaper. Recording each type of note on a separate card, and for bibliographical and content notes at least keeping the information from each separate document on a separate card, can save the research worker hours of work later.   For example, when criticizing the data, when preparing the presentation of the data, and when setting up the list of references, the investigator may from time to time wish to sort his information by author, by source of information, or by topic in various ways.   And having the data on cards (or even further, using marginal codes or punches) will greatly facilitate this task.

Types of data   In addition to distinguishing among various types of notes, historical investigators have developed some special terminology to describe the different types of data which may be gathered.   One type of data is referred to as *consciously transmitted information*—information that has intentionally been prepared for posterity.   The documents and other materials included in the giant tubes buried at the various world fairs and the records of their existence would be of this type, since they have been created solely for the purpose of letting those in the future know what happened in our period of time.

On the other hand, *relics* represent unconsciously transmitted testimony to events of the time. These articles and documents are things which have been created for use at the time with no thought, or at least attention to, the possibility that the items might later be useful in describing life as it was. All of our mechanical gadgets, furniture, music, art, clothing, literature, structures, will someday be considered by some historian to be relics.

Finally, *memorials* are those things which seem to have some of the characteristics of both consciously transmitted information and of relics. Monuments, inscriptions, and public documents were created to commemorate certain events like births, deaths, and business transactions for the lifetime of those involved but not really to provide future historians with information. In an immediate sense, they are consciously transmitted, but in a broader sense they are created for use at a particular time and thus have the properties of relics.

Historical investigators also make a distinction between *primary sources* and *secondary materials*. Primary sources are records of what the writer of the document himself observed, while secondary materials are accounts prepared by those who themselves were not present to personally observe the events. Thus original reports of experiments found in the literature can be thought of as primary sources, while a review of the literature, a discussion in a handbook or an encyclopedia, and the like, would be classified as secondary materials. Obviously, one of the main concerns in doing historical research is to avoid an overdependence on secondary materials and neglect of the primary sources available because the latter are more difficult to find and organize than the former.

THE CRITICISM OF DATA   As a formal step in carrying out a research study, the criticism of the data is unique to the historical approach, although it might be well to incorporate it, as such, in the case study method also. If the criticism of data is done at all in the other approaches, it is done in the planning stages of the study, where the researcher examines and reexamines the logic which leads him to make certain observations rather than others, and where he satisfies himself that the necessary measuring devices, recorders, and other instruments to be used are accurate, dependable, and will not influence the outcome of the study. Obviously, in these other approaches, this critical examination of procedures is done before the investigation starts rather than after the data have been gathered. As contrasted with the experimental or the descriptive approaches, the investigator involved in a historical investigation (and sometimes in a case study) has no control over his data gathering devices. He must take his data where he can get them. As a result, no matter how carefully he plans his study, it is absolutely essential that he carefully examine whatever data he has been able to gather after they have been collected to determine their veracity.

In his critical examination of the data, the historical investigator seeks to answer two questions: (1) Is the document under examination a genuine one? and (2) Is the information contained in the document trustworthy? In the language of the historian, the first question involves *external* or *lower* criticism, while the second question involves *internal* or *higher* criticism. It is important to note that, while the two questions are different, they are not independent of one another. Certainly, the trustworthiness of the information in the document (its accuracy, its consistency, and so forth) may help determine whether the document itself is genuine; and similarly, the genuineness of the document may be an important consideration in deciding whether the information in it is trustworthy.

The historical worker sometimes also distinguishes between positive internal criticism and negative internal criticism. In negative criticism he momentarily assumes that the author of the document is fallible, foolish, or faking and seeks evidence that this is not so. In positive criticism, on the other hand, he assumes that the author is accurate, competent, and acting in good faith, but considers the possibility that the author was speaking figuratively and seeks the literal meaning of the statements in the document.

Advantages and Limitations of the Historical Approach

Keeping the general nature and the specific steps of the historical approach in mind, it is easy to see several important advantages and some major weaknesses in this method.

First, it should be noted that there are some problems which can be solved in no other way. For example, a study of the effect of the testing movement on school curriculum can only be studied historically. Since the question refers to a situation which can never be duplicated again (at least in this country), it represents a truly historical problem in the field of education.

Similarly, it sometimes is not feasible or even desirable to attempt to duplicate a past situation in the laboratory or in a small field situation to examine the effects of a set of variables. No one would advocate the creation of a war to study the effect of such an event on the social structure of a community. Rather, one can readily find many past instances and might therefore turn to the historical approach to examine antecedent and subsequent conditions.

Finally, some authors have suggested that the historical approach to research might be used as a practical device for alleviating an emotionally charged situation as well as for providing some useful information toward the solution of a problem. Whether a crisis has appeared within a community, a school system, or an individual, a study of what led up to the present situation can provide a dual service of solving a historical problem by supplying an accurate record of past events and equipping those involved with a new perspective of the present situation.

The major disadvantage of the historical approach is the lack of rigorous control in matching past situations with present ones. Because of this, only the gross effects can be detected, and seldom can the cause of these effects be directly attributed in a specific way to particular variables.

Unfortunately, where matching is difficult and imprecise there seems to be a greater (ignorance is bliss) rather than a more cautious tendency to generalize the happenings in one situation to other somewhat similar ones. While not really a weakness of the method itself, but rather a caution to those doing or reviewing historical research studies, there is a great tendency to generalize the findings far beyond the justified limits.

Finally, the historical investigator faces a problem which is not as bothersome in other fields: namely, how much data to gather before a conclusion can be reached. With other approaches it is possible to calculate the size of sample needed to ascertain accuracy within specified limits or to determine the likelihood of making the various kinds of decision errors at any point. This is not so with historical research. Here, each research worker must decide for himself whether he wishes to spend a lifetime in a particular area or whether he is sufficiently satisfied to turn to a new problem. Apparently, there are no guidelines which the worker can use to satisfy himself that further data in the area will not be fruitful.

THE TRADITIONAL CASE STUDY APPROACH

The case study approach to research in the behavioral sciences is peculiar. It carries with it some of the features of the historical approach: it has a dual purpose and it is difficult to fit into the general pattern of the basic logic of science. Yet, in some respects, it is much more like the descriptive approaches to be presented in the following chapter.

It is not always clear what is meant by a case study. Usually, the term refers to a rather intensive examination of some single unit. The unit, however, is not always restricted to one person. A case study might be made of a single school or a single school district or of a single community or, perhaps, of a single event (Morison, 1950). Sometimes, though, the case study label is used even when two or three "representative" instances have been selected and subjected to an unusually detailed description.

Finally, the case study seems unusual in the almost violent reactions that various researchers have toward it. Thus, Campbell and Stanley (1963) say of the one-shot case study: "It seems well-nigh unethical at the present time to allow, as theses or dissertations . . . case studies of this nature (i.e., involving a single group observed at one time only)." On the other hand, Young (1956) claims that: "The most meaningful numerical studies in social science are those which are linked with exhaustive case studies describing accurately the interrelationship of factors and processes." In a different context, Skinner (1963) says of operant methods: "Instead of studying

1,000 rats for 1 hour each, or 100 rats for 10 hours each, the investigator is likely to study 1 rat for 1,000 hours. The procedure is not only appropriate to an enterprise which recognizes individuality, it is at least equally efficient in its use of equipment and to the investigator's time and energy. The ultimate test of uniformity or reproducibility is not to be found in method but in the degree of control achieved . . . ." [1] There are some who feel that a case study is almost a complete waste of time and effort, while others argue that the use of larger numbers and statistics only hinders and obscures our discovery and description of laws of behavior.

The Distinctive Features of Case Studies

DUAL FUNCTION   Like the historical method, the traditional case study approach often serves a dual purpose. While intensive investigation of a single case is often made for the sole purpose of increasing our general knowledge in the area, perhaps more often than not it is carried on for the ultimate purpose of making a practical improvement in the specific instance examined, and only incidentally does it contribute to general knowledge. As a research method it must be examined with respect to the way in which it can help solve scientific problems rather than in terms of its effectiveness in improving the case investigated.

The results are hypotheses A second and exceedingly important distinctive feature is that the traditional case study leads not to well-established conclusions, but rather to what might better be described as empirically developed hypotheses. It has been said that *for example* is never proof, and certainly this is the situation when only one single instance of a unit which may vary in a number of ways from other units is examined. The case study alone can never be considered as adequate evidence for some particular hypothesis in a well-developed and highly structured situation except in those instances in which the contingencies are sufficiently controlled to guarantee generalizability of the results, or where the sole concern is with the particular instance at hand.

Flexibility Another characteristic of the case study approach seems to be the latitude and apparent general freedom which the investigator has with respect to the type and amount of data gathered, the sources of information, and the procedures used to gather the information. Sometimes even a well-done case study seems not to be a systematic study of a scientific problem at all, but a general hodgepodge of information gathered by an investigator following capricious whims and inclinations. This is not neces-

---

[1] Although both Young and Skinner argue for the study of individual units, the reader must not infer that the traditional case study approach described here is similar to the experimental analysis of behavior as described by Skinner. The latter is described in greater detail in another section of this chapter.

sarily the case, but a person reviewing studies which have followed the case study approach is likely to find a much greater variation in technique than other types of studies.

Application to trouble situations   Even though, fortunately, the case study is used more and more in a preventive way rather than as a therapy after a situation has broken down, it still seems safe to say that the most frequent application of the case study approach is in the study of persons or situations which have gone awry.   A riot suddenly occurs in what had been regarded a peaceful community; a respected and well-liked person is found wandering around with amnesia; Johnny, who seems to be bright enough, is failing in his schoolwork.   Immediately, the question is raised as to what went wrong, and a case study to answer the question why is begun.

The Specific Steps in the Case Study Approach

To help make the steps of the case study approach more meaningful, the example of Johnny, the apparently bright boy who is suddenly having scholastic difficulty, will be pursued to illustrate the procedures used at each stage of the study.   It should be recognized, too, that the steps in the case study approach are not, in practice, as distinct and clear as they may appear from the following discussion.   The main purpose here is to make clear all the essential components of a traditional case study.

DETERMINING PRESENT STATUS   Up to this point the investigator may have only a vague impression that something is wrong or, at most, have observed a single, specific, dramatic incident which indicates that a real problem exists.   The first step, then, is to gather descriptive information which will determine, as precisely as possible, the present status of the unit under investigation.   In Johnny's case the questions might be raised: Is he really having difficulty or did it just seem so to us?   If there is a real difficulty, how serious is the problem?   In precisely what areas is he having the most trouble?   Does the difficulty seem to be something which appeared quite suddenly, or has it gradually been growing and just recently come to our attention?

GATHERING BACKGROUND INFORMATION   Once an accurate description of the present situation has been obtained, it seems desirable to get background data. Thus, the second step of the traditional case study approach is to collect information about and examine the circumstances leading to the current status.   This step helps the investigator compile a reasonable list of possible causes of the present situation.   In a sense, this stage represents the process of formulating hypotheses about the true nature of the situation by making use of symptoms which appear in the data, of the researcher's past experience with similar situations, and of knowledge of the principles of human behavior. In Johnny's case, the list of possibilities might include such things as: a breakdown of family relations at home, an inadequate scholastic background, a problem of adjusting socially to the new school, a recent physical disability, a lack of scholastic ability (our earlier impression may have been wrong), a need to make an economic contribution to the family, a lack of interest in certain school subjects, and the like.

TESTING SUGGESTED HYPOTHESES   The third step of this approach is to gather specific evidence about each of the hypotheses suggested from the background information just gathered. Since behavior is often multideter-mined, it should be recognized that the investigator is not likely to come up with a single cause for the breakdown of the situation. Rather, the goal of this step should be that of eliminating some of the possibilities and gaining confidence that certain others are important contributors to the situation which resulted in the initiation of the study. This, therefore, would be the stage during which Johnny might be sent to a physician for a physical ex-amination, given a scholastic ability test and a series of achievement tests, and during which the teacher might make a sociogram of the class, interview the parents, and so forth.

INSTITUTING REMEDIAL ACTION   The fourth and final step of the traditional case study approach is to verify that one or more of the hypothesized diffi-culties actually contributed to the original difficulties. This is accomplished by instituting some remedial or corrective or improvement program *and then rechecking* the status to see what effect the change has brought about. Suppose, for example, that the main cause of Johnny's scholastic difficulties seems to be a serious deficiency in his ability to read. The final step would be that of putting the boy through a remedial reading course and subse-quently following up his academic performance to see if it did, in fact, change as a result of this particular action. If such a change were observed, it would probably be concluded that an important cause had been found; but if the anticipated result did not appear, it would be necessary to return to the third or perhaps even the second stage and repeat the process.

Advantages and Disadvantages of the Traditional Case Study Approach

Perhaps the great advantage of the case study approach, as far as adding to our body of knowledge is concerned, is that it is a tremendous producer of ideas, suggestions, and hypotheses about behavior. It seems almost an ab-solutely essential technique when exploring completely new fields. That is, when we have no idea of the communalities, the categories of variables which play a part in a situation, and where we are trying to formulate new concepts or a new framework within which to carry out controlled experiments later, then the case study approach will be highly productive.

Conversely, the greatest weakness of the traditional case study approach is its great inefficiency in situations which are already well structured and where the important variables have already been identified. Contributing to this general inefficiency in such a situation are several minor disadvantages which might in one sense be viewed as cautions to keep in mind when using or interpreting results from the case study approach.

First, the case study often assumes that all past experiences of the individual or past happenings in the situation have contributed to the final result. The consequences of this assumption is that much data are gathered which later turn out to represent more or less chance happenings with no real pertinence to the specific aspects of the situation under investigation. Second, more than other approaches, the traditional case study seems dependent upon the recall of others as to what has happened. Anyone who is aware of the fallibility of memory can easily imagine the extent to which this characteristic of case studies limits their effectiveness. Third, since case studies often involve a problem case, undesirable traits tend to be overemphasized and desirable characteristics tend to be underemphasized, thus limiting the extent to which results can be generalized to more typical situations. For example, a person reviewing case studies of racial strife in various communities is likely to be left with the impression that there are few, if any, places where serious antagonisms do not exist. Finally, the case worker is likely to become frustrated with the incompleteness of the data he can obtain, and, if more than one case is involved, with the variation in information from one situation to the next. For example, one child may have been administered one test of scholastic ability and a second child a different one and a third child none at all, or accurate community records might be available in one city while only hearsay reports must be used in a second.

Again, these disadvantages do not seem to be serious in purely exploratory situations where the main goal is a rich variety of suggestions, but they can become a real handicap when attempting to draw rigorous conclusions or determine precise and specific relationships.

THE CONTROLLED STUDY OF SINGLE ORGANISMS: DESCRIPTIVE EXPERIMENTATION

In the first chapter it was indicated that investigators who followed the informal scientific approach preferred to carry out their studies with single organisms, but, unlike those following the traditional case study method, used techniques involving a high degree of experimental control of both the experimental conditions and of the behavior under examination. In this section, the reader will be provided with a brief and introductory overview of the basic designs and techniques currently used by laboratory scientists working with single organisms in their research into behavior.

While studying the techniques of descriptive experimentation, the reader should remember that they were originally developed for use with lower organisms where intersubject variability was relatively small and where, as long as the animals were not mistreated, there was no great ethical concern about imposing a high degree of control on the subjects under study. As the approaches described in this section are extended to studies with human subjects (cf. Sidman, 1962; Schutz & Baker, 1968), both these problems become more acute. Further discussion of them will follow the presentation of the methods and techniques themselves.

Basic Experimental Designs

It is important to recognize that advocates of descriptive experimentalism in the study of behavior loudly disclaim any rigid rules of experimental design. Nonetheless, there does seem to be enough similarity from one experimental problem to the next to permit the description of a few basic prototype approaches. Before examining the specific designs it is worth recalling that, "The behavioral processes studied in . . . [this type of] . . . experimental analysis usually consist of changes in probability [or rate of response] as a function of manipulated variables" (Skinner, 1966, p. 216). In Figure 2.1 the height of the solid line represents the level of behavior as it is observed over time, while X stands for some experimental treatment or manipulation, and the series of 0's indicates the period over which the observations are made continuously, if possible.

STEADY STATE DESCRIPTIONS   The most primitive type of study, and one which should precede all others, is the descriptive investigation of a steady state of behavior. The strategy involved is simply that of: (1) setting up a precisely specified set of conditions expected to have an effect on behavior; (2) placing the subject in these conditions; and (3) carefully noting the kind of behavior which results. The outcome is a numerical description of the level of behavior as a function of time under the conditions imposed.

In this type of design, so-called control observations are not made in the given experiment, but are assumed to come from independent studies previously carried out. If no stable state of behavior is reached following the application of the conditions, then the experimenter must consider his study as a pilot investigation and try again, this time using a tighter control of the conditions or more highly refined measures of response level.

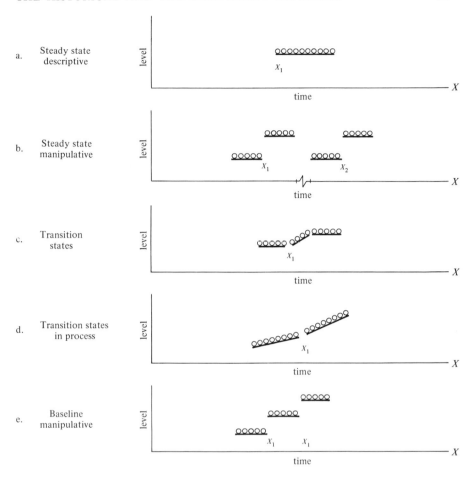

FIGURE 2.1   Schematic diagram of some basic designs used in the experimental analysis of behavior

STEADY STATE MANIPULATIONS   Once an experimenter can specify the particular antecedent conditions which will produce steady states of various sorts, he may take the next step of applying various experimental treatments to the steady state behaviors he can produce to see what effect they will have.   These treatments can involve either the separate application of different independent variables or the application of several different values of a single variable.

In general, studies which involve the manipulation of one steady state to another require a considerable period of time.   The most basic design is that shown in Figure 2.1b.   Once a steady state has been achieved, some experimental manipulation (such as the administration of a particular dosage of a drug) is carried out, and the resulting behavior noted.   Once the effects of the first experimental treatment have disappeared and the original stable behavior has returned, the second manipulation (a different dosage of the same drug, a different drug, etc.) is applied, and additional observations are made. The process continues until all manipulations of interest to the experimenter in the context of the investigation have been accomplished.

It should be obvious to the reader that whenever multiple treatments are applied to a single organism a major problem of concern is whether or not the effects produced are reversible. While there is no single-organism study design which will overcome the effects of true irreversibility, there are several techniques which an investigator can use to determine whether reversibility is possible.

When the effects of the treatment are anticipated to be relatively transitory the procedure already described will suffice. If the behavior returns to the original level between applications of the series of treatments, the effects can be considered to be reversible. Instead of waiting for the original behavior to be reached between each treatment, the experimenter can repeat an early treatment to see if the effects are the same after several intervening manipulations have been made. Another possibility is to complete the sequence of treatments and then to reverse the sequence of manipulations to determine whether the original behavior recurs. Finally, it is possible to make repeated applications of the possible different orders of treatments and to note whether a given treatment has the same effect no matter what series of manipulations precedes it.

TRANSITION STATES   Instead of waiting until the effects of some experimental manipulation have produced a stable behavior and describing it as the "product" of the conditions imposed, the investigator may concentrate on the *process* of the change itself. For example, an investigator may wish to see the effects of imposing a fatiguing condition on the rate of change in the acquisition of certain motor responses. It should be noted that the experimental condition might be imposed on a stable state and calculated to produce some gradual shift in behavior as in Figure 2.1c, or instituted in the midst of a change under the control of other conditions as shown in Figure 2.1d.

While studies of learning using rate of change as the major parameter to be related to the experimental conditions seem to comprise a great deal of the experimental literature today, what would appear to be the prior problem of ascertaining the precise limits under which change occurs has not been given nearly the attention it deserves. The reason for this state of affairs would seem to lie in the difficulty of ascertaining just when the transition state begins and when it ends. The problem of specifying the end points of a transition is complicated by the fact that many variables which ultimately seem to produce change do not seem to take effect immediately, and, conversely, seem to continue to influence behavior for some time after the operational procedure for terminating the experimental variable has been carried out. A purely operational definition seems inadequate. At the present time there seems to be no good way of determining exactly when the end points occur beyond that of providing careful specifications as to precisely what is meant by a steady state and then applying this steady state criterion to the observations themselves.

BASE LINE MANIPULATION   Another prototype investigation occurs when the research worker is interested in using the base line or original steady state behavior itself as a parameter to be investigated. As can be seen from Figure 2.1e, instead of applying several different treatments to a single base line, the investigator applies the same experimental treatment to different base lines. The result of this kind of study is a functional relationship between initial base line levels and final behavior states in the presence of a particular experimental variable.

Although the task of developing an adequate criterion of stability of behavior is important in all manipulative studies, it is crucial where the base line itself is to become the manipulated condition. All stability criteria involve a specification of the amount of variability in behavior which an experimenter considers permissible in a steady state. Although such criteria usually specify a fixed amount of variability over a given period of time (e.g., a difference in the number of positive responses of not more than three between any two out of three consecutive experimental periods), they may involve a sliding scale which adjusts to the magnitude or general level of frequency of the responses.

While stability criteria such as those described in the last paragraph are basically statistical in nature, they are always concerned with intrasubject rather than intersubject variability. They are also often judged by inspection of a plot of the data rather than by applying tests of statistical hypotheses as described in Chapter 6. Ultimately the test of an adequate criterion for determining when a steady state of responding has been reached is its usefulness in furnishing reproducible laws of behavior.

Establishing and Maintaining Behavior

To carry out any of the basic designs described above it is necessary that the experimenter be able to bring the behavior under his control. He must induce the subject to exhibit the behavior he wishes to study, and he must maintain the behavior exhibited at least until the application of the experimental treatment or condition. While the procedures by which this control is accomplished are becoming increasingly known among beginning students in psychology, and the skills involved can only be learned through practice in the laboratory, it would seem worthwhile to review the major concepts at this point, for research studies involving descriptive experimentation cannot be carried out without using these means of controlling behavior.

REINFORCEMENT SCHEDULES   The basic method of achieving the type of control over a subject's behavior required for descriptive experimentation is through the application of E. L. Thorndike's famous law of effect which, in brief, states that *those responses which are followed by satisfying consequences are more likely to occur again.*   If an experimenter rewards or reinforces a particular response, that response is more likely to occur again. Through repeated applications of the reward (usually by means of some automatic apparatus), the researcher may ultimately lead the organism to emit the desired response at various rates and under various conditions.   A wide variety of different reinforcement schedules or ways of applying the reward, each resulting in its own characteristic behavior, have been described by Ferster and Skinner (1957).   Chief among these are continuous reinforcement in which each response is rewarded, fixed interval reinforcement in which a response is rewarded only after a fixed interval of time since the last reinforcement, variable interval reinforcement in which reward is available following the occurrence of a response only after irregular periods of time, and a fixed ratio schedule in which the reward occurs only after a fixed number of responses have been made.

AVOIDANCE   In addition to controlling the behavior of an organism by providing it with a satisfying stimulus following a desired response, certain kinds of responses can be established and maintained by rewarding it with the removal of a noxious stimulus such as an electric shock.   It should be recognized that this procedure is not similar to the use of punishment which represents the application of a noxious stimulus to eliminate an undesirable response.   Punishment, unlike the application of avoidance procedures, generally reduces all responses and further, usually introduces unwanted physiological variables.   While the effects of punishment on behavior may be studied as an interesting phenomenon in and of itself, it is seldom used as a means for obtaining behavioral control in descriptive experimentation.

STIMULUS CONTROL AND CHAINING   If, over a period of time, the desired response is rewarded only in the presence of a particular stimulus, the organism will soon learn to make the response only in the presence of that stimulus.   When this happens, the behavior involved is said to be under stimulus control, and the particular stimulus used is labeled a *discriminative stimulus.*

The technique of stimulus control is especially useful to the investigator since, once the original training has taken place, he can in effect turn the behavior on and off by presenting or removing the discriminative stimulus.

Also, since a discriminative stimulus seems to acquire the properties of a reward, it can be used to reinforce some new response which then can be hooked up with or *chained* to the original response. The establishment of a series of responses by means of successive discriminative stimuli is called *chaining*.

SHAPING   All of the behavior controls described thus far have been concerned with getting a response which had already appeared in the organism with some degree of frequency to occur under certain specific circumstances. But a great deal of the applied work in education, in clinical psychology, and in other fields as well involves getting the organism to make responses which ordinarily do not occur in members of its species in the "natural" environment. An important additional type of experimental control which must often be brought into play by the researcher who is using descriptive experimentation is a method that enables him to shape whatever responses he desires within the morphological and physiological limits of the organism.

The shaping of a response occurs gradually by means of successive approximation. In the first stages of the process, the experimenter reinforces any frequently occurring response which even remotely approximates or is a component of the behavior ultimately desired. Once this remotely approximating response occurs with regularity, the experimenter withholds the reward until the next closer successive approximation appears. By carefully applying this process over a considerable period of time, the terminal behavior desired can finally be reached. Once the terminal behavior has been established, it can be brought under stimulus control and chained to other responses by the procedures already described. By careful and patient effort, the experimenter can establish and maintain a wide variety of highly complex behaviors.

EXTINCTION   In addition to getting the organism to make a response already in his repertory under specified conditions and to adding new responses to the repertory, the experimenter is sometimes faced with the task of eliminating a particular undesired response. It has already been noted that the application of a noxious stimulus (punishment) creates some unwanted side effects. Punishment reduces the rate of almost all responses of interest (not just the one to be eliminated), and it elicits a number of physiological responses which become associated with many stimuli similar to those present in the punishing situation, thus introducing unwanted variability. Therefore, the basic procedure for eliminating an undesirable response is not usually that of punishment, but rather that of *extinction*. The process of extinction, like the process of shaping, is generally a gradual one which occurs when the organism repeatedly makes the response without any subsequent reinforcement.

Reducing Variability

In our discussion of the informal approach to science it was noted that one of the hallmarks of descriptive experimentation was the view that variability was imposed on, rather than inherent in, behavior. Thus, when variability appears, it is up to the investigator to ferret out its cause and to reduce it. Several basic techniques have been generally found to be helpful in accomplishing this, and the reader who is interested in descriptive experimentation should at least be aware of what these procedures are.

STANDARDIZING TECHNIQUE   The failure to obtain intersubject replicability may occur because the apparatus used, the reinforcement schedule followed, the method of recording observations, or even the organisms themselves differed in what at first appeared to be minor ways. One solution to this problem is that of rigorously specifying and standardizing all the elements involved.

While such an approach would improve the situation in crudely devised and sloppily carried out experiments, it could easily lead to spending such a vast amount of effort on obtaining precision with minutiae as to become unfeasible. Worse, highly rigid standardization could prevent the observation of important behavioral phenomena. For example, behavior of humans outside the laboratory occurs in a relatively unstandardized environment; thus at some point in our investigations of the phenomena it will be necessary to study behavior in loosely controlled situations. While standardization of technique and apparatus will be helpful up to a point, there is a limit to the extent to which it can be usefully employed to reduce variability.

CONTROL OF ADVENTITIOUS CONTINGENCIES   Adventitious reinforcement can be defined as that reinforcement which strengthens behavior even though there is no causal relation between the two (Sidman, 1960, p. 349). The classic example of such accidental rewarding of specific behaviors is that previously described as "superstitious" behavior of pigeons under the heading of tenacity in the first chapter.

It is obvious that many accidental reinforcements will occur during the course of almost any experiment. These adventitious reinforcement contingencies will produce slight differences in response which do not appear in other replications and therefore must be classified as variability. Such occurrences are likely to become a major importance both in long-term experiments and in multiple-response situations, where their control is, as yet, beyond our capabilities. Further, it should be recognized that such contingencies also take place among the many responses which occur but which are not recorded as observations. These unrecorded responses become especially important because of their potential role as mediating responses.[2]

One way of controlling adventitious reinforcement in studies involving a discriminative stimulus is to arrange the presentation of the discriminative stimulus and the schedule of reinforcement in such a way that the patterns of behavior developed and maintained by the planned schedule and by the adventitious contingency will be distinctive. Instead of comparing the controlled behavior with a zero responding base, it would be compared with whatever behavior pattern occurred because of the adventitious contingency.

Instead of relying upon the adventitious reinforcement to produce a distinctive behavior pattern, the investigator can demonstrate his ability to control the behavior through the manipulation of specific variables by use of the process of chaining. That is, he can establish and maintain the behavior of concern by using the discriminative stimulus as a secondary reinforcer rather than by use of the original primary reinforcer which also will serve to produce the unwanted behavior patterns that result from adventitious reinforcement.

When it is desirable to have zero responding in the absence of the discriminative stimulus, a slight modification in the application of the chaining principle can be used to control the effects of undesirable adventitious reinforcement. Instead of using the discriminative stimulus as a secondary reinforcer to establish the behavior to be recorded, it can be similarly used to reinforce nonresponding. That is, the appearance of the discriminative stimulus can be made contingent upon the *absence* of responding during a specified period. During this period, the possibility of adventitious reinforcement is eliminated.

HANDLING BEHAVIORAL HISTORY   A third major source of variability which seems to interfere with intersubject replicability when findings are based upon the controlled study of a single organism stems from the fact that each different subject has a different past history of reinforcement and extinction experiences. Organisms which are similar in many superficial respects such as age, sex, body size, years spent in school, etc., may be quite different with respect to past reinforcement contingencies that have an important cumulative effect on their behavior in the specific situation under investigation.

The effects of behavioral history become increasingly important as more complex behaviors are studied, and the control of this source of variability becomes increasingly difficult with the study of higher organisms. At the present time, only three suggestions for handling the problem of behavioral history seem to be feasible. The first is to use experimental variables which are sufficiently powerful to overcome the effects of uncontrolled historical factors. The second is to gather explicit information about the general type

[2] Those readers not familiar with the basic concept of mediating behavior should see Kimble (1961).

of past contingencies which are brought into play in various culturally distinct subpopulations, and then to restrict the experiments, as well as the generalization of the findings, to the resulting homogeneous groups. The exception is in those instances in which specific evidence is to be gathered to show that particular past experiences have little effect on present manipulations. Finally, the experimenter can put the behavior to be studied under the control of a stimulus which is sufficiently unique as to preclude the possibility of stimulus generalization from past associations.

Special Problems in Application to Human Subjects

INCREASED VARIABILITY   The approach described in this section was originally developed in the animal laboratory where a great deal of control could be exercised to reduce the relatively small amount of intersubject differences which were found. In attempting to apply these techniques to the study of human behavior, however, the research worker is faced not only with the increased variability which results from larger genetic differences and from uncontrolled past histories of the subjects themselves, but also that which results from the fact that many complex human behaviors seem to vary in more dimensions than do single behaviors and to be irreversible.

One alternative in these circumstances is to confine investigations either to the study of those variables which produce powerful effects, or to a tedious series of experiments requiring the manipulation of one variable at a time in an endless number of different, highly restrictive conditions. The other is to make increasing use of some of the more recently developed statistical techniques which permit application to the study of single cases (Chassen, 1960). In connection with the latter, it should be noted that procedures which first provide for an analysis of repeated measures for a single organism, and then later combine the results to permit the researcher to ascertain the degree of intersubject replicability, are not the same as those which pool individual results to obtain a single curve. While the latter procedures may well obscure important information, the former do not. The objections which many persons who advocate the descriptive experimental approach have voiced to classical statistics tend to disappear as the method is applied to human subjects.

THE CONTROL OF HUMAN SUBJECTS   In the past, those who have most strongly urged the case study approach as a technique for providing information not obtainable through the traditional statistical experimental methods have been as much concerned with the task of improving the subject involved as with that of gathering data for scientific purposes. As a consequence, the data were often gathered haphazardly and analyzed intuitively. Thus, as Mefferd, Moran, and Kimble (1960, p. 354) point out: "It is true that there are many case history and similar reports in the literature where repeated measurements were made on the same subjects, but a typical case history does not incorporate the rigor, objectivity, precision of procedures, and controlled experimental design of a definitive scientific study."

Just what is required if the study of a single organism is to become as useful for scientific purposes as the traditional experimental-statistical approach becomes quite evident from the techniques of descriptive experimentalism as portrayed above. Unfortunately, the degree of control necessary to obtain adequate results far exceeds that to which most persons working with individual human subjects are either accustomed or are inclined to apply. The investigator seems faced with the dilemma of either attempting scientifically weak studies with human subjects or carrying out rigorous studies with lower organisms.

Ultimately, the ethical problem of conducting highly controlled studies with human beings is likely to result in the establishment of a pattern somewhat similar to that now followed in medical research. Basic and exploratory studies are most likely to be done with lower organisms first. Then, studies will be gradually replicated on organisms higher and higher on the phylogenetic scale until evidence from interspecies studies with subhuman organisms is sufficiently strong to provide confidence in a generalization to human beings. The first applications to humans will then be to those cases where all hope for improvement from traditional methods (e.g., of therapy in the case of clinical workers, or of instruction in educational situations) has been abandoned. Should the applications be successful in these first special instances, they will then be tried on a larger scale and with a more typical group of individuals. Finally, if the latter are successful, the findings will be incorporated into regular practice.

It should be noted that this question of the rigid control of human subjects in experimental situations is but one of several ethical considerations which have attracted the attention of both lay persons and scientific personnel in recent years. The final chapter of this book contains a more complete discussion of the whole problem of the conflict between individual and scientific values.

3.

The Descriptive Approaches

GENERAL CHARACTERISTICS OF THE DESCRIPTIVE APPROACHES

The Nature of the Descriptive Approaches

The characteristic that ties together the three approaches to be outlined in this chapter is their primary purpose: "painting a picture" of some particular situation rather than ferreting out so-called "cause-and-effect" relationships. Recognizing that the three approaches have a common purpose, the reader will not be surprised to learn that they also have in common a general breadth of application, a logical sequence of procedural steps, and a set of advantages and disadvantages. Before turning to a discussion of these points, however, it seems appropriate to note what the three methods are and to get clearly in mind the basis for distinguishing among them.

THE WAYS OF OBTAINING DESCRIPTIVE INFORMATION   Perhaps the simplest way to obtain descriptions of people and their behavior is to ask them to provide you with the necessary information, either by personal interview or by a mail survey, and the data thus obtained might relate to either factual information or to opinions. Research investigations which use this descriptive approach are often referred to as *questionnaire* or as *opinionnaire* studies.

The second basic method of obtaining information for descriptive purposes is observation, with little communication between the researcher and the subjects under investigation. Such observation might be of *the actual behavior* itself, in which case the study might be referred to as an activity analysis, a job analysis, or a process analysis. On the other hand, if the observations made concentrate on *the products of behavior,* the research might be referred to as a product analysis, a documentary frequency study, or a content analysis. Finally, the observations might concentrate on *the conditions in which the behavior occurs,* and the resultant study labeled a situation analysis.

The third way of obtaining descriptive information is to make measurements on the subjects included in the study. When this is done on a cross-sectional basis, the study is often referred to as a *normative survey;* but when a longitudinal approach is used or several cross-sectional studies are included together, the result is often called a *developmental study.*

The three basic methods of obtaining descriptive information have led to a wide variety of techniques which appear under many different rubrics. All of these minor variations need not be separately discussed, since what holds for one generally also holds for the other. Instead, the sections that follow our discussion of the common characteristics of the descriptive approaches will concentrate on the basic ideas involved in each of the three distinctly different approaches to gathering data.

THE EXTENT OF USE   Considering the behavioral sciences as a whole, it is probably still safe to say that the descriptive approaches are the most widely used of the three major varieties of research methods. While the natural trend toward the more experimental approaches which usually occurs as knowledge in the field increases is gaining momentum in both education and sociology, and currently represents much of the work in psychology, it is unlikely that descriptive research will ever represent only a small proportion of the work done in these fields.

One important reason for this is that the descriptive approaches have great value in both the preliminary and final stages of an experimental study. Thus, the descriptive approaches may serve as the "reconnaissance" phase of an investigation in a new area in which the purpose is to identify factors which are most promising for experimental investigation. The descriptive approaches may be used to portray the status of a situation after some procedure suggested by an experimental analysis has been put into effect.

A second reason for the rather widespread use of the descriptive approaches is that the kind of data yielded from such a study is highly regarded by applied workers as useful in coping with everyday practical problems. That is, the descriptive approaches often provide concrete facts describing the situation on the basis of which reasonably definite plans can be made for further action.

Finally, the descriptive approaches are widely used because they apply to a very broad class of problems. Thus, whenever a group of objects differs within itself, and one desires to know in what ways and to what extent these objects differ from one another, one of the techniques described in this chapter will be appropriate.

The Logical Sequence of Procedural Steps

All too often, naive researchers have a tendency to rush into a descriptive study and start gathering information immediately without taking time to stop and think what they are about. At best, the result is wasted effort gathering a great deal of unneeded data and, unfortunately, collecting data which cannot be adequately analyzed or which omits information crucial to an unambiguous solution to the original problem. A truly productive descriptive study requires much more careful planning than is generally supposed.

STATEMENT OF PURPOSE   The first requisite of a good descriptive study is a very clear statement of the purpose, goals, and specific objectives of the investigation. Starting with such a vague purpose as "to describe such and such a situation" is never enough, for such a statement fails to direct the attention of the worker toward appropriate sources of information. On the other hand, a specific statement as to why it is important to go to all the trouble of getting the descriptive information will immediately suggest the relevancy or irrelevancy of the various kinds of data which might be gathered.

Although a statement of purpose often represents a practical justification for the study, this need not be the case. It is just as important to indicate that the description is needed to check the implications of a theory as it is to say that the information is needed to overcome some practical difficulty. In either case, the question of *why* must be concisely answered before proceeding to the next step.

LISTING OF THE THINGS TO BE DESCRIBED   The second logical step of a descriptive study is spelling out in detail exactly what it is that will be described. This involves naming the sorts of things (processes, products, conditions, etc.) to be included, and then identifying the particular characteristics of the things which will be examined.

Obviously, a great deal of the effort at this stage will be devoted to a very careful definition of the variables which will be of major concern. Often, the most satisfactory definition will be an operational one in which the trait or characteristic is defined in terms of the way in which it is measured or observed.

PROCEDURES FOR GATHERING AND ANALYZING THE DATA   Once the specific characteristics to be examined have been identified, the next logical step is deciding precisely how the descriptive information will be gathered and analyzed. This includes, first, the selection (and sometimes the construction and evaluation) of the data gathering instruments in terms of their objectivity, reliability, and validity.[1]

Next, it is necessary to work out a detailed plan for obtaining the specific subjects to be included in the study. This usually involves spelling out procedures for carrying out one of the classical sampling plans (or a combination of them) as presented in Chapter 8.

Finally, it is essential to plan in detail just how the data to be gathered will be analyzed. This means: (1) determining exactly how the data will be categorized; (2) naming the descriptive indexes which will be used to summarize the information; (3) identifying which, if any, statistical tests of hypotheses will be applied; and (4) planning the charts, graphs, and tables which might be appropriate for the ultimate presentation of the results.

The importance of this last step cannot be overemphasized. Unfortunately, the research novice is prone to want to gather the data first and worry about how to analyze it later. All too often the result is to discover, too late, that an important assumption of the analysis technique has been violated in the data gathering process, or that a crucial bit of information has not been obtained. When this happens, the data gathered at great expense of time, effort, and money can often be only tenuously interpreted.

GATHERING AND ANALYZING THE DATA   The next major step of the descriptive approach is carrying out the procedures outlined in the preceding stage. If an adequate job of planning has been done, the researcher himself need not be involved except in a minor or supervisory role. Whenever possible, this task is relegated to a machine—an automatic recording device for gathering the data, and a computer for analyzing it. In some cases, of course, an interviewer or a special technician is used; but, always, the researcher himself is responsible for making certain that the specified procedures are accurately carried out. Nonetheless, it is true that the careful researcher now devotes much more of his time and energy to planning the study and to formulating the conclusions than to the relatively uninteresting process of gathering and analyzing the data.

DRAWING CONCLUSIONS   The final stage of a descriptive study is making inferences, and, perhaps, recommendations for whatever action is implied by the results of the analysis of the data gathered. While this step may seem too obvious to mention to persons who have read reports of research in psychology, education, and sociology, it is interesting to note that it is a step not always found in other fields. For example, many of the studies in the physical and engineering sciences end with the presentation of the results, leaving any interpretation to the reader.

[1] The technical meaning of these terms and the methods for getting evidence that a data gathering instrument is an effective one are presented in Chapter 7.

Just why the behavioral scientist traditionally is expected to present his own interpretations and conclusions as well as the results of his investigation is not entirely clear. Perhaps it is because there are so many possible misinterpretations to avoid with behavioral data; perhaps it is because the behavioral scientist is lazy and wishes the interpretation made for him; perhaps it is because, working with people, he is more aware of the problem of communication; or perhaps it is because he has so often been required to justify what he was doing (as contrasted with the physical, and to some extent the biological, sciences where enough concrete and immediately useful results have been produced so that the public no longer questions efforts in these areas). There is a basic danger in presenting a list of conclusions and recommendations at the end of a research investigation. The danger is that the particular biases and prejudices which the researcher carries with him into the study may show up in the final statement. Most often this leads to conclusions and recommendations which are in no way, or at best, only partially, supported by the data at hand. Sometimes, however, the result is that the researcher refuses to accept the findings of his own study. For example, in one study (cf. Fisher & Fisher, 1955) the investigators set up the hypothesis that scientists who preferred a more objective approach to psychological methodology would be less secure than those who took an intuitive attitude toward methodology. Their idea was that "the scientist pressed by anxiety might . . . take refuge in the symbols of objectivity so easily available to him in his science." When the data gathered showed just the opposite—that objectively oriented doctoral students in psychology were *more* secure than intuitively oriented students—the authors suggested that: (1) the more objectively oriented persons *became* less anxious because their precise answers gave them security; and (2) the greater anxiety of the intuitively oriented person was really a healthy dissatisfaction with current modes of interpreting phenomena. The possibility that the opposite of their original hypothesis was true—that the more anxious scientists took refuge in an ambiguous approach which would never prove them wrong— was conveniently ignored.

The best antidote for the tendency to reflect one's biases in the list of conclusions at the end of a study is to go down the list item by item, asking for each one: "Which of the data in this study lead to this particular conclusion?" Even experienced researchers are sometimes surprised to discover how many of the items listed come from outside the study being reported.

Common Advantages and Disadvantages of the Descriptive Approaches

Quite rightly, the descriptive approaches are frequently used as a check on laboratory findings. To isolate the specific efforts of important variables it is necessary to subject them to tight controls, and, no matter how elaborate the design, it is not possible to observe under controlled conditions all the characteristics and interactions present in a "real-life" situation. Seldom is it possible to lift findings from the laboratory and apply them directly in the field. In this sense, there is no substitute for a descriptive study.

Another important advantage of the descriptive approach is that, more than other approaches, it is amenable to the cooperative efforts of both layman and researcher. Whenever a study is carried out for the purpose of creating good public relations as well as to provide some information, the descriptive approaches stand out as most reasonable. Finally, as with each of the major approaches, there are some problems which cannot be carried out in any other way. A study that seeks to establish normative information or to examine the distribution of certain traits in the population requires the descriptive approach.

In examining the disadvantages of any approach it is important to distinguish between faults of the method per se and faults of the method when poorly used. One of the faults of a method, however, is that it is easily misused, and this is certainly one of the difficulties of the descriptive approaches.

Unfortunately, the descriptive approaches appear so simple on the surface that they are often selected by novice researchers who feel they can get by without a great deal of careful thought about the problem and, further, can avoid a statistical analysis. Generally when this happens, the descriptive study becomes merely information gathering and not research. Such an approach almost always leads to overgeneralization, results in gathering only that evidence which will support the ideas of the investigator, and becomes a one-shot study of only transitory significance.

A second disadvantage of the descriptive approaches is that they do not provide very much information about the effects of the variables under investigation. Because the important variables are not isolated and manipulated while others are held constant, no real evidence of cause and effect is provided. Descriptions of the natural situation can supply us with information about the concomitants of causation, but *not* of a causal sequence of events in and of itself. At best, a described relationship can be thought of as a necessary condition, but never a sufficient reason, for inferring causation.

A third major disadvantage is that it often requires the cooperation of persons, as subjects, over whom the investigator has no direct control. A great deal of time and effort must be expended in securing the interest and cooperation of those involved. Even though a subject has volunteered, he may have done so under peer pressure to conform, but is actually hostile. The result is almost always a great deal of missing information and some obviously useless data. Unfortunately, some deliberate distortions of the information provided can also occur and often remain undetected.

Finally, it should be mentioned that descriptive studies sometimes lead to complacency and satisfaction with a status quo rather than to improvement in the situation under investigation. For example, the discovery that a child is average, that a school or community situation is typical, or that most people have some feelings of insecurity often leads to the judgment that everything is satisfactory without any thought as to how adequate the situation is or what it could be like under ideal conditions. By contrast, the experimental approach is almost always oriented toward ultimate improvement.

THE SPECIFIC DESCRIPTIVE APPROACHES

Now that the general characteristics of all the descriptive approaches have been examined and some of the major advantages and disadvantages reviewed, it is time to concentrate on specific techniques. In each instance the unique characteristics will be described, the important variations noted, and the special advantages and disadvantages pointed out.

Questionnaire and Opinionnaire Studies

MAIL SURVEYS It will be recalled that a basic approach to obtaining descriptive information is to ask people for descriptions of themselves. One of the ways this can be done is by means of a mail survey. The obvious reason for carrying out a descriptive study by mail is cost; it is much less expensive and far less time consuming to put questionnaires in envelopes than it is to travel about and interview the subjects of the study. But, like almost everything else, the researcher gets what he pays for in terms of time and effort. The main question is whether in this day and age any mail study is worth the price no matter how low it may be.

Following a careful review of the advantages and disadvantages of mail questionnaires, Wallace (1954) concluded, "The safest rule in deciding whether or not to use direct-mail questionnaires is Don't." Anyone who is contemplating a mail study should read Wallace's arguments pro and con before he comes to a final decision about the wisdom of such an approach in his own situation.

It is not necessary to say a great deal about mail surveys since the same methodological statements that could be made about them are also true of interview studies. That is, the same care must be exercised in selecting respondents whether they are to be contacted by mail or in person, and almost the same suggestions apply for the construction of interview schedules as hold for the construction of mail questionnaires. In fact, about the only important difference between a mail survey and an interview study is that in mail studies the percent of return is small—between 20 and 40 percent on the average—as compared with interviews which typically result in about 95 percent return. The investigator who uses a mail survey is almost always faced with the question of how to estimate the effect the nonrespondents may have had on his results.

Most persons in the field now feel that, with our present day knowledge of small sample techniques, it is almost always better to spend what money is available on a small interview sample than it is on a larger mail sample. In general, the mail survey should be used only as a last resort, if then.

THE VARIETIES OF INTERVIEW APPROACHES   When the expression *interview study* is used, most people think of an investigation in which the investigator or his agents contact a large number of individuals in the community for a personal interview. While this approach is probably the most commonly used one, it is not the only one possible. Two other kinds of studies which depend upon interview techniques have been described in detail by Jahoda, Deutsch, and Cook (1951).

The first of these variations is the *panel study*. In the typical panel study the same group of individuals is interviewed on two or more occasions which surround the exposure of the subjects to some naturally occurring event. Often, some of the subjects have been exposed to the event and others not, and differences between the two groups noted. While the group involved is usually smaller than is the case for the typical individual interview study, the panel study provides an exceptional opportunity for the study of the causes and effects of change. With the panel technique it is possible to identify those who themselves changed or experienced the change in their community, to obtain direct and immediate, if subjective, statements about the reasons for change, and to obtain a personal description of the attitudes and feelings of those who are experiencing the change.

The second variation from the traditional technique is the *community self-survey*. In this approach it is not an outside agent who enters the homes in the community to obtain information, but the members of the community themselves who become involved in obtaining the information. Although an outsider may serve as a catalyst and a consultant, it is persons within the community itself who develop the questionnaire, do the interviewing and interpret the results in terms of implications for their particular community. The major purpose of this sort of "action research" is, of course, to motivate the community members to bring about the desirable social changes themselves.

SPECIAL CHARACTERISTICS OF INTERVIEW STUDIES   The primary characteristic of the interview study is that the observer, as the interviewer, is a vital part of the total situation.   Unlike experimental studies, or even other kinds of descriptive studies where the observer is a part of the background and has little influence on the results, in an interview study of any sort the interaction between subject and observer cannot be regarded lightly.

The interview study also poses the important question of how much structure is to be introduced into the data gathering process.   Structure means the extent to which the person doing the interviewing is required to ask every respondent the very same questions in exactly the same way—as contrasted with being allowed to ask different subjects slightly different questions, or, at least, to ask them in different ways, so as to take advantage of the exigencies of the moment.

At first it might seem that considerable latitude in structure should be permitted so as to take advantage of the personal situation.   It must be remembered, however, that in science the search is for what are called invariants.   That is, in research, the goal is primarily that of developing general concepts and laws which apply to and thus remain constant for many different situations.   The main advantages of an unstructured interview, on the other hand, come from clinical experiences where the main purpose is to provide help for a single individual as a unique human being.   In the latter circumstance, it can be legitimately argued that, since the causes of particular behaviors may vary from person to person, the questions appropriate for one person may not be relevant for another.   However, the scientist is not generally interested in the idiosyncrasies of the individual case, and only if what is discovered in one instance can be applied to another is a finding of value in a scientific sense.   Except in rare cases where there are compelling reasons for doing otherwise, a structured interview is used in research.

BASIC STEPS IN OBTAINING INFORMATION BY ASKING PEOPLE   The first step of any questionnaire or opinionnaire study is that of translating the stated general purpose of the study into the specific information needed from the individual subject.   This task requires little technical knowledge.   The researcher must simply sit down and carefully write out in detail exactly what information is needed to answer the questions raised by the research problem.   This step should not be forgotten or skipped over lightly because it appears so obvious and simple.

The next step is that of preparing the actual questionnaire that will be used.   As contrasted with the common sense approach taken in the first step, much technical help can be obtained from books devoted entirely to the topic of surveys (cf., for example, Parten, 1950).   Without going into all the technical details, several important general suggestions can be made which will start the beginner in the right direction in his first draft of a questionnaire.

1. The investigator should keep in mind, when writing each item, that

the major purpose of the questionnaire or interview schedule is twofold: to translate the research objectives into specific information; and to assist the interviewer in motivating the respondent to communicate the required information.

2. The language used must be gauged to both the level of the group to be interviewed and the precision of the data needed. Sometimes, when these two principles are in conflict, the researcher may be required to turn to another approach to get the information needed.

3. The writer must take into account the frame of reference of the respondent. A classic example of the difficulty involved here is described by Bancroft and Welch (1946) who report that in one investigation an estimate of the number of employed persons in the United States was increased by 2,500,000 when a question on an interview schedule changed from the general form of, "Was this person at work on a private or government job last week?" to whether the person "did any work for pay or profit during the census week." Apparently, homemakers and students who held part-time jobs did not see themselves as employed workers even though almost half worked 35 or more hours during the week in question.

4. The information level of the respondent must be kept in mind. Accurate results are not likely to be obtained from questionnaires which ask whether paleontology should be taught in the local high school or whether special prison facilities should be provided for recidivists.

5. The social acceptability of the possible alternative answers must be considered. Most respondents will lie or refuse to respond rather than destroy their ego by giving a socially unacceptable answer, though there will always be some who attempt to attract attention to themselves by exaggerating under such circumstances.

6. Leading questions must be avoided. It is not difficult to see that completely different results will be obtained if the question is "Do you want an expensive new city library?" than if the statement were more neutrally phrased. Sometimes, if a way cannot be found to state the question neutrally, a so-called "split-ballot" technique is employed where the question is phrased in a positive way on half the questionnaires and in a negative way on the other half.

7. Each question should be limited to a single idea. Double-barreled questions such as, "Was the speaker clear and concise?" can only lead to ambiguous results (unless by chance there is a direct one-to-one relationship between the two characteristics).

8. It is usually best to arrange the sequence of questions from the more general to the more specific.

9. The questionnaire should be pretested. It must be tried out on a small sample of persons who are from the same population (but not final sample) to which the results will be generalized. This is probably the most important suggestion of all. No matter how carefully written the first draft

or two of the questionnaire is, some ambiguities always seem to appear when respondents attempt to answer the questions.

The third step in carrying out that type of descriptive research asking people for information concerns the selection of the respondents to be contacted. This involves a careful definition of the universe to which inferences are to be made and the selection of an appropriate sampling design for the specific situation at hand. An adequate choice from among the possible sampling plans cannot be made without some knowledge of sampling concepts and a familiarity with some of the characteristics of basic sample designs. Before carrying out this step, the reader will need to study the material covered in the first section of Chapter 8.

Once the respondents have been identified, the next logical step is that of selecting and training interviewers. Again, it is recommended that the inexperienced investigator take the time to carefully study the interviewer selection and training techniques which are described in great detail in books concerned solely with surveys. In general, the adequate training of interviewers includes three basic elements:

1. A Clarification of the Goal of the Interview   This is provided so that the interviewer can properly handle any unique situation which may arise. It is absolutely essential, however, that the instructions given identify only what information is desired and *not* what the researcher's hypothesis is as to the likely outcome of the study. Unfortunately, no matter how honest an interviewer is or how impartial he tries to be, the possibility exists that he might favor certain responses over others through a gesture, a facial expression, a tone of voice, or another cue of which he is not aware. Also, it is essential that the interviewer report in detail to the researcher any situation which requires something out of the ordinary. Only in this way can the investigator determine whether the results from a particular respondent have been spoiled and whether a new respondent needs to be selected.

2. Motivation of the Interviewer   It is important to convince the person who will be gathering the data of the importance of the study as a whole. If this is not done, some interviewers, no matter how carefully selected, may tend to become lax in the accuracy with which they record information. Even worse, when the motivation of being paid for a job is not coupled with a feeling that the data are important, an occasional interviewer has been known to actually fake the results.

3. Practice in Interviewing   Although not yet carefully verified experimentally, there are a number of guidelines for interviewers which have been developed through experience. These should be provided to the interviewer. More important, however, is that each interviewer can be provided with both vicarious and actual practice in the task of interviewing. One highly effective approach is to have prospective interviewers listen to recorded interviews and discuss them critically with the investigator, pointing out both the things to imitate and the things not to do. Almost without

exception, the training should end with actual practice on persons who have been selected from the "target population" but who were not drawn to be included in the payoff sample. This affords one last opportunity to clear up in advance any difficulties which may arise because of the uniqueness of the respondents in this particular study.

When the interviewers have been adequately trained, the process of gathering data begins. With an adequately developed interview schedule and with well-trained interviewers, this step should go smoothly and reasonably automatically. About the only additional thing which can be mentioned is that every effort must be made to convince the respondent that he is a part of a legitimate research study. Usually, this can be accomplished by: (1) explaining the purpose of the study; (2) describing briefly the method by which he (the respondent) was selected; (3) identifying the sponsor or agency conducting the research; and (4) stating the anonymous or confidential nature of the answers given.

The final step, as with other types of studies, is the analysis and interpretation of data. This is best accomplished through the use of standard statistical techniques as described in Chapter 6.

SPECIAL ADVANTAGES AND DISADVANTAGES OF THE SURVEY APPROACH   As with other approaches to research, there are some kinds of information which are virtually impossible to obtain by any other means. For example, reactions to past experiences (or even data as to what the experiences were if no record is available), anticipated future behavior, and a report of one's thoughts while carrying out an activity (such as solving a problem or confronting a person toward whom one has strong feelings) can only be obtained by asking for a verbal report from those who have had the experience. Also, where the intent is to study *perceptions* or *stated attitudes* per se, then asking persons to describe what they see and how they feel is the only possible way to obtain the information.

A second advantage is the directness involved. As long as the circumstances are such that the researcher can assume that the respondent has no reason, conscious or otherwise, to distort his report, then asking persons to describe their attitudes and perceptions is the most simple and direct approach to use. It avoids the difficulties and disagreements which occur in an attempt to infer the attitudes and the perceptions from the behavior observed.

A third advantage to the interview approach stems from the fact that the interviewer can modify the situation when necessary. He can clear up a misunderstanding about a question and keep the respondent on the track of providing only essential information, something especially important when working with childen. Also, the interviewer can note special happenings and pick up clues which might prove to be highly valuable in interpreting the results and for future study—something that an aloof observer or a measuring device may not be able to do. Finally, in "action research" where the interest is as much to bring about change in those involved as it is in finding out information, the interviewer can set the stage for the development of certain attitudes in the respondent.

While the fact that the interviewer can actively participate in the data gathering process represents an advantage under certain circumstances, it also represents the greatest danger and therefore a potential weakness in the approach to getting information by asking for it directly. This danger is that interviewer characteristics will influence the responses. It must never be forgotten that when information is obtained through an interview the description is not just of the observed, but of the observed responding to an observer. There is always the question of how much of what has been observed is attributable to the respondent himself and how much is attributable to the special traits of the person doing the observation. While such techniques as training the interviewer to maintain a uniform pattern of behavior toward all respondents, selecting interviewers with somewhat similar characteristics, having several interviewers visit the same person on separate occasions, or using a sufficiently large number of interviewers and respondents in the hope that interviewer characteristics will cancel themselves out can minimize the problem, they can never completely eliminate the effects of the observer's role in the situation.

A second major disadvantage of the direct approach of asking persons for information is that it assumes that the respondent is not only willing but able to provide reliable results. While ideally such an assumption is valid, practical experience suggests that all too often such conditions do not, in fact, obtain. Even a skilled interviewer cannot always overcome the respondent's motivation to consciously influence the results by distortion if he has a mind to. Nor is the interviewer likely to be able to prevent every respondent from preserving his self-esteem in conflict situations by not responding or by lying. Further, even when the respondent is completely honest and forthright, there is no way yet known to overcome the memory bias which leads us to remember certain things and forget others and to fill in when recall is hazy. The respondent also may not possess the necessary information or the ability to provide accurate answers. Those who are aware of the length of time effective psychotherapy usually requires will readily recognize how difficult it is for persons to gain insight into their own behavior, and thus how unlikely it is that a short interview can lead a respondent to provide accurate descriptions of the causes and effects of his own behavior.

In time, it may be possible to reduce these two major disadvantages of the interview approach. For the present, however, sufficient knowledge of the dynamics of interviewing simply does not exist to be able to do so. To be sure, past experience has provided many rules of thumb which we think can be used to help alleviate some of the problems.   Unfortunately, few of the principles of interviewing as now formulated have been put to rigorous experimental test.

Observational Studies

One of the ways to overcome the major disadvantages of asking people for descriptions of themselves is to obtain the data by watching and recording what happens in the situation under examination.   It will be recalled that when this is done the study is referred to as an observational study and, as such, may concentrate on the behavior (including verbal behavior) of the subjects involved, on the environmental conditions under which the behavior is exhibited, on the products of the behavior, or on some combination of these.

UNIQUE CHARACTERISTICS OF OBSERVATIONAL STUDIES   A major feature that distinguishes observational studies from interview studies is the role of the observer.   Rather than taking an active part in adjusting each new situation to each specific subject to try to get maximum information, the person gathering data in an observational study remains aloof.   This is accomplished either by having the observer physically removed from the situation (for example, through the use of a one-way vision screen or a hidden camera or tape recorder) or by having the observer become so much a part of the situation that he is completely ignored or fully accepted as a member of the group.   Further, the research observer, unlike the teacher, the clinician, or the social case worker, all of whom must react immediately as each new piece of information is obtained, records what happens, withholding his analysis and recommendations for a later time.

A second thing to note about observational studies is that they involve much more than casual observation.   It is a serious mistake to assume that a broad overview of a situation will reveal those specific things which are relevant for some particular research purpose.   Thus, an adequate observational study must be carried out systematically.

As a systematic investigation, an observational study first requires careful identification of the specific things to be observed.   Further, it involves immediate recording of the information as the observations are being made rather than the preparation of reports of what has happened based on memory.   Finally, in so far as possible, the observations should be made quantitatively.   For example, the observer might count the number of times an event occurred or rate the product or environment on a numerical scale rather than attempt to portray the situation in the form of verbal, anecdotal descriptions.

VARIETIES OF OBSERVATIONAL STUDIES   Although observational studies may vary in a great many ways with respect to details, there are three major types: participant-observer studies, systematic observation of small groups, and content analysis.

Participant-observer investigations are characterized by the fact that the observer, to a certain extent, plays the part of a member of the group that is being observed.   While this is generally done to preserve the naturalness of the situation and to reduce the effect of an observer in the situation, its main advantage is to enable the observer himself to participate in the experiences of the members of the community or group.   The latter may be of considerable importance in helping the researcher formulate tenable hypotheses which might be impossible to do without both intimate familiarity with the situation and the actual feelings of the persons directly involved.

Obviously, the participant-observer study requires a special kind of devotion to research.   To gather data the investigator must give up, temporarily at least, his own comfortable way of life and adopt that of others.   In addition, the participant-observer must be especially skillful in maintaining his objectivity.   While the research worker may not be able to ask intelligent questions without considerable familiarity, becoming too friendly may lead him to become personally involved or to take as commonplace the very behavior he should be carefully describing as relatively unique and interesting.   Furthermore, it should be apparent that the success of such a study is often highly dependent upon those personal characteristics of the observer which determine whether he is fully accepted into the group rather than upon his skill as a researcher.   Finally, participant-observer studies are generally quite unstructured in nature, because, until he has been in the situation, the research worker may not know which variables are most relevant.   In general, participant-observer research is likely to be most efficient in exploratory work.

Whenever the investigator knows what specific aspects of group action or of individual action in the group are particularly relevant, then systematic observations of small groups are usually in order.   When a great deal is known not only can the investigator formulate specific hypotheses to test in the observational study, but he may even be able to inject enough control into the situation to eliminate some extraneous outside influences without disturbing the important features of the situation which are under scrutiny.

Thus, small group observation is usually quite structured in nature, and a great deal of effort goes into the task of developing appropriate instruments and devices for recording the observations.   It is also necessary to give considerable attention to what to do with the observer, for no matter how unobtrusive, the presence of a person obviously doing research may change the behavior of those being observed.   Selltiz Jahoda, et al. (1959) report that many investigators feel that members of a group soon get used to an observer and that: "it makes little difference in the observed behavior of the group whether the observer sits in the room with the group, behind a one-way screen with the group aware that he is there or behind a one-way screen with the group left to wonder if he is there or not." However widespread this belief among investigators, a review of the literature on the effects of the experimenter by Kintz, Delprato, et al. (1965), as well as a book by Rosenthal (1966), strongly suggests that the effect of the experimenter on results is far greater than might be suspected, even in laboratory studies where rigid control is maintained on everything except the variable of the experimenter himself.

Earlier, mention was made of the fact that observational studies included those in which observations were made of the products of behavior as well as those concerned with either the behavior itself or the situation in which the behavior occurred. One kind of product—man's verbal communications—is observed so often in the course of research investigations that the special name of *content analysis* has been given to the process. It is important to note that content analysis does not involve just a casual reading over of many documents but rather a systematic approach which usually results in quantitative information. Although early studies of this type involved simple frequency counts of convenient, ready-made categories, modern content analysis often requires both considerable ingenuity in devising measures which permit valid inferences about more complex relationships, and technical skill in the development of a sophisticated sampling design for describing a precisely specified content universe.

Content analysis is a very laborious process requiring painstaking attention to detail, much like historical research. Like historical research, content analysis also requires careful consideration of not only what the documents, records, graphs, photographs, etc., portray, but the trustworthiness of the information as well. A person who feels that content analysis might be appropriate for a research problem he has should consult a more detailed reference like Berelson (1952), who points out the many ways content analysis can be helpful, provides specific procedural information, and carefully cautions the reader against the weaknesses of the method.

SPECIAL PROBLEMS IN OBSERVATIONAL STUDIES Regardless of the type of observational study, the major tasks with which the research worker will be faced include: (1) deciding exactly *what* to observe; (2) establishing observational procedures which will specify exactly *when* the observations are to be made and *how* they will be recorded; and (3) the training of the observers.

There is no simple prescription for deciding exactly what to observe. The investigator begins with the hypothesis about the way in which the characteristics of concern manifest themselves, and sets about devising ways of noting and recording information about the behaviors expected.

In observational studies as well as in other applications of the scientific method, the researcher is faced with this question: "If such and such exists, then what will occur that I can see?"

Some writers have suggested that an adaptation of Flanagan's (1949) "critical incidents" technique might be helpful in deciding what to observe. This technique was originally developed in connection with job analysis as a way of determining what traits to measure in a test to best predict job success. Basically, the idea is that observations need be made only of those specific incidents which are critical—i.e., only those things which have been found to have a marked effect on success or failure of some activity. At first this seems to be a valuable suggestion: concentrate only on those things which are crucial to the relationships under consideration; but there are some special problems connected with the use of critical incidents in this way. First, such an approach requires judgment by the observers as to what is and what is not critical—and judges do not always agree on this, especially when the judgment is made during the observational period. Second, even if the decision as to what is critical is determined by the researcher rather than the observer, only rarely occurring phenomena will be included. Truly critical incidents do not occur very often. Finally, the apparently critical occurrence which brings about the crucial change may be only the culmination of many important events leading up to the incident, or simply a catalytic agent which precipitates an action, the primary determinants of which were apparently static conditions that were present long before the ostensible critical incident occurred.

Others (e.g., Whithall, 1949) have felt that since verbal behavior is so important in human affairs, verbal interactions are of prime importance. There is even here the problem of deciding whether the assumed reaction of the listeners (Bales, 1950) or the intention the speaker had (Steinzor, 1949) should be of greatest concern. Further, since most researchers do not feel that the verbal interactions are the only things of importance, few are willing to restrict themselves to just these kinds of observations. On the other hand, a researcher who fails to take note of verbal interactions along with other observables is going to be remiss. At the present time, most investigators will reason from the specific hypothesis to be tested as to what must be observed, and include in their study only those characteristics which they believe to have direct relevance to the problems at hand.

Even though it is not possible to be specific as to what to observe, some definite suggestions can be made with respect to the task of developing adequate observational procedures. First, it should be apparent that it is not possible to make continuous observations from the beginning to the end of time, so the first step is to decide when to observe. The most acceptable solution is to follow a time-sampling procedure. In developing a time-sampling procedure, the research worker carefully defines a universe of time and then makes use of one of the sampling designs described in Chapter 8 for selecting a sample of persons or objects. For example, the investigator might make his observations for a ten-minute period of each hour randomly selected after stratification by time of the year and day of the week. It is most important to note at this point that just dropping in every now and then or arbitrarily selecting a convenient day is not likely to produce a time sample which will yield observations that are representative of ongoing occurrences.

In addition to developing a time-sampling plan, it is necessary to devise a system for obtaining accurate records of the happenings. In general, best results are obtained when checklists or tally sheets listing the specific behaviors of concern are used. Thus, the task of the observer should be that of checking off a behavior which he sees or of making a tally each time it occurs. Observational schedules which require considerable judgment or reflection on the part of the observer are to be avoided, and simply taking notes on what happens can produce no information of any value except in the most exploratory of studies, if then. Observers who are required to make judgments on the spur of the moment usually produce inconsistent data, and when time is taken to think about whether a particular action is worth recording or writing down as an anecdotal description, much of crucial importance might be missed. It is also recommended that observational checklists be kept as short as possible, preferably of such a length as can be printed on one side of a single sheet of paper and as can be easily memorized by the observers. Keeping a list of items short may sometimes require the use of categories of behavior rather than the specific behaviors themselves. Whenever this is necessary, it is important to provide the observers with specific examples of the behaviors as well as the category names and to give the observers considerable practice in using the check sheet.

Much of what has already been said about the training of interviewers is also applicable to the training of observers. There are, however, some things which are different, and these need to be mentioned. While it is possible to develop an interview schedule first and then later bring in and train persons to use it, ideally, observers should participate in the development of a check sheet for recording ongoing events. While the interviewer can wait until the answer to one question is adequately recorded before going on to the next, events just won't wait for an observer to get his information down. Actual practice with the preliminary forms of an observational schedule often brings to light psychomotor limitations in recording information which might otherwise have been missed. Similarly, the interviewer can always take the time to record in detail a response which is sufficiently novel to raise doubts about how it should be classified; obviously, no such opportunity arises when describing continuous events. Thus, it is absolutely essential that the observer is perfectly clear as to how each and every different action he may see is to be handled.   This requirement can most effectively be met only when observers themselves have the opportunity to modify the schedule on the basis of some trial runs.

While it was suggested that interviewers be told the general purpose (though not the specific hypotheses) of the study so that they could clarify questions which the respondents may have had, the investigator who is training observers must be exceedingly cautious in this respect.   While it may sometimes be desirable to explain why a certain behavior is to be observed, doing so will more than likely lead the observers to see only certain things and ignore others.   Seldom does an observer have to know why he is observing something in order to make an accurate record of what happens.   A classic example of the danger in letting observers know the purpose of the observation is the study by Sheldon and Stevens (1942) in which a substantial relationship was found between body types as determined from photographs and certain personality traits measured by means of a rating scale that was filled out on the basis of a personal interview. Unfortunately, the persons doing the rating of the personality knew what Sheldon's hypothesis was and obviously could judge the body type at the same time that they made the observations of personality.   When this methodological error was corrected by using raters who did not know the purpose of obtaining the ratings (and also when personality tests were used instead of ratings; cf. Fiske, 1944), none of the postulated relationships could be found.

Finally, in the selection of observers, it is essential that no great cultural differences exist between the observers and the observed.   Otherwise much of what happens may pass unnoticed—or be completely misinterpreted.   A gesture, or grimace, or even a particular verbal phrase may be meaningless, or even worse, mean one thing in one culture and signify something entirely different in a second.   For example, in certain Oriental cultures sticking out one's tongue is a sign of happiness, while in Western culture this is usually taken as an indication of displeasure.   Similarly, among the Maori people raising the head and chin means "yes," while among Sicilians the same gesture means "no."

SPECIAL ADVANTAGES AND DISADVANTAGES OF THE OBSERVATIONAL APPROACH   The major advantage of the observational approach is its directness.   It avoids the necessity of dealing with hypothetical constructs inferred from behavior and works directly with the behavior itself.   If done carefully, there is less need to worry about the problem of conscious faking or unconsciously protecting one's ego in responding to direct questions.   It is especially useful for getting at such things as judgment in choosing companions, aesthetic appreciations, and cooperation.

On the negative side, a really satisfactory instrument for recording observations is much more difficult to construct than a typical interview schedule, and, sometimes, preparing a satisfactory observational schedule requires even more effort than developing a psychological test. Finally, in terms of time efficiency, the observational study ranks lower than the other two basic descriptive approaches. In the informal situation, the researcher is obliged to "live in" with the observed for a considerable length of time; and in the more formal observation studies, such a limited aspect of the situation can be accurately observed at one time that, in a given period, not nearly as much information can be gathered as by asking or by measuring people.

Normative Surveys and Developmental Studies

NORMATIVE SURVEYS The major difference between the normative survey approach and the questionnaire and observational approaches already discussed is in the system for quantifying observations. The steps are very much like those we have already seen: translate the problem into specific characteristics to be measured; choose or develop a test (by procedures described in Chapter 7) to measure the traits of concern; gather the data by administering the test; and finally, analyze the data by computing various descriptive indexes (as described in Chapter 6) and by making appropriate comparisons among groups.

Whenever the characteristic the research worker is interested in observing is one for which appropriate measuring devices are available (or can be readily constructed), this approach should be used. The chief advantage of the normative survey approach, then, is that it can make use of all the technical knowledge and experience which has been gained in the field of psychological, educational, and sociological measurement. The major drawback or danger is that of selecting things to include in a descriptive study simply because a good measuring instrument is available rather than because they are important to the problem. There is also a danger in failing to recognize that even the best tests and inventories are not perfect but rather are only representative of the most effective system for measuring many human characteristics that has been developed up to the present.

DEVELOPMENTAL STUDIES In one sense, developmental studies are simply normative surveys applied to the task of studying changes over time (i.e., to the task of investigating maturation and aging effects). Traditionally, developmental studies have been described as following one of two basic designs: the cross-sectional or longitudinal approaches as mentioned in Chapter 2. When applied to a developmental problem, a cross-sectional study involves gathering different samples of persons considered to be representative of various specified age groups and making comparisons among these. For example, a research worker might first obtain a sample of five-year-olds, of eight-year-olds, of eleven-year-olds, of fourteen-year-olds, and of seventeen-year-olds, and then obtain various measures of interests, social attitudes, personality, etc., on each subject. Finally, the research worker using the cross-sectional approach would note how the average scores obtained by the various groups change with age. On the other hand, an investigator following a longitudinal approach would select a single group of five-year-olds and measure them repeatedly—for example, at the present time and again at succeeding three-year intervals—until they reach the age of seventeen. The longitudinal research workers would similarly note changes with age by noting the average score at each age for the one group.

Different studies of the same developmental characteristic which approach the problem from these two different designs do not always lead to similar results. A great deal of discussion has been generated about the relative advantages and disadvantages of the two designs. Recently, however, Schaie (1965) has developed a general model which subsumes the two traditional designs as special cases and which makes apparent the reasons why the cross-sectional and longitudinal designs sometimes produce results which are not in agreement.

An example of the complete model is given in Table 3.1. The body of the

TABLE 3.1
Ages of Cohorts Studied over Age Ranges of Five to Seventeen with Three-Year Measurement Intervals

Time of Birth	Ages								
1948	5	8	11	14	17				
1951		5	8	11	14	17			
1954			5	8	11	14	17		
1957				5	8	11	14	17	
1960					5	8	11	14	17
	1953	1956	1959	1962	1965	1968	1971	1974	1977

Time of Measurement

SOURCE: Adapted from Schaie, K. A general model for the study of developmental problems. *Psychological Bulletin*, 1965, **64**, Table 1. P. 93.

table presents the ages of cohorts (i.e., of persons who were born during the same year) between the ages of five and seventeen which might be studied at three-year intervals. In this schema, a cross-sectional study would occur when samples of cohort groups in a given column were taken. For example, a study done in 1965 would select samples of children born in 1960, 1957, 1954, 1951, and 1948 in order to get information about children at three-year intervals beginning with age five and ending with age seventeen. Similarly, a longitudinal study would be made by sampling groups described in a given row. A study beginning in 1965 would sample

1960 cohorts (i.e., children born in 1960) in 1965, again in 1968, and again in 1971, in 1974, and in 1977. It should be noted that the traditional longitudinal study is a special case of this more broadly conceived longitudinal design in which the same sample of children is used in successive measurement years rather than drawing a new sample of children born in 1960 every third year.

From this general model it is readily seen that, in a cross-sectional study (which involves comparisons among age groups in a vertical direction), it is not possible to determine to what extent differences that are observed are attributable to actual age differences or to differences resulting from the fact that the children were born in different years. That is, age and time of birth differences have been confounded. In the same way, the longitudinal approach, which compares groups in a horizontal direction, confounds age differences with time of measurement differences. It is impossible to determine to what extent differences that have been observed are attributable to true differences in age and to what extent they are attributable to the fact that the measurement was obtained at different times. In addition, when the same sample of children is used over and over again, as in the case of the traditional longitudinal approach, problems of the effects of repeated measurement with the same test arise.

Schaie points out that it is possible to overcome confounding of the various possible sources of developmental change only by using so-called sequential strategies—strategies which involve more than one row or column in the study design. Thus, it is possible to use a *cohort-sequential* method, a *time-sequential* method and a *cross-sequential* method.

In the cohort-sequential method longitudinal studies for two or more cohort groups are made simultaneously: for example, by taking two or more rows of Table 3.1. Only if changes in the characteristic under study are independent of changes which might result from doing the measurement at different points in time, will this study result in evidence about true age change. As Schaie points out, this condition is likely to hold only in the case of physical or other genetically determined characteristics. The time-sequential method, on the other hand, involves a design which includes at least two columns of the table. With this strategy, true age differences can be separated out whenever such changes are independent of the effects of being born in one year rather than another. This assumption is most likely to be violated in the case of genetically controlled variables (each successive generation is taller and heavier than the preceding) and least likely to be violated by those traits which are primarily determined by culture. Finally, a cross-sequential design requires comparisons involving at least two rows and two columns (for example, the trapezoidal area encircled with a broken line in Table 3.1). Results from this method are unambiguous only when changes in the characteristic of concern are independent of true age changes—i.e., for those characteristics which would be constant with age were it not for the fact that measures were obtained at different times in our culture or for the fact that there are genetic differences which result from being born at different times. As Schaie points out, such a design is not likely to be useful for studies during childhood but could provide unambiguous evidence about the effects of environment over time on adults.

In conclusion, Schaie suggests that:

the most efficient design for a developmental study consists of the following scheme:
(1) Draw a random sample from each cohort over the age range to be investigated, and measure at time k. (Score A)
(2) Get a second measurement on all Ss tested at time k at time l. (Score B)
(3) Draw a new random sample from each cohort in the range tested at time k plus one cohort below that range, and test at time l. (Score C)

An example of this ideal design applied to the study of developmental changes at three-year intervals from ages five through seventeen beginning in 1965 is shown in Table 3.2. As can be seen from this table, such a design

TABLE 3.2

Ages of Groups Studied at Three-Year Intervals in an Efficiently Designed Investigation of Developmental Changes over Age Range Five to Seventeen

Time of Birth	First Sample (Score A) Age	Group	First Sample (Score B) Age	Group	Second Sample (Score C) Age	Group
1948	17	a	20	f	20	k
1951	14	b	17	g	17	l
1954	11	c	14	h	14	m
1957	8	d	11	i	11	n
1960	5	e	8	j	8	o
1963					5	p

1965 (time k)   1968 (time l)

Time of Measurement

requires data from sixteen different groups (labeled a through p in Table 3.2) fathered at two points in time and separated by a three-year interval. With the information thus gathered, Schaie recommends that the four comparisons summarized in Table 3.3 be made. According to Schaie, "Almost all questions of interest to the developmental researcher can be handled by this strategy which should yield interpretable results in practically all empirical situations."

It should be emphasized that the effective use of the various models described by Schaie requires careful consideration of the characteristic under investigation. In particular, it is essential to know the extent to which the trait being studied is primarily a function of cultural or of genetic changes.

TABLE 3.3

Groups Compared to Permit Study of Appropriate Age Changes
According to Schaie's (1965) Optimal Design

Number	Comparison Model Followed	5 to 8	Age Changes Studied 8 to 11	11 to 14	14 to 17
1	cross-sequential	*e* and *p* vs. *d* and *o*	*d* and *o* vs. *c* and *n*	*c* and *n* vs. *b* and *m*	*b* and *m* vs. *a* and *l*
2	time-sequential	*e* vs. *o*	*d* vs. *n*	*c* vs. *m*	*b* vs. *l*
3	cross-sequential repeated measures	*e* vs. *d* and *j*	*d* and *j* vs. *c* and *i*	*c* and *i* vs. *b* and *h*	*b* and *h* vs. *a* and *g*
4	cross-sequential practice controlled	*p* vs. *j* and *o*	*j* and *o* vs. *i* and *n*	*i* and *n* vs. *h* and *m*	*h* and *m* vs. *g* and *l*

In the past, such information was obtained by examining correlational data showing the degree of similarity between pairs of individuals sampled from various groups. Examples of such data as compiled by Ruch (1948) and Burt (1958) can be seen in Table 3.4.[2] It can be noted, for example, that the drop in between the first and second row, which results from a shift in genetic similarity while cultural background remains essentially constant, is just slightly less for the I.Q. than it is for height. Similarly, the drop in similarity is going from the second to third row, which results from a shift in cultural similarity while genetic similarity remains the same, is nil for height and slight for I.Q. Thus, one could reasonably conclude that both height and I.Q. are primarily functions of heredity, though I.Q. is slightly more influenced by environment than is height.

Now, however, Schaie has provided a set of decision rules that can be followed when interpreting the results from an analysis of variance [3] to enable the researcher to determine whether a trait under investigation meets the various assumptions required for the different sequential models. Thus, the modern researcher who is investigating developmental problems can determine from his own data which designs and comparisons are the most appropriate.

---

[2] The reader not familiar with the correlation index as a measure of similarity should be aware that a value of zero indicates a complete lack of similarity and a value of 1.00 would be found only if the pairs of individuals compared were completely similar to one another. Since the correlation index is *not* a percentage scale, however, the person who wishes to fully appreciate the meaning of the above information would refer to the discussion of correlation in Chapter 6.

[3] The basic concepts underlying the analysis of variance are given in Chapter 6.

TABLE 3.4
Degree of Similarity Between Pairs of Individuals Sampled from Different Groups

Data Compiled by	Source of Change in Similarity from Row Above (C = culture; G = genetic)	Group Sampled	Height	Intelligence
Ruch (1948)	C and G same	identical twins	.90	.90
	C same; G reduced	fraternal twins	.50	.55
	C reduced; G same	siblings	.50	.50
	C reduced; G reduced	parent and child	.30	.30
	C reduced; G reduced	grandparent and child	.15	.15
	C reduced to 0; G reduced to 0	unrelated individuals, random pairing	.00	.00
Burt (1958)	C and G same	identical twins, raised together		.94
	C reduced; G same	identical twins, raised apart		.77
	C increased; G reduced	fraternal twins, raised together		.54
	C reduced; G same	siblings, raised together		.52
	C same; G reduced	unrelated children, raised together		.28

CAUTIONS IN THE USE OF THE DESCRIPTIVE APPROACHES TO RESEARCH

Before leaving the discussion of the descriptive approaches to research, it is essential to point out three things which the user of any of the descriptive methods must keep in mind if the research results are to make a contribution to our knowledge.

The first thing which must be remembered is that the common characteristics which may be found when describing any particular group of individuals may not be traits that are unique to that group. Failure to keep this in mind can lead to what D. G. Patterson (see Blum and Balinski, 1951) has referred to as the P. T. Barnum effect. This effect can be readily demonstrated by following a procedure similar to that described by Forer (1949). The instructor announces to a class, following an essay examination, that it is possible for him to read the student's character from his handwriting on the exam. Then the instructor can pass out to each of the students a written character analysis especially prepared for him and placed in a sealed envelope. After each student has had an opportunity to examine the statements describing him, the instructor can ask for a show of hands to indicate how many felt the analysis was accurate. While a few will always claim it did not describe them, most students will feel the handwriting analysis did provide a fairly accurate picture. Then, just as the students are about to accept handwriting analysis as an effective way of describing character, the instructor will ask that the students exchange descriptions. When this is done, the students will discover that the descriptive statements are identical for each person.

The point is, of course, that there are a certain number of things which are descriptive of all of us no matter how we are classified or grouped. In a research setting, the same sort of thing all too often occurs when an attempt is made to describe delinquents, men who had a mental breakdown during military combat, persons from a particular social class, or children of a given age. The results are often simple descriptions of the common characteristics of the special group observed. A researcher might report that a certain percentage of subjects come from broken homes, a specified percentage had enuresis beyond age eight, etc. The trouble is that the same descriptive phrases apply to all teen-age children, delinquent and nondelinquent alike, to all combat soldiers, to all social groups, or to children of most other ages, as well as to the one particular sample of persons under study. Thus, the researcher who uses the descriptive approaches must find not only characteristics which are common to the group under study, but those traits which are unique to this particular group as well.

A second thing which must be kept in mind by those using the descriptive approaches is that seldom is description per se an end in and of itself. We do not describe the common and unique characteristics of school dropouts just so we can hang their psychometric pictures on the wall for all to admire. Rather, the ultimate hope is that from the description, dropouts can be identified and helped to achieve their potential before it is too late. And so it is with other groups. We describe a social class not just to be describing it, but in the hopes that ultimately such a description will enable the various cultural groups to get along better with one another. A taxonomy of behavioral disorders is useful not because it helps us distinguish among the various types of psychotics, but because such a classificatory scheme will suggest (i.e., predict) which therapies will and which therapies will not work with the individual so classified according to symptoms. In short, description which does not ultimately facilitate prediction or control is meaningless. Keeping this in mind will be of tremendous value in helping the researcher whose immediate concern is purely description to decide which of the infinite number of characteristics that might be observed should be examined and which of the characteristics may be safely ignored.

Finally, it must be emphasized that seldom, if ever, is the interest of the researcher confined solely to those particular individuals included in his study.   Almost always the hope is to discover some relationships, some laws, or some characteristics which will also be true of other individuals, perhaps similar with (but of course not identical to) those persons on whom the actual observations have been made.   Almost always, a descriptive researcher must concern himself with the principles of drawing inferences from a sample to a population as described in Chapter 6.   The person who seeks to do descriptive research in the hope of avoiding the use of statistics is only kidding himself and attempting to rationalize away the necessity of being rigorous in drawing conclusions.

4.

The Experimental Approaches

THE NATURE OF THE EXPERIMENTAL APPROACHES

The Concept of Experimentation

The experimental approaches are considered to be the prototypes of the scientific method of problem solving. They have been described as procedures for gaining knowledge by collecting new or fresh observations under controlled conditions. They set up relatively simple cause-and-effect situations where one or more variables are manipulated and their effects observed while other conditions are held constant.

BASIC TYPES OF VARIABLES   The term *variable* as used by the experimental researcher refers to any aspect of behavior or any condition which can change. Investigators using the experimental method identify three major types or categories of variables which must be considered in any given study. The aspects of behavior or the conditions which are manipulated in a given experiment are referred to as the *experimental* variables. Experimental variables represent one type of a broader class of variables called independent variables. The other type of independent variable is represented by those characteristics and conditions which the researcher tries to hold constant or control during his experiment. While these variables might be labeled controlled variables, they are more frequently referred to as *independent* variables. In common usage, those independent variables that are to be controlled are called independent variables, while those independent variables which are to be manipulated are referred to as experimental variables. The final category of variables represents those conditions or aspects of behavior which the researcher expects to change as a result of the manipulation of the experimental variables. The variables which are expected to change (i.e., the ones which the researcher anticipates will reflect the effects in the study), are usually called *dependent* variables. Sometimes, however, they are referred to as *criterion* variables since they represent the criteria by which it can be determined whether the experimental manipulations had any effect.

It is essential to note that the identification of a particular variable as experimental, independent, or dependent holds only for a given experiment. This is so because the same condition or characteristic of behavior might be regarded as an experimental variable in one study, as a dependent variable in a second investigation, and as an independent variable in a third. For example, "time spent in practice" might well be an experimental variable which is manipulated to determine its effect on a dependent variable of level of performance; or, in a study of the effects of different types of incentives, time in practice might be an important dependent variable. Finally, in a study of different instructional approaches, the amount of time spent in practice might be an independent variable which was essential to control. The investigator must classify his variables anew under the labels independent, dependent, and experimental for each different investigation.

CONTROLLED STUDIES IN FIELD SITUATIONS Traditionally, the experimental approaches have been appropriate only for the laboratory where all sorts of gadgetry and special restrictions can be used to hold all variables but one constant, while that one is systematically varied to note the effect. Beginning about 1926 with the work of R. A. Fisher and continuing up to the present time, various contributions to the field of statistics have made such a practice obsolete. A special laboratory can no longer be regarded as a necessary (and it never should have been regarded as a sufficient) condition for an adequately controlled research study. At the present time, thanks to the concepts of *replication* (repeating the experiment on several groups), *randomization* (assigning subjects and/or treatments to groups by a random process), and specific *statistical control* (mathematically adjusting the results to account for the effects of experimentally uncontrollable variables), it is possible not only to carry out a study in a field situation with little interference with the ongoing activity but also to manipulate several variables at once, noting the effects of each alone as well as the interaction effects among them.

An illustration of the way in which several variables can be manipulated in a single experiment is provided in Table 4.1. This table suggests the schema for studying the effects of class size and teaching approach on whatever dependent variable or variables (such as amount of learning, rate of learning, number of dropouts, etc.) might be of interest. The design illus-

TABLE 4.1

Possible Study Design to Assess the Effects of Class Size
and Teaching Approach

Teaching approach	Size of Class			
	Small (1–10)	Medium (11–30)	Large (31–75)	Very Large (over 75)
Lecture				
Recitation				
Independent study				

trated calls for twelve groups of subjects, each group to be taught by the method indicated in the row and in the size of class suggested by the column heading. Information about the effects of teaching method without regard to class size would be obtained by comparing row totals, that is, by comparing groups classified by rows only. Similarly, information about the effects of class size without regard to teaching method would be obtained by contrasting groups classified by column alone, that is, by comparing column totals. Finally, the interaction—the extent to which the efficiency of the method depended upon the class size—would be determined by comparing cells, that is, by comparing all groups classified by both size and method of instruction. There is, of course, no mathematical reason to stop with just two dimensions. A third factor, such as subject matter taught, could also be added as a third dimension to the schema. Then, in addition to the three main effects of class size, teaching method, and subject matter, there would be four interaction comparisons which could be made: between class size and teaching method, between class size and subject matter, between subject matter and method of instruction, and the higher order interaction among class size, teaching method, and subject matter. With modern computers there is no limitation to the number of variables which can be included in a single study as far as the mathematical analysis of results is concerned. However, the practical limitations of finding an adequate number of groups and of making comprehensible interpretations of third- and fourth-order interactions would seem to suggest that no more than five or six different experimental variables can be feasibly handled in any one investigation. This number, however, far exceeds what could be accomplished in the days when the classical paradigm of varying only one factor at a time had to be followed.

From these general remarks, it should be apparent that the term "experiment" as used by the research worker is quite different from the common lay interpretation of the word as representing a "tryout" of something new or different. In a sense, such a lay usage of the term implies only the earliest form of research: trial-and-error learning. True experimentation, however, is much more involved than instigating a new procedure and casually observing the outcome. It is important to examine carefully the logic of experimental design, to note the varieties of experimental designs which have been developed for studying human behavior, and to see clearly the specific steps which need to be followed in carrying out any such investigation.

The Logic of Experimental Designs

Careful experimental design is a rigorous exercise in logic. Superficial approaches have long provided many humorous anecdotes, such as that of the individual who was studying the jumping behavior of a flea:

After carefully conditioning a flea to jump out of a box on an appropriate auditory signal the "experimenter" removed the first pair of legs to see what effect this had. Observing that the flea was still able to perform his task, the second pair of legs was removed. Once again noting no difference in performance, the researcher removed the final pair of legs and found that the jumping behavior no longer occurred. Thus, the investigator wrote in his notebook, "When all the legs of a flea have been removed, it can no longer hear."

Perhaps one of the most famous attempts to spell out the logical requirements of good experimental design is that of John Stuart Mill (1874) who set forth five canons of logic by which so-called cause-and-effect relationships could be determined. The methods he suggests are as follows:

1. Method of agreement:
If two or more instances of the phenomenon under investigation have only one circumstance in common, the circumstance in which alone all the instances agree, is the cause (or effect) of the given phenomenon.

2. Method of difference:
If an instance in which the phenomenon under investigation occurs, and an instance in which it does not occur, have every circumstance in common save one, that one occurring in the former; the circumstance in which alone the two instances differ, is the effect or the cause, or an indispensable part of the cause of the phenomenon.

3. Joint method of agreement and difference:
If two or more instances in which the phenomenon occurs have only one circumstance in common, while two or more instances in which it does not occur have nothing in common save the absence of that circumstance, the circumstance in which alone the two sets of instances differ, is the effect, or the cause, or an indispensable part of the cause of the phenomenon.

4. The method of residues:
Subduct from any phenomenon such part as is known by previous inductions to be the effect of certain antecedents, and the residue of the phenomenon is the effect of the remaining antecedents.

5. The method of concomitant variation:
Whatever phenomenon varies in any manner whenever another phenomenon varies in some particular manner, is either a cause or an effect of that phenomenon or is connected with it through some fact of causation.

As useful as Mill's guides are, they must not be applied automatically or carelessly. Without thoughtful attention to the requirements of each approach, inappropriate conclusions are all too easy to come by. Becker (1964) has provided a humorous illustration of the way in which a careless application of Mill's canons led to erroneous conclusions. Becker's story is as follows:

It seems that a "cocktail party" researcher decided to apply the method of agreement to ascertain the cause of inebriation. By carefully observing his sociable companions, he soon noted that one drank scotch and water, one bourbon and water, and one gin and water. As the evening wore on and all three became quite drunk, it became obvious that the only common element, water, was the cause of the phenomenon observed.

But, being of a cautious nature and of an experimental bent, our amateur researcher decided to apply the method of residue to be certain that drunkenness was not caused by elements other than water. Thus, he concocted a mixture of scotch, bourbon, gin, and water, and systematically replicated his earlier finding by noting that the mixture did in fact produce inebriation. Next, our investigator mixed a similar concoction but left out the scotch.

Since the phenomenon of drunkenness still occurred, scotch could be safely eliminated as a cause. Not wishing to complicate things by manipulating more than one variable at a time, our naive researcher remixed the original concoction, this time omitting only the bourbon. Since, once again, inebriation occurred, bourbon could safely be eliminated as a cause. Similarly, gin was shown to have no effect on behavior. There was, of course, no need to test the water by this method since his previous study had already proved that it did produce inebriation.

Our researcher, of course, was a completely ethical individual. In the report of his findings he gratefully acknowledged the financial support he had received from the American Association of Liquor Distributors.

A wealth of background information about the effects of alcohol prevents us from accepting the conclusions reached by the "cocktail party" investigator, and leads us to search for the fallacies in his design. That such sophistication is not always present when exploring new areas of research is amply illustrated by Becker's description of a number of studies in the area of programmed instruction which sought to identify important elements of learning in practical situations, but which were designed along the lines of the investigation carried out by our naive research worker described above.

To help guide investigators in overcoming some of the fallacies commonly found in experiments, Campbell and Stanley (1963) have examined over twenty research designs with respect to their susceptibility to (or immunity from) a variety of common threats to valid inference. The remainder of this discussion on the nature of the experimental approaches is largely based on their concepts.

INTERNAL DANGERS TO VALIDITY OF EXPERIMENTS   It has been noted that the essence of experimentation as the prototype of the scientific method is control. As yet, however, little has been said about what it is that must be controlled. The answer is that the things to be controlled are those factors other than the experimental condition under investigation which may have produced the observed results. In the study of human behavior, there are a number of very specific rival hypotheses which always pose threats to what Campbell and Stanley have called the *internal validity* of research studies. These rival explanations of observed events, which *must* be accounted for if the results of a study are to be at all usable, are as follows:

1. History   Because human beings interact so greatly with their environment, it is almost impossible to achieve the experimental isolation from external events that is possible in the physical sciences—at least without bordering dangerously close to unethical practice. Since it is impossible to carry out an experiment at a single point in time, there is always the possibility that some external environmental event will occur between the beginning and the end of an experiment which will have an effect on all the subjects under observation. Any effect of the occurrence of such an event on the behavior of the subjects, therefore, will be confounded with the effects of the experimental variable itself.

2. Maturation   Since the human organism seems continually to change with time in ways which are almost independent of any specific environmental event, those processes which seem to occur from within the organism and which make subjects different at the end of the experiment than they were at the beginning regardless of environmental manipulation, must either be controlled or accounted for.

3. Testing   Again unlike the situation in the physical sciences where measuring devices may be applied without significantly changing the object under examination, the very process of obtaining many behavioral measures alters that which is measured. Care must be taken to demonstrate that the process of measurement itself did not contribute to that which was observed during the experiment. This is a particularly bothersome effect when both pre and post measures are used, and the act of taking the first test is likely to have an effect on the act of taking the second test.

4. Instrumentation   Unfortunately, many of the instruments used to measure behavior characteristics may themselves change during the course of the study. For example, observers may learn to do their job better or may become fatigued and do it less well at the end of an experiment than they did at the beginning. Or it might be necessary to use parallel but slightly different forms of a test for the initial and the final measure. In these situations some control is needed to rule out the possibility that the observed effect resulted entirely or in part from such "calibration" changes in the measuring instrument itself.

5. Statistical regression   All measures of behavioral characteristics (as contrasted with physical aspects of behavior) are sufficiently fallible that the error involved cannot be ignored as it may in the measurement of many physical properties.   The result is that those initially high on a measure are there, in part, because they were "lucky" on the day they were examined, and chance errors favored them.   Similarly, those low on an initial measure fell down, in part, because chance errors worked to their disadvantage on this testing.   Since chance seldom strikes in the same way on two successive occasions, it is a stochastic expectation that both those originally high and those originally low would regress toward the mean.   Whenever a group is selected for treatment *because* they were high on an initial measure, the effect of the treatment will be, in part, counteracted by the regression effect; and, when a group is selected for treatment *because* they were low on an initial measure, at least part of their gain on a second testing can be attributed to the rival hypothesis of regression effect.

6. Selection   Whenever the subjects selected for observation in a study have not been chosen by random procedures from the population to which it is hoped the findings may be generalized, it is always possible that a bias has produced the results thought to be attributable to the experimental variable.   An experimenter may have (unconsciously) selected subjects because they already exhibited the behavior the treatment was expected to bring about, or, it could happen that a difference found between two groups may have been the result of the different ways they were recruited.   Any differences observed were there to begin with and occurred as a result of the selection procedures rather than as an effect produced by the experimental treatment.

7. Experimental mortality   Just as a bias in the initial selection of subjects for observation can produce an effect, so can a differential dropout of persons during the course of the experiment make it seem as if the treatment had an effect when in fact it did not.   Campbell and Stanley use the example that few would be willing to infer that college experience adversely affects feminine beauty because a smaller number of girls were judged to be beautiful as seniors than was true of the freshman class four years earlier. This particular alternative hypothesis to the one that the experimental variable produced the observed effects is most serious when the experimental group consists of persons who have volunteered for or have been invited to participate in some remedial treatment.   In any group process work where the members are free to discontinue at any time they wish, those who remain until the end are those most determined to improve.

8. Selection maturation   Just as those who continue with a therapy or remedial instruction to the end are the ones who are most determined to overcome their difficulty, so those who even volunteer or accept an invitation when it is offered may be more mature or further along the road to recovery than those who refuse to acknowledge a difficulty. Those who "select themselves" for a study may, because of their higher level of maturation, be those who would recover or find a way to improve regardless of any specific treatment offered.

9. Reactivity Although not listed as a source of internal validity by Campbell and Stanley, it is certainly possible to consider the reactive effect of the experimental arrangement as an alternative hypothesis to the treatment effect as an explanation of any observed change in the dependent variables. The reactive effect occurs when the subjects of the investigation become aware that they are part of an experiment, and when this knowledge causes the subjects to behave differently than they might in a nonexperimental situation. The classic example of what can happen under such circumstances is the now famous Hawthorne study (Roethlisberger & Dixon, 1940) in which changes in working conditions, such as improving the lighting, allowing rest pauses, providing refreshments, and changing the ventilation appeared to result in increased productivity. Subsequent manipulation of the variables showed, however, that when the original working conditions were reintroduced, output continued to climb. The observed effects could not be attributed to any of the specific changes introduced. Rather, the gain in productivity was explained by the fact that the girls involved, recognizing that they were subjects of an experiment, came to feel that the company was finally interested in their individual welfare and responded with increased effort. It is to be expected that, in studies where the persons observed are aware that they are subjects of an experiment, the participants may be on their "best behavior," may develop a special *esprit de corps,* or may exhibit the behavior which they think the experimenter is looking for. All such possibilities must be ruled out if an observed effect is to be attributed to the experimental variable under investigation.

EXTERNAL DANGERS TO VALIDITY OF EXPERIMENTS   In addition to ruling out reasonable rival hypotheses as threats to the *internal* validity of an experiment, it is always necessary when studying human behavior to ask the question of the extent to which results found with one particular set of individuals can be generalized to the population as a whole. Specific conditions or effects which prevent us from generalizing the findings to all human beings represent what Campbell and Stanley have called threats to *external* validity. Unlike the situation with internal validity, where careful experimental design and use of appropriate statistical tests can rule out certain alternative hypotheses, there is no specific and precise way to identify the limits to which the results of a study can be generalized. In effect, the investigator must be willing to make the assumption of all science which was mentioned earlier—that insofar as things are similar, what has happened in one instance will also happen in another—and then proceed to describe those situations which he feels are similar (or dissimilar) in the essential ways. As Campbell and Stanley have put it: "The sources of external validity are thus guesses as to general laws in the science of a science: guesses as to what factors lawfully interact with our treatment variables and, by implication, guesses as to what can be disregarded."

Campbell and Stanley have identified at least four things which can seriously limit the generalizability of results from an experiment on behavior. While it is not absolutely essential that these threats to external validity be eliminated, an acquaintance with them will help prevent both the research worker himself and the consumer of research from overgeneralizing.

One factor which may limit the extent to which results from a study can be applied to the population as a whole results from the possibility of a testing-treatment interaction. Such an effect occurs whenever a measure applied at the beginning of an experiment "sensitizes" the subjects to the treatment. It is sometimes possible that the very act of taking a pretest alters the subject's likelihood of benefiting from the treatment, and thus, any resulting generalizations as to the effects of the treatment must be limited to populations to which the pretest is given. This, of course, is no problem in a practical situation where taking a pretest is routine and can be considered part of the treatment as is often the case in schools or in clinics. But, in a study designed to isolate specific effects, or a study in which the introduction of a pretest is a special event, as might be the case in a sociological investigation, a potential testing-treatment interaction can be seriously limiting.

A second possible limit to drawing broad generalizations from some experimental studies is an interaction effect between any selection bias and the treatment. If the individuals selected for treatment are those who are most likely to respond to the treatment, then any conclusions about the effectiveness of the treatment must be limited to those displaying the specific characteristics which make them responsive to the treatment. Such an effect is most obvious in a medical setting where a particular treatment for cancer is most effective with persons over fifty, and it happens that in the experimental trial the method was applied primarily to persons of this age. Obviously, it is inappropriate to draw the general conclusion that the treatment for cancer is effective with persons of all ages. The most common example in psychology and education is a study in which volunteers are divided into an experimental and a control group. As contrasted with the internal validity problem of selection-maturation interaction, it is, in this case, possible to conclude that the treatment is effective when definite differences are found between the control and the experimental group. Generalizations about the effectiveness of the treatment must be limited to those who volunteer for the therapy or special instruction.

The reactive effect of the experimental arrangement which was described as one important source of a lack of internal validity can sometimes be interpreted as a limit to generalization rather than a rival alternative hypothesis to the experimental effect. It may sometimes happen that the treatment does, in fact, have an effect, but that this effect occurs only when people are playing the kinds of roles they play while participating in an experiment.

One final condition that limits generalization is a multiple-treatment effect which may occur when several different treatments are applied to the same group of subjects in what has sometimes been called a "rotated group" design. The problem here results from the fact that the effect of prior treatments cannot be erased, and that the effect of treatment may not be the same when it is applied after Treatment 1 as it is when Treatment 2 is given by itself or prior to Treatment 1. Under these circumstances, the experimenter can generalize his findings only to those individuals who have experienced the treatments in the same order as did subjects of his particular experiment.

Varieties of Experimental Design

No single experimental design can account for all thirteen factors enumerated as possible threats to valid inference from an experiment. Some commonly used designs are quite weak, for they control very few of the sources of invalidity; other designs rule out a large number of such factors and are, therefore, considered to be quite powerful. Any design which controls some factors but not others will thus be weak or strong in a particular situation depending upon which rival hypotheses are most plausible and which limitations to generalizations are the most restrictive for the specific variables under investigation. The task of the research worker, then, is to ascertain which of those designs that are feasible within his practical limitations of time, money, and available subjects will rule out those sources of invalidity that are most crucial when dealing with the kinds of variables he is investigating. To aid in this task, a checklist similar to that illustrated in Figure 4.1 might be used. For each alternative design the researcher might simply place a checkmark in the appropriate column to indicate the status of each of the sources of validity indicated by the different rows and make a comment as to its importance in that particular research problem. A visual scanning or a weighted summing of the + and − factors should provide some information as to the efficiency of the design under the particular circumstances at hand.

PSEUDOEXPERIMENTAL DESIGNS   It is important to note that a research design which involves rigorous measurement and a test of a statistical hypothesis is not necessarily an experimental design. It should be remembered that the essence of experimentation is the control which the experimenter has of the situation, and that, unless some manipulation of one or

Check sheet for design _____ ____

Final reaction _____

Source of Invalidity	Status			Comment
	Controlled +	Not Sure* ?	Not Controlled −	
Internal (alternative hypotheses)				
History				
Maturation				
Testing				
Instrumentation				
Regression				
Selection				
Mortality				
Interaction between sel. and mat.				
Reactivity				
External (restrictions on generalization)				
Testing inter.				
Selection inter.				
Reactivity				
Multiple treat.				
Other				
Other				
Other				

* Depends partly upon presently unknown characteristics of the variables and their relationships.

FIGURE 4.1   Check sheet for use in comparing the efficiency of alternative experimental designs

more characteristics in order to note their effects has been involved, no true experimentation has been carried out.   Studies in which the researcher attempts to note the effects of naturally occurring treatments by observing either a wide sample of persons over a wide range of characteristics, or a highly selected sample of persons who fall naturally into particular groups, are not to be confused with experimental studies. Chief among these *pseudoexperimental* designs are the "one-shot" case study in which a follow-up is made of single groups of persons who have experienced some specific treatment or event; a "pre and post" comparison of a single group which underwent some treatment; and the so-called "static-group" comparison in which a group of persons which has not experienced the treatment is found for comparison with one which has. In all three of these designs, the number of plausible rival hypotheses is so great as to preclude any interpretation of cause and effect. Studies using these three approaches are, therefore, best thought of as varieties of descriptive analysis and should be classified along with correlational studies, panel studies, and ex post facto studies, all of which are described elsewhere in this volume.

Occasionally, it is possible to reach some approximation to experimentation by using two (or perhaps more) of the pseudoexperimental designs in combination. The approach here is to start with an originally weak design and patch it up by adding specific controls to eliminate various rival explanations as to the cause of the observed effects. As Campbell and Stanley (1963) point out, "The result is often an inelegant accumulation of precautionary checks, which lacks the intrinsic symmetry of the 'true' experimental designs, but nonetheless approaches experimentation."

QUASI-EXPERIMENTAL DESIGNS   Even though a research worker cannot control the exact time and the specific persons to whom an experimental variable is applied, it is sometimes possible for him to determine the time and persons on whom the observations will be made, and thus gain some form of control. Carefully done research studies in which something like experimental control is obtained by means of scheduling data collection, by means of the selection of particular groups, and the like can often reduce the plausibility of rival hypotheses to a sufficient extent to permit at least a low level of causal inference. Such investigations have been labeled *quasi-experiments* by Campbell and Stanley. When true experimentation cannot be carried out, the quasi-experimental designs described in this section are much to be preferred over the complete abandonment of investigation for the alternatives of purely logical analysis or of personal opinion. At the same time, it should be recognized that the greatest usefulness of these quasi-experimental designs will be to reduce the number of theories that need to be put to rigorous test by means of true experiments, rather than to build up any real confidence in hypotheses which they fail to reject.

It will be helpful to retain the schematic notation used by Campbell and Stanley in their discussion in describing the many varieties of quasi-experimental approaches. Each row of the paradigm of a research design will represent a different group of subjects, and each column a different point in time. Various letters symbolize different experimenter operations. *R* stands for the process of randomly assigning individuals to the group, *O* stands for making observations (usually as measurements), and X represents the application of the experimental treatment. A broken horizontal line between the rows representing the different groups indicates that the two groups were not equivalent in either a matching or a sampling sense at the beginning of the investigation.

In this system, a "nonequivalent control group" design is represented as follows:

$$O \quad\quad X \quad\quad O$$
$$\overline{}$$
$$O \quad\quad\quad\quad\quad\quad O$$

These symbols tell us that the investigator using this design has selected two naturally occurring groups (such as two classrooms at the same level) and designated, preferably by a random process, one to be the experimental group and one to be the control group. Observations were made on relevant variables prior to the application of the experimental variable, X, and again following it.

This design, although not a true design because the experimental and control groups are not known to be equivalent, is still a considerable improvement over a single-group pre- and posttest study because it controls the main effects of history, maturation, testing, and instrumentation; for these variables would produce similar effects in both the experimental and control groups. Any difference between the two groups must be attributed to factors other than these four. The major weakness of this design is its sensitivity to any interaction among the main effects mentioned above and to differences between the groups in characteristics related to the dependent variable under observation. For example, a current event that is independent of the study itself but which might "sensitize" people to the treatment, and which is more likely to affect one group than another (i.e., because it concerns their particular race, religion, socioeconomic level, etc.), might be a plausible hypothesis for an explanation of any observed differences. As Campbell and Stanley point out, any attempt to compensate for a lack of matching of the initial groups by later selecting a subsample of the control group which is matched with the experimental group for analysis will only exaggerate the difficulties. The correct approach is to use the statistical technique called the analysis of covariance (see page 115) to "adjust for" any difference in the posttest which would be expected on the basis of the size of initial differences in the pretest. When the analysis of covariance is used, this design may even be preferred over some of the true experimental designs in which reactive effects—effects that result from knowledge that an experiment is being carried on—are likely to result from the disruption of the normal situation by assigning specific persons into a control and an experimental group.

A second useful quasi-experimental design makes use of a separate sample of randomly equivalent groups for the pre- and posttest, and thus is represented as:

$$R \quad O$$
$$R \qquad\qquad X \quad O$$

Even though it is sometimes referred to as a simulated before-and-after study, this separate sample approach actually is preferable to a single-group pre- and posttest study because it controls the effects of testing whereas the single-group investigation does not. This separate sample design is used primarily when it is possible for the experimenter to select the time and persons on whom the observations are to be made (though not to whom the X is to be applied) or when it is possible to make only one observation on each person, and the treatment occurs for all or for none of the members of a group. The major weakness of this design is that it does not control for the effects of history, since an event occurring between the observation of the first group and the observation of the second group could have produced whatever difference between the two groups was observed. Also, when used in a sample survey situation where the observations are made by the interviewers, instrumentation can be a serious problem. These two weaknesses can be overcome, however. For example, if the design is replicated at different times, the problem of history is lessened, and if randomly matched groups of interviewers who are not aware of the hypothesis under investigation are used, the instrumentation problem is minimized. Under these conditions, this design is an acceptable one internally and has an added advantage in that it moves the laboratory out into the field situation to which the researcher wants to generalize, and thus assures external validity.

Perhaps the best of the quasi-experimental designs is one which modifies the separate sample pre- and posttest design just described by adding a separate sample control group as indicated by the schema:

$$R \quad O$$
$$R \qquad\qquad X \quad O$$
$$\text{---}$$
$$R \quad O$$
$$R \qquad\qquad\qquad\quad O$$

The addition of the separate sample control groups (even though they may not necessarily be equivalent to the separate sample pre- and postexperimental groups) ruled out the bothersome problems of history and instrumentation. About the only question that remains is that of a possible interaction between selection and one of the other sources of invalidity. Such an interaction may occur because of some local trend which affects the experimental groups but not the control groups, and might be confounded with (i.e., mistaken for) the effects of the treatment. When such interaction effects are not plausible, this design may, in fact, be preferred to the true experimental designs (described in the next section) which, while controlling on all internal validity factors, are always subject to questions of external validity.

A different form of quasi-experimental design from those already described is that represented by so-called "time-series" studies. Such investigations involve a series of measurements over a period of time and the introduction of an experimental variable at some point during the sequence. The result is the following paradigm:

$$O \quad O \quad O \quad O \quad X \quad O \quad O \quad O \quad O$$

While experiments of this form are typical of much of the successful early experimentation in the physical and biological sciences, they have a serious weakness when applied to the study of human behavior. As is true of all studies that are done with human subjects and which lack a control group, the effects of history represent a rival hypothesis which somehow must be ruled out. In the physical and biological sciences, extraneous natural influences are easily eliminated by taking the objects under investigation into the isolation of the laboratory. When working with people, however, it is seldom either feasible or ethical to isolate them completely from the rest of the world during the course of the study. At the very least, if the simple time-series design is to be useful in studying human behavior, the experimenter will need to specify *in advance* the time relationship between the application of the treatment and the appearance of the effect. It also is especially important to note that any examination of a natural time series which has occurred in the past capitalizes on chance happenings in such a way as to greatly exaggerate the effects of the experimental treatment. Therefore, the results of historical time-series studies can be considered to be nothing more than empirically based hypotheses about cause-and-effect relationships. In addition, if time-series experiments are to be accepted, they must be repeated by many researchers in separate situations as is done in the physical sciences. Under these conditions the design is quite useful since the repeated observation, both before and after the introduction of *X*, eliminates all internal sources of invalidity except history and, under some circumstances, instrumentation.

One possible modification of the simple time-series experiment described above which does attempt to reduce the likelihood of history as a possible alternative explanation is the equivalent time-samples design which can be represented as:

$$\begin{array}{cccccccccc} R & R & R & R & R & R & R & R & R & R \\ XO & O & O & XO & O & XO & XO & O & XO & XO \end{array}$$

In this design, the total possible times for making observations are divided into "equivalent time periods," and it is randomly decided which times to make the observation. This has been indicated in the paradigm above by placing the R's in the columns instead of the rows. Obviously, this design will be meaningful only where the experimental variable is repeatedly introduced to the same subjects (as in many educational and clinical situations where practice, remedial help, or various forms of therapy are applied on many successive occasions) and where the total number of time units sampled is sufficiently large so as to result in both a number of observations made immediately after the application of the X and a number of observations made independently of the introduction of the experimental variable. By comparing those observations made directly after a treatment with those made somewhat independently from it, some evidence as to the effect of the experimental variable may be obtained. This design effectively controls history in that it is quite unlikely that the same external historical event would appear with each application of the X while never appearing when the observations were made independently from the application of X. The greatest danger in this design is the external source of invalidity described as multiple-treatment effect. The results of experiments using this design are applicable only to those populations of persons to whom multiple treatments have been given and must never be used in an attempt to infer what the effect of a single application might be.

A second modification of the simple time-series approach which eliminates the problem of history is the multiple time-series design, diagrammed as:

$$O \quad O \quad O \quad O \quad X \quad O \quad O \quad O \quad O$$
$$\overline{O \quad O \quad O \quad O \quad X \quad O \quad O \quad O \quad O}$$

Although the addition of a second group does control the main effect of history, there remains the minor possibility of an interaction of selection and history as a possible source of invalidity. In another sense, this design might be thought of as a modification of the nonequivalent control group approach which eliminates the effects of any interaction between selection and maturation as well as the possibility of regression effects. As such, this design is quite powerful, and its chief difficulty, as with all time-series approaches, is that of external validity. Inferences simply cannot be made to situations in which repeated observations are not part of the natural ongoing series of events if there is any likelihood of a testing experimental variable interaction, nor, because the experimental and control groups are not randomly equivalent, to any situation where selection-treatment interactions are not free to occur.

One additional quasi-experimental design, which should be mentioned because it is quite different from those already presented, is the "regression-discontinuity" analysis. This design essentially asks the question of whether the introduction of an experimental treatment disrupts an observed relationship between two variables and can be represented schematically as:

$$
\begin{array}{cc}
X & O \\
\hline
X & O \\
\hline
X & O \\
\hline
 & O \\
\hline
 & O \\
\hline
 & O
\end{array}
$$

Here, the solid line has been used to indicate that the groups are not only lacking in equivalence but actually represent persons who differ by known amounts along one of the variables. Further, it should be noted that the treatment is not assigned randomly but applied only to those individuals who have reached or exceeded a certain level on one of the variables. The example given by Campbell and Stanley is that where scholarships may be awarded to persons above a certain point on a scholastic ability test, and the question raised is whether such an award will alter the relationship between ability and performance. Similarly, this approach might be used in any learning situation where a special treatment is given to all those who have reached or exceeded some specified stage of practice (e.g., giving a special privilege or other award to all those who have completed a specified number of exercises or spent at least so many hours in practice), and the question, as illustrated by Figure 4.2, is whether this treatment alters the learning curve.

In general, this design controls for history, maturation, regression, selec-

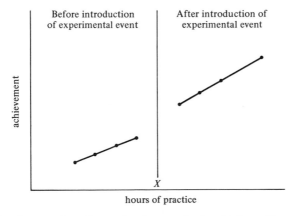

FIGURE 4.2   Regression-discontinuity analysis (After Campbell, D., & Stanley, J. *Experimental and quasi-experimental designs for research.* Chicago: Rand McNally, 1963, Fig. 4. P. 62.)

tion, and the main effects of testing when the comparison is interpreted for groups near the point of application of the treatment. While instrumentation and mortality may be a problem in some special cases, the biggest difficulty with this design is in external validity. The dilemma which the researcher faces is that even though the various sources of invalidity are controlled for persons near the cutting stone, the rival alternative hypotheses become more and more plausible as one attempts to generalize to groups higher and lower on the variable used to determine whether the treatment should be applied. In spite of this difficulty, Campbell and Stanley point out that the regression-discontinuity design is much to be preferred to an ex post facto approach which, in the past, has been applied to similar situations.

TRUE EXPERIMENTAL DESIGNS   It will be recalled that in true experimental designs, the researcher has complete control over the situation in the sense of determining precisely who will participate in the experiment as subjects and which subjects will or will not receive the experimental treatment. One of the simplest forms of true experimentation which can be used in the study of human behavior is the pre- and posttest control group design represented as:

$$R \quad O \quad X \quad O$$
$$R \quad O \qquad \; O$$

Although quite similar to the first of the quasi-experimental designs described in the previous section, this approach is different in one essential way: the experimental subjects are randomly divided into the two groups to be compared, and it is randomly determined which group will serve as a control group and which group will be the experimental group (the one to which the experimental treatment will be applied). The two groups may be said to be equivalent at the time of the initial observations, and, when the final observations are made, different only in that the variable under study has been applied to one but not the other.

Unfortunately, the process of obtaining equivalent groups by means of randomization does not seem to be easily accepted by novice researchers. Apparently, there is an intuitive uneasiness in leaving things to chance, and a tendency to want to make certain the two groups are the same by some sort of matching process. It is, of course, true that the random process does not *guarantee* that the groups will be equivalent,[1] but only insures that, if the sample size is sufficiently large, the groups are very unlikely to be different in any important respect. The problem with matching is that equating groups with respect to one characteristic does not guarantee that they are also equivalent in other respects; and, even when matched on suc-

---

[1] Randomization does, however, guarantee that the sampling is unbiased in the sense defined in Chapter 8.

cessive characteristics to the limit of practicality, there is no guarantee that the two groups are alike in all respects. Further, there is the possibility that the experimenter actually biased the results by the very matching process with which he sought to make them equal. As Campbell and Stanley point out, randomization "is a less than perfect way of assuring the initial equivalence of such groups. It is, nonetheless, the only way of doing so, and the essential way." It is possible to combine matching and randomization procedures by a process called "blocking." In the simplest form of blocking, subjects are first assigned to matched pairs, and then randomization is used within the pair to determine which member should be assigned to the experimental group and which to the control group. Where circumstances permit (and this is in most instances) it is generally considered better to use randomization to obtain groups, and then correct for any differences which still remain in important control variables by means of a covariance analysis.

As is the case with all true experimental designs, all seven of the factors discussed earlier as sources of internal lack of validity are well controlled. The major weakness of the pre- and posttest control group design is the possibility of an interaction between testing and the experimental variable. Results of an experiment of this sort are generalizable only to those situations in which a pretest is given (perhaps as a regular part of the treatment) or in which independent data suggest that the process of taking a test does not in any way sensitize the subjects to the experimental variable.

As is also true of all true experimental designs, the possibility of a selection-treatment interaction occurs if some of the subjects drop out during the course of the experiment, and a further limitation to the generalization of results is imposed whenever the subjects are aware that an experiment is in progress.

The external validity problem of a testing-treatment interaction can be overcome whenever it seems an important rival hypothesis by using a posttest-only control group design which takes the form:

$$R \quad X \quad O$$
$$R \qquad\;\; O$$

This latter design, however, limits the dependent variable to an ultimate level of achievement or other performance index. Where gain or change in behavior is the desired dependent variable, the so-called "Solomon Four-Group Design" must be used:

$$R \quad O \quad X \quad O$$
$$R \quad O \qquad\;\; O$$
$$R \qquad\;\; X \quad O$$
$$R \qquad\qquad\;\; O$$

As Campbell and Stanley have pointed out, the simple posttest-only control group design has been greatly underused in studying human behavior, probably because of the general uneasiness mentioned earlier which some researchers feel in using randomization as a procedure for obtaining equivalent groups. These feelings of uneasiness can often be relieved by using a stratified sampling design. In any case, such feelings are unwarranted when the samples are of sufficient size. Where a pretest is quite difficult or awkward to obtain, or where the use of a pretest is likely to tip off the subjects that an experiment is being carried on and, therefore, result in a reactive effect, this posttest-only approach may be much preferred to the pre- and posttest control group design.

The Solomon Four-Group Approach is the most desirable of all the really basic experimental designs, both quasi and true. While it does not really *control* any more sources of invalidity than does the posttest-only control group approach, the four-group design permits the estimation of the extent of the effects of some of the rival hypotheses. Both the main effects and the interaction effects of testing are determinable, and also one can note the combined effects of maturation and history. Further, the design has the important advantage of permitting the investigator to examine the effects of the treatment in four independent comparisons: the before measure with the after measure in the first group; the after measure in the first group with the after measure in the second group; the after measure in the third group with the after measure in the fourth group; and the before measure in the second group with the after measure in the third group.

FACTORIAL AND COUNTERBALANCED DESIGNS   If not actually dictated by the hypothesis generated from his theory, it is often to the experimenter's advantage to extend the basic designs presented here to include several levels of a treatment (for example, various amounts of therapy rather than some fixed amounts versus no therapy) or to include more than one experimental variable. In general, when the situation is under the complete control of the experimenter, and the extension of the true experimental design includes observations of some subjects at all levels of all experimental variables, the result is labeled a *factorial* design; and, when the extension requires observations of all subjects under all treatments, the result is called a *counterbalanced* design.[2]

In addition, a wide variety of practical attempts to achieve even greater efficiency with these latter extensions have produced a myriad of specialized designs such as "Latin squares," "split-plots," "fractional replication," "randomized blocks," "nesting," "Greco-Latin squares," and the like, which can be used by the sophisticated researcher. While it is beyond the intent of this book to go into such specialized designs, it is important for the begin-

---

[2] The rubrics "rotation experiments" and "cross-over" designs, as well as other descriptive phrases, have also been used to identify designs of this sort.

ning student to recognize that such elaborations and extensions are not only possible but have been fully developed (cf. e.g., Cox, 1958, Winer, 1962, and others) and are often extremely useful in studies of human behavior.

While the basic designs discussed here provide the student with an understanding of the experimental approach, he needs to recognize that, as Campbell and Stanley point out: "The goal of science includes not only generalizations to other populations and times but also to other nonidentical representations of the treatment, i.e., other representations which theoretically should be the same, but which are not identical in theoretically irrelevant specifics." And, further: "Again, conceptually, the solution is not to hope piously for 'pure' measures with no irrelevant complexities, but rather to use multiple measures in which the specific vehicles, the specific irrelevant details, are as different as possible, while the common content of our concern is present in each."

This latter point—the necessity for multiple observations, and indeed multiple approaches to testing the same hypothesis—cannot be emphasized too strongly. The words of Campbell and Stanley quoted above represent but one sample of a growing clamor (see among others, Barber, 1961; Chamberlain, 1965; Cronbach, 1957; Dunnette, 1966; Platt, 1964) for greater eclecticism in both theory and method if science, especially as applied to the study of human behavior, is to be more than what Dunnette (1965) has suggested might be labeled "A Game We Play."

THE LOGICAL STEPS IN EXPERIMENTAL RESEARCH

Having examined the logic of experimentation and noted the many varieties of experimental design, the reader will recognize readily that effectively carrying out an experiment requires going through some rather definite (if not always explicit) logical steps. In the subsequent parts of this section, each step will be identified and briefly described.

Refining the Problem

Once a research worker has identified what appears to him to be a problem (i.e., a gap, a contradiction, or a fuzziness in our knowledge) and, through a careful review of the literature has ascertained that the problem is a research problem and not a communications problem, he turns his attention to the refinement of the problem. Usually, this takes the form of careful specification of both the variables of importance and the role they will play in his experiment.

Typically, the experimental variables are identified first. The investigator decides what variable or variables he will manipulate, and thinks through the distinguishing characteristics of the two or more treatments or levels of treatments to be examined. When this has been carefully done, the research worker next turns his attention to the dependent variables which will be of prime concern. At this stage, the investigator asks himself what kinds of variables are likely to be affected by his manipulations of the experimental conditions. In working with human behavior, the number of potential, meaningful dependent variables is many, and in this writer's opinion it is a tragedy that so many studies of behavior consider the effects of an experimental variable on only one (and even that often an easily measured, rather than an important) dependent variable. In view of the tremendous effort it sometimes takes to set up appropriate experimental conditions and to cajole the desired persons into serving as subjects, it would seem that the little additional effort entailed in observing a variety of dependent variables is well worthwhile. It is recommended that, at this stage, the investigator should identify as many different effects as seem at all reasonable, listing them all as potential dependent variables to observe. Later, he can trim them down to fit the practical limitations of the study.

Once the various important dependent variables have been listed, a decision must be reached as to which variables will need to be controlled. This can be accomplished by asking, "Which characteristics or conditions other than the experimental variables will influence the results?" Again, the experimenter is likely to discover that there are many more such variables than he can hope to control tightly in a single situation. Thus, it will be necessary to place the "control" variables in rank order according to the extent to which they will influence the results and take the greatest pains with those at the top of the list. If it should turn out that crucial variables cannot be controlled because of practical limitations, the researcher may have to face the reality that an experimental approach to the study would not pay off under the present circumstances. Sometimes, of course, the researcher need not give up entirely, but rather will be able to break the study down into smaller, more feasible components, each of which can be investigated separately.

Occasionally, the refinement of the problem will include a specific, operational definition of terms to be used. It should be obvious that words and concepts which are in common use in the field and for which there is little ambiguity need not be included. However, it is essential to indicate precisely what will be meant by a technical term which may be interpreted in several ways or which will be used in the particular experiment at hand in a slightly different way than has been the case heretofore. In instances where the characteristic is a hypothetical construct to be inferred from observations, the task of providing a clear definition may involve simply spelling out the operations by which the observations will be obtained. For example, intelligence can be defined as a score on the Weschler Adult Intelligence Scale, response strength as number of responses required for extinction, family cohesiveness as the number of times one family member expresses concern for another during an hour interview with each of the parents, and degree of identification as the number of times during a standard set of observational periods that a child imitates the model. When the investigator feels the concept requiring definition involves more than the measurement or the measurement is indirect (e.g., using vocabulary as an indirect measure of intelligence), then it will be necessary to relate the construct in highly specific ways to other concepts or terms which are themselves unambiguous or directly tied to specific empirical observations. This latter involves in essence the establishment of construct validity as described in Chapter 7.

Formulating the Hypothesis

In addition to identifying precisely what characteristics or conditions will be affected by the experimental variable or variables, it is essential to indicate, as precisely as possible, the way in which the dependent variables will change. Although it is often not possible to specify in advance the exact relationship between the experimental variable and the dependent variable, the investigator should at least be able to state the direction of the expected change. An investigator who feels he does not have enough information at least to do the latter possibly is not yet ready to carry out an experimental study and might better turn his attention to other research approaches which are likely to prove more valuable for exploratory work.

It is at this point also that the investigator will want to make a clear distinction between his scientific hypothesis and his statistical hypothesis. Because of considerations noted in Chapter 6, the statistical hypothesis will often be restricted to a null (no difference or no relationship) hypothesis which the researcher typically hopes to be able to reject. In contrast, the scientific hypothesis will reflect directly that which the investigator expects to find. The important thing with respect to the latter is that if the hypothesis is to be scientifically meaningful, it must be stated in such a way that it is capable of being refuted.

Specifying the Population to Be Sampled

Ideally, the research worker should carefully specify in advance the population of both persons and settings to which he hopes to be able to generalize his results, and then sample from it, using one of the sampling designs described in the chapter on special methods and techniques. In many practical situations such an ideal approach can never be realized, and the researcher, if he is to make any attempt at all, must use a "sample of convenience"— that is, a group of subjects which are available to him. Under these latter circumstances, it is the obligation of the researcher to describe his subjects and his situation as carefully as possible so that others who read the results can make their own intelligent judgment as to how far the results of the study can be generalized. In general, a sensible answer can be realized if the sample is clearly described in as much detail as possible by asking the question: "Of what population might these subjects be a representative sample?"

In any case, overgeneralizing (i.e., generalizing beyond the population originally specified or the one clearly seen as that from which the subjects used could be representative) is to be avoided. To extend the results beyond such populations requires additional evidence. Again, the novice research worker is less likely to err if he remembers that he is formulating a hypothesis which may be useful within certain limits and not necessarily a hypothesis that is true for all situations and all times.

Instituting Proper Controls

Once the specific hypotheses of an experimental study have been formulated, it is time for the research worker to get down to the business of developing a specific experimental design. This consists of arranging the situation so that none of the rival hypotheses described earlier can be claimed to have produced any of the results which might be observed. Sometimes this involves nothing more than selecting one of the basic designs already outlined. On the other hand, it may require a careful analysis of all the subject variables, all the situational variables, and all their interactions which are likely to occur, and then developing unique ways of bringing each under the control of the experimenter.

The three classic ways of maintaining the desired control are: (1) holding conditions constant; (2) using randomization; and (3) making statistical adjustments. Holding situational variables constant has long been the primary means of control in the physical sciences and still is the preferred method. This approach becomes less and less practical, however, as one moves through the biological sciences to the behavioral sciences.

The problem of subject differences remains; the situational conditions are quite adequately controlled by carrying out studies in the laboratory. In the early days of psychology these problems could be ignored simply by defining psychology as the study of the "normal human adult mind." But, as our knowledge of behavior expanded, such a position became less and less tenable. Not being able to ignore human differences, the next reasonable step was that of carefully matching subjects, person for person. Thus, paired control grouping, co-twin control, and the like became the watchword of the day.

Unfortunately, as our knowledge expanded further, and more and more interrelationships were examined, it became quite apparent that once subjects were carefully matched with respect to one characteristic, they were often still markedly different with respect to another; and once they were matched with respect to a second, there was still another way in which they differed, and so on—always the subjects still seemed to be different, and different in a way which could very well have an effect on the results. Thus, gradually, research workers have more and more come to accept the process of gaining control by randomization—that is, by randomly assigning subjects to groups and randomly determining which groups will receive which treatments. Again, it should be emphasized that such a procedure does *not* guarantee equivalent groups, rather only that there is no bias in the formation and selection of the groups; and, further, that as the sample size increases, it will become less and less likely that the two groups are not the same.

When matching is not possible and randomization has not eliminated relevant subject differences, the researcher can employ statistical control. Actually, statistical control does not involve holding variables constant or obtaining equivalent groups, but rather making a statistical adjustment on the final observations to account for any measured lack of initial equivalence. For example, in a study to determine the effectiveness of two approaches to instruction, it might be necessary to employ two groups of subjects which differ with respect to past accomplishment. If a measure of past accomplishment is available and it is related to future performance, then, by means of an analysis of covariance, it is possible to determine how many of the differences in the final performance would be expected because of the initial differences in achievement and to make an appropriate adjustment. When interpreting results, only differences larger than those to be expected on the basis of initial differences would be considered.

There is no reason why all three of the techniques for obtaining control cannot be employed in the same study. Subjects could be matched on the most important variable to control, and random assignment be made to the experimental and control groups from within the matched pairs. Then, any differences observed to remain on characteristics for which a measure can be obtained could be handled by means of a covariance analysis or the Neyman-Johnson technique.

Measuring the Criterion Variables

No aspect of an experimental study is more fundamental than obtaining a satisfactory measure of the dependent variables against which the presumed differential effects of the experimental variable can be evaluated. All the thoughtful effort in designing a careful study, in obtaining subjects, and in applying the experimental treatment will be wasted if the criterion used is not a relevant one or the measurement of it is not dependable. The effect of using a criteria which is invalid is to reduce the study to a trivial one, since it will demonstrate nothing of real concern. The effect of using an unreliable measure will be that of making it more difficult to find differences among the experimental group; thus, if no differences are found, the investigator has no way of knowing whether this occurred because the experimental variable had no effect or whether what effect it had could not be detected because of the great amount of error in the measurement of the dependent variable. Of course, if differences *are* found in such a situation, the investigator can be sure they would be even more obvious were the criterion measured with greater reliability.

The best guard against using an invalid or irrelevant criterion is a crystal clear statement of the objectives of the study. In fact, if the objectives are spelled out in specific, operational terms, the appropriate criterion measures will have been defined. Knowing precisely the nature of the needed criterion variable, the researcher next goes about selecting the appropriate instrument from among those already available or constructing one which will serve his purposes. In either case, he will need to keep in mind the criteria for a good measuring instrument as described in Chapter 7. When no satisfactory measuring device is available, the researcher will need to carry out test development procedures fully, not only writing the items (or developing the task in the case of a psychomotor performance) but planning and carrying out substudies to establish the reliability and validity of the instrument.

Gathering Data

The actual process of gathering data is of even less significance in the case of an experimental study than it was in the case of descriptive studies. Whenever possible, the task is relegated to instruments, or, at most, to a technician who has been carefully trained to record observations as automatically and as precisely as possible. Except, perhaps, for watching the first few observations come in to make certain all his careful planning up to this point has not been in error, the investigator often takes little interest in this phase. In fact, if the study were such that very much of value could be obtained by observing the data gathering process, the experimental approach is, itself, not likely to be the most appropriate one at this stage of knowledge in the area of concern.

Analysis and Interpretation of the Data

The final step in applying the experimental approach to the study of behavior involves a careful analysis and interpretation of the data gathered in the previous step.   In spite of the advent of modern computers which make the necessary computations and even the application of the appropriate decision rules quite automatic, the investigator himself needs to become deeply involved in this stage of the experimental study.   Since the computer will do nothing but what it is told, it is the researcher himself who must determine what kind of analysis is appropriate and make the value judgments necessary to the development of the decision rule which is to be applied.

While an understanding of the specific techniques to be applied here must await the discussion of the logic of statistical methods in Chapter 6, the reader should be aware at this point that an adequate analysis and interpretation of data will involve both the estimation of one or more descriptive indexes and the testing of hypotheses.   Further, the research worker will need to make a clear distinction between a result which is statistically significant and that which is of practical importance.   In brief, the test of statistical significance only involves the question of whether the observed results can be considered to be a chance phenomenon.   If the results are significant statistically (i.e., are *not* attributable to chance fluctuations), then the investigator must turn to his estimates of the size of the difference between his experimental groups or to the magnitude of the relationship between the experimental and the dependent variables [3] in order to determine whether the results he expects to get are going to be of much practical import.

SPECIAL CONSIDERATIONS IN USING THE EXPERIMENTAL APPROACHES

Because the experimental approach is the prototype of the scientific method, it has often been the special target of various antiscience and antibehaviorist critics who somehow see this method as representing an inhumane or irrelevant approach to studying human beings.   Since such general reactions would seem to fall more properly in the realm of philosophy than in a discussion of scientific approaches, the general arguments which have been raised against the use of scientific techniques in the study of human behavioral phenomena will not be considered here.   Rather, at this point, it seems more appropriate to concentrate on the various specific arguments for and against the use of the experimental approach as contrasted with the other alternative scientific approaches to doing research on behavioral phenomena.

---

[3] In an experimental study, this involves determining the proportion of the variance in the criterion variable which can be attributed to the experimental manipulations. See Hays (1963).

Arguments for the Use of the Experimental Methods

Perhaps the most obvious advantage of the experimental approach is its rigor. By instituting control over irrelevant variables and by manipulating crucial ones in specified ways, the experimenter is clearly able to be more specific in his answers and to achieve a higher degree of certainty with respect to his conclusions than is possible with other approaches.

A second distinct advantage of the experimental approach is that it is not limited to the particular combinations and magnitudes of variables and the timing that occurs in natural events. Because of this, the experimental approach can add a great deal to science. As McDonald (1965) points out: "Obviously we learn from our experience; at least, we draw conclusions from what we observe. Simply having more experience, however, does not guarantee greater understanding."

A third basic argument in favor of the experimental method is the purely pragmatic one that (perhaps because of the two features just mentioned) the study of simplified phenomena in admittedly artificial situations of the laboratory has paid off in the past, not only in the physical sciences, but in the behavioral sciences as well. That is, again and again, the experimental methods as a rigorous approach to the study of "cause-and-effect" relationships have provided results which are lasting over time, which have led to fruitful new studies, and which have suggested more practical applications. In short, they have proved to be the most useful of all approaches when they can be applied.

Arguments Against the Use of Experimental Methods

The most frequently heard criticism of the experimental approach to the study of behavior is that the laboratory is so artificial as to preclude any generalization of results to a real-life situation. As Underwood (1959) has noted in a discussion about verbal learning:

there are clear individual differences among psychologists in the zest for such extrapolation. To take extreme cases, a physiological psychologist who long ago convinced himself that there are no basic differences in the principles underlying the learning of planaria, white rats and men, would probably show little hesitation in generalizing from the laboratory to the classroom. At the other extreme is the ultra-conservative scientist who is so reluctant to generalize he refuses to say "Good Morning" until noon.

Many research workers in the behavioral sciences seem caught between the twin dangers of doing a study which may be rigorous but has little application, and of carrying out an investigation which may be highly applicable but of such a tenuous nature as to be of little actual use.   Solutions to this apparent dilemma vary all the way from Corey (1953), who would shift the task of carrying out research to the applied person, to Dunnette (1966), who might be thought to have implied that research should only be done by the professional research workers when he said that we should: "Press for new values and less pretense in the academic environments of our universities . . . by enabling those scholars who may be ill-fitted for the research enterprise to appropriate rewards in other endeavors."   Most of the persons in the behavioral sciences today, however, probably would agree with Dunnette (1966) when he elaborates by further stating that: "the advantages to both of close association between basic researchers and those practicing the art of psychology should become more apparent.   The researchers would thereby establish and maintain contact with the real world and real problems of human behavior, and the professional practitioners would be more fully alert to the need for assessing their methods by generating and testing alternate deductions and hypotheses growing out of them."   Campbell and Stanley (1963) who, in speaking of research on teaching, suggest that the most appropriate procedure is: "for the ideas for classroom research to originate with teachers and other school personnel, with designs to test these ideas worked out cooperatively with specialists in research methodology, and then for the bulk of the experimentation to be carried out by the idea-producers themselves."

On the other hand, some writers do not see the question of rigor versus application as a dilemma at all, but rather see experimental studies as serving different purposes.   Thus, for example, McDonald (1965) points out that "an experiment does not replicate life in all its complexity; it simulates aspects of it," and Underwood (1959) states that:

One may view the laboratory as a fast, efficient, convenient way of identifying variables or factors which are likely to be important in real-life situations.   Thus if four or five factors are discovered to influence human learning markedly, and to influence it under a wide range of conditions, it would be reasonable to suspect that these factors would also be important in the classroom.   But, one would *not* automatically conclude such; rather, one would make field tests in the classroom situation to deny or confirm the inference concerning the general importance of these variables.

In the same vein, Underwood explains why it is that the experimental researcher is not particularly disturbed when he is accused of concentrating on variables which have effects so small or so specific as to be of little practical consequence.   He points out: "A 'small' phenomenon may be very important in leading to a scientific understanding of learning and yet be of little practical importance.   A scientist's major interest is usually with advancing the understanding of the learning process and such advancement might well be brought about by studying 'little' phenomena as well as 'big' ones."

HOW TO RUN AWAY FROM AN EDUCATIONAL PROBLEM

Paul B. Diederich, University of Chicago

1. Find a scape-goat and ride him. Teachers can always blame administrators, administrators can blame teachers, both can blame parents, and everyone can blame the social order.
2. Profess not to have the answer. This lets you out of having any answer.
3. Say that we must not move too rapidly. This avoids the necessity of getting started.
4. For every proposal set up an opposite and conclude that the "middle ground" (no motion whatever) represents the wisest course of action.
5. Point out that any attempt to reach a conclusion is only a futile "quest for certainty." Doubt and indecision "promote growth."
6. When in a tight place, say something which the group cannot understand.
7. Look slightly embarrassed when the problem is brought up. Hint that it is in bad taste, or too elementary for mature consideration, or that any discussion of it is likely to be misinterpreted by outsiders.
8. Say that the problem "cannot be separated" from other problems; therefore no problem can be solved until all other problems have been solved.
9. Carry the problem into other fields; show that it exists everywhere, hence is of no concern.
10. Point out that those who see the problem do so by virtue of personality traits; e.g.: they are unhappy and transfer their dissatisfaction to the area under discussion.
11. Ask what is meant by the question. When it is clarified, there will be no time left for the answer.
12. Discover that there are all sorts of "dangers" in any specific formulation of conclusions; dangers of exceeding authority or seeming to, of asserting more than is definitely known, of misinterpretation, misuses by uninformed teachers, criticism (and of course the danger of revealing that no one has a sound conclusion to offer).
13. Retreat from the problem into endless discussion of various techniques for approaching it.
14. Retreat into analogies and discuss them until everyone has forgotten the original problem.
15. Appoint a committee.
16. Notice that the time is up. If other members of the group look surprised, list your engagements for the next two days.
17. Point out that some of the greatest minds have struggled with this problem, implying that it does us credit to have even thought of it.
18. Be thankful for the problem. It has stimulated our best thinking and has, therefore, contributed to our growth. It should get a medal.

FIGURE 4.3   Some socially acceptable ways to avoid a problem

Actually, the most serious criticism of the experimental approach is that it is often subject to the source of external invalidity which has already been labeled as *reactivity*. There seems to be little doubt that, in working with human subjects, knowledge that an experiment is in progress can, and does, have an influence on the findings. This fact, coupled with recent evidence (e.g., Kintz, et al., 1965; Rosenthal, 1966) that the experimenter himself can unconsciously influence his subjects, be they men or animals, should serve to remind the reader of the extreme caution required when interpreting even experimental studies. While it is true that the reactive effect can occur in the use of the other basic approaches as well as with the experimental approach, it must be remembered that it is much more difficult to hide the fact that a research study is in progress when carrying out an experiment than is the case with other methods of investigation.

Other arguments which are sometimes offered against the use of the experimental approach include statements that experimentation makes no real contribution itself, but merely consolidates gains made by the other approaches; that many variables of extreme importance are exceedingly difficult or impossible to manipulate, control, or measure; and that even a single experiment is so difficult to carry out that the payoff can seldom be sufficient to compensate for the effort. It should be readily apparent that the first statement is a specious argument somewhat akin to early discussions of whether heredity or environment was the most important: obviously, both the creation and testing of scientific hypotheses and theories are vital if we are to increase our understanding of behavioral phenomena. The latter arguments are reminiscent of Diedrich's list of ways to avoid solving a problem, which has been reproduced in Figure 4.3.

Common Errors in the Design of Research Studies in the Behavioral Sciences

Because experimentation *is* difficult to carry out adequately, it seems reasonable to conclude this chapter on the experimental approach and, indeed, that part of the text devoted to research methods per se with a discussion of some of the common errors in the design of research studies in the behavioral sciences.

Perhaps there is no better place to start than with an examination of the reasons why research grant applications are disapproved. Allen (1960) made a tabulation of the characteristic shortcomings of rejected applications for research grants submitted to the National Institutes of Health in April and May of 1959. This tabulation, reproduced in Table 4.2, is based on 605 proposals which were rejected by a panel of jurists after a "round-table discussion of a research proposal from fifteen to twenty scientists in the same general field . . . ." While the studies involved cover the entire field of medical and related biological sciences, they do include investigations in the behavioral sciences (particularly mental health), and the defects listed will be quite familiar to those who have served on similar panels concerned primarily with research studies in education, psychology and sociology.

The shortcomings listed in the table have been classified into four main types: the first type was those related to inadequacies in the problem itself, that is, the question which the proposed research was to answer was judged to be unimportant or to be unclearly stated or thought out; the second category was concerned with the approach by which an answer to the questions raised would be sought; the third category concerned the estimated competence—the scientific judgment and technical skill—of the investigator himself; and the fourth category, labeled other, consisted mainly of practical considerations of the situation in which the research was to be done.

TABLE 4.2
Shortcomings Found in Study-Section Review of 605 Disapproved Research
Grant Applications, April–May 1959
(All percentages are to the base number 605)

Number	Shortcoming	Percentage
	Class I: Problem (58 percent)	
1	The problem is of insufficient importance or is unlikely to produce any new or useful information.	33.1
2	The proposed research is based on a hypothesis that rests on insufficient evidence, is doubtful, or is unsound.	8.9
3	The problem is more complex than the investigator appears to realize.	8.1
4	The problem has only local significance, or is one of production or control, or otherwise fails to fall sufficiently clearly within the general field of health-related research.	4.8
5	The problem is scientifically premature and warrants, at most, only a pilot study.	3.1
6	The research as proposed is overly involved, with too many elements under simultaneous investigation.	3.0
7	The description of the nature of the research and of its significance leaves the proposal nebulous and diffuse and without clear research aim.	2.6
	Class II: Approach (73 percent)	
8	The proposed tests, or methods, or scientific procedures are unsuited to the stated objective.	34.7
9	The description of the approach is too nebulous, diffuse, and lacking in clarity to permit adequate evaluation.	28.8
10	The overall design of the study has not been carefully thought out.	14.7
11	The statistical aspects of the approach have not been given sufficient consideration.	8.1
12	The approach lacks scientific imagination.	7.4
13	Controls are either inadequately conceived or inadequately described.	6.8
14	The material the investigator proposes to use is unsuited to the objectives of the study or is difficult to obtain.	3.8
15	The number of observations is unsuitable.	2.5
16	The equipment contemplated is outmoded or otherwise unsuitable.	1.0
	Class III: Man (55 percent)	
17	The investigator does not have adequate experience or training, or both, for this research.	32.6
18	The investigator appears to be unfamiliar with recent pertinent literature or methods, or both.	13.7

TABLE 4.2 (*continued*)

Number	Shortcoming	Percentage
19	The investigator's previously published work in this field does not inspire confidence.	12.6
20	The investigator proposes to rely too heavily on insufficiently experienced associates.	5.0
21	The investigator is spreading himself too thin; he will be more productive if he concentrates on fewer projects.	3.8
22	The investigator needs more liaison with colleagues in this field or in collateral fields.	1.7
	Class IV: Other (16 percent)	
23	The requirements for equipment or personnel, or both, are unrealistic.	10.1
24	It appears that other responsibilities would prevent devotion of sufficient time and attention to this research.	3.0
25	The institutional setting is unfavorable.	2.3
26	Research grants to the investigator, now in force, are adequate in scope and amount to cover the proposed research.	1.5

SOURCE: Allen, E. Why are research grant applications disapproved? *Science*, 1960, **132**, 1532–1534.

It is worth taking special note that the largest proportion of shortcomings fell under Class II—approach to the problem. Seventy-three percent of the shortcomings involved inadequate methodology, as compared with 58 percent for the statement of the problem, and 55 percent for the qualifications of the investigator. Of the 26 specific shortcomings listed, 4 appeared much more often than any of the others. These four were as follows:

The proposed tests, or methods, or scientific procedures are unsuited to the stated objective.   34.7%

The problem is of insufficient importance or is unlikely to produce any new or useful information.   33.1%

The investigator does not have adequate experience or training or both, for this research.   32.6%

The description of the approach is too nebulous, diffuse, and lacking in clarity to permit adequate evaluation.   28.8%

Although the remaining shortcomings appear much less frequently (the next greatest being cited only 14.7 percent of the time), the relatively inexperienced researcher would do well to note each defect and perhaps use the entire list as a check against which to compare any research study he is planning to do.

In addition to looking at specific inadequacies of research proposals, it would seem well worthwhile to consider also some of the more general criticisms which have been leveled at research in the various behavioral sciences from time to time. Typical is the rather delightful taxonomy of the "games psychologists play" which was presented by Dunnette (1966) in a talk entitled "Fads, Fashions and Folderol in Psychology."

According to Dunnette, a perusal of current psychological research literature reveals a surprising number of *fads* ("practices and concepts characterized by capriciousness and intense but short-lived interest"), *fashions* ("those manners or modes of action taking on the character of habits and enforced by social or scientific norms defining what constitutes the thing to do") and downright *folderol* ("those practices characterized by excessive ornamentation, nonsensical and unnecessary actions, trifles and essentially useless and wasteful fiddle-faddle"). Further, the fads, fashions, and folderol can be classified into a number of "games" which psychologists sometimes play in the process of (and sometimes instead of) attempting to carry out research on human behavior.

The first of these games has been labeled "Pets We Keep." "This game is characterized by an early and premature commitment to some Great Theory or Great Method." Its effect is "to distort research problems so that they fit the theory or the method," and it leads the researcher to "prove" something rather than to "find out" something. As Platt (1964) suggests, we all should: "Beware of the man of one method or one instrument, either experimental or theoretical. He tends to become method oriented rather than problem oriented; the method oriented man is shackled."

A second game described by Dunnette is called "Names We Love." This is the great word game which is characterized either by "the coining of new words and labels either to fit old concepts or to cast new facts outside the ken of a theory in need of protection," or by applying "new names in psychological research widely and uncritically before sufficient work has been done to specify the degree of generality or specificity of the trait being dealt with." The effect of this game is "to sustain theories even if facts seem to refute them," for "if facts appear that cannot be ignored, relabeling them or renaming them gives them their own special compartment so they cease to infringe on the privacy of the theory." Playing this game also is the main cause of fads in which a great deal of research energy is expended before discovering that the newly labeled concept is a spurious one or, at best, an older one in a new hat. "Another game, entitled 'The Fun We Have,' is characterized by: . . . a compulsion to forget the problem—in essence to forget what we are really doing—because of the fun we may be enjoying with our apparatus, our computers, our models or the simple act of testing statistical null hypotheses. Often, in our zest for this particular game, we forget not only the problem, but we may even literally forget to look at the data!" The result of this game, of course, is to build a science of human behavior on "a foundation of triviality."

A fourth "game" that psychological researchers sometimes play is called

"Questions We Ask." The researcher who plays this game determines the questions he will ask on the basis of whether they will enhance his pet theory, display his pet method, or increase his visibility among his colleagues. A particularly vicious variant of this game occurs when: "the investigator shrewdly fails to state the question he is trying to answer, gathers data to provide answers to simpler questions and then behaves as if his research has been relevant to other unstated but more important and more interesting problems."

The result of this kind of activity is similar to that found when playing "The Fun We Have." The "scholarly" journals become glutted with trivia and pseudoscientific conclusions.

Perhaps the most dangerous game of all to the behavioral sciences is that which Dunnette has called "The Delusions We Suffer." This game is best described as "maintaining delusional systems to support our claims that the things we are doing *really* constitute good science." Though dangerous, this game is so popular it has several different variants. One variant is arguing that "if a new theory or method stimulates others to do research, it *must* be good." The effect of this logic is that "an inestimable amount of psychological research energy has been dissipated in fighting brush fires spawned by faddish theories—which careful research might better have refuted at their inception." A second variant of this game results when the investigator discovers that gathering data from real people emitting real behaviors in the day-to-day world proves to be difficult, unwieldy and just plain unrewarding. Under these conditions the investigator quickly retreats "into the relative security of experimental or psychometric laboratories where new laboratory or test behaviors may be concocted to be observed, measured, and subjected to an endless array of internal analyses." The result of this variant is "elaborate theories or behavioral taxonomies, entirely consistent within themselves but lacking the acid test of contact with reality."

A third delusion research workers sometimes suffer is the rationalization of "certain practices on the grounds that they are intrinsically good for humanity and that they need not, therefore, meet the usual standards demanded by scientific verification." As examples of this game, Dunnette cites some of the uses of psychotherapy in clinical situations and the use of sensitivity training in industry. The effect of this game is, obviously, that of perpetuating empty rituals superstitiously believed to be of value, while drawing attention from using and finding practices and techniques which do have a beneficial effect.

Another delusion which researchers sometimes use is that of treating "individual differences as merely bothersome variation—to be reduced by adequate controls or treated as error variance in the search for General Laws." The effect is to construct an oversimplified image of man. As Dunnette points out, "We cannot expect a science of human behavior to advance very far until the moderating effects of individual variation on the functional relationships being studied are taken fully into account."

At the other extreme from those who ignore individual differences are those who maintain an even more detrimental delusion: that of regarding the differences between individuals "as so pervasive that it is assumed *no* laws can be stated." As Dunnette points out, "a strong commitment to this point of view must ultimately be an admission that the methods of science cannot be applied to the study of human behavior." Unfortunately, this latter implication is seldom recognized or honestly admitted by those who emphasize the ultimate uniqueness of the individual. Rather, such persons continually talk of "new approaches," less "mechanistic emphasis," and "humanistic endeavors." While no one denies the ultimate uniqueness of every individual, failure to recognize that there are degrees of similarity, by definition, can produce no "replicable or practically useful findings."

If "The Delusions We Suffer" represents the most dangerous of games, that called "The Secrets We Keep" is certainly the most despicable. This last game is characterized by "all the things we do to accomplish the aim of looking better in public than we really are." While the main variants of this game are those of burying negative results and using "subjective arithmetic" (i.e., letting one's hopes and strong commitments lead to errors in calculating with the data), it can also be played by dropping certain subjects from the analysis, consciously or unconsciously biasing the observations, incompletely describing the methodology, and failing to carry out (or to report) cross-validation studies. According to Dunnette, the extent to which this game is played was suggested recently in an article by Wollins (1962). Wollins reports that he wrote to 37 authors asking them for raw data. Of the 32 who replied, 21 reported that the data had been "either misplaced, lost or inadvertently destroyed." In examining the seven sets of data ultimately received from 5 of the authors, it was discovered that three contained errors of calculation so great as to clearly change the outcome of the study as originally reported. If one were to generalize from this small, select sample, the conclusion might be reached that, at best, 43 percent of the information presently in our journals is erroneous. As Dunnette points out, "these tactics of secrecy can be nothing but severely damaging to any hopes of advancing psychology as a science."

It is quite apparent that if our knowledge of human behavior is ever to advance beyond the alchemy stage, it is up to each individual researcher to try and avoid the major errors described above as games. To help accomplish this task, Dunnette offers the following five major suggestions:

1. Give up constraining commitments to theories, methods and apparatus.
2. Adopt . . . "multiple working hypotheses" for every problem.
3. Put more eclecticism into graduate education.

4. Press for new values and less pretense in the academic environments of our Universities.
5. Establish more stringent requirements for the publication of research articles.

As Dunnette himself points out, if all investigators were to use appropriate research designs and avoid playing the games, which, while personally satisfying, are detrimental to the advancement of the behavioral sciences, we would have reached Utopia. But surely Utopia is not too much to ask of a science in its second hundred years, and indeed, no less can be demanded if research in the behavioral sciences is to fulfill its basic function of and potential for advancing mankind.

III.
Tools of
Research

5.
The Library

INFORMATIONAL SYSTEMS OF THE FUTURE

The Information Explosion

The day has long passed when an investigator in any of the areas of the behavioral sciences can do without the library. Our knowledge has expanded so rapidly and the number of persons involved has increased so greatly that the likelihood of a study so unique or novel as not to be related in any way to any other prior investigation is practically nonexistent. Thus, the traditional functions of the literature search—preventing duplication of effort, providing suggestions for new hypotheses and for new interrelationships, and, in applied work, justifying the importance of the problem—have become more and more essential.

The same knowledge explosion which has increased the need for a careful review of the literature is also making the current practice of each individual investigator performing the task manually less and less practical. With the number of research articles published doubling every ten years, the amount of time and energy devoted to the task of hunting down and recording the results from relevant studies done by others is reaching horrendous proportions. As the American Library Association itself has pointed out (1963), "unless we inject some effective anti-coagulants into our information-processing system, we can look forward to gradual hardening of the research arteries."

As long ago as 1945, Bush (1945) saw these problems and their importance and, by 1962, a vision of what may be accomplished well within the
lifetime of most of the readers of this book was described by Cahn (1962).
In that same year, an exhibit which gave concrete form to the notions of a
completely automated information system was displayed at the World's Fair
in Seattle by the American Library Association, and was seen by some
1,800,000 visitors.

The General Problem of Information Storage and Retrieval

While a truly comprehensive information system might provide for the storage and presentation of materials for instructional as well as for informational purposes, it is the latter which is of prime interest to the investigator.
The discussion to follow will concentrate on the general problem of information storage and retrieval without concerning itself with instructional
systems per se.

Both the investigator's informational need and the current manual system of fulfilling it has been aptly described by Becker and Hayes (1964),
as follows:

He perhaps asks for a list or bibliography of all available literature which touch
his field of interest. He would like, if possible, to have brief descriptions or
abstracts of the more important documents on the list in order that he may decide, without much time consuming research, which are most likely to be of
value for his particular purpose . . . . He gets from the library's card catalogue
a list of volumes which deal with his problem. Then he consults the bibliographies given in each of them for additional titles. Little by little he builds up
an imposing bibliography for his own study, and over a period of months he
sifts the books one by one for the chapters, sections and statistical tables which
have a specific meaning for his job.

Although the complete mechanization of the task as described by Becker
and Hayes may not be possible, a tremendous amount of the research worker's time and effort could be saved through the utilization of a specialized
information system which included the following major components: a remote inquiry station; a unit for automatic catalogue search and bibliographic listing; a facsimile transmission unit which would permit both display
and duplication; an automatic abstracting device; and a language translation
unit. Although many of these units are presently under separate development, and some are even now in actual use, no attempt has yet been made
to integrate them all into a single functioning system. Each component
will be discussed separately in the following sections.

THE REMOTE INQUIRY STATION   The main function of this unit is to eliminate the travel of the individual research worker to the place where the

documents of interest are stored. While it may seem unnecessary, or even frivolous at the present time, to want to eliminate a short walk to the library, the expansion of knowledge will soon make it impossible for a copy of every published journal to be stored in every library in the country. It will soon be necessary to develop a more complete system for cooperation among libraries whereby each will store only its designated part of the research literature. Under these circumstances, a personal search by an investigator who wished to cover all the journals in his own and related fields would require travel to points considerably distant from his home base of operations. When this occurs, much time and energy can be saved by a fully developed remote inquiry station.

As it is presently envisioned, an investigator may use, in his office (or even in his home), a typewriterlike keyboard to transmit his request for a literature search to the appropriate central computer storage unit. The response, in the form of a complete bibliography, a set of abstracts, the complete documents themselves, or some combination of these, will be beamed directly to the inquiry station by means of masers or lasers which according to the American Library Association (1963) "will be, for the library of the future, an optical transmission line . . . ."

AUTOMATIC CATALOGUE SEARCH AND BIBLIOGRAPHIC LISTING   Now, because of the work accomplished in a field labeled by some as *intellectronics* or *artificial intelligence,* it has been possible to develop a literature searching machine which can carry out this most uninteresting and arduous task in about 2 percent of the time it would take to complete the job by hand (Becker & Hayes, 1964, p. 127).

As a result of the efforts of a group of persons at Western Reserve University (Perry, Kent, & Berry, 1956; Vickery, 1959) it is now possible for a worker in the metallurgy industry to ask the "library reference machine" several questions relevant to the topic at hand, and to receive a list of articles which have been written on that subject. Suppose a worker in industry gets the idea that titanium might be just the thing for some new product. Some of the questions he must ask and answer, even before laboratory studies begin, might be: Will it hold certain acids? What temperatures can it stand without deteriorating? How heavy is it? What stresses can it take? Where are supplies of it available? Are the supplies limited or large? How much will it cost? Each question can be put to the machine (in a coded machine language, of course), and the output will be a complete list of all articles pertinent to each question.

In the first applications of the library reference machine, the bibliographic listings, the indexing of key words and the necessary abstracting was all done by hand and fed, in coded form, into a regular computer with an extra large storage capacity. The search always required a complete scanning of every item listed in the memory. While these procedures transferred much of the effort from the research worker to professional abstracters and bibliographers, the process was still much too slow. It was necessary to develop special-purpose equipment which used a coordinate system approach, now referred to as random access, to seek appropriate documents, rather than the traditional linear search of every item in the memory. The output system was modified so as to yield either the location of an abstract or the document or the complete abstract, as well as the bibliographic citation.

Obviously, the effectiveness of any such system of automatic search will depend upon the quality of the indexing. While this is true of even the complete linear search, the difficulties become even more apparent when a random access approach is used. Becker and Hayes (1964) point out: "the reliability and completeness of any search, as with most other systems, were found to be wholly dependent upon the quality of the human indexing and the effectiveness of the decision process for compatibility of index and search terms."

In attempting to improve the situation, the first difficulty noted was that: "the larger and more detailed the index and catalogue, the less the information loss, but the greater the difficulty in searching" (Becker & Hayes, 1964). Further, it was noted that (p. 141) unfortunately "traditional subject classification schemes, alphabetic subject heading listings, and even the prescribed vocabularies of the documentalists tend to pigeonhole information and restrict its use." The problem is further complicated when, as seems to be required as our knowledge increases, many persons of quite different backgrounds need to concentrate on a common problem. Under these circumstances, as Becker and Hayes indicate (1964): "different individuals . . . each concerned with a common area . . . seem to be using the same language and talking about the same thing. Thus, similar words all too frequently are used to represent superficially similar concepts which are, in fact, fundamentally different."

To help overcome these difficulties, several varieties of automatic indexing have been developed and tried. For example, Tasman (1958) has described a system in which statements were obtained from scholars indicating the kind of information they wanted to know about each word. Next, the scholars went through the text indicating the extent to which each word was related to each of the kinds of information previously listed. With this kind of system, the machine was able to prepare an index and catalogue of the information in the Dead Sea Scrolls which was especially useful for carrying out concordance studies and for preparing specialized word lists which are useful in the type of document analysis described in the chapter on historical research.

Another system called "key word in context" (KWIC) has been developed by Luhn (1960). This approach makes use of what is now referred to as "permutation indexing" and results in an index made up of individual words which appear in document titles and abstracts. Words such as prepositions, articles, conjunctions and the like are eliminated from the indexing process automatically by the machine which maintains in storage a list of such words which are to be removed from the final index. This approach has already been successfully applied to research reports published in the *Chemical Abstracts* to produce a separate volume for more rapid reference called *Chemical Titles*.

Another approach has been tried for the indexing of names rather than subject matter and title information. Here, the chief difficulty seems to result from misspelling or a misunderstanding of the names on the part of the inquirer. To overcome this problem (for example, confusing Burke, Birk, Burck, and Bherk), systems have been developed which use a phonetic coding of input names.

While the systems described above are adequate for concordance and similar studies where exact duplication of words is important or in highly technical fields where there is little ambiguity of words, such approaches are simply not powerful enough to handle the more complex indexing tasks which arise so often in the behavioral sciences, where the terminology is far from precise, let alone standardized. However, more recent work by Doyle (1962), by Maron and Kuhns (1960), and by Stiles (1961) shows some promise for this area. Essentially, these newer techniques make use of counts of various associations among the indexing terms and of ratings of the relevancy of the index terms to particular documents. The result is a weighted index which can be used to assess the similarity of the content of various documents, and this measure of similarity, in turn, used to clarify documents into categories, for listing by group in answer to any inquiry for information in a given area.

An excellent illustration of the premise which these latter approaches to automatic indexing have for duplicating that which is presently accomplished by hand, is provided in a study by Borko (1961). Using a set of 618 psychological abstracts, key words from a list of 90 possible index terms were assigned to each of the documents. Next, a table was set up showing the similarity of each document to the other as indicated by the communality of terms used. The technique of factor analysis (see Chapter 8) was then applied to determine the factors which would be necessary to classify the 618 documents. As it turned out, the resulting ten factors corresponded to labels used in the classification system developed manually and independently by the American Psychological Association.

FACSIMILE TRANSMISSION The possibility that tomorrow's investigator may not be able personally to travel to the place that stores the document he needs demands some system for the rapid transmission of exact copies of the materials over great distances. Modern television systems provide a means for the immediate transmission of visual materials, and it should be apparent that each central storage unit will need a transmitter and each remote inquiry station will need to be equipped with a receiver and a screen. In addition, each remote inquiry station will need equipment, such as that presently used in making wirephotos, and audio and video tapes, which can provide a permanent record of the information transmitted, whether it be auditory or visual. The researcher would not need to be personally present to receive the messages from the information center and could study the documents at length at his later leisure.

ABSTRACTING   It has been noted that one of the outcomes of the automatic literature search might be an abstract of the research report. Although, at the present time, many publications require the author himself to provide, along with the full article, an abstract which could be stored and later transmitted in total to the inquirer, work is currently progressing on the automatization of the abstracting process itself. Already, according to the American Library Association Report (1963): "Several researchers have produced computer programs which embody sophisticated mathematical principles for searching natural language text after it exists in machine readable form. Research work has explored ways of extracting meaning from text by means of word association, syntactical analysis and even contextual analysis."

The initial work in this field seems to have been done by Luhn (1958) whose approach involved: (1) the identification of those sentences in the article which contained the most information; and (2) the verbatim reporting of them in the sequence in which they appeared in the original text. To identify the "meaning-bearing sentences" a total count of "notion" words, i.e., verbs, nouns, and adjectives (as contrasted with common words such as prepositions, articles, conjunctions which rarely characterize meaning in English sentences), is first made. Then, each sentence is rated according to the number of high-frequency (in the total count over the entire article) "notion" words which they contain. After all sentences have been rated, they are ranked and those with the highest rank printed as the abstract. An excellent example of the results of Luhn's approach has been reproduced as Figure 5.1. Those readers who are especially interested in this area may enjoy comparing this abstract with the original article by Marrazzi (1957).

It should be apparent that Luhn's system is based upon the assumption that authors of articles stress the importance of certain ideas through the repetition of certain words and further tend to express the relationship of ideas through the physical nearness of the words in the text. Because of a wide variety of writing in terms of style, complexity of material, etc., it may be anticipated that this approach will not work equally well with all types of articles. One might suspect that highly technical articles in which the researcher goes to great pains to eliminate redundancy will not be as successfully abstracted as will newspaper articles (where the same thing is said again and again, each time with more details), as will scientific information written for popular consumption, or as will materials written for instructional purposes.

Attempts to overcome some of the limitations of Luhn's approach have been made by Oswald (1959) and by Baxendale (1958). Essentially,

---

134   Information storage and retrieval

Exhibit 1

Source: The Scientific American, Vol. 196, No. 2, 86–94, February, 1957
Title: Messengers of the Nervous System
Author: Amodeo S. Marrazzi
Editor's Subheading: The internal communication of the body is mediated by chemicals as well as by nerve impulses. Study of their interaction has developed important leads to the understanding and therapy of mental illness.

Auto-Abstract *

It seems reasonable to credit the single-celled organisms also with a system of chemical communication by diffusion of stimulating substances through the cell, and these correspond to the chemical messengers (e.g., hormones) that carry stimuli from cell to cell in the more complex organisms. (7.0) †

Finally, in the vertebrate animals there are special glands (e.g., the adrenals) for producing chemical messengers, and the nervous and chemical communication systems are intertwined: for instance, release of adrenalin by the adrenal gland is subject to control both by nerve impulses and by chemicals brought to the gland by the blood. (6.4)

The experiments clearly demonstrated that acetylcholine (and related substances) and adrenalin (and its relatives) exert opposing actions which maintain a balanced regulation of the transmission of nerve impulses. (6.3)

It is reasonable to suppose that the tranquilizing drugs counteract the inhibitory effect of excessive adrenalin or serotonin or some related inhibitor in the human nervous system. (7.3)

* Sentences selected by means of statistical analysis as having a degree of significance of 6 and over.
† Significance factor is given at the end of each sentence.

FIGURE 5.1   Sample auto-abstract produced by means of a system developed by Luhn (1958) (Becker, J., & Hayes, R. *Information storage and retrieval: Tools, elements, and theories.* New York: Wiley, 1964. P. 134.)

Oswald expanded Luhn's original rating of sentences to include all possible juxtapositions of meaning-bearing words, not just their sequential arrangement. Baxendale, on the other hand, took quite a different tack. She felt that in the English language prepositional phrases reflected the important subject content more than words alone, and thus developed a rating system based on the frequency counts of only those words which appeared among the first four following any of the fifty common prepositions of the English language.

Although current systems of automatic abstracting are far from perfect, they do seem sufficiently successful to enable the researcher to make, for a wide variety of subject matters, an accurate judgment as to whether or not he should review the entire article. And, as Savage (1958) has pointed out, it is now only a matter of collecting large samples of data from a wide variety of writings before completely adequate systems for almost all written materials can be developed.

MACHINE TRANSLATION   The translation of foreign language journals has not been given as much attention in this field as it has in the physical and biological sciences because of the apparent lead which the United States has enjoyed for some years in the behavioral sciences. However, important work is being done in other countries and the results of such studies are not always published in English language journals. The day is past when a competent investigator in the behavioral sciences can afford to ignore foreign journals; his literature search must be worldwide, not just nationwide. Although an individual investigator might become sufficiently proficient in one or two other languages to accurately translate research articles relevant to his own work, life is just too short to enable any one person to become an expert in his field and in many foreign languages as well. So, once again, it is an automatic machine approach which seems to hold the only promise of effectively overcoming this difficulty.

It is now apparent that the simple, statistical technique of making frequency counts of words or phrases, which seems to work so well in producing the auto-abstract, is simply not powerful enough to perform the task of translating a foreign language. A full-blown linguistic analysis is necessary —not only of the English language, but of each foreign tongue from which translations are desired. Without going into the details of process itself, it is sufficient to say that, although progress has been hampered because no completely satisfactory criterion yet exists for judging the adequacy of a translation, sufficient advancement has been made to lead Becker and Hayes (1964) to conclude that: "translations adequate for conveying the general sense of a foreign-language technical article in a sufficiently circumscribed field can now be prepared by any one of several operating programs and . . . the quality of the translation will significantly improve with time."

CURRENT BARRIERS TO THE RAPID DEVELOPMENT OF AUTOMATIC LIBRARIES
Although the technical possibilities of a highly efficient and largely automatic information system can be clearly seen, and fragments of the system are already being put to use in certain limited areas, there are a number of very practical difficulties which are inhibiting the full development of the idea system as described in the previous section.

The first inhibiting factor is that of cost. While all of the equipment described is technically feasible, its manufacture, its installation, and its maintenance will require initial expenditures which far exceed monies now spent or available for library facilities. It is quite likely that future developments will appear first in those areas where the pressure for increased efficiency is greatest. Judging from past experience, this is most likely to be in applied areas in business and industry where competition requires increased efficiency in the acquisition of accurate information, and, most especially, in the military, where results are specific and concrete and where emotional attachments have a way of overcoming fiscal timidity. In the long run pure research and education will also benefit, since they will be permitted to use, as time and money permit, the equipment constructed for applied work in other areas.

In addition to cost, there is a problem of standardization. One of the obvious requirements of automatic search, automatic abstracting, machine translation, and document reproduction is uniformity, not only in the size of the pages of reports and in the method of bibliographic citation, but in the format of topic presentation, and perhaps even in the style of writing as well. While many research workers will be reluctant to yield some of their current flexibility, they will need to recognize that the place to be creative is in the formulation of their hypotheses and the design of their studies, not in the reporting of their results. Without some conformity in the latter area, the information bottleneck will relegate the results of their creativity to oblivion.

Various professional organizations, like the American Psychological Association, the American Educational Research Association, and the American Sociological Society have for some time required a reasonable standardization in the organization of articles submitted to the various journals they sponsor; and the cooperative use of the National Union Catalog, which is maintained by the Library of Congress, has necessitated some uniformity in the cataloging process. The greatest pressure toward standardization will come from those government agencies which have formed rudimentary information networks. Most prominent among such networks is the one developed by the Armed Services Technical Information Agency (ASTIA) which, as an arm of the Department of Defense, is responsible for collecting and maintaining files of reports of all groups doing research under contract to the Department of Defense. The civilian counterpart to ASTIA is the Office of Technical Services (OTS) of the Department of Commerce. This agency is responsible for the dissemination of research literature sponsored both directly and indirectly by the government. Smaller information networks also providing pressure toward standardization which will make the library of the future possible are the Atomic Energy Commission, the Mid-West Interlibrary Center and the Association of Research Libraries.

Another barrier to the rapid development of the ideal information system is the communication problem. One aspect of this, the use of similar terms for different concepts, has already been mentioned in connection with the problems which arise in automatic indexing. Another stems from the inability or reluctance of the user of the information system to formulate his needs in precise terms rather than in vaguely stated generalities based on intuition.

Even though it is well recognized that the fundamental aim of the user of any information system is to make decisions and that the crucial point, as far as getting the most useful information is concerned, is almost always a clear definition and understanding of the research question, it turns out that the definition of a research problem is not always a simple, straightforward process. Work which has attempted to assess the value of information to the research worker has already shown that seldom is it the individual fact which is important; but rather, usually, it is some analytical combination of the facts which turns out to be most useful. It is becoming more and more essential that the investigator state his problem so precisely that it is possible to determine not only what individual facts, but what combination of facts are relevant.

It may well be, however, that a fully automatic literature review which is completely satisfactory can never be accomplished. As Doyle (1961) has pointed out, a formal literature search in terms of expected associations can lead only to confirmation, yet it is the casual browsing which leads to the unexpected associations that provide the real "new" information which makes the search worthwhile for research purposes. While the formal literature search may be carried out automatically at a great saving of time, the heuristic value of a personal examination of the literature must neither be overlooked nor jeopardized in any way.

A final block to the automatization of information systems is the human resentment of machines. This resentment appears every time a machine takes over a task previously performed by persons, without any attempt on the part of the critics to discriminate between an automatic activity performed by a human and a truly human endeavor. Following Wiener's lead in suggesting the human use of human beings, Becker and Hayes (1964, p. 280) distinguish among three different roles which man can play in an information system. The first is that labeled "machinomorph" in which man is simply a cog in a machine, performing a simple routine task. The second, coming closer to the human use of humans, involves man as a communications link. Even though some communication functions can be automatized in highly rigid situations, no equipment has yet been devised which can operate efficiently in highly flexible situations where complex judgments are required to handle an endless variety of special cases. The third role, which represents the human being performing a truly human task, is that of making value judgments. It is for this reason that the browsing portion of the review of literature function described above is not likely to be automatized. Obviously, the ideal information system will make use of machines in tasks that machines can perform best and use humans only for human tasks. It is not likely that this ideal will be achieved, however, until the overgeneralized negative reaction of some individuals toward machine use is overcome, and man is freed from serving as a machine so that he can perform truly human tasks.

BASIC TYPES OF REFERENCE MATERIALS

While the library of the future may require only that the investigator be able to formulate his needs clearly and concisely and given this, can then carry out the formal literature search automatically, today's investigator must still be familiar with the various types of reference materials and know what kinds of information they contain.

Just how vast the literature is in this day and age usually comes as quite a shock to most persons who are doing their first thorough search of previous work. A recent National Science Foundation report (1964) which describes the characteristics of some 300 hard-core journals (i.e., journals publishing over 50 percent of pagination in reports of original research which was basic rather than applied, and which were national in scope) noted that the number of such journals has doubled approximately every 15 years since 1899, as seen in Figure 5.2. Assuming that there is no reason for such a trend to change and noting that in 1964 the *Psychological Abstracts* regularly reviewed 349 journals, including major ones in education and sociology, and sporadically covered (i.e., abstracted a relevant article which was brought to the attention of the editorial staff) an additional 205 publications, the reader can extrapolate to determine just how many publications he might have to scan, at any given time, were he to make a thorough search of original sources.

It is not possible, in a text like this, to describe in detail the contents of every publication which might be of interest to a research worker in the behavioral sciences. The discussion in the remainder of this chapter will be restricted to presenting only a brief description of the various *types* of publications which are of use to the research worker and listing a few examples which illustrate the variety of materials that are classified under each heading.

It will become apparent to the reader as he examines the literature that a completely "errorless" classification system is impossible. In the first place, it is not always possible to categorize a publication properly by its title alone. For example, the *Handbook of Psychological Terms* is really a technical dictionary, the *Dictionary of Occupational Titles* possesses more of the characteristics of a handbook than of a dictionary, the *Mental Measurement Yearbook* is *not* published every year and the *Handbook of Experimental Psychology* can be thought of as an encyclopedia. In the second place, many publications contain information typical of several different

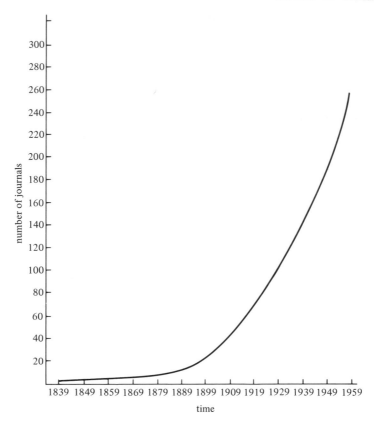

FIGURE 5.2   Accumulated growth of journals 1839–1959 (National Science Foundation, Office of Science Information. Characteristics of scientific journals 1949–1959. *National Science Foundation Report,* Washington, D.C.: NSF, 1964, **64-20.**)

types of source materials, yet, are listed only under the heading which describes the major portion of their contents.   Finally, the boundaries themselves are not always clear cut and there is an overlapping of even the definitions of the different types of publications.   The distinction between a handbook and an encyclopedia or between a handbook and a directory is not always clear.   Under these circumstances, the classification used in the following discussion must not be thought of as an immutable taxonomy, but simply one useful way of describing various types of materials.

Sources Providing Overview Information

While an experienced investigator who is well familiar with the field in which he is working may turn directly to sources of original materials, the beginning research worker or an experimenter whose work has led him into a new and somewhat unfamiliar area will probably start background readings with one or more of the types of sources described in this section. Never, however, would a careful worker stop with the secondary materials listed under this heading. Rather, he would use these sources for gaining a general orientation which would enable him to more precisely search out the particular studies of particular importance.

GUIDES TO REFERENCE MATERIALS   In general, the term *guide* is used to designate a publication which is intended to aid the researcher by providing him with systematized lists and descriptions of various research publications. In a very real sense, a guide is an elaboration and an exhaustive coverage of the material presented in this portion of this chapter. In short, it is a thorough discussion of literature sources.

Typical publications of this type which are of interest to workers in the behavioral science area are the following:

Alexander, C., & Burke, A. *How to locate educational information and data.* (4th ed.) New York: Columbia University, Teachers College, Bureau of Publications, 1958.

Daniel, R., & Louttit, C. *Professional problems in psychology.* New York: Prentice-Hall, 1953.

Graves, E. (Ed.) *Ulrich's periodical directory: A classified guide to a selected list of periodicals, foreign and domestic.* (12th ed.) New York: Bowker, 1967.

Walford, A. (Ed.) *Guide to reference material.* London: The Library Association, 1959 (Suppl., 1963).

White, C. et al. *Sources of information in the social sciences: A guide to the literature.* Totowa, N.J.: The Bedminster Press, 1964.

Winchell, C. *Guide to reference books.* (7th ed.) Chicago: American Library Association, 1951 (Suppls.).

A typical page from a guide is presented in Figure 5.3.

INDEXES AND BIBLIOGRAPHIES   In contrast to guides, which provide the investigator with lists of publications, bibliographies and indexes give the direct citation of individual research studies and articles. Typically, the listing is organized by subject, title, author, date, or some other scheme.

Because our literature is already so vast, most bibliographies are restricted to some specific subject matter area or topic, and some are delimited as to the years covered. Typical of such specialized bibliographies are the following:

Albert, E. et al. *A selected bibliography on values, ethics and esthetics in the behavioral sciences and philosophy, 1920–1958.* Glencoe, Ill.: Free Press, 1959.

D216. Gittler, Joseph B., *ed.* Review of sociology; analysis of a decade. New York, Wiley, 1957. 588 p.
22 specialists survey the most significant literature and developments in all areas of sociological inquiry for the period 1945-1955. Each of the 14 essays (Sociological theory, Population research, Collective behavior, Marriage and the family, Racial and cultural relations, etc.) is followed by a bibliography. A total of 2,158 items are listed. Five annotated bibliographical appendices (Sociology of education, politics, religion, art and culture change) list an additional 423 titles.

D217. Kölner Zeitschrift fur Soziologie und Sozialpsychologie. v. 1 + 1949 + Cologne, Westdeutscher Verlag. quarterly.
An important German journal which reviews 150-200 monographs a year. Long (1,000-2,000 words) critical single reviews are supplemented by extensive essays reviewing groups of books.

D218. Population. v. 1 + 1946 + Paris, Institut National d'Études Démographiques. quarterly.
One half of each issue is devoted to surveying current literature. "Analyses" carries 150-200 short critical reviews (150-600 words) of monographs in all fields of population study. "Notes" analyzes in short reviews (100-300 words) between 200 and 250 periodical articles selected from major scholarly journals. Reviews included in general index.

D219. Social service review. v. 1 + 1927 + Chicago, Univ. of Chicago Press. quarterly.
This journal, devoted to the scientific and professional interests of social work, surveys the current literature in long (385-2000 words), critical, signed reviews. The 100-150 reviews a year are generally restricted to English language titles but included are reviews of important government reports and public docu-

ments. Annual index of book reviews. Since 1954 "Doctoral dissertations in social work" has been a regular feature. See (D298)

See also: F256

ABSTRACTS AND DIGESTS

D220. Excerpta criminologica. v. 1 + 1961 + Amsterdam, Excerpta Criminologica Foundation. bimonthly.
Abstracts articles from criminological periodicals and pertinent material from related fields. International in scope. Some books (manuals, texts, etc.) are abstracted as well as composite monographic studies. Abstracts are classified under 14 major headings with an author index in each issue and annual author and subject indexes. 1,655 items included in 1961.

D221. Sociological abstracts. v. 1 + 1952 + New York. 5 times a year.
An important journal which abstracts 200-250 books and 1,500-2,000 articles a year appearing in ca. 250 periodicals. 31 major sociological journals from 12 countries are indexed in full, the remaining journals in cognate areas are partially abstracted for articles of significance to sociologists. The entries are classified under 42 major subject areas with annual indexes of authors, subjects, and periodicals. Category 42 abstracts current texts, readers and reference books. All titles in foreign languages are translated into English.

D222. Tumin, Melvin M. Segregation and desegregation. New York, Anti-Defamation League of B'nai B'rith, 1957. 112 p.
Comprises one page reviews and digests of 107 significant articles from professional journals (1951-1956) classified under 12 general

FIGURE 5.3   A typical page from a guide (White, C. et al. *Sources of information in the social sciences.* Totowa, N.J.: The Bedminster Press, 1964.   P. 211.)

Goheen, H., & Kavruck, S. *Selected references on test construction, mental test theory and statistics,* 1929–1949. Washington, D.C.: U.S. Government Printing Office, 1950.

Halpern, J. (Ed.) *Bibliography of anthropological and sociological publications on eastern Europe and the U.S.S.R.* Los Angeles: University of California at Los Angeles, Russian and East European Studies Center, 1961.

Young, M. *Bibliography of memory.* Philadelphia: Chilton Company Book Division, 1961.

Since titles are sometimes deceiving, some bibliographies go a step beyond just listing references to the articles and provide brief objective descriptions of these articles. Such bibliographies are labeled *annotated* bibliographies, and, when available in an area of interest to a researcher, can be of considerably more help than a straight bibliography. Three examples of good annotated bibliographies are these:

Mack, R. *Social mobility! Thirty years of research and theory.* An annotated bibliography. Syracuse, N.Y.: Syracuse University Press, 1957.

Schramm, W. *The research on programed instruction: An annotated bibliography.* Washington, D.C.: U.S. Office of Education, 1964.

Stein, M., & Heinze, S. *Creativity and the individual: Summaries of selected literature in psychology and psychiatry.* Glencoe, Ill.: Free Press, 1960.

A bibliography or list of references which appears as a periodical [1] is commonly labeled an index. The *Education Index* which appears monthly except for June and August is considered by many as the basic source for keeping up with the literature in the field of education. A typical page from this publication is presented in Figure 5.4. Other examples of basic indexes are:

British education index. London: Library Association. Vol. I = Aug. 1954/ Nov. 1958+.

Current sociology: An international bibliography of sociology. Paris: International Sociology Association Quarterly, 1952–.

Mental health book review index. Flushing, N.Y.: Queens College, Library, Editorial Committee and Contributing Libraries. Semiannual, Vol. I = 1956+.

Quarterly cumulative index medicus. Chicago: American Medical Association. Vol. I = 1927–.

Since references to research articles which have been published can be obtained from sources other than special bibliographies and general indexes, one special kind of index is especially important. This is an index which lists unpublished materials. Often information for this type of publication

---

[1] According to the American Library Association Glossary of Terms (1943), a periodical is "a publication with a distinctive title intended to appear in successive (usually unbound) numbers or parts as stated at regular intervals, and, as a rule for an indefinite time."

704 EDUCATION INDEX

TESTS and scales—Item analysis—*Continued*

Effects of instructions and item content on three types of ratings. H. A. Borresen. bibliog Ed & Psychol M 27 pt 1:855-62 Wint '67

Failure strategies of third grade arithmetic pupils. G. H. Roberts. Arith Teach 15: 442-6 My '68

Haiman's revised open-mindedness scale: a comparative study of response patterns. K. D. Frandsen. Speech Mon 34:389-91 Ag '67

Index of an individual's agreement with group-determined item difficulties; pattern analysis. T. F. Donlon and F. E. Fischer. bibliog Ed & Psychol M 28:105-13 Spr '68

Investigation of item bias; Preliminary scholastic aptitude test (PSAT) T. A. Cleary and T. L. Hilton. Ed & Psychol M 28:61-75 Spr '68

Item sampling for achievement testing. H. G. Osburn. bibliog Ed & Psychol M 28:95-104 Spr '68

Method for assessing racial attitudes in preschool children. J. E. Williams and J. K. Roberson. bibliog Ed & Psychol M 27:671-89 Autumn '67

Old problem solved? item bank. J. Watts Times Ed Sup 2752:525 F 16 '68

Simplified item analysis for better grading. T. B. Milligan. Sch Sci & Math 68:177-80 Mr '68

Systematic construction of distractors for ability and achievement test items. L. Guttman and I. M. Schlesinger. bibliog il Ed & Psychol M 27:569-80 Autumn '67

Test construction; a technique for producing and verifying a normal distribution of items. N. France. Brit J Ed Psychol 38:21-6 F '68

Test content as a determinant of response habits. C. I. Chase. H Sch J 51:254-61 Mr '68

Validity as a function of empirical scaling of test items by a logistic model. M. J. Ferris. Ed & Psychol M 27 pt 1:829-35 Wint '67

What skills do reading tests measure? J. R. O'Connor. H Points p23-5 Spr '67

Length

SVIB key length: dissident data. N. M. Abrahams. J Ap Psychol 51:266-73 Je '67

Misuse

See Tests and scales—Use

Norms

Condensed norms: ACS cooperative examinations (cont) American chemical society. Division of chemical education. Examinations committee. J Chem Ed 45:273-4 Ap '68

Determination of a method to predict 1-RM chin and dip from repetitive chins and dips. R. A. Berger. Am Assn Health Phys Ed Rec Res Q 38:330-5 O '67

Estimating test norms from variable size item and examinee samples. D. L. Cook and D. L. Stufflebeam. Ed & Psychol M 27:601-10 Autumn '67

Evaluation of the norms and reliability of the PPVT for pre-school subjects. W. L. Bashaw and J. B. Ayers. Ed & Psychol M 27 pt2:1069-75 Wint '67

Interrelationships between physical fitness scores. D. R. Mohr. Am Assn Health Phys Ed Rec Res Q 38:725-6 D '67

Study of an assumption about high school and college equivalency in language training. R. E. Spencer and R. L. Flaugher. Mod Lang J 51:331-5 O '67

Vocational interests of female computer programmers. D. K. Perry and W. M. Cannon. J Ap Psychol 52:31-5 F '68

See also

Tests and scales—Scores

Reliability

Comparability and validity of three forms of SCAT. T. M. Goolsby, jr. Ed & Psychol M 27 pt2:1041-5 Wint '67

Construction of and acquisition of reliability data for a test of qualitative levels in creative problem solving; Lundsteen tests. I. Rickborn and S. W. Lundsteen. Calif J Ed Res 19:53-8 Mr '68

Dependence of test reliability upon heterogeneity of individual and group score distributions. D. W. Zimmerman and others. Ed & Psychol M 28:41-6 Spr '68

Evaluation of the norms and reliability of the PPVT for pre-school subjects. W. L. Bashaw and J. B. Ayers. Ed & Psychol M 27 pt2:1069-75 Wint '67

Evaluations of three factors that might influence responses to tests of academic achievement motivation. C. E. Buxton. Brit J Ed Psychol 37:241-7 Je '67

Examinations and higher education: a survey of the literature. R. Cox. bibliog Univ Q 21:292-340 Je '67

Extension of the Rulon formula for test reliability: the case of correlated true and error components of scores. R. H. Williams and D. W. Zimmerman. J Exp Ed 36:94-6 Spr '68

Factorial analysis of the semantic structures of retarded adolescents. G. A. Rybolt. bibliog Am J Men Deficiency 72:512-17 Ja '68

GATB longitudinal validation study. R. C. Droege. il J Counsel Psychol 15:41-7 Ja '68

High school characteristics index: a study of scale reliabilities. E. L. Herr and H. R. Kight. J Ed Res 60:334-6 Mr '67

Interactions among interests, abilities, and career plans. W. W. Cooley. bibliog il J Ap Psychol Mon Sup 51:1-16 O '67

Interrelationships among personality scale parameters: item response stability and scale reliability. R. R. Jones and L. R. Goldberg. bibliog Ed & Psychol M 27:323-33 Sum '67

Inter-scorer reliability on the Bender Gestalt test and the revised Visual retention test. B. Egeland and others. Am J Men Deficiency 72:96-9 Jl '67

Investigation of the reliability of the French pictorial test of intelligence. R. N. Sawyer. J Ed Res 61:211-14 Ja '68

Maximum reliability of a multiple-choice test as a function of number of items, number of choices, and group heterogeneity. G. J. Burkheimer and others. bibliog J Exp Ed 35:89-94 Sum '67

Multiple choice and essay tests. A. S. Andrews. bibliog Improving Col & Univ Teach 16:61-6 Wint '68

Rating of competence of counselors and psychotherapists. R. M. Schumacher. J Counsel Psychol 14:440-3 S '67

Reliability of a group form of the Peabody picture vocabulary test. B. S. Tillinghast, jr. and J. S. Renzulli. J Ed Res 61:311-14 Mr '68

Reliability of different methods of scoring throwing accuracy. R. M. Malina. bibliog Am Assn Health Phys Ed Rec Res Q 39:149-60 Mr '68

Reliability of measures of reading achievement. H. A. Robinson and E. Hanson. Read Teach 21:307-13+ Ja '68

Reliability of observations of teachers' classroom behavior. B. B. Brown and others. J Exp Ed 36:1-10 Spr '68

Reliability theory and research decision in selection of a criterion score. W. Kroll. bibliog Am Assn Health Phys Ed Rec Res Q 38:412-19 O '67

SVIB key length: dissident data. N. M. Abrahams. J Ap Psychol 51:266-73 Je '67

Sex differences in aptitude maturation during high school. R. C. Droege. J Counsel Psychol 14:407-11 S '67

Significance levels for the Kuder-Richardson twenty: an automated sampling experiment approach. W. H. Payne and D. E. Anderson. bibliog Ed & Psychol M 28:23-39 Spr '68

Stability of the WISC in a psychiatric group. R. K. Turner and others. bibliog Brit J Ed Psychol 37:194-200 Je '67

Statistical investigation of the Ryhming step test. J. A. P. Day. Am Assn Health Phys Ed Rec Res Q 38:539-43 D '67

Study of the stability of the Illinois test of psycholinguistic abilities. M. V. Wisland and W. Many. bibliog Ed & Psychol M 27:367-70 Sum '67

Technique for the assessment of high school examinations: rapid impressionistic marking by suitably paired assessors (RIMSPA) N. France. bibliog Can Ed Res Digest 7: 252-65 S '67

Validities of the D-48 test for use with college students. M. E. Boyd and G. Ward, 2d. Ed & Psychol M 27 pt2:1137-8 Wint '67

Vocabulary and non-verbal reasoning components of verbal analogies tests (Miller analogies test and Concept mastery test) N. E. Wallen and M. L. A. Campbell. J Ed Res 61:87-9 O '67

Response set

Acquiescence and social desirability response sets and some personality correlates. D. M. Pedersen. bibliog Ed & Psychol M 27:691-7 Autumn '67

Answer-changing behavior on objective examinations. J. A. Bath. J Ed Res 61:105-7 N '67

FIGURE 5.4 A typical page from the education index (*Education index*, New York: H. W. Wilson 1967, **36**(4), 194.)

is obtained by means of a regular questionnaire sent to members of an association or to professional staff members of an institution or agency which carries out a great deal of research. Three such indexes are:

Current sociological research. New York: American Sociological Association. Annual, 1953+.

A list of researches in education and educational psychology. London: National Foundation for Educational Research. Biennial, 1950+.

Research studies in education: A subject index of doctoral dissertations, reports and field studies and a research method bibliography. Bloomington, Ind.: Phi Delta Kappa. Annual, 1955+.

A final variety of index which may seem to the reader to be the ultimate, but, in fact, which is most useful to the investigators working on a highly specialized topic, is the bibliography of bibliographies. The classic example of this kind of publication is the *Bibliographic Index*. This cumulative bibliography of bibliographies is published semiannually by H. W. Wilson Company of New York.

ENCYCLOPEDIAS The encyclopedia is generally a giant volume which attempts to provide the reader with a relatively exhaustive treatment of the subjects it covers. Its articles may be either major essays or rather concise discussions in which specialists attempt to synthesize what is currently known in their field. A typical page from an encyclopedia is presented in Figure 5.5 and the major general encyclopedias of interest to the behavioral science researcher are these:

Gray, P. *Encyclopedia of the biological sciences.* New York: Reinhold, 1961.

Harriman, P. *Encyclopedia of psychology.* New York: Philosophical Library, 1946.

Harris, C., & Liba, M. (Eds.) *Encyclopedia of educational research,* 3rd ed. New York: Macmillan, 1960.

Sills, D. (Ed.) *International encyclopedia of the social sciences.* New York: Macmillan, 1968.

Smith, E., Krouse, S., & Atkinson, M. *The educator's encyclopedia.* Englewood Cliffs, N.J.: Prentice-Hall, 1961.

Encyclopedias which restrict themselves to special topics within a general subject field are often labeled handbooks. However, since many such publications are intended to provide the reader with general information rather than a large number of specific and detailed facts, as in a true handbook, these publications are best thought of as specialized encyclopedias. Typical examples of these specialized encyclopedias are the following:

Beigel, E. (Ed.) *Encyclopedia of sex education.* New York: Stephen Daye Press, 1952.

in other schools. These variations in amount of time are due to many factors: differences in school standards and attitudes toward scholarship, in students' home backgrounds, in their intelligence, in the kinds of examinations and assignments given, and in the ways homework is introduced. If the homework is interesting, students say they spend more time on it; read it thoroughly and carefully; comprehend, enjoy, and remember what they read; and read further along the same lines (**35**).

It does not necessarily follow that the more hours a student spends in home study, the higher marks he receives. One survey of high-school students showed practically no relation between study time and marks, although in a certain school the high achievers in the ninth grade, where the curriculum was challenging, were spending more time in study than the low achievers (**33**). In college, students of low intelligence did not seem to compensate for their handicap by studying more than the average number of hours (**41**).

Relation of Homework to Scholastic Success. Even the best of the experimental work on the relation of homework to scholastic success is inconclusive because of (*a*) the impossibility of controlling all the variables that may influence scholastic achievement; (*b*) inadequate information on the age, ability, and background of the subjects; (*c*) failure to define the kinds of homework under discussion and to assess the effectiveness with which it is introduced.

One experiment with eighth-grade students (**1**) may be cited as quite typical of these investigations. In general, when home study was appropriate to the students concerned and when it was carefully assigned, their marks improved. With students of average intelligence, home study was equally valuable for English, social studies, and mathematics; the brighter students in the "homework group" made proportionally higher achievement scores than the group that was given no homework; both average and below-average students seemed to be handicapped when homework was not assigned. Similar results have been obtained with older students, with different school subjects, and with different research designs (**19, 29**). Another research design—subjecting the same students to different procedures, rather than setting up an experimental and control group—might yield more conclusive evidence. In certain situations, the sum total of achievement did not seem to be affected by reduction in the amount of homework (**17**).

Problems Associated with Homework. Many problems are associated with homework. Some types of assignment encourage copying. In a large city system (**11**) the amount of copying increased as students progressed through the grades; copying was admitted by almost three times as many ninth-graders as seventh-graders. Most of those who made the admission did not feel guilty about it. The bright students copied less than the slow learners.

When excessive tension and pressure are associated with homework, it may affect mental health; conscientious students may become depressed and anx-

ious; conflicts may arise between parents and children (**40**).

Conditions Affecting Home Study. Research on the ways in which distractions affect learning, especially reading efficiency, has been conflicting and inconclusive. However, several hypotheses have emerged: that variety programs and popular music are more distracting than classical music; that able learners suffer fewer adverse effects than those of below-average ability; that the effect of the distraction is related to the complexity of both the learning task and the radio program; that students who are used to studying with the radio on are distracted just as much as those who are not used to studying under these conditions; that even though certain individuals maintain a high level of concentration in the face of distractions, they do so at a cost of increased effort; that certain musical programs seem to aid the reading comprehension of certain individuals at certain times. Studies by Fendrick (**14**), Freeburne and Fleischer (**15**), Hall (**18**), and Leipold (**23**) are representative. It may be that the younger generation is evolving new adaptations to the distractions of modern life; some of them may be learning to shift their attention from one stimulus to another with great rapidity, or to suppress one sensory appeal while concentrating on another.

When asked what conditions made studying easy or difficult for them, 536 students in Grades V to XIV emphasized privacy, quiet, interest in the subject, freedom from worries and competing interests, absence of distracting radio and television programs, effective teaching, and well-spaced and clearly understood assignments (**36**, p. 266–71). In general, conditions opposite to these were named as making studying difficult.

On the basis of these limited investigations, surveys, and descriptions, certain recommendations may be made (**34**):

More school time should be devoted to the guidance of learning.

Students should be encouraged to do more reading and studying of the kind that will have continuing value in later life.

Students should be allowed more initiative and choice in the matters of what and how and when and with whom to study.

Homework should be more individualized, meaningful, and useful; students should uncover new problems in school which they solve at home.

Approval should be accorded to homework that is well planned and successfully completed.

The general trend seems to be not to abandon homework, but to evaluate and improve it.

GUIDED STUDY IN SCHOOL. Practices with respect to guided study vary with changes in the concept of the teacher's function. The very concept of supervised study has changed. In 1925, Brownell (**4**) clarified the subject by his critical and creative review of sixty investigations reported up to that time. He pointed out that evidence from the few controlled experiments indicated that supervised study had a slight advantage over undirected independent study

FIGURE 5.5   A typical page from an encyclopedia. (Harris, C., & Liba, M. Eds. *Encyclopedia of educational research,* 3rd ed. New York: Macmillan, 1960. P. 678.)

Birren, J. (Ed.) *Handbook of aging and the individual; biological, social and psychological bases of aging in individuals.* Chicago: University of Chicago Press, 1959.

Dorcus, R., & Jones, M. *Handbook of employee selection.* New York: McGraw-Hill, 1950.

Eysenck, H. *Handbook of abnormal psychology: An experimental approach.* New York: Basic Books, 1961.

Fryer, D., & Henry E. (Eds.) *Handbook of applied psychology.* New York: Rinehart, 1950.

Gage, N. (Ed.) *Handbook for research on teaching.* Chicago: Rand McNally, 1964.

Gruenberg, S. (Ed.) *The encyclopedia of child care and guidance.* New York: Doubleday, 1954.

Knowles, M. (Ed.) *Handbook of adult education in the United States.* (4th ed.) Chicago: Adult Education Association, 1960.

Lindzey, G. (Ed.) *Handbook of social psychology.* Cambridge, Mass.: Addison-Wesley, 1954.

Stevens, S. (Ed.) *Handbook of experimental psychology.* New York: Wiley, 1951.

Winn, R. (Ed.) *Handbook of child guidance.* New York: Philosophical Library, 1943.

REVIEWS   Overview inventories of current research which appear regularly are often labeled reviews. Reviews are integrated and critical discussions of recent research on particular topics written by a variety of different authors. Some reviews attempt to cover all fields in each issue, while others include, on a regular rotating basis, only certain topics in each issue. A page from a typical review is presented in Figure 5.6 and the publications of this sort which are of primary interest to the behavioral researcher are as follows:

Annual review of physiology. Stanford, Calif.: Annual Reviews. Annual, 1939+.

Annual review of psychology. Stanford, Calif.: Annual Reviews. Annual, 1950+.

Current sociology. London: Blackwell. Quarterly, 1952+.

International social science journal. Paris: UNESCO. Quarterly, 1941+.

Psychological bulletin. Washington, D.C.: American Psychological Association. Monthly, 1904+.

Psychological review. Washington, D.C.: American Psychological Association, Bimonthly, 1894+.

Review of educational research. Washington, D.C.: American Educational Research Association. Five issues yearly, 1931+.

Social service review. Chicago: University of Chicago Press. Quarterly, 1927+.

Sources of Original Research

As contrasted with the reference materials described above, all of which provide the research worker with a general background, those types of publi-

ASSESSMENT   337

The generality of original thinking was investigated by Barron (4) in a group of 100 Air Force officers. A number of measures whose composite correlated .55 with originality as rated by the Institute for Personality Assessment and Research staff were used to select 15 high and 15 low cases. Twelve of 15 predictions made on the basis of hypotheses about preference for complexity, complexity of personality structure, self-assertion and dominance, and rejection of suppression as a mechanism for control of impulse reached what would be the .05 significance level if the predictions had been independent. Originality is thus regarded as a rather pervasive trait.

Flanagan (47) defined ingenuity as inventing or discovering an unusually neat, clever, or surprising solution to a problem and then proposed an ingenious(!) way of constructing objective test items to measure it. Six criteria for the items are listed and the item format is multiple choice with only the first and last letters of key words in the optional solutions given.

Harmon (74) described an attempt to develop a criterion of scientific creativity in a follow-up study of Atomic Energy Commission fellowship candidates. Number of publications correlated highest with creativity ratings by a panel of judges, suggesting that the panel was using that factor in their own ratings. None of the variables which had formed the basis for the original decision to accept or reject a candidate showed up very well. The criterion problem was also treated by Bloom (10) who cited experience in assessing academic potential for particular environments in which the original assessment procedures were very costly, but led to the development of inexpensive and practically useful instruments. He believes the same procedure might prove fruitful in developing creativity criteria.

Stein (169) described his rationale for the study of environmental influences on creativity, but did not have sufficient outcome data to make a report. Four roles a scientist may play were identified: scientist, professional, employee, and social.

REACTIONS AGAINST ASSESSMENT

There have been more than the usual expressions of resentment against psychological testing in the last five years, and in some instances action has been taken. Nettler (144) and Eron & Walder (44) report two cases of community action against personality testing. Three professional educational organizations joined hands to put out a pamphlet (93) on the problem of external testing in the schools. A number of the recommendations made at the end are sensible, others are extraordinarily naive and impractical, and all the good ones could have been written by a knowledgeable committee in a two-day conference, without benefit of the two-year study that was undertaken. The recommendations are preceded by a popular exposition of mixed truths, half-truths, and emotionally based arguments. Neither the committee in charge nor the sponsoring organizations should be proud of this publication.

The use of multiple choice tests for selection for college admissions and

FIGURE 5.6   A typical page from a review (Milholland, J.   Theory and techniques of assessment.   *Annual Review of Psychology*.   Stanford, Calif.: Annual Reviews, 1964, **15,** 337.)

cations in this section bring the investigator into direct contact with specific, individual studies, or articles.

ABSTRACTS   The investigator who is reasonably well up to date in terms of the major trends of research in the area of concern often starts his literature search with those publications which provide abstracts of original works. In general, abstracts are preferred to bibliographies because the titles of articles are often quite misleading as to actual content. The bibliography, however, may be checked later, when a more exhaustive survey of the literature is necessary. Although the abstract is sometimes thought of as a periodical annotated bibliography, the annotated bibliography often includes critiques of the research, while the abstract is generally a very brief and noncritical summary of the contents of the original work. It is often prepared by the author of the original research himself rather than by someone else. In addition, the abstract can be distinguished from the review in that each article of the abstract is described and indexed completely independently from every other one, rather than integrated and discussed in relation to the general trend of results as is the case with reviews.

A sample page from an abstracting publication is shown in Figure 5.7, and examples of classic abstracts are the following:

Biological abstracts. Philadelphia: University of Pennsylvania. Semimonthly, 1926+.
College student personal abstracts. Claremont, Calif.: College Student Personal Institute. Quarterly, 1965+.
Dissertation abstracts. Ann Arbor, Mich.: University Microfilms. Monthly, 1938+.
Education abstracts. Paris: UNESCO. Monthly except July and August, 1949+.
International journal of abstracts; statistical theory and method. Edinburgh: Oliver and Boyd. Quarterly, 1959+.
Psychological abstracts. Washington, D.C.: American Psychological Association. Monthly, 1927+.
Sociological abstracts. New York: Eastern Sociological Society and the Midwest Sociological Society. Nine times a year, 1952+.

JOURNALS   The vast majority of reports of original research and theoretical papers are contained in technical periodicals which are known as journals. The journals represent the major source of primary materials available to the research worker, and it is here that investigations are described in detail sufficient to enable the researcher to repeat the study in his own laboratory if he desires.

As indicated earlier, the number of different publications reporting original research is so vast as to preclude the possibility of preparing a complete list. A page from one such journal is presented in Figure 5.8, and only five typical journals from each of the fields of psychology, sociology, and education are listed below.

Psychology
Journal of Abnormal and Social Psychology. Washington, D.C.: American Psychological Association, 1906+. Monthly since 1962.
Journal of Applied Psychology. Washington, D.C.: American Psychological Association. Bimonthly, 1917+.

after the game, were correlated with cooperative responses. There were no significant differences in cooperative behavior between ethnic groups. Significant relationships with cooperation were found for a number of attitude scales and trait ratings. (19 ref.)—*Journal abstract.*

Socioeconomic Structure & Social Role

8774. **Levenson, Bernard, & McDill, Mary S. Vocational graduates in auto mechanics: A follow-up study of Negro and white youth.** *Phylon,* 1966, **27**(4), 347–357.—The earnings of graduates in automotive mechanics from 2 racially homogeneous vocational high schools in Baltimore are about 50% lower for Negroes than whites throughout a follow-up period of 4½ yr. Comparative data are furnished for the 2 groups with regard to socioeconomic background, postgraduation nonemployment, and curricula at the 2 schools.—*A. R. Howard.*

8775. **Roach, Jack L., & Gursslin, Orville R.** (U. Connecticut) **An evaluation of the concept "culture of poverty."** *Social Forces,* 1967, **45**(3), 383–392.—The concept of a "culture of poverty" figures prominently in analyses of contemporary poverty and in explanations of the behavior of the poor. An examination of this concept indicates logical and empirical deficiencies in its use. Many of these deficiencies stem from basic problems in the use of the subculture framework, of which the concept of a culture of poverty is an instance. Some suggestions for a more appropriate use of the concept are offered. An alternative approach for understanding the behavior of the poor is proposed in which the material conditions of economic deprivation are given greater emphasis. (44 ref.)—*Journal abstract.*

Religion

8776. **Barocas, Ralph, & Gorlow, Leon.** (U. Rochester) **Religious affiliation, religious activities, and conformity.** *Psychological Reports,* 1967, **20**(2), 366. —The study was undertaken to explore differences in response to social influence as a function of religious affiliation and activity. 1-way analyses of variance failed to reveal significant differences among 3 religious groupings or among religious activity groupings in their susceptibility to social influence.—*Author abstract.*

8777. **Goldstein, Sidney, & Goldscheider, Calvin.** (Brown U.) **Social and demographic aspects of Jewish intermarriages.** *Social Problems,* 1966, **13**(4), 386–399. —Focuses on the extent and character of Jewish intermarriage—specifically (1) on trends and generational changes in the rate of intermarriages and conversions to Judaism, (2) residential differences in intermarriages, (3) changes in the age at marriage and fertility patterns of intermarried couples, and (4) religious identification of the children of intermarried couples. Data covering 1603 households containing at least 1 Jewish member indicate a relatively low rate of intermarriage, although it is increasing among the young, the native-born, and the suburbanites. The findings also suggest that a high proportion of these intermarriages result in the conversion of the non-Jewish spouse to Judaism and that a large proportion of the children are being raised as Jews. Increased similarity of the fertility and age-at-marriage patterns of younger intermarried and nonintermarried couples suggest a greater social acceptability of interfaith marriages.—*S. L. Warren.*

8778. **Tracy, James J.** (Sister Formation Program, Los Gatos, Calif.) **Faith and growth: A psychology of faith.** *Insight: Quarterly Review of Religion & Mental Health,* 1967, **5**(3), 15–22.—Suggests a "psychology of faith based on reflections on the experience of faith, on reading the reflections and research of others, and also on exchange with both believers and non-believers." Erik Erikson's 8 stages of man's development are defined in terms of contributing directly to forming a psychology of faith, and adult problems at each of these stages are analyzed. Trust is stressed as 1 of the prime factors in forming an adequate and integral faith psychology and also of the 8-point life cycle of Erikson.—*J. L. Ahlberg.*

Cross-Cultural Comparison

8779. **Abraham, H. H. Social distance and patterns of prejudice in Germany and Sweden.** *Archiv für die gesamte Psychologie,* 1966, **118**(3–4), 229–252.—Psychological investigations of prejudice and social distance are relatively rare in Europe and nonexistent in Sweden. A Bogardus-type distance scale was constructed and standardized on 2 samples of university students in Mainz and Stockholm. Germans and Swedes agreed in choosing 9 out of 10 most popular nations, although the rank orders were slightly different. Catholic Ss were significantly more tolerant than Protestants. Men Ss were generally less distant socially in their mean racial distance scores than were women. Ss whose fathers had higher education had more tolerant attitudes. The similarity of attitudes of German and Swedish students toward various nations and peoples may be an effect of mass communication.—*K. J. Hartman.*

8780. **Berkowitz, William R.** (Lafayette Coll.) **Use of the Sensation-Seeking Scale with Thai subjects.** *Psychological Reports,* 1967, **20**(2), 635–641.—This report describes the use and validation of the Sensation-Seeking Scale (SSS) with Thai Ss. Based upon anthropological and popular reports about Thailand, it was predicted that (1) Thai students would have lower SSS scores than American students, (2) Buddhist monks would have lower scores than Thai students, and (3) Thai students in teacher-training schools would have lower scores than those in schools of commerce. The 1st 2 hypotheses were confirmed; the 3rd was not. In addition, Thai males had significantly higher SSS scores than females. The advantages of the SSS as a measuring instrument are discussed.—*Journal abstract.*

8781. **Berrien, F. K., Arkoff, Abe, & Iwahara, Shinkuro.** (Rutgers State U.) **Generation difference in values: Americans, Japanese-Americans, and Japanese.** *Journal of Social Psychology,* 1967, **71**(2), 169–175.—A comparison was made between college students and their parents on the EPPS using Japanese, Japanese-American (Hawaiian), and American respondents. Postwar changes in Japanese culture were expected to show up in greater differences in that country than in the other 2 settings. This hypothesis was not confirmed; instead much greater similarity was found between the 3 types of mothers or the 3 types of fathers than between the parents and their own children.—*Author abstract.*

8782. **Gordon, Leonard V.** (State U. New York, Albany) **Q-typing of Oriental and American youth: Initial and clarifying studies.** *Journal of Social Psychology,* 1967, **71**(2), 185–195.—Intercorrelations among 19

FIGURE 5.7   A typical page from an abstract (American Psychological Association. *Psychological abstracts,* Washington, D.C.: APA, 1967, **41,** 881.)

Table 2

Effects of the shock-off ("OFF") and shock on ("ON") procedures on several behavioral measures when pre-shock periods were not accompanied by an exteroceptive stimulus.

Subject*	Discrim. Index		CER Index		Rate in S^Δ (rpm)		Rate in S^D (rpm)		Total Reinforcements	
	"OFF"	"ON"	"OFF"	"ON"	"OFF"	"ON"	"OFF"	"ON"	"OFF"	"ON"
No. 62	0.43	0.85	0.92	0.90	11.4	11.6	27.1	11.8	63.0	36.0
No. 64	0.64	0.92	0.83	1.01	4.9	30.3	8.3	33.0	54.0	65.0
No. 65	0.31	0.95	0.99	1.01	18.0	11.1	60.4	13.3	67.5	61.0
No. 66	0.30	1.21	1.06	0.99	4.0	12.9	12.8	13.5	59.0	47.0
Group Mean	0.42	0.98	0.95	0.98	9.6	16.5	27.2	17.9	60.9	52.3

*Subjects No. 60 and 63 are not included in this table because under the shock-on procedure their responding continued to be almost completely suppressed throughout experimental sessions, even after 18 sessions of exposure to this procedure.

from medians over the last three days of exposure to each procedure.

Table 2 shows an even greater impairment of the S^D *vs* S^Δ discrimination than Table 1; when shocks occurred, the mean discrimination index of Table 2 approximated 1.00, which signifies no discrimination whatever between S^D and S^Δ. However, with regard to absolute response rate in S^Δ, rats No. 64 and 66 exhibited a pronounced facilitation under the procedure with shocks, whereas No. 62 and 65 showed either very little change or a decrease. The absence of S^Δ facilitation in these latter subjects, which does not match the results of Table 1, may well be due to the extremely strong opposing influence of the suppressive factors in the situation. This is suggested by the fact that response rates in S^D for No. 62 and 65 were markedly suppressed by the delivery of shocks. In Table 1 the S^D rates of these subjects had been much less affected by the shock procedure than they were here.

Since no exteroceptive stimulus accompanied pre-shock periods, CER ("dummy") indices were, as expected, close to 1.00 under both experimental conditions. Therefore, the results shown in Table 2 indicate that a discriminative impairment will occur even when there is no specific suppression of response in another component of the multiple schedule.

Figures 2 and 3 present daily discrimination and CER indices over most of Exp. I and II for rats No. 65 and 66 respectively. The only sessions omitted from the records were (a) a few sessions on which apparatus failures occurred, and (b) some early training sessions, including those for No. 65 before the change to a compound (auditory-visual) CER stim-

ulus.[3] There was very little overlap in discrimination indices between the procedure with shock and the procedure without shock. A virtually complete and immediate recovery of discriminative performance occurred whenever shock was eliminated.

EXPERIMENT III

Comparison of CER and Punishment

Procedure. Exp. I and II showed that delivery of unavoidable shocks, with or without warning, produced a breakdown of the discrimination between S^D and S^Δ. Next, a comparison was made between response-correlated shock and unavoidable shock. Is it likely that another method of response suppression in the CER stimulus would also be accompanied by a discriminative impairment?

The former CER stimulus was restored to the procedure but, instead of signalling unavoidable shock, it now served as a signal that all responses in its presence would be punished. The procedure was essentially the same as in Exp. I except that each lever press during the former CER stimulus produced a brief electric shock of approximately 0.3 ma for 0.11 sec. To obtain a degree of stimulus-specific suppression approximating that on the unavoidable-shock procedure, and to minimize the possibility of a permanent overall suppression of lever-pressing rate, it was necessary to use a lower intensity and duration of shock than on the CER procedure (by inference from the results of Azrin, 1956, and Appel, 1963). Experiments with a punishment procedure that employed the same high shock intensity and duration as on the CER pro-

FIGURE 5.8   A typical page from a journal (Hearst, E. Stress induced breakdown of an appetitive discrimination. *Journal of the Experimental Analysis of Behavior.* 1965, **8,** 139.)

Journal of Comparative and Physiological Psychology. Washington, D.C.:
American Psychological Association. Bimonthly, 1921+.
Journal of Experimental Psychology. Washington, D.C.: American Psycho-
logical Association. Bimonthly, 1916+.
Psychometrika. Chicago: Psychometric Society. Bimonthly, 1936+.

Sociology

American Journal of Sociology. Chicago: University of Chicago Press. Bimonthly, 1895+.
Journal of Marriage and the Family (formerly *Marriage and Family Living*).
Menasha, Wis.: The National Conference on Family Relations. Quarterly,
1939+.
Public Opinion Quarterly. Princeton, N.J.: Princeton University Press. Quarterly, 1937+.
Rural Sociology. Ithaca, N.Y.: Cornell University, Department of Rural Sociology. Quarterly, 1936+.
Sociometry. Washington, D.C.: American Sociological Association. Four
times a year, 1937+.

Education

American Educational Research Journal. Washington, D.C.: American Educa-
tional Research Association. Four times a year, 1964+.
Educational and Psychological Measurement. Chicago: Science Research As-
sociates. Quarterly, 1941+.
Journal of Educational Psychology. Washington, D.C.: American Psychologi-
cal Association. Bimonthly, 1910+.
Journal of Educational Sociology. New York: Payne Educational Sociology
Foundation. Nine issues a year, 1927+.
Journal of Experimental Education. Madison, Wis.: Dembar Educational Re-
search Services. Quarterly, 1932+.

MONOGRAPHS   Second only to the journals as a source of direct information about original research are the monographs. Technically speaking a
monograph is a type of serial [2] which, in contrast to the periodical, another
major variety of a serial, is published irregularly. A monograph appears
whenever its sponsors feel there is a need, and it contains reports of research
which are too long to be published as a journal article. Many monographs
are sponsored either by institutions of higher learning or by a professional
society, as is indicated in the following list of but a few examples.

British journal of psychology monograph supplements. London: Cambridge
University Press, 1911+.
Comparative psychology monographs. Berkeley, Calif.: University of Cali-
fornia Press, 1922+.
Harvard studies in education. Cambridge, Mass.: Harvard University, 1914+.
Psychological monographs: General and applied. Washington, D.C.: American
Psychological Association, 1895+.

[2] According to Daniel and Louttit (1953), "a serial or continuation is a publication
appearing more than once under the same title and having some indication of con-
tinuity such as continuous pagination over a period of time or by numbering each issue in sequence of issue."

Psychometric monographs. Chicago: Psychometric Society, 1938+.
Social science research council monographs. New York: Social Science Research Council, 1948+.
Sociological review monograph supplements. Keele, Staffordshire, England: University College of North Staffordshire, 1958+.
Sociometry monographs. New York: Beacon House, 1941+.

Sources of Special Information

In addition to knowledge of the research in the field in general, and to the specific methods and results of particular studies, the research worker often needs detailed factual information about instruments or other equipment, about specific persons or organizations, about the precise definition of highly technical words, and about the location of things. To obtain such data, he may use one or more of the various sources labeled manuals, handbooks, yearbooks, directories, dictionaries, atlases, and gazetteers. The types of information contained in the major varieties of this type of source material has been summarized and presented along with typical examples in Table 5.1.

Sources of Government Publications

The research worker who is willing to become acquainted with and make use of all of the types of basic reference materials described in the previous sections will be able to locate almost all of the literature of importance which is pertinent to his problem. The only exception to this, is the possibility of overlooking an important paper prepared for government use but not published in any of the professional journals. As Daniel and Louttit (1953) point out: "Unfortunately, there is no simple, convenient way for psychologists to keep track of material which may be of interest. For a number of years *Psychological Abstracts* has endeavored to include government publications but because of the complexity of finding them, its coverage has been far from complete."

In view of this situation—and the problem is becoming more and more acute as an increasing number of government agencies carry out and report an increasing number of significant studies in their own departmental bulletins—about the best the research worker can do is to regularly examine the monthly publication *U.S. Government Research Reports* [3] or at least search index lists such as the Title Announcement Bulletin, Armed Services Technical Information Agency. For a really thorough search of government literature, the investigator will want to make extensive use of an up-

[3] Issued by the Office of Technical Services, Business and Defense Services Administration, Department of Commerce.

TABLE 5.1

Information Contained in and Examples of Major Sources of Special Information

Type of Publication	Subvarieties	Information Contained	Typical Examples
Handbooks	manuals	a variety of facts and figures arranged for ready use, plus specific instructions as to "how to" accomplish some specific objective	U.S. Navy Dept. Special Devices Center. *Handbook of human engineering data.* (2nd ed.) Medford, Mass.: Tufts College, 1951.
			Farris, E. (Ed.) *The care and breeding of laboratory animals.* New York: Wiley, 1950.
			Krathwohl, D. *How to prepare a research proposal.* Syracuse, N.Y.: Syracuse University Bookstore, 1965.
	yearbooks	a variety of facts, figures, and other information which may become dated and therefore which may be superseded by information in later (usually annual) editions	Buros, O. *Mental measurements yearbook.* Highland Park, N.J.: Gryphon Press, 1938+ (irregular).
			Armstrong, E., & Stinnetl, T. *A manual for certification requirements for school personnel in the U.S.* Washington, D.C.: NEA, 1951+ (biennial).
Directories	persons	an alphabetical or other systematized list of persons, giving names, addresses, and other biographical information	American Psychological Association. *Directory of the American Psychological Association.* Washington, D.C.: A.P.A., 1948+ (annual).
			Phi Delta Kappa. *National register of educational researchers.* Bloomington, Ind.: Phi Delta Kappa, 1966.

organizations	an alphabetical or other systematized list of organizations of a specific type, together with addresses, officers, major functions, and similar information	Social Science Research Council. *A directory of social science research organizations in universities and colleges.* New York: SSRC, 1950. Phi Delta Kappa. *A directory of educational research agencies and studies.* Bloomington, Ind.: Phi Delta Kappa, 1957+ (irregular).
Dictionaries	detailed definitions of both technical words and common words as used in a technical sense	English, H., & English, A. *A comprehensive dictionary of psychological and psychoanalytical terms.* New York: David McKay, 1965. Good, C. *Dictionary of education.* (2nd ed.) New York: McGraw-Hill, 1959. Zadrozny, J. *Dictionary of social science.* Washington, D.C.: Public Affairs Press, 1959.
Geographical sources atlases	a collection of graphic materials such as diagrams, charts, and maps	Gibbs, F., & Gibbs, E. *Atlas of electroencephalography.* Reading, Mass.: Addison-Wesley Press, 1951. Hathaway, S. *An atlas of juvenile MMPI profiles.* Minneapolis, Minn.: University of Minnesota Press, 1961. Millett, J. (Ed.) *An atlas of higher education in the United States.* New York: Columbia University Press, 1952.
gazetteers	a systematic listing of places and their location or other brief description—in essence, a geographical dictionary	Seltzer, L. (Ed.) *Columbia Lippincott gazetteer of the world.* New York: Columbia University Press, 1962.

to-date guide which specializes in the area, such as Schmeckebier, L. and Eastin, R., *Government Publications and Their Use,* 2nd ed., Washington, D.C.: Brookings Institute, 1961.

OTHER INFORMATIONAL RESOURCES

In addition to the basic types of library materials described in the last section, other informational resources are available to the research worker. First of all, there is his own store of personal knowledge gleaned from previous reading of textbooks and periodical materials and from his own personal experiences. Second, there are professional meetings and direct communication with colleagues, both of which are likely to provide information (1) which is more timely (i.e., which has not yet been published or stored); (2) from which the extraneous material can be readily sifted out; and (3) which can be obtained in a meaningful form without undue attention to the details of making a highly precise inquiry. Third, there are information centers and exchanges now in existence which can provide the researcher with either direct observations, such as is the case with the Project Talent Data Bank, or with publications of current research and collections.

Several typical information service centers are described below. More complete and detailed information can be obtained from the *Handbook on Informational Services* (1968).[4]

I. Science Information Exchange (SIE), 209 Madison National Bank Building, 1730 "M" Street, N.W., Washington, D.C. 20036, telephone: (202) 381-5511

A. Purpose The SIE is designed to provide the community with timely information about currently active scientific research. The National Science Foundation supports SIE through a contract to the Smithsonian Institution.

B. Users Information from the exchange is available to recognized granting agencies, research institutions, and to investigators associated with recognized research organizations. Information may not be used for publication or publication reference without approval of principal investigator.

C. Structure SIE consists of three divisions: (*a*) the Life Sciences Division (biological sciences, behavioral sciences, medical sciences, agriculture and applied biological sciences, and social sciences and community programs); (*b*) the Physical Sciences Division (chemistry, earth sciences, electronics, engineering, materials, and physics and mathematics); and (*c*) the Data Processing Division (registry, reports, systems and program-

---

[4] These descriptions represent slight modifications of those presented at a *Seminar on Information Sources in the Behavioral Sciences* conducted by the American Institute for Research and held at the 75th Annual Convention of the American Psychological Association, September, 1967.

ming, computer operations, and science support). Each division is staffed by specialists in the several fields.

D. Services Provided   1. Acquisition of Data   Information on current research is accepted from organizations that support research programs and from individual investigators who wish to register their current projects. SIE provides registration forms free of charge. A summary, 200 words or less, of current research projects can be mailed directly to SIE. This summary is used as a means of communication among research scientists.

2. Analysis of Information   SIE's system for registering, indexing, organizing, and retrieving information is complex since it involves not only the collection of data from many different sources, the indexing and retrieval of technical material in detail, but also the compilation of information extracted from thousands of records for program management purposes. In essence, 30 information elements dealing with such areas as authorship, institutional membership, geographical location, subject matter area, etc., are extracted from each record received at the exchange. These elements are compiled in such a way that any single element, or any combination of elements, can be retrieved.

3. Recording Results of Analysis   Information about research planned or in progress is registered on a single-page Notice of Research Project. This is the basic document of the exchange, and includes: (*a*) the name of the granting agency; (*b*) names and addresses of principal and associate investigators; (*c*) location of the work; (*d*) title; (*e*) a 200-word summary of technical detail; (*f*) the level of effort; and (*g*) the duration of the grant.

4. Storage of Source Documents   Notices of research documents are coded and indexed to electronic-computer files to provide ready access to any item or combination thereof. Fiscal data are privileged information submitted by and released only to officials of authorized cooperating agencies. All information in the exchange is restricted from unauthorized publication or publication reference, since it is furnished by investigators prior to their own publication.

5. Development of Search and Retrieval Strategy System   SIE has search and retrieval systems for both scientific and nonscientific requests. Scientific requests are channeled to an appropriate specialist who makes a specific identification of the requested subject area. A computer search is then made to determine the acquisition numbers of the various Notices of Research Projects which are applicable to the request. These NRP's are then pulled off the stacks and sent to the requester. The procedure for nonscientific requests is much the same, the main difference being that the nonscientific request is screened by a reports analyst, not a scientific analyst. SIE is currently developing a computer search and retrieval system designed to eliminate the need for NRP stacks. In the near future, the computer will print out NRP's directly.

E. Procedure for submitting inquiries   SIE should be informed of the specific research or problem on which information is desired. Written requests should be sent to Science Information Exchange, 209 Madison National Bank Building, 1730 "M" Street, N.W., Washington, D.C. 20036. Requests may also be phoned in by calling (202) 381-5511. Since screening of the request is done by a scientist or engineer, requests should be made in a straightforward, technical manner. A narrow definition of the specific information area needed by the requester will enable requests to be handled more quickly, easily, and efficiently.

F. Anticipated response SIE will promptly forward pertinent Notices of Research Projects. Requests are usually filled within ten days to two weeks, although this time may be increased if there is a backlog of requests within any one subject matter area. Services of SIE are currently provided free of charge.

II. Human Relations Area Files, Inc. (HRAF), P.O. Box 2054, Yale Station, New Haven, Connecticut 06520

A. Purpose HRAF was established in 1949 as a nonprofit organization to collect, organize, and distribute information of significance to the natural and social sciences and the humanities. HRAF materials are basic research sources for investigators in the social sciences interested in cross-cultural research and area studies. Broadly stated, the function of HRAF is to facilitate research and comparative study in the sciences concerned with mankind, thereby promoting a general understanding of the peoples of the world, their ways of life, their problems, values and ideas. To carry out this program, HRAF systematically places the information at the outset where it will be sought by the investigator.

B. Users The files are intended to provide data essential to the theorist, the analyst, the synthesizer, and the critic. At some universities, only graduate students and members of the faculty are allowed to use the files; at others, all students are permitted to use them; at still others, they are open to the public. For information on this point, the research worker should consult the file supervisor at the institution where he plans to do his research.

C. Structure The new HRAF library is located in its entirety at each of the member institutions; it contains maps, line drawings, and pictures in addition to organized files of textual materials. There are 23 member institutions in the HRAF system. These are:

University of Chicago	Kyoto University
University of Colorado	Maison des Sciences de l'Homme, Paris
Cornell University	University of Michigan
Harvard University	State University of New York at Buffalo
University of Hawaii	University of North Carolina
University of Illinois	University of Oklahoma
Indiana University	University of Pennsylvania
State University of Iowa	University of Pittsburgh

Princeton University
Smithsonian Institution
University of Southern California
Southern Illinois University

University of Utah
University of Washington
Yale University

D. Services provided   1. Acquisition of Data   Selection of documents
to be used in the files is carried out at Yale University.   A survey is made
of books, journals, periodicals, government publications, etc., to determine
what is to be included in the files.   Foreign language sources pertaining to
HRAF interest areas are translated, and both the foreign text and the English translation are placed in the file.

2. Analysis of Information   Incoming materials are coded as to the
particular category to which they refer.   Each document is considered not
only as a single source in itself, but segments of the document are also
treated as individual bits of information.   The standard unit of analysis is
the paragraph, but this will vary according to the author's organization of
his material and the analyst's judgment of the best method for codifying it.
An entire section, series of paragraphs, or even a single sentence could serve
as a unit of analysis in any particular instance.   Source materials are coded
with reference to the *Outline of Cultural Materials* (*OCM*), since it is assumed that the research worker will investigate all of the categories to
which he is referred by the *Outline*.   Categories which follow each other
in OCM (and which are, therefore, very closely related) are not normally
used for the same passage.   The three-digit OCM category is the standard
unit of classification.   The classification system identifies the particular
subject with which each unit of analysis is concerned.   In addition to the
three-digit category, other marking conventions have evolved in response
to the necessity of making the files as useful as possible to the researcher.
Forms of classification other than the three-digit type have been used to alleviate problems of excessively broad subject areas, large amounts of information in a single category, cursory reference to a subject in a given article, notation of a large amount of material within any one document, and
passages which have no reference to any category in OCM.

3. Recording Results of Analysis   There are several publications with
which the investigator should be familiar in order to use the files efficiently.
These are: (*a*) *Outline of Cultural Materials* (*OCM*): This is one of the
two basic guides to the files.   It contains a brief history of the files, the
theoretical basis of their organization, the complete list of categories that
are used in marking or analyzing material together with definitions of these
categories.   The OCM may be consulted at the member institutions or
purchased by mail from HRAF, New Haven. Its cost is $3.75.   (*b*) *Out-
line of World Cultures* (*OWC*): This is the second basic guide to the files
and consists of a classification by area and key number of the files upon
which the research staff at HRAF is working at present or may possibly
work in the future.   The purpose and organization of the OWC is ex-

plained in a preface to the manual. Like the OCM, the OWC may be consulted at the member institutions or purchased by mail from HRAF, New Haven; its price is $3.75. The investigator should be warned, however, that the OWC is only a preliminary classification of the culture of the world and since its publication, it has been extensively revised in the light of actual research. The member institutions have received bulletins from HRAF which include the various additions and revisions to the manual, and for a knowledge of its present status, the research worker is advised to consult the file supervisors at the institution where he is doing his work. (*c*) *Function and Scope of the Human Relations Area Files, Inc.:* For investigators completely unfamiliar with the files, *Function and Scope* provides a brief history of the organization, its aims, and its methods of operation. It may be obtained free of charge from HRAF, New Haven. (*d*) *Behavior Science Notes:* This is a quarterly journal designed to provide current information about the files and about HRAF's member institutions. In addition, it includes at least one bibliographic feature in each issue, in line with HRAF's continuing role as a center of bibliographic information. Subscription price is $3.00 per year; single copies are available at $1.00 each. (*e*) *HRAF Information Bulletins:* Information bulletins are sent to the member institutions whenever a change is instituted in the HRAF method. They may concern revisions in the OWC, additions to the index of the OCM, decisions regarding particular files, instructions about filing, and so forth. To remain informed of these changes, the research worker should consult the file clerks at the member institutions. These publications may be ordered from New Haven.

4. Storage of Source Documents   Actual source documents are included in the files at each member institution. These documents are the primary information resource of HRAF, and as such they are stored according to HRAF's system for use by those persons using HRAF.

5. Development of Search and Retrieval Strategy   All search and retrieval operations are performed by the research worker himself. The OWC and the OCM are designed to assist the researcher in these operations, and the publications of HRAF give more detailed information on the correct and efficient use of the files. The file supervisor at each institution will assist users in their initial experience with the files.

E. Procedure for submitting inquiries   A prospective user of the files should contact the member university nearest him to determine whether or not the files are available to him. If they are, the investigator should familiarize himself with the workings of HRAF in order to make best use of the resources.

F. Anticipated response   Users of HRAF can make use of the extensive filing, indexing, and cataloging resources of HRAF in order to locate pertinent documents. Research workers may take notes or make photocopies of these documents.

III. Educational Resources Information Center (ERIC), United States Office of Education, Washington, D.C. 20202

A. Purpose The purpose of ERIC is to gather, catalog, index, abstract, and disseminate currently available educational research and research-related materials to a wide variety of people desiring information on educational research or allied fields.

B. Users Anyone with an interest in educational research or research-related fields can make use of ERIC's services. Users of the ERIC system may include teachers, administrators, other educational specialists, researchers, public officials, commercial and industrial organizations, and the public.

C. Structure At present, ERIC consists of: (*a*) a headquarters office, or Central ERIC, which is responsible for overall development, coordination of full activities, operation of the system, and the dissemination of the results of research; (*b*) nineteen decentralized clearinghouses, each focused on a different subject matter area; and (*c*) several contractors who provide specialized services.

The nineteen ERIC clearinghouses have been established to deal with various areas in educational research. The addresses of the clearinghouses are:

1. ERIC Clearinghouse on Adult and Continuing Education, Syracuse University, 107 Roney Lane, Syracuse, N.Y. 13210
2. ERIC Clearinghouse on Counseling and Personnel Services, University of Michigan, 611 Church Street, Ann Arbor, Mich. 48104
3. ERIC Clearinghouse on the Disadvantaged, Teachers College, Columbia University, New York, N.Y. 10027
4. ERIC Clearinghouse on Early Childhood Education, University of Illinois, 805 West Pennsylvania Avenue, Urbana, Ill. 61801
5. ERIC Clearinghouse on Educational Administration, University of Oregon, Eugene, Oreg. 97403
6. ERIC Clearinghouse on Educational Facilities, University of Wisconsin, 606 State Street, Madison, Wis. 53703
7. ERIC Clearinghouse on Educational Media and Technology, Institute for Communication Research, Stanford University, Stanford, Calif. 94305
8. ERIC Clearinghouse on Exceptional Children, Council for Exceptional Children, NEA, 1201 Sixteenth Street, N.W., Washington, D.C. 20036
9. ERIC Clearinghouse on Higher Education, George Washington University, Washington, D.C. 20005
10. ERIC Clearinghouse on Junior Colleges, University of California at Los Angeles, 405 Hilgard Avenue, Los Angeles, Calif. 90024
11. ERIC Clearinghouse on Library and Information Sciences, University of Minnesota, 2122 Riverside Avenue, Minneapolis, Minn. 55404
12. ERIC Clearinghouse on Linguistics and Uncommonly Taught Languages, Center for Applied Linguistics, 1717 Massachusetts Avenue, N.W., Washington, D.C. 20036
13. ERIC Clearinghouse on Reading, Indiana University, 204 Pine Hall, Bloomington, Ind. 47401
14. ERIC Clearinghouse on Rural Education and Small Schools, Box AP,

University Park Branch, New Mexico State University, Las Crues, N. Mex. 88001

15. ERIC Clearinghouse on Science Education, Ohio State University, 1460 West Lane Avenue, Columbus, Ohio 43221
16. ERIC Clearinghouse on Teacher Education, American Association of Colleges for Teacher Education, 1156 Fifteenth Street, N.W., Washington, D.C. 20005
17. ERIC Clearinghouse on Teaching of English, National Council of Teachers of English, 508 South Sixth Street, Champaign, Ill. 61820
18. ERIC Clearinghouse on the Teaching of Foreign Languages, Modern Language Association of America, 62 Fifth Avenue, New York, N.Y. 10011
19. ERIC Clearinghouse on Vocational and Technical Education, Ohio State University, 980 Kenny Road, Columbus, Ohio 43210

D. Services provided. 1. Acquisition of Information Selection of documents to be included in the ERIC collection is made by the subject matter specialists at the ERIC clearinghouses. Investigators and others can assist ERIC in the acquisition of significant documents by: (*a*) keeping the director of any clearinghouse informed of any new projects which relate to the specialty of the clearinghouse; and (*b*) sending two copies of every report, reprint, or document to the director of the appropriate clearinghouse.

2. Analysis of Information Documents selected are catalogued, abstracted, and indexed by assignment of retrieval terms from the *Thesaurus of ERIC Descriptors.*

3. Recording Results of Analysis Resumes for all documents, including the abstracts, retrieval terms, and bibliographic information, from all ERIC clearinghouses are forwarded to North American Aviation where they are merged, stored on magnetic tape, and prepared for announcement in *Research in Education* (RIE), ERIC's monthly announcement bulletin. A subscription to RIE may be obtained by sending $11.00 in check or money order to: Superintendent of Documents, U.S. Government Printing Office, Washington, D.C. 20402. There is an additional charge of $2.75 for foreign subscriptions, and single copies are available at $1.00 per copy.

4. Storage of Source Documents Many users will want the full texts of documents. These documents can be obtained from ERIC Document Reproduction Service which is operated by the Micro Photo Division, Bell and Howell Company, 1700 Shaw Avenue, Cleveland, Ohio 44112.

5. Development of Search and Retrieval Strategy Systems The first priority within ERIC is to have clearinghouses focus on information analysis functions, selective search and dissemination activities, and initiation of current awareness searches on request. The objective is to have in ERIC files at least one copy of every significant document on educational research or research-related concerns from anywhere in the world, with citation access to users in minutes and copy availability in hours.

E. Procedure for submitting inquiry. Direct inquiry should be made to the appropriate clearinghouse according to the subject matter area of interest.

F. Anticipated response ERIC provides high accessibility to all users. Documents can be obtained in microfiche (usually 9¢ per fiche) or in hard copies (prices quoted in RIE) by following the instructions outlined in RIE. User requests for documents are generally filled within five days after receipt of request.

IV. National Clearinghouse for Mental Health Information (NCMHI), National Institute of Mental Health, 5454 Wisconsin Avenue, Chevy Chase, Maryland 20203

A. Purpose The purpose of the NCMHI is: (*a*) to collect, abstract, index, and store information related to mental health; (*b*) to regularly disseminate scientific and program information among research workers and practitioners concerned with mental health and mental illness; (*c*) to analyze, evaluate, and interpret trends in the mental health field; and (*d*) to serve as an informational resource at the request of individuals working and studying in disciplines related to mental health.

B. Users Individuals and groups who need scientific and program information for work or study related to mental health may use NCMHI services. Individuals who regularly receive NCMHI publications and who request specialized information from NCMHI generally include scientists, educators, administrators, hospital personnel, practitioners, students, and other professionals concerned with mental health. Groups generally include federal and state agencies, professional associations, hospitals, schools, and community organizations.

C. Structure The NCMHI is part of the Office of Communications, National Institute of Mental Health. Three major sections comprise the clearinghouse:

1. The Program Analysis and Development Section analyzes, evaluates, and makes recommendations concerning work flow, resources utilization, information processing procedures, and use of the computer.

2. The Professional Services Section analyzes and interprets trends in mental health, research and programming; its members also act in a consultative capacity for projects in other parts of the Institute.

3. The Technical Information Services Section is divided into two units. (*a*) The Acquisitions Unit, which secures documents for use in the NCMHI publications and automated information storage and retrieval system; and (*b*) The Information Processing Unit, which provides quality control for input and output of the information system and determines how to respond to demands on the system.

D. Services provided 1. Acquisition of Data The selection and acquisition of documents to be included in NCMHI's computerized information storage and retrieval system is made by the NCMHI Acquisitions Unit in consultation with the NCMHI Professional Services Section and the Chief, NCMHI. NCMHI governs its acquisition of serial literature through the maintenance of the NCMHI Master List of Published Periodical and Serial Sources, a classified list of more than two thousand sources of mental health information. The Acquisitions Unit arranges for the regular procurement of as many Master List sources as is feasible. The acquisition may take any of several forms: e.g., subscription, exchange, loan. NCMHI systematically selects books, reports, project data, and other nonserial sources of information relevant to mental health from appropriate lists, announcements, and publishers' indexes.

2. Analysis of Information   Upon obtaining a document, NCMHI analyzes it, processes it, and forwards it to a "processor" (either in-house or contractual) for the necessary preparation of abstract, index, or other product.

3. Recording Results of Analysis   A processor receives a batch of documents from NCMHI, generates from each document unit the designated products (index, citation, abstract, etc.), then returns each item of source material, together with its generated resume, to NCMHI. NCMHI quality controls the processed documents, refines them, and includes them in the computerized storage and retrieval system.

4. Storage of Source Documents   NCMHI includes only the document resume (citation, abstract, index terms) in the computerized information system. The original or source document is placed on microfilm (mylar jackets) and maintained in the NCMHI Document Files. The microfilmed source documents are presently available only for NIMH archival uses.

5. Development of Search and Retrieval System Strategy   The NCMHI computerized information storage and retrieval system provides for the accumulation and maintenance of an unlimited number of document resumes. The computerized document collection may be readily searched for any subject or combination of subjects through the application of controlled retrieval logic. A search will yield a printout of all document resumes which meet the criteria specified in the search statements.

E. *Procedure for submitting inquiries*   Anyone desiring an NCMHI publication or information from the automated storage and retrieval system should describe the precise nature of his inquiry in a letter or phone call to the National Clearinghouse for Mental Health Information, 5454 Wisconsin Avenue, Chevy Chase, Maryland 20203.

F. *Anticipated response*   Responses to inquiries may be in the form of comprehensive bibliographies, short lists of literature citations, selective bibliographies with abstracts, or referrals to individuals and organizations qualified to give more complete and accurate information pertaining to inquirer's request.

V. Scientific Information Centers Branch, National Institute for Child Health and Human Development (NICHD), National Institutes of Health, Bethesda, Maryland 20014

A. Purpose   The Scientific Information Centers Branch of NICHD has the mission of assisting scientists in the furtherance of their research in the interdisciplinary areas of investigation, as defined by the NICHD programs, by keeping them current with the world's literature and the ongoing research programs.

B. Users   The services of the branch are intended primarily for the use of qualified research workers in the fields covered by NICHD.

C. Structure   The Scientific Information Centers Branch is organized into information centers which reflect the Institute's program areas.   These centers are: (*a*) Adult Development and Aging Center; (*b*) Growth and Development Center; (*c*) Reproduction and Population Research Center; and (*d*) Perinatal Biology and Infant Mortality Center.

D. Services provided   1. Acquisition of Information   Information for the Branch is acquired through a continuing survey of published literature in the field.   Information is collected in an interdisciplinary manner; that is, the physiological, psychological, and social aspects of the areas covered by the work of NICHD are examined.

2. Analysis of Information   Incoming information is analyzed in such a way as to promote the interdisciplinary nature of the branch's method of operation.   Documents are coded and indexed according to a common vocabulary developed for the information centers.   Thus, a single article may appear in the biological sciences under "Drugs and Chemical Substances" and "Body Substances," and in the behavioral and social sciences under "Learning" and "Social Controls."   Also, documents may appear under a related sciences area, which would include subjects such as ecology, nutrition, demography, and administration which pertain to both the other divisions.

3. Recording Results of Analysis   The primary media of dissemination will be abstract journals, published monthly by each information center. Each center will also provide other services including request bibliographies, current research surveys, and directories of research workers.

4. Storage of Source Documents   Abstracts of source documents will be stored on computer tapes.

5. Development of Search and Retrieval Strategy   Three distinct sets of descriptors are used in the computer search system.   The lowest applicable descriptor of a field of study in the common hierarchy vocabulary will establish the starting point of the search.   The second set, the control parameters, specify the organism, population, nationality, or location, etc., required by the question.   To reach the very specific, the third set of descriptors is used, the "free or natural language" (these are words and phrases taken from the article), which is searched as single words or as

phrases and can be permuted. The search program to be used for request and recurring bibliographies is comprehensive and has the capabilities to: (a) search out phrases containing up to nine words; (b) select a single word and/or a broad phrase from a specific phrase; and (c) make a numerical range selection, such as age or temperature. The second part of the search program allows the selection of elements of the citation. These elements can be searched separately or in combination: the author, the institution, the periodical, etc. Searching by elements can be done very rapidly and specifically by the computer.

E. Procedure for submitting inquiries   In the near future, NICHD will prepare forms for information requesters to use in submitting requests. At present, requests for information should be sent to the Scientific Information Centers Branch, National Institute for Child Health and Human Development, National Institutes of Health, Bethesda, Maryland 20014.

F. Anticipated response   As soon as the branch is fully operational, most information requests will be handled by computer printouts. There will be no cost for investigators who have a qualified need for the branch's services.

VI. National Referral Center for Science and Technology (NRCST), Library of Congress, Washington, D.C. 20540

A. Purpose   The NRCST is essentially an organization to provide information about sources of information (including the social sciences). It is designed to provide anyone with an interest in science and technology with a single place to which to turn for advice on where and how to obtain information on specific topics.

B. Users   Anyone with an interest in science and technology—the physical, biological, social, and engineering sciences, and the many areas related to them—may use the center.

C. Structure   There are two main sections within the NRCST. The Referral Services Section answers requests for referral service and the publication functions of the center, while the Systems Identification and Analyses Section registers new information resources and provides machine processing of data regarding requests and information resources.

D. Services provided   1. Acquisition of Information   Through a continuing survey, the NRCST is building up a central register of detailed data on information resources in terms of their areas of interest and the services they provide. The center solicits registration of organizations or individuals who have specialized information capabilities in the physical, biological, social, or engineering sciences. The center will provide registration forms for those wishing to register specialized capabilities. These forms can be obtained by calling (202) 967-8341, or by writing the National Referral Center for Science and Technology, Library of Congress, Washington, D.C. 20540.

2. Analysis of Information   Data on information resources are indexed in such a way as to provide the NRCST's referral specialists with multi-dimensional access routes to the information resources registered.   Resources are indexed as to geographic location, type of organization, nature of information activity, services provided, conditions of use, collections, publications, etc.

3. Recording Results of Analysis   The NRCST has issued three directories covering a broad range of information resources.   These are: (a) A Directory of Information Resources in the United States: Physical Sciences, Biological Sciences, Engineering ($2.25); (b) A Directory of Information and Resources in the United States: Social Sciences ($1.50); and (c) A Directory of Information Resources in the United States: Water ($1.50).   These directories may be purchased from the Superintendent of Documents, U.S. Government Printing Office, Washington, D.C. 20402. A fourth directory of information resources in the federal government will be available in September.

4. Storage of Source Documents   At present, all data relating to information resources and referral requests are stored on punch cards.

5. Development of Search and Retrieval Strategy System   The punch-card system now in operation was developed by the NRCST.   Conversion to a tape-retrieval system is planned for the immediate future.

E. *Procedure for submitting inquiries*   For prompt and efficient service, inquiries should contain: (a) a precise statement of the information desired; (b) a statement of information resources already contacted; and (c) a statement of special qualifications of the inquirer (e.g., participation in a government contract, affiliation with a recognized research project, membership in a professional society) which may entitle him to use resources not otherwise available.   Referral requests can be made by calling (202) 967-8265; by writing to the National Referral Center for Science and Technology, Library of Congress, Washington, D.C. 20540; or by visiting the center on the fifth floor of the Library of Congress Annex, Second Street and Independence Avenue, S.E.

F. *Anticipated response*   In answer to inquiries the NRCST provides names, addresses, telephone numbers, and a brief description of information services that can be expected from the information resources.   A response can be expected about five working days from date of receipt.   Answering requests by telephone normally takes less than three working days.   The center has developed a feedback program to assess user satisfaction with the center's services and the services of the information resources cited to the user.   There is no cost for the center's services.

VII. Neurological Information Network (NIN), National Institute for Neurological Diseases and Blindness (NINDB), National Institutes of Health, Bethesda, Maryland, 20014

A. Purpose   Essentially, the NIN consists of a number of specialized information centers designed to identify, collect, and store for retrieval all information items relating to each center's specific area of responsibility. These centers would also distill and repackage the information contained in these items so that physicians and research scientists could get their appropriate information in a useful form as soon as possible.

B. Users   Anyone with an interest in the types of information handled by the NIN may use the services of the system. The network is designed primarily for use by physicians and research scientists.

C. Structure   At present, the network consists of four large specialized centers: (*a*) Parkinson's Disease Information and Research Center at Columbia University; (*b*) The Special Information Center for Hearing, Speech, and Disorders of Human Communications at Johns Hopkins University Medical School; (*c*) The Brain Information Center at U.C.L.A.; and (*d*) Information Center for Vision and Diseases of the Eye at the Harvard Medical School. With full development, each of these large documentation centers will support several information analysis satellites in subareas of its field.

D. Services provided   1. Acquisition of Data   At present, the large centers are developing their input systems. Major sources of input material will include journal articles, books and monographs, technical reports from any source, other audiovisual aids, special indexes, abstract services, or information in any other form which might be useful to people in the field.

2. Analysis of Information   Since the NIN is still in a developmental stage systems for analysis of information and documentation are not yet fully operational. A common language or glossary, indexing philosophies, and a design for computer use are being developed for the information center.

3. Recording Results of Analysis   When fully operational, the output of the NIN's information will include, in addition to bibliographies and current awareness service: data arrays; synthetic and critical analyses; monographs; state-of-the-art reports; authoritative answers to pertinent scientific questions; knowledge about unpublished materials; and identification of research workers.

4. Storage of Source Documents   Systems for storage of documents are currently being developed by the network information centers.

5. Development of Search and Retrieval Strategy   A system for search and retrieval of pertinent information is currently being developed for use by the network information centers. Increased mechanization of the system is planned for the near future.

E. Procedure for submitting inquiries   Queries should be sent to the appropriate NIN information center. The addresses for the three semi-operational centers are: (*a*) Parkinson's Disease Information and Research Center, 640 West 168th Street, New York, New York 10032; (*b*) The

Brain Information Center, University of California at Los Angeles, Los Angeles, California 90024; (*c*) The Special Information Center for Hearing, Speech, and Disorders of Human Communication, Johns Hopkins University Medical School, Johns Hopkins University, Baltimore, Maryland 21218. The fourth information center of the network (Information Center for Vision and Diseases of the Eye at the Harvard Medical School) is just getting underway with recruitment and initial planning so that there are no substantive developments at this time.

F. Anticipated response   The three semioperational information centers are currently providing such services as weekly citations lists, demand bibliographies, and current awareness or alerting services. Potential information users should contact individual centers for information as to their specific information output capabilities.

VIII. Clearinghouse for Federal Scientific and Technical Information (CFSTI), U.S. Department of Commerce, Springfield, Virginia 22151

A. Purpose   CFSTI is a system designed to supply the industrial and technical community with unclassified information about government-generated science and technology in defense, space, atomic energy, and other national programs.

B. Users   The services of CFSTI are intended for use by the scientific and technical community and are also available to the general public.

C. Structure   CFSTI is a division of the Institute for Applied Technology and is a component part of the National Bureau of Standards of the U.S. Department of Commerce.

D. Services provided   1. Acquisition of Data   CFSTI processes unclassified documents produced by Department of Defense research and development contractors and other agencies. The Clearinghouse also processes translations of significant technical literature originally published in foreign languages. (*Note:* Organizations participating in defense programs may be eligible to receive classified scientific and technical data through the services of the Defense Documentation Center (DDC). Potential DDC users should contact DDC Headquarters, Cameron Station (Building 5) 5010 Duke Street, Alexandria, Virginia 22314. The telephone number is (202) OX8-1981.)

2. Analysis of Information   Incoming documents (consisting of reports based on federally sponsored research and development projects and translations of foreign technical material) are cataloged and indexed according to a system developed by CFSTI.

3. Recording Results of Analysis   New documents are announced semimonthly in: (*a*) *U.S. Government Research Reports:* Department of Defense and other agencies except AEC and NASA (which announce their reports separately as indicated below). Sold by the Superintendent of Documents, U.S. Government Printing Office, Washington, D.C. 20402,

$30 a year ($37.50 foreign); (*b*) *Technical Translations:* Translations of significant technical literature originally published in foreign languages, available from CFSTI and other sources, including the Special Libraries Association and the European Translations Center. Sold by Superintendent of Documents, $12 a year ($16 foreign); (*c*) *Government-wide Index to Federal Research and Development Reports:* The *Index* is a monthly consolidated index to government-sponsored technical literature. It contains subject, author, source, and report number—the standard points of access to the total report literature. This *Index* permits scientists, engineers, and research managers to scan one publication in reviewing report literature in their fields of interest. The *Index* is available from CFSTI at $22 a year ($27.50 foreign), $3.00 for a single copy; (*d*) *Fast Announcement Service:* The *Service* is designed to announce by direct mail reports of special industrial significance. To get this service, write CFSTI (Attn.: Customer Relations Branch), U.S. Department of Commerce, Springfield, Virginia 22151. The cost is $5.00 per year for any or all of 57 categories.

4. Storage of Source Documents   Source documents (government reports and foreign translations) are stored at CFSTI in both microfilm and hard copy.

5. Development of Search and Retrieval Strategy   CFSTI cross-indexes its reports on the basis of acquisition number, title, author, corporate author, and contract number.

E. Procedure for submitting inquiries   Specific information on how to use the resources of the clearinghouse is given in each of CFSTI's periodical document announcements. More general information about the clearinghouse can be obtained by writing: Clearinghouse, U.S. Department of Commerce, Springfield, Virginia 22151. Information about CFSTI can also be obtained by writing any of the U.S. Department of Commerce Field Offices. The locations and addresses of these fieldhouses are listed below.

U.S. Department of Commerce Field Offices:

Albuquerque, N. Mex. 87101
  U.S. Courthouse
Atlanta, Ga. 30303
  75 Forsyth Street, N.W.
Birmingham, Ala. 35203
  Title Bldg., 2030 Third Avenue, North
Buffalo, N.Y. 14203
  117 Ellicott Street
Charleston, W. Va. 25301
  500 Quarrier Street
Chicago, Ill. 60604
  219 South Dearborn Street
Cleveland, Ohio 44101
  East 6th Street & Superior Avenue

Anchorage, Alaska 99501
  Room 306, Loussac-Sogn Bldg.
Baltimore, Md. 21202
  Gay and Lombard Streets
Boston, Mass. 02110
  Room 230, 80 Federal Street
Charleston, S.C. 29401
  No. 4, North Atlantic Wharf
Cheyenne, Wyo. 82001
  16th Street and Capitol Avenue
Cincinnati, Ohio 45202
  550 Main Street
Dallas, Tex. 75202
  Rm. 1200, 1114 Commerce Street
Denver, Colo. 80202
  19th & Stout Street

Des Moines, Iowa 50309
509 Grand Avenue
Greensboro, N.C. 27402
Rm. 412, U.S. Post Office Bldg.
Honolulu, Hawaii 96813
1022 Bethel Street
Jacksonville, Fla. 32202
208 Laura Street
Los Angeles, Calif. 90015
1031 S. Broadway
Miami, Fla. 33130
51 S.W. First Avenue
Minneapolis, Minn. 55401
110 South Fourth Street
New York, N.Y. 10001
350 Fifth Avenue
Phoenix, Ariz. 85025
230 N. First Avenue
Portland, Oreg. 97204
520 S.W. Morrison Street
Richmond, Va. 23240
400 North 8th Street
Salt Lake City, Utah 84111
125 South State Street
Santurce, Puerto Rico 00907
Rm. 628, 605 Condado Avenue
Seattle, Wash. 98104
909 First Avenue

Detroit, Mich. 48226
445 Federal Bldg.
Hartford, Conn. 06103
18 Asylum Street
Houston, Tex. 77002
515 Rusk Avenue
Kansas City, Mo. 64106
Rm. 2011, 911 Walnut Street
Memphis, Tenn. 38103
167 N. Main Street
Milwaukee, Wis. 53203
238 W. Wisconsin Avenue
New Orleans, La. 70130
610 South Street
Philadelphia, Pa. 19107
1015 Chestnut Street
Pittsburgh, Pa. 15219
1000 Liberty Avenue
Reno, Nev. 89502
1479 Wells Avenue
St. Louis, Mo. 63103
1520 Market Street
San Francisco, Calif. 94102
450 Golden Gate Avenue
Savannah, Ga. 31402
125–29 Bull Street

F. Anticipated response Research reports can be obtained from CFSTI in either microfiche or hard copy. Cost for a report in microfiche form is usually $.65, while hard copy reports are usually $3.00. To simplify ordering and handling, the clearinghouse sells coupons for the purchase of documents. The coupon is a tabulating card with a face value of the purchase price. The coupon serves as the medium of payment, as well as the order form and the shipping label. In addition to the research reports described above, CFSTI provides several other information services, including a literature searching service, referral services, reports on research in progress, development of selective bibliographies, and regional dissemination of selected government research reports in "packaged" forms. Potential users of these clearinghouse services should contact CFSTI in Springfield or any of the U.S. Department of Commerce Field Offices.

6.
Statistical Reasoning

THE NATURE AND FUNCTION OF STATISTICS

In his article "Parlez-Vous Statistics," Darrell Huff (1963) suggests that in a personal and subjective sense, statistics is like a foreign language to many people. Closer examination, however, reveals that the learning of statistics is not so much the substitution of a different vocabulary and symbols for common concepts as it is getting used to a new way of thinking about things—a way of examining groups of objects as a whole rather than as a sum of a set of individual objects and a way of coming to rational conclusions in the face of uncertainty. Statistical reasoning represents a unique and highly useful tool to the research worker concerned with the phenomena of human behavior. This chapter is designed to provide the reader with insights into the logic by which some types of scientific problems can be solved and is not a substitute for good solid courses in statistics.

A Definition of Statistics

To many lay persons, the word *statistics* refers to a mass of facts and figures, and *statistical analysis* is the process of gathering and tabulating these facts and figures. Statistics involves working with a mass of observations and arranging the results of these observations in a way which makes sense. However, this falls far short of telling the entire story. Actually, what the layman calls statistics, the statistician generally refers to as data. To the professional, statistics are descriptive indexes or a combination of his observations which can be used to test a hypothesis and statistical analysis is a logic for making inferences about general laws from a set of specific observations.

Perhaps the most complete definition of statistics is that given by Anderson and Bancroft (1952) who see it as: "the science and art of the development and application of the most effective methods of collecting, tabulating and interpreting quantitative data in such a manner that the fallibility of conclusions and estimates may be assessed by means of inductive reasoning based on the mathematics of probability."

Careful examination of the above definition reveals that the statistician is concerned with three different but related aspects of scientific problem solving: the description of observations, the drawing of inferences about scientific hypotheses from observations, and the design of studies so that appropriate inferences can be made.

The descriptive function of statistics has grown out of attempts in the social sciences (i.e., history, economics, and political science) to picture entire populations of persons through tabulations of births, marriages, residences, salaries, employment, disease incidence, etc.—in short, out of what some have called "political arithmetic." Such demographic studies have not been entirely independent of statistical inference ever since the staggering cost and practical difficulties of obtaining a complete census suggested the possibility of using samples for reasonable estimates, and the latter, in turn, required a procedure for assessing the degree of accuracy of such estimates. Nonetheless, descriptive statistics still maintains as its primary goal the development and application of procedures for obtaining indexes that summarize observations in such a way as to portray the major characteristics of groups.

The analytical function of statistics arose out of a body of pure "basic" research done simply to satisfy the curiosity of mathematicians about games of chance. From the concern with mathematical games came concepts of probability which, in turn, have led to modern logic for the testing of scientific hypotheses in the face of uncertainty. Such a procedure cannot be divorced from descriptive statistics, since the hypotheses of concern are generally about the way and extent to which various groups differ when subjected to various kinds of experimental treatment.

The third area of interest of modern statistics, that of experimental design, has gained increasing prominence as research workers became more and more aware that unless data were appropriately gathered, statistical analysis would not make the study valid. It cannot be too strongly emphasized that statistical concepts need to be introduced at the beginning of a research investigation and not after all the observations have been made. All too often the research worker who first collects his data and then brings it to a statistician or takes it to a computer and expects an "appropriate" analysis to be made finds, to his dismay, that there simply is not a defensible way to analyze data gathered in this manner. The student who has carefully read and understood the basic ideas presented in the discussion of the experimental method is not likely to make this error. The student should recognize, however, the tremendous importance of working out a careful statistical design before carrying out his investigation and should be aware that more elaborate designs than those presented in Chapter 4 are available.

The Need for Statistical Analysis

Even recognizing that statistics involves the design of experiments, the description of data, and the testing of hypotheses, a student may legitimately ask, But why statistics? Isn't it possible to use rational analysis to design adequate studies and to use "ordinary" mathematics to describe and test hypotheses about scientific phenomenon? What is so different about human behavior that requires us to depend so heavily on statistics, while workers in the physical sciences make so little use of it?

The answer represents what Senders (1958) calls nature's "gigantic practical joke" on the scientist: variability. No two things in nature, whether they are trees, leaves, atoms, snowflakes, or people, are exactly alike. If no two people are exactly alike, then no two people will behave in exactly the same way; and, if no two people behave in exactly the same way, how can we possibly come up with any understanding of or any laws of behavior? How is it possible, under these circumstances, to make observations of one person's behavior with any hope that our observations may provide suggestions about the behavior of another? We have seen in Chapter 1 that the answer given to this question by Skinner and others advocating descriptive experimentalism is that the appearance of variability results from the lack of adequate controls. These research workers would contend that if we would concentrate on appropriate observable phenomena and would take into consideration enough of the variables we would find relationships of human behavior which could be expressed with the same precision as can be found in the physical sciences. Others would argue that the similarity of one object to another is a matter of degree and that it is obvious that men are more like one another than any man is like a monkey. These investigators feel, therefore, that it is both possible and useful to examine the grosser aspects of behavior and to attempt to derive laws of behavior which are true in general, even though there may be some deviation from them in specific, individual cases. For those who take the latter point of view, statistics is essential, for it provides the means by which it is possible to rigorously describe "people in general" and to say with some degree of confidence when a particular hypothesis holds "in general" in spite of some degree of deviation from it in particular instances.

In this latter connection, it is an interesting paradox that a great number of persons shy away from or even condemn statistics when applied to human beings because it assumes that everybody is alike or because it leads to conformity, when, in actuality, exactly the opposite is the case. The *raison d'être* of statistics is that the objects examined are different from one another. The only way to avoid statistics is either to assume that all humans behave identically and impose greater and greater controls until that behavior can be seen or to give up the enterprise of studying and communicating about human behavior except as an interesting pastime of describing what has happened once with no thought that it will be of any value in connection with future cases.[1]

DESCRIBING A SET OF OBSERVATIONS

The Nature of Data

The way in which observations can be described (and, indeed, the way in which hypotheses can be tested on the basis of observations) will depend upon the characteristics of the observations themselves. The first step in any appropriate analysis of data is a careful consideration of the nature of that data.

QUALITATIVE OR QUANTITATIVE   The first distinction that can be made is between those observations which describe objects or persons on a numerical scale and those which do not. Descriptions of the characteristics of persons or objects which involve numerical concepts are labeled *quantitative*, and those which do not involve numerical concepts are labeled *qualitative*.

In making the distinction between qualitative and quantitative, it is essential to recognize that the difference between these two types of data rests upon numerical *concepts* or the use of numbers and not on the type of symbol (numeral [2] or verbal) which happens to be employed. For example, it is sometimes convenient to use numerals as labels for qualitative description as when we let 1 = male and 2 = female; and sometimes convenient to use verbal labels to represent essentially quantitative description as when we use the categories very good, good, average, poor, and very poor.

It is also essential to recognize that the use of the word quality does not necessarily correspond to the use of the word qualitative. *Quality* refers to a judgment of value, while qualitative refers to a type of description. It is clearly recognized that the quality of one's performance can be described on a quantitative scale.

---

[1] An enlightened plea to avoid either of the two extremes suggested here has been made by Cronbach (1957).

[2] It is important to remember the distinction between *number* (the concept) and *numeral* (the symbol). Thus, when we write 2 and 4, we say that 2 is the largest numeral but that 4 is the largest number.

The clue to the distinction between quantitative and qualitative description, then, does not lie in the distinction between the types of symbols used, nor in the distinction between value judgments or empirical facts. The difference depends upon the way in which the symbols are attached to the categories of persons. If the symbols are used only as labels to distinguish among different categories and nothing more, the data are qualitative; but if the symbols are used not only to distinguish among categories but to infer a relationship of order among them as well, then the description is quantitative. One simple way to determine in which of the two ways the symbols have been used is to reassign the labels and see if it would make any difference in the interpretation involved. It makes little difference whether we use 1 = male and 2 = female or whether we use 1 = female and 2 = male, but it makes a great deal of difference if we label those whose performance is best "good" and those whose performance is next best "very good" as contrasted with the reverse assignment of category names. The former case is thus labeled qualitative description and the latter is labeled quantitative description. Essentially, quantitative description results in the classification of persons into ordered categories, while qualitative description results in the classification of persons into nonordered categories.

LEVELS OF MEASUREMENT   Because the definition of statistics which was given earlier mentions only the handling of quantitative data, the reader may at first conclude that the statistician is never involved with qualitative information, i.e., with a set of unordered categories. However, the investigator is often concerned with differences in quantitative observations found when persons have been classified into nonordered groups, i.e., when they have been described qualitatively. If the quantitative information of interest is simply that of an enumeration or counting of how many units fall into each category, the measurement used is said to be at the *nominal level*. At this level, the only measurement operation involved is the judgment of "equal to" ($=$) or "not equal to" ($\neq$), and the data become quantitative in any useful sense *only* when the researcher becomes interested in the numerical concept of the size of group (proportionally or absolute).

A danger arises at this nominal level of operation if numerals are used as category names and the researcher then attempts to apply the ordinary rules of arithmetic to those numerals. For example, just because we assign 1 = male and 2 = female does *not* permit us to say that it takes two males to equal one female. In this case, the digits 1 and 2 have no numerical properties per se but are simply used as category names.

If the measurement operation permits judgments of "greater than" ($>$) or its opposite, "less than" ($<$), the data are said to be at the *ordinal level*. With this level of measurement, we certainly can analyze the data with respect to the ranking of persons or objects, but we must be careful to avoid any arithmetical operation which makes assumptions about the differences between ranks. The danger of interpreting the values of numerals assigned to objects or persons when only rank order information is available is well illustrated in the following example which was described by Senders (1958). Imagine that, through a series of singles tennis matches, it had been ascertained that the four persons, A, B, C, and D fell in the following rank order with respect to their performance on the court: A = first, B = second, C = third, D = fourth. Can you infer that you would have a fairly even doubles match if you pitted A and D against B and C? (Note that the average of the ranks of the players for each team is 2.5.) The answer is no, for it could be that players A, B, and C were professionals, while player D was a visitor who had never held a tennis racket in his hand until the singles tournament began. In this case, the difference between the rank orders of 3 and 4 is not the same as the difference between 1 and 2, or between 2 and 3; and the two teams would not be evenly matched, even though the average of the ranks for each team is 2.5.

Whenever the measurement operations are such as to permit judgments of differences between persons or objects in terms of magnitude, but do not provide for judgments of single individuals in terms of distances from some absolute zero point, the *interval level* of measurement has been achieved. At this level, the arithmetical operations of addition and subtraction are permissible, but misinterpretations are likely to result if multiplication and division (e.g., taking ratios) are employed. For example, suppose it were necessary to measure height, not in terms of the distance from the floor to the top of the head of a standing person, but rather in terms of how much higher than some arbitrarily selected zero point (such as the top of a convenient table) he stands. If the reported observation for Person A were 1.5 feet, and for Person B were 3 feet, it is certainly possible to say that Person B was taller than Person A and even state that the difference in height between the two persons was 1.5 feet. However, there is no basis for saying that Person B was twice as tall as Person A, even though 3 is twice 1.5. (If the table were 36 inches high, Person A's actual height would be 4.5 feet and the height of Person B would be 6 feet.)

Whenever a numerical description is accomplished with a scale that has an absolute zero as well as equal units of measure throughout, the so-called *ratio level* of measurement has been achieved. When data are on a ratio scale, all mathematical operations permissible with real, as opposed to imaginary, numbers can be performed without danger of gross misrepresentation. The reader should be aware, however, that while physical measures generally meet the requirements of the ratio scale,[3] measures of behavioral characteristics seldom do. For example, even the best standardized test defines as its arbitrary zero point exactly none of the answers to the set of questions included. Someone may know a little about the material in question or have

[3] Familiar exceptions are the Fahrenheit scale of temperature and the scale of hardness of minerals.

a little ability but not enough to show on the test. Under these conditions the highest possible measurement achieved is an interval scale.

DISCRETE AND CONTINUOUS VARIABLES   Thus far, measurement, at its various levels, has been discussed only in the abstract. But, when a measurement is made, something is measured. This something which is being measured is an attribute or a characteristic of some phenomenon, and further it is a characteristic which can change or vary. This characteristic can take on different values from person to person, from time to time, or from object to object. Such a characteristic we have already learned to call a *variable*. Now it is important to make a distinction between *continuous* variables and *discrete*, or discontinuous, variables.

A continuous variable is one for which all possible subdivisions of the units in which observations of the variable are recorded turn out to be conceptually meaningful. For example, height is a continuous variable because it is meaningful to record height in inches, half-inches, a tenth of an inch, a hundredth of an inch, or any other subdivision of an inch. The only limit to the refinement is the accuracy of the observations which can be achieved. In contrast with this, the number of children in a family, the size of a class, or the number of bar presses a rat makes before extinction all represent discontinuous or discrete variables. It is simply not meaningful conceptually to speak of $3\frac{1}{4}$ children in a family, a class size of $34\frac{3}{4}$, or of 156.03 bar presses. In these latter cases, the variable of concern can take on only certain specific values which are separated by a gap along the number line (a line representing all possible numbers).

It is important to remember that the distinction between continuous and discrete is based upon the conception of the *variable* or characteristic itself and *not* on the *variate* or measurement of it. For example, test scores are treated as measures of a continuous variable even though they may be recorded only in terms of whole numbers, as long as the trait being measured is conceived to be continuous. Scholastic ability is thought of as being continuous even though the variates (the scores) by which scholastic ability may be numerically described represent the number of items marked in such a way as to agree with some key. With continuous variables, the limits are imposed by the technique of measurement (as might be the case if we could measure height only to the nearest inch) rather than by the meaningfulness of the concept.

It has been noted that the way in which data can be described and the techniques for testing hypotheses with observations depend in part upon the nature of the observations themselves. In this respect, the distinction between discrete and continuous variables is especially important. It should be recognized that perfect accuracy of measurement *can* be achieved with discrete variables but cannot be accomplished with continuous variables. It is possible to make a completely errorless count of the number of children in a family, of the number of bar presses made by an animal during extinction, and the number of pupils in a class, but when height is measured persons are grouped into categories represented by certain limits. That is, when measurement is made to the nearest inch and it is reported that someone is 6 feet tall, the information conveyed is that this individual is one of those persons whose height places him in the category ranging from 5' 11.5" to 6' 0.4999"; if we were to measure to the nearest tenth of an inch, a person reported as being 6 feet tall could be anywhere from 5' 11.95" to 6' 0.0499", and so forth. Never would perfect accuracy be achieved, and, in this respect, the only difference

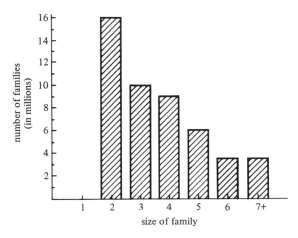

FIGURE 6.1   Number of families of a given size in the United States (Data from: U.S. Department of Commerce, U.S. Bureau of Census. *Statistical abstract of the United States,* 88th ed.   Washington, D.C.: U.S. Dept. of Commerce, 1967, Table 40.   P. 38.)

between the measurement of physical quantities and behavioral characteristics is that the limits of inaccuracy can be reduced much further for the former than the latter.

Because perfect accuracy can never be achieved with a continuous scale, the investigator is always confronted with the problem of grouping and with the problem of rounding in such a way as to avoid the accumulation of errors when an analysis of this kind of data is made. When making graphic representations of data, you must remember that the numerical description of observations of a continuous variable must occupy an *interval* along a line and cannot be represented by a point, as is true with discrete data. The number of families of various sizes should be represented by a bar graph, as in Figure 6.1, while the number of persons of various ages would be represented by a histogram, as in Figure 6.2.

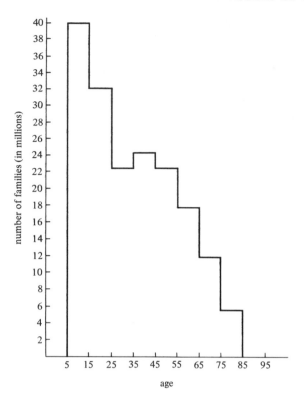

FIGURE 6.2   Number of persons of various ages between 5 and 85 in the United States (Data from: U.S. Department of Commerce, U.S. Bureau of Census. *Statistical abstract of the United States,* 88th ed.   Washington, D.C.: U.S. Dept. of Commerce, 1967, Table 8.   P. 10.)

The Characteristics to Be Described

At the beginning of this chapter, it was noted that statistics involved the description of observations of a group of objects or events as contrasted with observations of single objects or events in and of themselves.   It is necessary to consider the characteristics of a *group* as contrasted with the characteristics of the single individuals of which the group is comprised.   To help make the discussion more concrete, the student might keep in mind the example of attempting to describe college freshmen with respect to their reading speed. The characteristic of the individual—the variable of concern—is reading speed.   The task is to determine the ways in which an entire group can be described in terms of the reading speeds of its members.

One question that might be asked is: How fast do college freshmen read? One answer to this would be to provide the questioner with several hundred thousand numbers, each representing the reading speed of one college fresh-man. This is not what the person asking the question intended. What is wanted is an indication of the rate of reading of college freshmen *in general:* a single number which is representative or typical of what might be expected from a college freshman. In statistics an index which describes a typical level of performance is called a *measure of central tendency* or a *measure of location*. Such an index indicates where the group as a whole tends to centralize, i.e., where the set of individuals as a whole are located along the line of all possible reading speeds. Thus, in Figure 6.3, a measure of location might indicate whether college freshmen as a whole are located near Point *A*, Point *B*, or Point *C* or at some other place along the line.

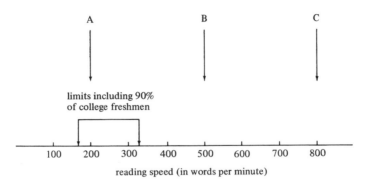

FIGURE 6.3   Illustration of the concepts of location and variability

A second thing a researcher might wish to know about the reading speeds of college freshmen is the extent to which they vary or differ from one an-other. If all the reading speeds of the members of the group were quite similar, the research worker would describe the group as *homogeneous* with respect to this characteristic; but, if the reading speeds varied from very low to very high from one college freshman to the next, the researcher would describe the group as *heterogeneous* in reading rate.

In statistics an index of the extent to which members of a group differ from one another, i.e., the extent to which there are individual differences in the group, is called a measure of *variability* (or sometimes, a measure of disper-sion or a measure of spread). Ideally, an index of typical performance (the measure of location) should never be reported without an indication of the extent to which deviation from this typical performance is expected (i.e., the measure of variability). In Figure 6.3, for example, it would be appropriate to indicate not only where the group as a whole fell, but also the limits within which most, say 90 percent, of the observations fell, as is shown with the brackets.

In addition to locating the group along the line of possible reading speeds and obtaining a measure of the extent to which the reading speeds differed from one another, an investigator might also be interested in knowing something about the *way* in which the reading speeds of the individual college students were distributed along the line.   An index of *skewness* would indicate whether the distribution was symmetrical about the point of central tendency, and an index of *kurtosis* would indicate whether the observations were largely concentrated near the center of the distribution with only a few at the extremes, or whether the observations distributed themselves fairly evenly throughout the limits.   Few research workers, however, bother to compute these particular descriptive indexes.   The more common practice would be to prepare a graphic representation of the data called a *frequency distribution*.   The frequency distribution presents an overall picture of the data from which it is possible to get a visual indication of the level of overall performance, the variability, and the shape of the distribution as well.

Another descriptive index of considerable importance is that which provides an indication of the extent to which two characteristics are found to go together in a group of individuals.   For example, it might be interesting to know whether reading speed tends to fluctuate with classroom performance (as indicated by grades) among college freshmen.   That is, when a freshman with a high reading speed has been located, has the investigator also found a person who earns good grades?   Or, might a person who reads rapidly be just as likely to have middle grades or low grades as he is to have high grades? In statistics an index of the extent to which two characteristics are found to go together is called a *measure of association*.

In summary, then, the properties of a set of observations in which a researcher might be interested are: (1) the typical level or magnitude; (2) the extent to which the values differ from one another; and (3) the extent to which two characteristics fluctuate together.   These properties are indicated respectively by measures of location, by measures of variability, and by measures of association.   The researcher may obtain an overall picture of his data by means of a graphic representation called a frequency distribution. Each of these major ways of describing data will be discussed more fully in the following sections.

The Frequency Distribution

The chaotic appearance of variation in making observations of human behavior led many early psychologists to conclude that this variation was a characteristic of the phenomenon of behavior itself and that the study of psychology was limited to an examination of the individual.[4]   These persons saw no hope of applying the scientific method which had been so successful in the study of the physical universe to the process of attempting to under-

[4] Interestingly,Treloar (1951) has pointed out that this was also true of early-day biologists.

stand human beings. Other more scientifically oriented psychologists argued that the variations were primarily a result of inadequate observations or inadequate formulation of the principles of behavior, and that the orderliness would come through refinement of technique and with a more complete inventory of the variables which interacted with one another to produce the effect observed.

The statistician, however, takes a third approach. According to Treloar (1951), "The semblance of confusion among magnitudes which differ among themselves, yet belong properly to the same class, is a natural consequence of a simple fact. The sequence in which determination of magnitude is made must ordinarily be quite independent of the magnitudes themselves. It follows directly, therefore, that any variation pattern will not be revealed without reorganization of the data."

If one writes down the scores obtained by fifty students on a test in the order in which the papers were turned in (as has been done in Table 6.1), there is no apparent pattern in the variation. If, however, the lead of the early mathematical astronomers is followed, and the data are organized by

TABLE 6.1

Test Scores and Grade Completed by Fathers of Fifty Hypothetical Subjects

Number	Subject Name	Score on Test L (X_i)	Grade Completed by Father (Y_i)
1.	John Jones	$X_1 = 50$	$Y_1 = 16$
2.	Alice Smith	$X_2 = 45$	$Y_2 = 12$
3.	Roger Brown	$X_3 = 43$	$Y_3 = 13$
4.	. . . . . .	. 37	. 12
5.	. . . . . .	. 39	. 16
6.	. . . . . .	. 27	. 4
7.	. . . . . .	. 40	. 16
8.	. . . . . .	$X_8 = 36$	$Y_8 = 6$
9.	. . . . . .	41	17
10.	. . . . . .	36	9
11.	. . . . . .	46	16
12.	. . . . . .	44	16
13.	. . . . . .	42	18
14.	. . . . . .	28	8
15.	. . . . . .	38	16
16.	. . . . . .	40	10
17.	. . . . . .	33	4
18.	. . . . . .	46	19
19.	. . . . . .	41	14
20.	. . . . . .	38	11
21.	. . . . . .	37	11
22.	. . . . . .	25	6
23.	. . . . . .	39	13

TABLE 6.1   (*continued*)

Subject Number	Name	Score on Test L (X_i)	Grade Completed by Father (Y_i)
24.	. . . . . .	36	12
25.	. . . . . .	29	4
26.	. . . . . .	39	9
27.	. . . . . .	35	6
28.	. . . . . .	40	13
29.	. . . . . .	37	10
30.	. . . . . .	35	9
31.	. . . . . .	34	12
32.	. . . . . .	44	15
33.	. . . . . .	43	14
34.	. . . . . .	41	17
35.	. . . . . .	30	5
36.	. . . . . .	42	13
37.	. . . . . .	40	18
38.	. . . . . .	44	15
39.	. . . . . .	39	15
40.	. . . . . .	38	13
41.	. . . . . .	34	5
42.	. . . . . .	40	17
43.	. . . . . .	47	19
44.	. . . . . .	42	13
45.	. . . . . .	37	12
46.	. . . . . .	44	16
47.	. . . . . .	40	8
48.	. . . . . .	38	16
49.	. . . . . .	41	11
50.	Barbara Doe	$X_{50} = 45$	$Y_{50} = 17$

a plot of the *number of observations* of a given size against the *magnitude, or numerical value, of the observations*, a kind of orderliness does appear in the form of the *frequency distribution*.   (See Figure 6.4.)

PREPARING THE HISTOGRAM   Although the logic of a frequency distribution as an organization of the data which shows the relationship between the number of observations and the magnitude of the observations is straightforward, the actual plotting of a frequency distribution, like that of Figure 6.4, often involves some intermediate steps.   It might be noted that the observations were grouped according to their magnitude into units or class intervals of size two.   This was done for the same reason that the distance between two cities is measured (for most practical purposes) in miles rather than inches or to the nearest 1000 miles: to measure in inches requires far more effort than is required, and to measure to the nearest 1000 miles would provide a description so gross as to hide many important relationships.

Without going into the details at this point, it is sufficient to recognize that the compromise between amount of effort and the loss of information is reasonably well achieved if the data are ultimately organized in such a way as to result in between 7 and 20 groupings of magnitude. In the present case, the highest value was 50 and the lowest score was 25. Taking the difference between these two scores, it is seen that the entire interval to be divided into between 7 and 20 parts is of length 25. Because 10 is an easy number to divide by, assume that 10 groups are desired. To get 10 groups in an interval of 25, each group will need to be 25/10, or 2.5, units long. Remembering that there is some flexibility in the number of groups to be used, the simple

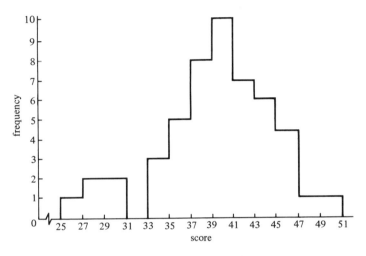

FIGURE 6.4   Frequency distribution of a set of scores

way out is to first try groupings of size two (which will require a larger number of groups, but will result in less error than groups of size three).

The next step is to decide whether to start the process of grouping by two's with the value 24 (placing 24 and 25 together) or with the value 25 (placing 25 and 26 together) and to decide whether to let whole numbers indicate the boundaries or the midpoints of the groupings. Remembering that the function of the graphic representation is to provide a general visual portrayal of the data—for exact information, calculations should be made from the original data—the choice should be that which seems simplest and most reasonable to the researcher himself.

In the example of Figure 6.4, the decision to begin with 25 seemed simplest because that was the lowest score recorded. Using whole numbers as boundaries seemed most sensible because test scores representing numerical descriptions of behavioral characteristics are usually treated verbally more like ages than like heights. That is, when someone is said to be 8 years old, it is inferred that he is between 8.00 and 8.99, while a report that someone is 6′ 2″ tall usually means between 6′ 1.5″ and 6′ 2.49″ tall. Like the former, when someone is said to have 30 items correct on a paper-and-pencil test, it is inferred that he got at least 30 items correct, but not quite 31. (For example, even if he were able to eliminate three out of five choices in a multiple-choice test on the thirty-first item, his score would still be 30.)

The last step before preparing a histogram like that of Figure 6.4 is to set up the frequency distribution in tabular form as in Table 6.2. To construct

TABLE 6.2

Frequency Tabulation of Scores on Test L (X_i)
Using Class Interval of Length Two

X	Tally	f_x	Cum f_x
49.0–50.9	|	1	50
47.0–48.9	|	1	49
45.0–46.9	||||	4	48
43–	✚ |	6	44
41–	✚ ||	7	38
39–	✚ ✚	10	31
37–	✚ |||	8	21
35–	✚	5	13
33–	|||	3	8
31–		0	5
29.0–	||	2	5
27.0–28.9	||	2	3
25.0–26.9	|	1	1

this table, the scores were first listed by two's starting with 25 at the bottom of the first column and continuing through the group which contains the largest score reported in Table 6.1. Next, a tally was placed in the appropriate row of the frequency table for each of the raw scores reported in Table 6.1. Finally, the number of tallies in each row has been indicated in arabic numerals in the frequency column, labeled f_x.

To plot the histogram itself, a horizontal line is drawn at the height indicated by the frequency directly above the corresponding score interval as indicated on the horizontal axis. In Figure 6.5 a horizontal line has been drawn at a height of 1 above the interval 25 to 26.9; a horizontal line has been drawn at a height of two above the interval 27 to 28.9, etc. The horizontal lines at the various heights have been connected to the base line with vertical lines drawn at the boundaries of the groupings or class intervals. Broken horizontal lines have been sketched within each interval to demonstrate the very important relationship that the area under the curve (i.e., under the histogram) corresponds to the number of observations. Because 10 observations fell in the interval 39.0 to 41.9, ten blocks of area form the column above

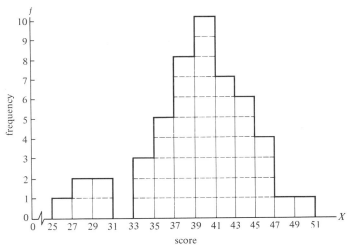

FIGURE 6.5 Frequency distribution showing the relationship between the number of observations and the area under the curve

that score interval on the base line; and because there were 50 observations in all, the total number of blocks forming the entire histogram is 50.

THE CUMULATIVE FREQUENCY DISTRIBUTION   A second kind of frequency distribution, particularly useful for determining certain measures of central tendency, for calculating some measures of dispersion, and for locating the position of certain observations within the group of observations, is the *cumulative frequency distribution* shown in Figure 6.6. By definition, a cumulative frequency is the number of observations which fall *in and below* a given score interval. Thus, the height of the curve at any point indicates the *number* of observations which are *equal to or lower than* the value indicated by that point.

The information necessary for plotting a cumulative frequency curve is readily obtained from the tabular form of the frequency distribution previously presented in Table 6.2. The cumulative frequency is recorded in the final column of that table and labeled cum f_x. Each figure in this column is the *sum* of the frequencies which are listed in its row and those below it. Thus, 5 in the row representing the interval 29.0 to 30.9 is the sum of 2, 2, and 1. Instead of re-adding the long column of figures to obtain each new cumulative frequency, it is easier to simply add the value recorded in the *cumulative* frequency column *of the row below* to the frequency in the row in which one is working. To obtain the cumulative frequency for the interval 37.0 to 38.9, simply add 13 to 8; for that for the interval 39.0 to 40.9, add 21 to 10; etc. Obviously, the cumulative frequency for the top row should be the total number of observations since they all fall below the upper boundary of that interval.

When plotting the cumulative frequency distribution, it is important to re-member that the cumulative frequency was defined as the number of obser-vations within and below a given score interval.   Thus, the cumulative fre-quency recorded in the last column of Table 6.2 always represents the value to be plotted against the point on the horizontal scale which represents the

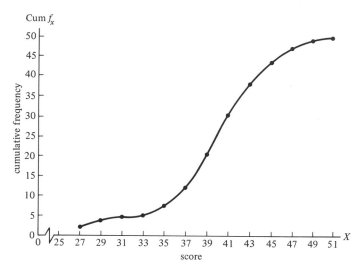

FIGURE 6.6   Cumulative frequency distribution

upper boundary of the interval in which it is found.   For example, the cumu-lative frequency eight found in the interval 33.0 to 34.9 must be plotted against 34.9 (or what looks to be 35 on the graph) and *not* above the value 33.0.

THEORETICAL FREQUENCY DISTRIBUTIONS   The frequency distribution repre-sented by the histogram is referred to as an *empirical* frequency distribution because it portrays data gathered through observation.   The researcher con-cerned with human behavior sometimes speculates as to what would happen under certain idealized conditions.   When this approach is applied to statis-tical reasoning the result is often a theoretical frequency distribution—a distribution for which a mathematical function can be written and which further represents what the researcher feels the actual data would look like if certain idealized conditions prevailed.

By far the best-known theoretical frequency distribution is the normal dis-tribution of error, commonly called the *normal curve*.   This frequency distri-bution can be expressed as follows:

$$y = f_{(x_i)} = \frac{N}{\sigma_x \sqrt{2\pi}} \exp \frac{1}{2} \left(\frac{x_i - \mu_x}{\sigma_x} \right)^2$$

where $f_{(x_i)}$ = a function of x and represents the frequency of occurrence of x_i
       N = total number of observations
       π = pi = 3.1416
   exp = e = base of natural logarithms = 2.71813
      μ_x = arithmetical mean of the distribution
      σ_x = standard deviation of the distribution

The expression above represents not just a single normal curve, but a whole
set of possible (i.e., a family of) normal curves. The formula for the normal
curve is the same no matter which particular normal curve is described, and
the specific curve in any instance will depend upon the specific value assigned
to the so-called *parameters* of N, μ_x, and σ_x.

All of the curves shown in Figure 6.7 are normal curves, even though they
differ with respect to their location along the line, with respect to the number
of cases they represent, and with respect to the extent of variation represented.

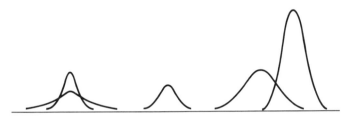

FIGURE 6.7   A variety of normal curves

It has already been noted that N, the total number of cases involved, is indicated by the area under the curve. The arithmetical mean, μ_x, represents the
place along the number line that the center of the curve falls, and the standard
deviation, σ_x, represents the distance from the center of the curve to the point
where it changes curvature from convex to concave (since the curve is symmetrical, this distance is the same moving in either direction from the center
point). In addition to their general bell shape, the characteristic which all
of these curves have in common, and which is true only for normal curves, is
the percentage of cases which falls between the mean and certain distances
along the base line. If σ_x is used as a convenient unit, the appropriate percentages are those shown in Figure 6.8. In all of the curves shown in
Figure 6.7, 68.26 percent of the cases fall between the mean plus and minus
one standard deviation unit, 95.34 percent of the cases fall between the mean
plus and minus two standard deviation units, etc.

It has already been noted that the values N, μ_x, and σ_x are called the *parameters* of the normal curve. The label parameters is used to distinguish
between these three semiconstants and the true constants of π, e, and the number 2, which also appears in the formula for the normal curve. The true con-

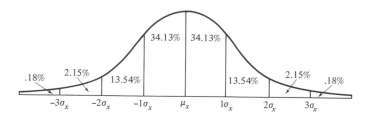

FIGURE 6.8   Relationship between distances along the base line and the percent of observations under a normal curve

stants are always the same no matter what particular normal curve is represented. Two is the number 2, π is 3.1416, and e is 2.71813 for each one of the distributions of Figure 6.7. On the other hand, the values of N, of μ_x, and of σ_x vary from one particular normal curve to the next, though they remain constant for any given normal curve. In this latter respect, these characteristics are different from the true variables, X, which takes on a different value for each observation and Y, which is different for each different X, even within a given distribution. When reading the formula for the normal curve, it is necessary to note that it involves three classes of numbers: the constants, the parameters, and the variables.

At this point the student may be wondering about the tremendous emphasis which seems to be given to the normal curve in the behavioral sciences. He may be wondering why it is that the normal curve is used rather than some other curve and, even more importantly, whether researchers force their data to come out a particular way when the normal curve is assumed in the development of the various hypothetical constructs called mental traits. Actually, it just happens that most biological traits, such as height, weight, the length of index fingers, when recorded for a large sample of human adults and cast into a frequency distribution, follow the normal curve. Also, most products of human endeavor which can be measured in terms of physical quantities (such as the actual diameters of metal washers manufactured by hand in a shop) follow the normal curve when a large sample is obtained. Because many biological traits are normally distributed and because many products of human effort measured on physical scales turn out to be normally distributed, it simply seems reasonable to *assume* that other biological traits, such as intelligence, and other products of effort, such as knowledge of history, are also normally distributed. Exactly what the true underlying distribution is cannot be known. At the present state of our knowledge, it seems more reasonable to assume that many traits are distributed normally rather than some other way.

There are, however, some very well-known exceptions to this general rule and it is important to know what a few of them are. One of the most obvious times when a researcher should *not* expect to obtain a normal distribution is when a measure of behavioral characteristics which is too easy or too difficult for the group involved is used. For example, an ability test designed for six-year-old children but administered to adults is not likely to result in a normal curve, but rather one in which the scores pile up at the high end of the distribution and is said to be skewed to the left (the direction of the long tail in Curve A of Figure 6.9). Similarly, if a high school mathematics test were given to fourth-graders, the resulting distribution would likely be skewed to the right, as in Curve B of Figure 6.9.

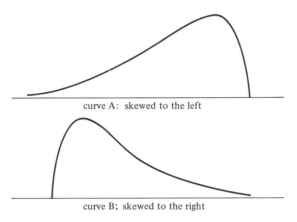

curve A: skewed to the left

curve B: skewed to the right

FIGURE 6.9   Hypothetical frequency curves which would be obtained if a test were too easy or too difficult for the group observed

Skewed curves are also likely to be obtained in any situation in which there is social pressure to conform in a particular direction. Thus, if 24-hour records are kept of the minimum rate of speed at which motorists travel when going past a stop sign, a highly skewed curve will result. Similarly, in the use of rating scales in this country, there seems to be social pressure not to rate anybody below average. Thus, in any use of personal rating systems where special efforts have not been made to compensate for the problem (e.g., by listing many more categories at the high end of the scale than at the low end or by forced-choice techniques), a skewed distribution is likely to result.

A third situation in which the researcher should not expect to find a normal frequency distribution is that in which the data have been obtained on persons representing a mixture of two or more distinct groups with respect to the characteristic measured. For example, if one were to measure the heights of a group composed of both three-year-old and five-year-old children, or if one were to measure knowledge of statistics among a group of students composed of some persons who have had and some persons who have not had a course in the subject, the results would form a *bimodal* distribution similar to that of Figure 6.10. Usually such a distribution is considered to be composed of two overlapping normal (or approximately normal) distributions. When such a distribution is obtained, the research implications are that the two groups should be separated and handled independently in any analysis or experimental treatment.

Another widely used theoretical frequency distribution is the counterpart

FIGURE 6.10   A bimodal distribution

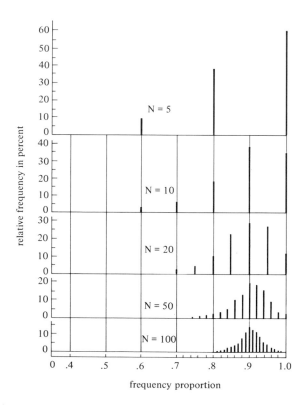

FIGURE 6.11   Five different binomial distributions (A. Treloar, *Biometric analysis: An introduction.* Minneapolis: Burgess, 1951, Fig. 37. P. 171.)

to the normal curve when the variable under consideration is discontinuous. This is the *binomial* distribution, various forms of which are presented in Figure 6.11. The binomial distribution arises whenever a series of events each having two possible outcomes occurs in such a way that each event has the same probability of coming out in a particular way, and a frequency distribution is made of the number of times the event did come out in that

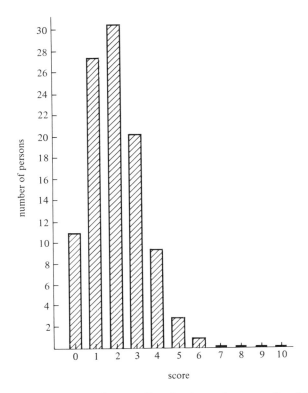

FIGURE 6.12   The theoretical chance distribution of scores for 100 students taking a 10-item multiple-choice test

particular way. For example, the number of times each of the possible number of heads appears in flipping 10 coins 100 times would follow the binomial curve. So would the frequency distribution of test scores achieved by 100 students who responded to a 10-item test composed of multiple-choice items with five alternatives each (only one of which was correct) if the students marked the answers without looking at the questions. The "chance" distribution of scores obtained under the above circumstances is that presented in Figure 6.12. This distribution was obtained from the following formula for the binomial distribution:

$$Y = f(X) = \frac{Nn!}{X!(n - X)!} p^X q^{n-X}$$

where   ! = symbol for factorial (0! = 1)
         n = number of trials
         X = number of successes in n trials ($0 \leq X \leq n$)
         p = likelihood of success on any one trial
         $q = 1 - p$
         N = sample size (i.e., number of observations of n trials)
         $f(X)$ = frequency with which X successes occur in N observations

To obtain the distribution of Figure 6.12, let $N = 100$, $n = 10$, and $p = \frac{1}{5}$. Then, to discover how many students would get none right, $f(X)$ is calculated when $X = 0$; to find out how many might be expected to get one right by chance, $f(X)$ is calculated for $X = 1$; to find out how many would get two right, $f(X)$ is determined for $X = 2$, etc. One does *not* expect everyone who marks the answer sheet without looking at the questions to end up with $\frac{1}{5}(10) = 2$ items correct. The value 2 represents only the average of the chance distribution, and it is the entire binomial distribution which represents the frequency distribution of scores to be expected when the responses are purely a matter of chance.

Several additional well-known theoretical frequency distributions are presented in Figures 6.13 through 6.15. An examination of these distributions reveals that the t distribution, which is used primarily for testing hypotheses about mean differences and about correlation, is symmetrical about zero, has a range from $-\infty$ to $+\infty$, is leptokurtic (i.e., tall and thin as compared with the normal distribution), and is *asymptotically normal* (i.e., approaches a normal curve as the number of cases increases but never quite duplicates the normal curve). The chi-square distribution (χ^2), however, is not symmetrical but is skewed to the right. Its range is from zero to $+\infty$ and it is also asymptotically normal. The chi-square distribution is used most often to test hypotheses about proportions and other frequency counts. Quite similar to the chi-square distribution is the *F distribution*, which is probably the most widely used distribution in modern experimental design. The F distribution occurs in the testing of hypotheses about the differences among two or more means and about differences in variability.

One final important theoretical frequency distribution, the *bivariate-normal*, is shown in Figure 6.16. This distribution indicates the frequencies with which observations occur when categorized (or measured) with respect to two characteristics. In a truly bivariate normal distribution, the marginal distributions for X and for Y (i.e., the distribution of the X values without regard to the Y values, and the distribution of the Y values without regard to the X values, respectively) are normal, and all the conditional distributions are normal. A conditional distribution is the frequency distribution of Y values for a given X score or a distribution of X values for a given Y score.

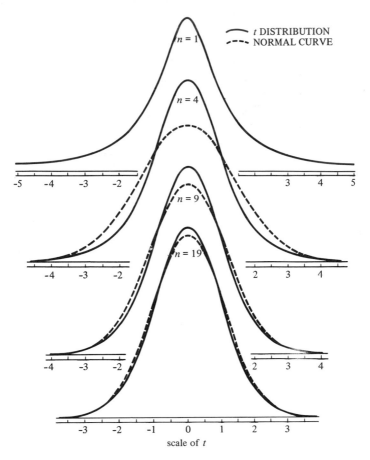

FIGURE 6.13 The *t* distribution for different sample sizes as compared with the normal distribution (A. Treloar, *Random sampling distributions.* Minneapolis: Burgess, 1942, Fig. 20. P. 57.)

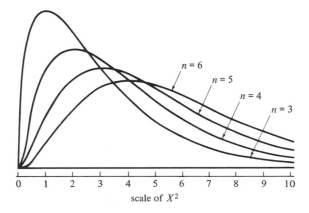

FIGURE 6.14 The x^2 distribution for several different sample sizes (A. Treloar, *Biometric analysis: An introduction.* Minneapolis: Burgess, 1951, Fig. 32. P. 156.)

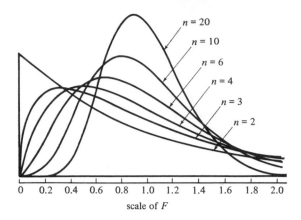

FIGURE 6.15 The *F* distribution for several different sample sizes (After A. Treloar, *Biometric analysis: An introduction.* Minneapolis: Burgess, 1951, Fig. 33. P. 156.)

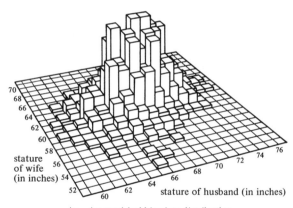

A: An empirical bivariate distribution

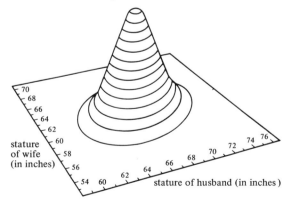

B: Corresponding bivariate-normal distribution

FIGURE 6.16 Empirical and theoretical bivariate frequency distributions (A. Treloar, *Biometric analysis: An introduction.* Minneapolis: Burgess, 1951, Figs. 37 and 38. P. 171.)

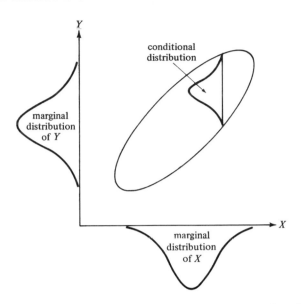

FIGURE 6.17 A plan view of a bivariate frequency distribution with marginal and conditional distributions.

These special frequency distributions are most easily seen in Figure 6.17, in which the normal bivariate is viewed from above and the marginal distributions and one conditional distribution have been rotated to lie flat in the plane of the X dimensions. A numerical example of a bivariate distribution is presented as Table 6.3. In this table, the number in the cells represents the

TABLE 6.3

A Numerical Example of a Bivariate Frequency Distribution in Tabular Form

$Y\downarrow$ $X\rightarrow$	1	2	3	4	5	6	7	8	9	10	f_y
11									1	1	2
10								1	2	1	4
9						1	2	4	1	1	9
8					1	4	3	2		1	11
7				2	5	4	5	1	1		18
6			1	4	3	6	4	1			19
5			2	4	5	1					12
4		1	3	2	1						7
3		1	3	2							6
2	1	2	1								4
1	1	1									2
f_x	2	5	10	14	15	16	14	9	5	4	94

number of observations which were found to have the X value shown in the column heading and the Y value shown in the row heading. For example, there were four observations for which the X value was 6 and the Y value was 7; two observations for which the X value was 3 and the Y value was 5; etc. The marginal distribution of Y values (i.e., the frequencies of Y values without regard to X) are given in the column headed f_y, and the marginal distribution of X is given in the bottom row (headed f_x). Each row and column represents a different conditional distribution. For example, the conditional distribution for $X = 6$ (i.e., the distribution of Y's on the condition that X has a value of 6) is found in the column under the heading 6 and indicates that of those 16 observations where X was equal to 6, one of the Y values was 9, four of the Y values were 8, four of the Y values were 7, six of the Y values were 6, and one of the Y values was 5.

The concept of the bivariate distribution can be easily extended to observations along any number of dimensions. The discussion of these so-called *multivariate* distributions is, however, beyond the scope of this book, as are other theoretical frequency distributions with which sophisticated students of statistics may be familiar.

Measures of Location

The frequency distributions studied in the previous section provide a general, overall description of observations. From a graphic plot of the frequency distribution, it is easy to see whether the same number of observations occurs at each different value or whether there are a few low and a few high observations with most falling somewhere in between, etc. Usually, such a graphic description is not enough. More specific information is desired about the *location* of the frequency distribution along the line which represents all possible values which the observations might have. It would be helpful to have one number which indicated whether the group as a whole was at the high end, the low end, or somewhere in the middle of the scale. All measures of location are designed to provide such information by yielding a single point along the line which designates the position of the group as a whole.

THE MODE   Once a frequency distribution has been plotted, an obvious index of location is the point on the line under the highest part of the curve. This point is called the *mode* and can generally be located by inspection of the frequency distribution when plotted in graphic form. In a strict sense, the mode is defined as the most frequently occurring observation or, if grouping has been carried out, as the midpoint of the class interval with the greatest frequency. In the data represented by Figure 6.5, the class interval containing the largest number of observations is that from 39.0 to 40.9. Therefore, the midpoint of this interval, 40.0, is the mode.

The mode is very simple to obtain, and this is, perhaps, its principal advantage. Another advantage is that it *does* represent a real observation (in fact, by definition, that observation which occurred most often). When a statement is made to the effect that there is no such thing as the average person, the type of average referred to is most certainly not the mode.

Unfortunately, the mode has some rather serious disadvantages. First, the mode shows considerable variation with small changes in the relatively ar-

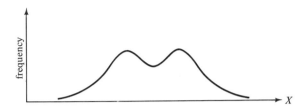

FIGURE 6.18   A bimodal frequency distribution

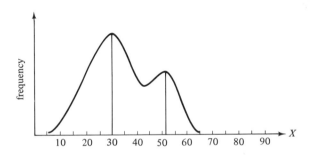

FIGURE 6.19   A bimodal frequency distribution with a major and a minor mode

bitrary decisions as to the length of class interval used and as to whether a whole number is used to represent the midpoint or the lower boundary of an interval. Second, the mode is not stable in sampling. That is, if all possible samples of some given size were taken from a population of observations and a mode calculated for each sample, the various modes thus found would vary from one another to a considerable extent. Third, the mode is difficult—almost impossible—to handle algebraically. (For example, it is not possible to write a meaningful formula for it.) Finally, the mode is not always unique. Since both humps on the curve shown in Figure 6.18 rise to the same height, the curve has two modes and is referred to as a bimodal curve. Contrast this curve with that shown in Figure 6.19. In the latter figure, since one hump is much higher than the other, the mode, by definition, has the value 30. However, to indicate that there are two peaks in the frequency distribution, curves like those of Figure 6.19 are still described as bimodal—with a

major mode at 30 and a minor mode of 52. In either case, the classic definition of the mode simply does not provide a satisfactory measure of the location of the group as a whole.

THE MEDIAN   Given a bimodal distribution like that shown in Figure 6.19,
a much more sensible way to locate a single point along the line which can be
used as an index of central tendency is to pick the middle value—that is, the

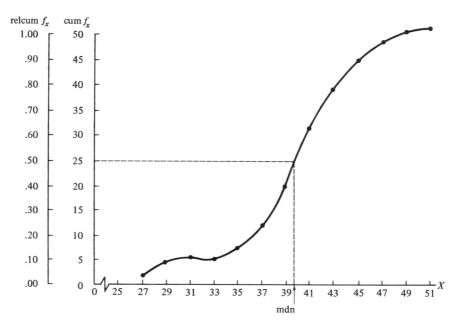

FIGURE 6.20   Calculation of the median from a cumulative frequency
curve

point above and below which exactly half of the observations fall. This second measure of location is called the *median*. The median is often referred
to as a "counting" measure, because it can be obtained by laying the observations in order from low to high and counting to the halfway point. While
there are many ways of calculating the median of a distribution (it can be
done by formula, or it can be done logically, remembering the definition of
the median as the point above and below which exactly half the observations
fall), the simplest procedure is to read the value from the cumulative frequency curve, as previously plotted in Figure 6.6. Since the cumulative frequency curve gives the number of observations found at or below each score
value, the median can readily be found by reading the score corresponding to
a cumulative frequency equal to exactly half the number of observations. In
Figure 6.6, the total number of observations represented was 50; exactly

half is 25. Drawing a horizontal line at a height of 25 (see Figure 6.20), it is seen that this line intersects the cumulative frequency curve at a point directly above 39.8 on the score scale. Thus, the median of the set of scores represented is 39.8. (See Table 6.1.)

The median is always specifically defined, and therefore it has a distinct advantage over the mode as a measure of central tendency. It is readily obtained and easily understood as the middle point. It is also of special value when measurement is at the ordinal level, for it only makes use of the order of numbers, and not the actual values. That is, if the highest value of the set of 50 observations used in the calculations above was 60 or 44 instead of 50, the median would remain the same. It is the rank position of the numbers which counts in obtaining a median, not their magnitude.

As contrasted with these advantages, the median still fluctuates with arbitrary choices in representing the data and is still somewhat unstable in sampling. It is also quite difficult (though not impossible) to express algebraically. Thus, although superior to the mode, the median still does not represent a completely satisfactory measure of location.

THE ARITHMETICAL MEAN   For most purposes, the most satisfactory index of central tendency yet devised is the *arithmetical mean*. By definition, this index is the *balancing point* of the frequency distribution and is often referred to as a computational measure because it does require some calculation in order to find it. To obtain the mean,[5] one adds up the scores and then divides the sum by the number of scores used in getting the sum. Since the sum of the 50 scores of Table 6.1 is 1945, the arithmetical mean is 1945/50 = 38.9. Thus, if a fulcrum were placed along the score line at exactly 38.9, the frequency distribution would be perfectly balanced and would not tip (i.e., rotate in the plane defined by the score and frequency-dimension axes).

A number of readers will recognize the arithmetical mean as precisely that index to which many persons refer as the "average." It should be noted, however, that in the language of the statistician all measures of central tendency (or location) are averages. The mode is an average, the median is an average, and the arithmetical (as well as other kinds of) mean is also an average. To be precise, then, it is essential to refer to this most popular and widely used measure of central tendency not as an average, but as a mean.

In symbolic form, the computational procedure for obtaining the mean is given as follows:

$$\overline{X} = \frac{\Sigma X_i}{N}$$

[5] Although there are actually many kinds of means, viz., arithmetical, geometric, harmonic, contraharmonic, the word *mean* without any adjective preceding it is taken to refer to the arithmetical mean.

where $\overline{X}$ = arithmetical mean[6]
         N = number of observations
         $\Sigma X_i = X_1 + X_2 + X_3 + \cdots + X_N$

Because the arithmetical mean is the most stable (in sampling) of the indexes of central tendency described, because it is easy to express and handle algebraically, and because it appears as a parameter in frequency distributions, it is preferred to the mode and the median. The mean does have one serious disadvantage that limits its usefulness in some situations: in small samples it is very greatly affected by one or two highly unusual observations. For example, consider the two sets of observations shown in Table 6.4. For

TABLE 6.4
Two Sets of Five Fictitious Observations

Observation Number	Set A	Set B
1	3	3
2	3	3
3	4	4
4	5	5
5	5	25

Set A, the mode is undetermined, the median is 4 and the mean is also 4. Set B, which is composed of the same observations, except for one extreme value of 25, has a mode of 3 and a median of 4 but an arithmetical mean of 8. Note that while the value 8 does not seem to be very representative of the five observations in Set B, it is a legitimate average. It cannot be said that the mean is wrong in this instance any more than it could be said that the Mercator projection of the earth's surface on a flat map is wrong and the Lambert projection is right. It can only be said that the mean is different (and perhaps a little misleading) as compared with the other two indexes of central tendency.

In general, then, the arithmetical mean is the preferred index of central tendency, except when the frequency distribution is highly skewed (as a result of an unusual observation), when the sample size is quite small (when it is possible to have a skewed population distribution and not know it), or when the original level of measurement is only at the ordinal level (and the magnitudes of the observations reported have no meaning anyway). In situations where the mean is not appropriate, the median is the preferred index. The mode is used only for quick, crude approximations or when it is essential that the average found represent some *real* (i.e., actually found) observation.

[6] When a population mean is indicated rather than a sample mean, the symbol for the mean becomes μ_x.

Measures of Variability

In addition to knowing where along the line of possibilities the group lies, it is also essential to determine the extent to which observations of the group are spread out or bunched together. From such an index, it is possible to make statements about the extent to which one expects the observations to deviate from the average and about the relative heterogeneity or homogeneity of the group involved.

Basically, there are two major varieties of indexes which provide information about variability. One variety, called the *range*, notes the distance between two points along the scale which are determined by specifying a proportion of cases which must lie in between. The other basic approach involves averaging deviations from some specified point.

THE RANGE   The easiest index of variability to obtain is the simple range or difference between the highest and the lowest observation.[7] Unfortunately, the range makes use of only two observations of the many available; and worse yet, it makes use of those very two which are likely to contain the greatest amount of error. In the measurement of behavioral characteristics, the person with the highest score is a person who not only has a great amount of the characteristic described but also for whom a great amount of plus error occurred on that particular measurement. Similarly, a person with the very lowest score is likely to be that person who possesses only a small degree of the trait under consideration and for whom a great amount of negative error occurred on that measurement.[8] To avoid this problem, T. L. Kelley has suggested that the two points to be used should not be the highest and the lowest but rather that below which 90 percent of the cases fall and that below which 10 percent of the cases fall. The difference between the ninetieth percentile and the tenth percentile has thus become known as the *Kelley range*.

The Kelley range can most readily be obtained by making use of the cumulative-frequency curve. Reading across from a relative cumulative frequency of 90, one finds the ninetieth percentile (for the data represented in Figure 6.6) to be 45.2; and reading across from a relative cumulative frequency of 10, one finds the tenth percentile to be 32. Thus, the Kelley range for the example given is 13.2.

A third and much more popular variety of range as an index of variability

[7] Strictly speaking the number 1 should be added to this difference, just as if one were counting tickets by subtracting the number on the lowest ticket from the number on the highest. For most practical purposes, however, it is not necessary to be so fastidious in obtaining a measure of variability.

[8] Evidence that this is so comes from studies in which a regression toward the mean from both extremes has been found upon repeated measurement.

is the so-called semi-interquartile range, which is obtained by taking half the difference between the seventy-fifth percentile and the twenty-fifth percentile. Again, by means of the cumulative frequency curve, the semi-interquartile range for the 50 observations of Figure 6.6 is found to be

$$\frac{42.8 - 36.8}{2} = 3$$

Because all the ranges depend upon counts of numbers of observations and therefore upon their rank positions rather than the actual magnitudes of the numbers themselves, these indexes of variability are primarily used in work with ranked data, with small samples, or with skewed distributions. They are used in precisely the same situations in which the median, as a measure of central tendency, is preferred to the arithmetical mean. Of the three indexes, the semi-interquartile range has come to be the preferred measure, even though the simple range is still widely used because it is so easy to obtain.

THE DEVIATIONS   Faced with the logical task of developing an index of the extent to which observations differ from one another that would preserve the information contained in the magnitude of the values, it would seem reasonable to consider all possible differences among the observations. Just taking the sum of all possible differences, however, would tend to result in larger indexes for large groups and smaller indexes for small groups. To eliminate the effect of group size it is essential to take the average of the difference between all possible pairs of observations. While such an index satisfies the logical requirements of an ideal index of variability, it obviously becomes awkward for large samples. For example, with 100 observations there would be $\frac{1}{2}(100)(99) = 4950$ subtractions to make.

To overcome this practical problem and develop a simpler index that still retains the desired properties, it would seem reasonable to select just *one* observation and determine the difference between it and all the others, rather than to take each observation from each other one. The question then arises as to which observation to choose. The logical answer is the one which is typical—the arithmetical mean. Logically, then, a simple index would be obtained by taking the average of the deviations of all the observations from the mean. If one were to do this, however (see the third column of Table 6.5), the sum of these deviations and consequently the average of them would be zero. This occurs because of the way the mean was defined—the balancing point of the distribution. Thus, while taking the sum of the deviations of the observations from the mean can serve as a check upon calculations thus far carried out, it cannot be used as an index of variability.

At this point, it could be reasoned that, since the primary interest is in the *amount* of deviation or variation in the observations and *not* in the *direction*

TABLE 6.5
Calculating Deviation Measures of Variability

Column 1 Observation i	Column 2 Raw Score X_i	Column 3 Deviation Score $X_i - \overline{X}$	Column 4 Absolute Deviation $\mid X_i - \overline{X} \mid$	Column 5 Squared Deviation $(X_i - \overline{X})^2$
1	50	11.1	11.1	123.21
2	45	6.1	6.1	37.21
3	43	4.1	4.1	16.81
4	37	− 1.9	1.9	3.61
.	.	.	.	.
.	.	.	.	.
.	.	.	.	.
50	45	6.1	6.1	37.21
Sum (Σ)	1945	0	197.8	1342.50
N	50	50	50	50
Average	38.9	—	3.96	26.85
Index:	mean	—	average dev.	standard dev.

of the deviation, the algebraic signs of the differences obtained can, logically, be ignored. If this were to be done and the average of these absolute deviations from the mean taken as in the fourth column of Table 6.5, the measure of variability known as the *average deviation* would be obtained. In the example given, the average deviation is

$$\frac{\Sigma \mid X_i - \overline{X} \mid}{N} = \frac{197.8}{50} = 3.96$$

To some persons, the process of ignoring the algebraic signs is illogical because algebraically ignoring the signs involves doing different things to different observations: multiplying some by −1 and others by +1. When there is no interest in the direction of the deviations and it is desirable to eliminate the algebraic signs, it can be done by squaring the deviations found. Of course, carrying out the process of multiplying a number by itself also has the effect of giving large deviations relatively more weight than small ones. But this is not unreasonable, because the primary interest is in a measure of variability, and when there are large deviations, there is considerably more variability than when the deviations from the mean are small.

The average of the squared deviations from the mean results in an index called the variance. The symbol for the variance is s_z^2 when the reference is to a sample statistic, and its Greek counterpart, σ_x^2, when referring to a population parameter. In the numerical example,

$$s_x^2 = \frac{\Sigma(X_i - X)^2}{N} = \frac{1342.5}{50} = 26.85$$

While the variance is widely used in testing hypotheses by a statistical approach, there is still one final logical limitation in its use as an index of the extent to which the observations differ from one another. Suppose the observations in the example used were measurements of height. The average height would be reported in inches, and the deviation of each observation from the mean height would also be in inches. However, the squared deviation from the mean would be in square inches. The variance, as the average of the squared deviations from the mean, would also be in square-inch units. Somehow, it does not seem reasonable to describe the extent to which persons differ in height in square inches, so to get back into the original units of measurement, the square root of the variance is used. In symbolic form, this most useful descriptive index, known as the *standard deviation*, becomes [9]

$$s_x = \sqrt{\frac{\Sigma(X_i - \overline{X})^2}{N}}$$

Higher Moments of a Distribution

It has already been noted that the two other major characteristics of a frequency distribution which might be described are skewness and kurtosis. In most instances, however, it is unnecessary actually to calculate indexes of these two characteristics. Rather, it is sufficient to note that while the variance represents the second moment about the mean, a comparable measure of skewness represents the third moment about the mean; and a comparable measure of kurtosis can be obtained by calculating the fourth moment about the mean (the mean itself representing the first moment about zero). Also, one might note that when a unimodal distribution is free from skew, the mean, median, and mode will all be identical. When the distribution is skewed to the right (i.e., the long tail is toward the right), it is said to be positively skewed, and when the distribution shows the long tail toward the left, it is said to be negatively skewed. In any nonsymmetrical distribution, the mean, median, and mode will appear in alphabetical order starting from the tail of the curve, as seen in Figure 6.21.

[9] For computational purposes, a simpler equivalent formula is: $\sqrt{\Sigma X^2/N - (\Sigma X/N)^2}$; and for small samples (say, $N < 20$), a correction for bias should be made by multiplying the result by $\sqrt{N/(N-1)}$.

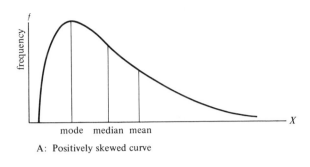

A: Positively skewed curve

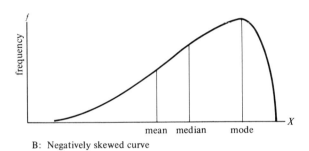

B: Negatively skewed curve

FIGURE 6.21   The relationship among measures of central tendency in nonsymmetrical curves

Locating a Particular Observation

PERCENTILE RANKS   In addition to describing a group of observations, it is often necessary to describe the location of one particular observation in relation to the others which comprise the frequency distribution.   One straightforward way to accomplish this would be to put all the observations in order and assign ranks.   This, however, is not perfectly satisfactory, because the logical meaning of a rank depends, in part, upon the size of the group.   That is, being the tenth highest in a group of 10 observations is quite different from being tenth highest in a group of 3000 observations.

One way of locating a particular observation that overcomes the problem of group size is to determine the *percentile rank* (P_r).   By definition, a percentile rank of a particular observation is the percentage of observations which have the *same* or *lower* value than the given observation.   It is important to distinguish clearly between a percentile *rank* and a percen*tile*.   A percen*tile* is a score below which a given percentage of people fall.   Thus, the median is the fiftieth *percentile*, since it is the score such that 50 percent of the observations fall below it. In contrast, the *percentile rank* of the median is 50, because 50 percent of the observations in the group fall at or below this score.

The task of finding a percentile rank, then, is just the opposite of that which was faced when trying to locate the median and when finding the necessary scores to use in determining the Kelley range and the semi-interquartile range. In the previous calculations, a percentage of persons was given and the task was to find the score at or below which this percentage of observations fell. In determining a percentile rank, a score is given and the task is to find what percentage of the observations fall at or below this value.

The relationship between these two problems can most clearly be seen in the formula which permits a conversion from the score scale (the percentile) to the frequency scale (the percentile rank) and back again. This conversion formula can be written as

$$\text{score scale} \qquad \text{frequency scale}$$

$$\frac{S_{p_r} - b}{h} = \frac{\dfrac{P_r N}{100} - \text{cum } f_b}{f_w}$$

where S_{p_r} = score (or percentile) corresponding to a percentile rank of P_r
  b = lower boundary of the interval in which the score falls
  h = length of class interval of the score scale
  P_r = percentile rank or percentage of persons
  N = number of observations
  cum f_b = cumulative frequency *to the lower boundary* (i.e., below) of the interval in which the score falls
  f_w = frequency *within the interval* in which the score falls

---

	TABLE 6.6	
	Computational Example for Finding Percentiles and Percentile Ranks by Formula	

Finding a Percentile	Finding a Percentile Rank
Problem: Find the median (i.e., find the *score* such that 50 percent of the observations fall at or below this point).	Problem: Find the percentile rank for Roger Brown (i.e., find the percentage of observations which fall at or below a raw score of 43).

$$\frac{S_{p_{50}} - 39.0}{2} = \frac{\dfrac{(50)(50)}{100} - 21}{10} \qquad\qquad \frac{43.5 - 43}{2} = \frac{\dfrac{P_r(50)}{100} - 38}{6}$$

$$S_{p_{50}} = 39.8 \qquad\qquad\qquad\qquad\qquad P_r = 79$$

Data from Table 6.2, p. 188.

An illustration of the way in which this same formula can be used to solve the two types of problems described is presented in Table 6.6. The information used comes from Table 6.2.

In Table 6.6 the value substituted in the formula for Roger Brown's score was 43.5 rather than the raw score 43 reported in Table 6.2 because percentile ranks are defined as the percentage of the group which falls at or below the *midpoint* of the score interval. Since a score represents an interval, not a point, the score 43 occupies the interval 43.0 to 43.999 and the midpoint of this interval is 43.5.

For most practical situations, a far simpler way to locate a particular observation in a group of observations by means of a percentile rank is to make use of the cumulative frequency curve of Figure 6.6. Before, in Figure 6.20, this curve was used to find a score (percentile), given a percentage of persons. Now the task is to find a percentage of persons, given the score. Thus, the curve is used in the reverse direction. The midpoint of the score interval is first located on the base line. Then move in a vertical direction until the curve is intersected. Finally, move horizontally to the left to find the desired percentage. In Figure 6.22, the graphic solution to the problem of finding Roger Brown's percentile rank is presented.

While the percentile rank is a readily understood way of locating a particular observation in a group of observations, it is awkward to compute (especially when using the formulas), and, furthermore, it is not a linear trans-

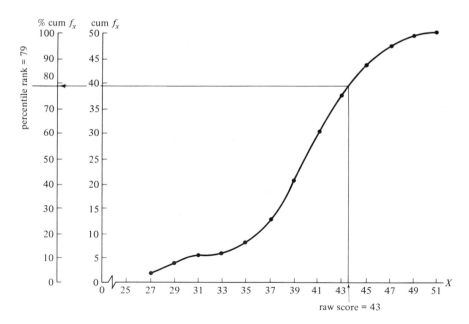

FIGURE 6.22   Graphic solution to finding a percentile rank for Roger Brown

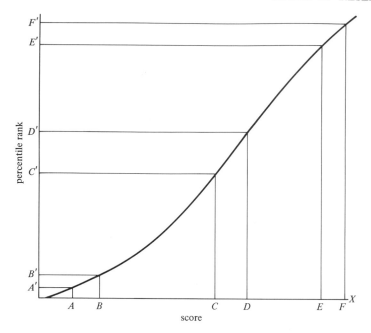

FIGURE 6.23   Changes in percentile rank for equal shifts in raw scores at three different places along the score scale

formation of the raw scores.   The difficulty with nonlinear transformations of raw scores is that equal differences in raw scores do not result in equal differences in percentile ranks and the relation between them shifts throughout the scale.   For example, small differences in raw scores near the center of the distribution result in marked differences in percentile ranks, while relatively large shifts in raw scores near the upper or lower end of the scale result in only small changes in percentile ranks.   This can readily be seen in Figure 6.23, in which the differences in raw-score points from A to B, and from C to D, and from E to F are all the same, but the differences in percentile

TABLE 6.7

Illustration That the Average of Percentile Ranks Does Not Equal the Percentile Rank of the Average

X_i	P_r	
		$\overline{P}_r = \dfrac{83}{3} = 28$
30	10	
45	18	
40	55	$\overline{X} = \dfrac{105}{3} = 35$
$\Sigma 105$	83	
$N = 3$		P_r for $35 = 18$

Data from Table 6.6, p. 210.

ranks are quite different for C' to D' than they are in the other two cases, i.e., from A' to B' and from E' to F'.

In practical terms, the result of a nonlinear transformation is to limit the interpretation of gain scores and to make it inappropriate to average percentile ranks. The average of percentile ranks, as seen in Table 6.7, is not necessarily the same as the percentile rank of the average of the raw scores.

STANDARD SCORES   There is a mathematically simple solution to the problem of locating a single observation in a group of observations by means of a linear transformation; it is called the *standard score*. By definition, a standard score represents the number of standard deviation units above or below the group mean where the particular score lies. Computationally, the formula for obtaining a standard is

$$z_i = \frac{X_i - \overline{X}}{s_x}$$

where z_i = standard score
X_i = raw score
$\overline{X}$ = mean of the group of scores
s_x = standard deviation of the group of scores

Graphically, the relationship between the standard-score scale and the raw-score scale for which the computed mean was 110 and the computed standard deviation was 10 can be seen in Figure 6.24.

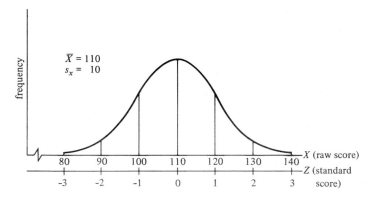

FIGURE 6.24   Graphic representation of the relationship between a raw-score scale and a standard-score scale

For practical purposes, it is sometimes inconvenient to use a numerical scale like the basic standard score as defined above, which ranges from -3 to $+3$ and which involves negative numbers. Various special standard

TABLE 6.8
Commonly Used Arbitrary Standard Scores

Score (Z_a)	Arbitrary Mean ($\overline{X}_a$)	Arbitrary Standard Deviation (s_a)
Army General Classification Test (AGCT)	100	20
Navy Aptitude Classification Battery (T-Score)	50	10
College Entrance Examination Board	500	100
Wechsler Intelligence Quotient	100	15
Wechsler Subscore	10	3
Stanford-Binet Intelligence Quotient	100	15
Stanine	5	2
In general	$\overline{X}_a$	s_a

$$Z_a = \overline{X}_a = s_a \left(\frac{X_i - \overline{X}}{s_x} \right)$$

scores have been developed for use in particular situations which specify some arbitrary mean, X_a, and some arbitrary standard deviation, s_a. Various such scales in common use at the present time are listed in Table 6.8, along with the values for means and standard deviations selected. The general formula which may be used to obtain a standard scale with any specified mean and standard deviation is

$$Z_a = \overline{X}_a + s_a \left(\frac{X_i - \overline{X}}{s_x} \right)$$

where Z_a = standard score on the arbitrary standard scale
X_a = selected arbitrary mean
s_a = selected arbitrary standard deviation
X_i = raw score
$\overline{X}$ = calculated mean
s_x = calculated standard deviation

It has already been noted that when the frequency distribution of raw scores is normal, there is a specific relationship between distances along the base line and the percentage of cases under the curve. (See Figure 6.8.) Thus, *when the distribution of observations is normal*, there is a specific relationship between percentile ranks and standard scores. The relationship between percentile ranks and standard scores, with a normal frequency distribution assumed and with illustrations given for three specific values, can be seen in Figure 6.25.

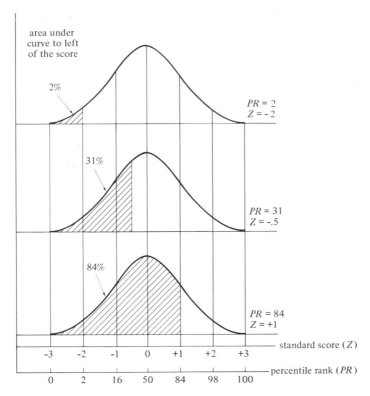

area under
curve to left
of the score

2%

$PR = 2$
$Z = -2$

31%

$PR = 31$
$Z = -.5$

84%

$PR = 84$
$Z = +1$

standard score (Z)

-3   -2   -1   0   +1   +2   +3

percentile rank (PR)

0   2   16   50   84   98   100

FIGURE 6.25   The relationship between percentile ranks and standard scores for a normal curve

Measures of Association

GRAPHIC REPRESENTATION   It is first necessary to understand precisely what is meant by association between two characteristics before developing an index of the extent to which two characteristics are related.   In general, when two variables are said to be related, it is meant that either

High values on one variable are associated with high values on the second variable, *and* low values on the first variable occur with low values on the second;

or

high values on one variable occur with low values on the second variable, *and* low values on the first variable are associated with high values on the second.

When the first situation occurs, there is a *direct* or *positive* relationship between the two characteristics; when the second occurs, there is an *inverse*, or *negative*, relationship between the two variables. When there is *no* relationship between the two measures, there is no tendency for one value of a pair of observations to fluctuate with the other value of the pair. That is, a person who gets a high score on one characteristic is just as likely to get a high as a middle or a low score on the other characteristic; and over a whole group of pairs of observations, it is likely to be found that one person who got a low score on the first variable will get a high score on the second variable; that a second person who got a low score on the first variable will have a high score on the second; and a third person with a low score on the first will have a low score on the second; and so on throughout the range of possibilities.

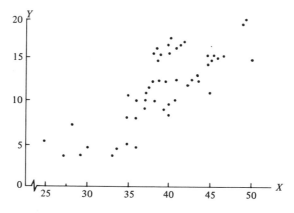

FIGURE 6.26.   Scatterplot representing the relationship between X and Y values of Table 6.1

A type of graphic representation of a bivariate frequency which clearly shows both the degree and type of relationship which occurs in the data is a *scatterplot*. In the scatterplot, each pair of observations (usually a person on whom two measures have been made) is represented by a single dot, the position of which is determined by the values of the observations. The distance to the right of one axis represents the value of the observation on the characteristic labeled X, and the distance above the base line indicates the value of the observation on the variable labeled Y. Figure 6.26 is a scatterplot of the data from Table 6.1, and Figure 6.27 shows several scatterplots representing correlations of different types and degrees. In general, a positive relationship is present when the slope of the dots is from lower left to upper right, while a negative relationship is indicated if the dots fall from upper left to lower right. When no relationship is present, the dots form what is termed a circular pattern; and the higher the degree of relationship (either positive or negative), the more elliptical the pattern becomes, until for a perfect relationship the dots all fall along a straight line.

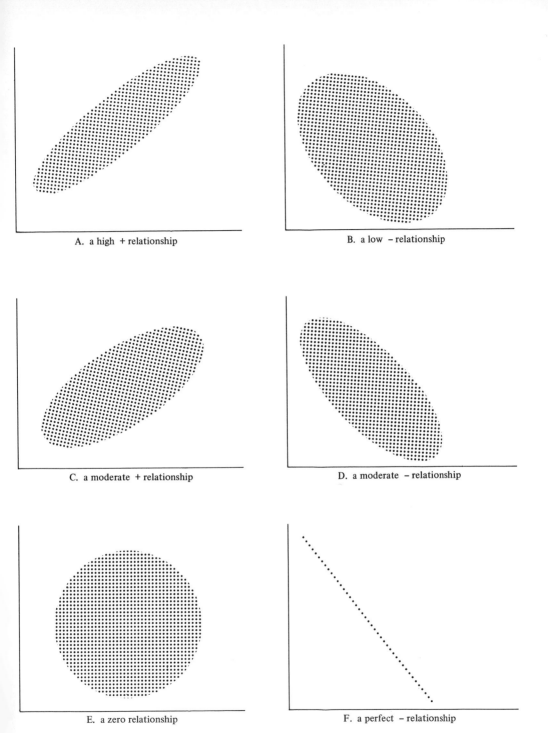

A. a high + relationship

B. a low – relationship

C. a moderate + relationship

D. a moderate – relationship

E. a zero relationship

F. a perfect – relationship

FIGURE 6.27 Scatterplots representing various types and degrees of relationships

PEARSON PRODUCT-MOMENT CORRELATION   While the scatterplot provides a general idea as to the direction and degree of relationship between two characteristics, it does not represent an accurate numerical description of the association involved.   An index which does provide an accurate measure of the degree of association when the two variables involved are measured on an interval or higher scale and when the relationship between them is linear (i.e., the dots in the scatterplot form about a straight line rather than a curve) is the product-moment correlation developed by Karl Pearson (1895).

The logical basis of the product-moment correlation is straightforward. Consider the possible distribution of the observational points in Figure 6.28,

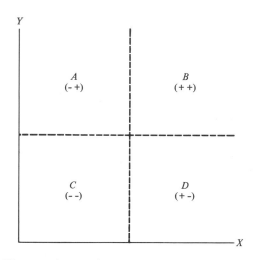

FIGURE 6.28   The quadrant of a scatterplot divided into four subregions

which represents the quadrant of a typical scatterplot divided into four subregions, *A*, *B*, *C*, and *D*.   If a positive relationship exists, there will be many dots which fall in Regions *B* and *C* and there will be only a few in Regions *A* and *D*.   On the other hand, if a negative relationship occurs, there will be a large number of observational points in Regions *A* and *D*, while only a few will fall in Regions *B* and *C*.   When there is no relationship, the dots will be approximately equally divided among the four regions.   If the subregions are then viewed as representing a new coordinate system with the origin (the zero point) at the intersection of the dotted lines, every dot which falls in Region *B* will be numerically represented by coordinates, both of which have a positive sign.   Similarly, every dot which falls in Region *C* will be represented by coordinates, both of which have a negative sign; and dots falling in Regions *A* and *D* will be represented by coordinates such that one has a plus sign and the other has a minus sign.   Remembering that when two positive numbers *or* two negative numbers are multiplied, the product is positive, and that when two numbers with *un*like signs are multiplied, the product is negative, it is apparent that multiplying the two numbers (i.e., the X coordinate and the Y coordinate) which locate the observation in the *new* coordinate system will result in a positive product for every dot in Region B or C and a negative product for every dot in Region A or D. Thus, by adding such products, a desirable index would be obtained because every dot in B or C would increase the size of the measure and every dot in Region A and D would decrease the size of the index. The only other problem is to eliminate the effects of sample size; and this, as in the case of the standard deviation, can be done by taking the average of the products rather than the sum.

Logically, then, a useful index is the average of the products of the coordinates in the new system. The only tasks that remain are the practical ones of deciding (1) where exactly to put the dotted lines and (2) how to eliminate the effects of different units in which the Characteristic X and Characteristic Y might be measured.

Since it would seem appropriate to locate the dotted lines somewhere near the center of the distribution along the X axis and somewhere near the center of the distribution along the Y axis, what better place than at the mean of X and Y, respectively? By taking deviation scores $X_i - \overline{X}$ and $Y_i - \overline{Y}$, values in the new coordinate system are obtained. That is, every pair of observations such that both measures are above average will fall in Region B and have two plus signs for coordinates; every pair of observations for which the X measure is above average and the Y measure is below average will fall in Region D and have an X coordinate which is plus but a Y coordinate which is minus, and similarly for those below average on both measures and those below average on Measure X but above average on Measure Y.

To eliminate the effect of the different units and achieve a purely numerical scale, it is a simple matter to divide the deviation scores just obtained by the standard deviation of the respective measures. Instead of the original raw scores, each observation will be transposed to the new coordinate system and new scale by using

$$\frac{X_i - \overline{X}}{s_x} \quad \text{and} \quad \frac{Y_i - \overline{Y}}{s_y}$$

The reader will immediately recognize the latter as the standard scores developed in the previous section. Averaging the products of the coordinates in this new system results in the desired index. In short, the Pearson product-moment correlation coefficient is the average of the products of the standard scores on the two variables and can be expressed algebraically as

$$r_{xy} = \frac{\sum \left(\frac{X_i - \overline{X}}{s_x} \right)\left(\frac{Y_i - \overline{Y}}{s_y} \right)}{N}$$

This "understanding" formula can be simplified for computational purposes
to

$$r_{xy} = \frac{N\Sigma X_i Y_i - \Sigma X_i \Sigma Y_i}{\sqrt{[N\Sigma X_i^2 - (\Sigma X_i)^2][N\Sigma Y_1^2 - (\Sigma Y_i)^2]}}$$

and the application of the latter to the data of Table 6.1 is shown in Table 6.9.
Traditionally, when we speak of population parameters rather than sample
estimates, the Greek symbol ρ_{xy} is used rather than the English notation shown
above.

The Pearson product-moment correlation coefficient is such that when a
perfect direct relationship exists, the index takes on a value of $+1.00$; when
a perfect inverse relationship occurs, the correlation becomes -1.00; and
when no relationship exists, the value of the index is 0.00. To interpret a
correlation coefficient properly, then, it is necessary first to note the numerical
value, which indicates the *degree* of relationship, and then to note the algebraic sign, which indicates the *direction* of the relationship. While, in general,
the larger the relationship, the closer the numerical value will be to 1, a corre-

TABLE 6.9
Illustration of the Calculation of the Pearson Product-Moment
Correlation Coefficient

i	X_i	X_i^2	Y_i	Y_i^2	$X_i Y_i$
1	50	2500	16	256	800
2	45	2025	12	144	540
3	43	1849	13	169	559
.	.	.	.	.	.
.	.	.	.	.	.
.	.	.	.	.	.
49	41	1681	11	121	451
50	45	2025	17	289	765
Σ	1945	77003	617	8515	24859

$$r_{xy} = \frac{N\Sigma X_i Y_i - \Sigma X_i \Sigma Y_i}{\sqrt{[N\Sigma X_i^2 - (\Sigma X_i)^2][N\Sigma Y_i^2 - (\Sigma Y)^2]}}$$

$$= \frac{50(24859) - (1945)(617)}{\sqrt{[50(77003) - (1945)^2][50(8515) - (617)^2]}}$$

$$= \frac{42885}{54997.46}$$

$$= 0.78$$

Data from Table 6.1, pp. 185–186.

lation must *not* be interpreted as a percentage. It can be shown that it is the *square* of the correlation coefficient which indicates the percentage of one characteristic that can be accounted for by the other. Thus, a correlation of .50 between an independent and a dependent variable indicates that about 25 percent (.50 × .50) of the variation along the dependent variable can be accounted for by differences in the independent variable.

One additional and very important point to remember about the interpretation of a correlation coefficient is that it is a descriptive index and therefore must *not* be interpreted to mean causation. As suggested in Chapter 3 and again in Chapter 4, an association between two characteristics is a necessary but not a sufficient condition for causation. To illustrate this point, it was reported in the *Journal of the Royal Statistical Society of England*, Vol. 89 (1926) that, based on data gathered for the years 1875 to 1890, there was a correlation of −.98 between the birth rate in Great Britain and the production of pig iron in the United States. This does *not* mean that the United States can control the birth rate in Great Britain or vice versa or that the British can control the production of pig iron in the United States but only that during the years of observation, when the production of pig iron in this country went up, the birth rate in Great Britain went down, and when the birth rate in Great Britain went up, the production of pig iron in this country went down. It can also be shown that there is a substantial correlation between the hardness of asphalt and the death rate of new-born infants or between the number of ministers in town and the amount of liquor consumed. In both these latter instances, it is more obvious that such occurrences result when a third (unobserved) variable produces simultaneous changes in both variables observed. Thus, temperature affects both the hardness of asphalt and the death rate of newborns, and the larger the city, the larger both the number of ministers and the amount of liquor consumed by the populace. Again, while a correlation may suggest the possibility of a causal relationship, it *alone* does not provide a basis for inferring causation.

OTHER MEASURES OF RELATIONSHIP   The Pearson product-moment correlation coefficient is the appropriate index to use to describe the degree of relationship when (1) two characteristics are involved; (2) both variables are continuous; (3) both variables are measured on at least the interval level of measurement; and (4) the relationship between the two characteristics can be assumed to be linear. When any one or several of these conditions are violated, the product-moment correlation will *not* accurately describe the amount of association among the variables under investigation. Some other correlational procedure must be used. While the development of the particular techniques which are useful under various circumstances is properly the topic of a book in statistics and not one in research methods, Table 6.10 summarizes the most commonly used of such indexes.

TABLE 6.10
Commonly Used Measures of Association for Different Types of Variables

Nature of Variables Involved	Restrictions, Assumptions, or Comments	Measure of Association to Use
2 continuous variables	linear relationship interval or ratio scales	Pearson product-moment correlation
2 continuous variables	ordinal scales	rank-order correlation or Kendall's tau
2 continuous variables both of which have been dichotomized	normal bivariate distribution of the two variables	tetrachoric correlation
1 continuous variable 1 variable, either continuous or a discrete set of categories	nonlinear relationship	correlation ratio (eta coefficient)
1 continuous variable 1 variable, a discrete set of categories	intent is to ascertain degree of similarity within groups interval or ratio scale	intraclass correlation
1 continuous variable 1 continuous variable which has been dichotomized	interval or ratio scale	biserial correlation
1 continuous variable 1 true dichotomy	interval or ratio scale	point biserial correlation
2 true dichotomies	nominal or ordinal scale	fourfold point correlation (phi coefficient)
2 sets of unordered categories	nominal scale	contingency coefficient
1 set of unordered categories 1 or more variables of any sort	intent is to determine degree of similarity among the group on basis of several measures	Mahalanobis' D^2 (from linear discriminant function) or multiple biserial correlation
3 or more continuous variables	intent is to find the degree of relationship between any two with the effects of the others held constant	partial correlation
3 or more continuous variables	intent is to determine predictability of one variable on basis of several others— linear relationships	multiple correlation (from multiple regression)
3 or more continuous variables	intent is to determine the overall amount of agreement—ordinal scale	Kendall's coefficient of concordance
3 or more continuous variables	estimates average of intercorrelations between pairs	intraclass correlation

Describing Functional Relationships

Whenever a correlation coefficient or one of the other measures listed in Table 6.10 indicates that there is a substantial degree of relationship between two characteristics, it certainly seems reasonable to try to specify the precise nature of this relationship by developing a curve that expresses the functional relationship (that is, shows exactly how one characteristic changes with shifts in the other) between the two variables. Once we have such a curve, it is possible to predict a specific value of one characteristic when given a specific value for the other. For example, if the precise nature of the relationship between test scores and grades in college can be plotted, then, given a test score for some particular person, it is possible to make a prediction about what his grade-point average will be.

In statistics this process of specifying the exact nature of the relationship between two characteristics is referred to either as *regression analysis* or as *curve-fitting*. Usually, the former term is reserved for those situations in which there is a scattering of points, each representing a pair of observations, and the task is to find a curve that best fits the scatterplot of observed data. The latter term is used when the task is to determine whether the data follow a particular frequency distribution or whether a trend of single observations made over a sequence of time (as in a learning curve) follows some predetermined pattern. In general, whenever a prediction is made (of grade-point, for example, or of the amount learned after so many trials), the predic*tor* variable is referred to as the *independent* variable and the predic*ted* characteristic is referred to as the dependent or the *criterion* variable. While full discussions of regression analysis and of curve-fitting are beyond the scope of this text, it is essential to have some knowledge of what is involved in these two processes.

REGRESSION ANALYSIS   Basically, the task of regression is that of finding some algebraic expression by which to represent the functional relationship between two (or more) characteristics, given some observations of one characteristic at specified values of another. For example, one might observe the grade-point averages of persons who received test scores of 50, 58, 73, 108, etc., and from this information try to fit a curve which would permit the prediction of the grade-point average of a prospective student who gets a score of 87.

The first thing to do is to determine the approximate shape of the relationship. That is, one must first make a judgment as to whether the relationship follows a straight line or is a parabola, an exponential curve, or some other form. And, while there are some elaborate "finite-difference" techniques for determining the relationship, the most common way is to make a scatterplot and by visual inspection judge the type of curve required.

Once the type of curve has been decided upon, the next task is to use the observations to obtain estimates of the parameters which are required to express that curve algebraically. For example, if a straight line is judged to be appropriate, the functional relationship is assumed to be $Y = a + bX$, and the values a and b are the parameters to be estimated from the observations; if the relationship is judged to be an exponential curve, the functional relationship assumed is $Y = AB^X$ and the parameters to be estimated are A and B, and similarly for other possible curves.

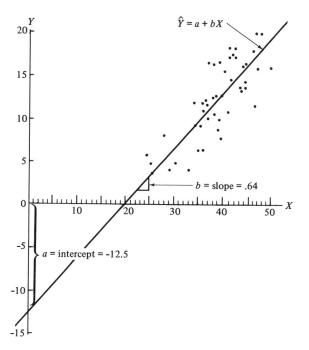

FIGURE 6.29   The regression line which best fits the data of Table 6.1

The logic involved in the estimation of a set of parameters in the process of fitting a curve is essentially to select those values for the parameters which produce the curve that gives the best fit of the observational points in the scatterplot. For example, in the case of the data of Table 6.1, it was felt that a straight line would adequately fit the scatterplot and those particular values of a and b which resulted in the best fit were: $a = -12.5$ and $b = 0.64$, as seen in Figure 6.29.

One important question, of course, is what is meant by "best fit." While there are several ways of deciding this matter, one of the most common criterion is that called the *least squares*. According to the concept of least squares, the best-fitting line is that for which the sums of the squares of the *vertical* deviations of all the points to the line is as small as possible. The use of the vertical distance rather than either the horizontal distance or the most direct distance (i.e., perpendicular to the line) is appropriate because, in most regression applications, the ultimate purpose is to predict the Y variable from the X variable, and under these circumstances, the vertical deviation from the actual observation to the line is the error in prediction. Using the square of the deviation rather than the actual distance itself has the effect of giving large errors heavier weight than small errors when fitting the curve.

Once the basic parameters of the curve have been estimated by the least squares or some other procedure (for example, the maximum-likelihood method, which selects those parameters that provide the maximum likelihood for the occurrence of the data actually observed) for obtaining the best fit, one substitutes these estimated values in the expression for the curve and uses this specific curve as representing the functional relationship between the two characteristics. Thus, in the example of this chapter, the relationship between the scores on the two tests can be expressed as $Y = -12.5 + 0.64X$.

CURVE-FITTING   The initial stages of the process of curve-fitting,[10] whether matching data to a hypothetical frequency distribution or to a learning curve, are logically the same as regression analysis. One estimates the necessary parameters of the plausible theoretical curves from the observations actually obtained. Once the specific functional relationship has been obtained, however, there is a slight difference in the two approaches. In regression analysis, the correlation coefficient (or multiple correlation coefficient if more than one predictor variable is involved) provides a numerical index of how good the fit of the actual points to the curve is. In fitting a frequency distribution or a learning curve, however, one additional step is necessary to get an indication of goodness of fit.

In these latter situations, a goodness-of-fit index is obtained by calculating a so-called chi-square (χ^2). By definition,

$$\chi^2 = \sum \frac{(O - E)^2}{E}$$

where O = observed value
       E = expected value

In the case of the frequency distribution, the observed and expected values are, respectively, the frequencies actually found and anticipated in the various class intervals and the sum is taken over all categories used. In the fitting of a learning curve, the values are the actual and estimated Y values, and the sum is taken over all values of X for which observations were actually made.

The interpretation of the chi-square is just the opposite of the correlation coefficient. While a large correlation indicates a high accuracy of fit, a large chi-square indicates considerable disagreement between the observed and the

[10] An excellent discussion of the process of curve-fitting can be found in Lewis (1960).

expected values. In both cases, it is possible to run a test of hypothesis to determine whether the observed deviations are larger than one would expect by chance, assuming the theoretical curve.

DISCRIMINANT FUNCTION   When expressing the functional relationship between two characteristics by means of either regression analysis or curve-fitting, we generally assume that the variables involved are continuous or at least ordered categories.   Sometimes, however, the characteristic to be predicted is qualitative rather than quantitative, and the task is not that of determining from other information to what extent some characteristic is possessed but of determining to what classification group an individual belongs. For example, on the basis of several measures, it might be desirable to try and predict one's occupation, one's socioeconomic category, or one's clinical grouping according to anticipated response to certain types of therapy.   In these cases, the predicted variable is a set of discrete and often unordered categories.

Whenever the criterion variable is a set of unordered categories, the relationship between the predictor variables and the criterion is expressed by means of the *discriminant function*.   Discriminant-function analysis is very similar to regression analysis, except that the criterion used in obtaining the best estimates of the parameters involved is that of minimizing the number of misclassifications rather than minimizing the sum of squares of errors of prediction.   The discriminant function itself is analogous to the regression equation, except that a different discriminant function is needed for every pair of criterion groups, while only one regression equation is needed for any criterion variable.   Finally, just as the correlation coefficient and the chi-square value can be used as an index of the goodness of fit of the functional relationship, an index called *Mahalanobis' D^2* can serve as an index of the accuracy of classification achieved by means of the discriminant function.   In this case, the larger the D^2 value, the greater the distance between the groups involved and the less likely it is that a person who belongs to one group will be misclassified into the other.

TESTING HYPOTHESES IN THE FACE OF UNCERTAINTY

The Necessity for Testing Hypotheses

There would be no need for any further statistics if the investigator was satisfied to limit the discussion of his results only to those particular individuals on whom actual measurements were made.   The calculated mean *does* describe the group's typical performance, the calculated standard deviation *does* provide an accurate description of the homogeneity of the group on whom the measurements were obtained, and the calculated correlation *does* describe the extent of association between two traits as possessed by those individuals on whom observations were made.

But very seldom is the research worker satisfied to let things rest with a description of only those particular persons on whom he has gathered data. Rather, the achievement of this year's class, which was taught by Method A, is described in the hope that it will tell us something about the likely accomplishment of *next* year's class if it is to be taught by the same method. The research worker calculates the degree of relationship between intelligence and achievement on one sample and assumes that the same relationship will hold with other similar groups. The research worker almost always wants to apply the results and conclusions of his study to persons other than those particular ones on whom the observations were actually made.

The minute an attempt is made to apply any results or conclusions to even one person who was not in the group on whom data were gathered, the investigator is generalizing from a specific sample of instances to a larger population. That is, he is saying that there exists an entire universe of individuals of which those on whom he has made observations are but a subset or sample; and he is inferring that what he found in the sample will also hold true for the entire universe.

Making inferences from a specific instance to a general case is a perfectly legitimate though risky process called *inductive reasoning*. It is risky in that there is a great tendency to overgeneralize and draw conclusions far beyond the limits strict logic allows; and it is legitimate in that, if the logic is carefully followed, generalizing from the specific observations to new cases from the same population does provide useful information. As suggested in Chapter 1, no one starts out each new day from scratch; it is always assumed that what happened in one instance yesterday will also happen in a similar instance today.

The problem is that only *some* of what is observed in a particular instance is generalizable; the rest is attributable to the uniqueness of the particular time or the particular individual—that is, unique to the particular sample at hand. When a test of a statistical hypothesis is made, the question raised is whether what has been observed can be generalized to the population or whether what has been observed can be explained entirely as attributable to the particular circumstances under which the sample was measured.

If the observations are generalizable, it is said that the result is statistically significant; if the data can be explained as only a sampling fluctuation, then the result is described as not significant. It is especially important to see that statistical significance indicates only *whether* what was observed in the sample can be inferred for the entire population and *not* how important what was found is in any practical sense. It is essential to distinguish between statistical significance and practical importance. The latter is a value judgment as to how much the result is worth for some particular practical or theoretical use;

the former simply answers the question, can these results be attributable to chance fluctuations in sampling? If the answer is yes, the result is not significant; if the answer is no, the result is significant. Obviously, it is possible to judge the practical importance of a result *if and only if* the result is, first, statistically significant.

The General Steps in Statistical Problem Solving

FORMULATING A STATISTICAL HYPOTHESIS   The first step in statistical problem solving is that of translating the verbally stated scientific hypothesis into a meaningful statistical hypothesis. For example, if the scientific task is to determine whether a particular treatment will have an effect on the performance of persons to whom it is applied and the procedure has been to administer the treatment to one group and not to a second, the statistical hypothesis could be that there is no difference between the mean performance of the two groups after the treatment. Or, if the scientific task is to determine whether persons who are highly intelligent are also highly creative, the statistical hypothesis might be that there is no correlation between the two characteristics as measured.

Note that the statistical hypothesis refines the scientific hypothesis first by stating precisely the particular descriptive characteristic which is relevant and second by specifying exactly an assumed condition (or set of conditions) about the population. In the first case above, the descriptive index specified by the statistical hypothesis was the arithmetical mean, and the population condition assumed was that of no difference between the two groups. In the second case above, the descriptive index specified was that of correlation, and the condition assumed for the population was that the relationship was zero.

The reader will be quick to realize that the specific set of conditions assumed about the population may or may not be true. As a matter of fact, that is what the investigator is trying to find out. He will also recognize that, often, the statistical hypothesis specifies a set of conditions which are just the opposite of that which the experimenter really expects to find. (Note that in the two cases cited above the statistical hypothesis was that of no difference or of no relationship—the *null* hypothesis—when it is likely that the researcher actually anticipated a difference between the treated and nontreated groups and probably expected to find intelligence and creativity to be related.)

The crucial aspect of the set of conditions specified about the population in stating the statistical hypothesis is that the conditions be such that *if* (and only if) they exist, then they will yield a set of sample observations which themselves (or some combination of them) will have some particular mathematical frequency distribution in repeated sampling. That is, the research worker first pretends the hypothesis is true. Then he says, "Suppose I took all possible samples of a particular size from this population (in which the hypothesis is true) and computed a combination of the observations, C (perhaps a mean), for each different sample. Then, if I make a frequency distribution of all the C's, the result, if I have a usable statistical hypothesis, will be a normal distribution, a *t* distribution, an *F* distribution, a chi-square distribution, a binomial distribution, or some other known mathematical frequency distribution."

It is precisely because the assumed set of conditions specified about the population by the statistical hypothesis must yield a known mathematical frequency distribution that the statistical hypothesis is so often a null hypothesis. If the statistical hypothesis were to assume a difference (in the population) of 18 points between performances of treated and untreated groups, the resulting sampling distribution is not generally known.[11] Also, the state of knowledge about human behavior is not yet such that the investigator can specify a particular mean difference or a particular value for the anticipated correlation between two characteristics. Some day it may be possible that a highly developed theory of human behavior will suggest a difference of exactly 18 points between treated and untreated groups or a correlation of precisely .76 between creativity and intelligence, and it will then no longer be necessary to make use of the null hypothesis. Until this time, however, most of the statistical hypotheses in practical use will specify no difference or no relationship in the population.

MAKING THE OBSERVATIONS   The second step in the process of statistical problem solving is that of making observations—that is, of taking one of all the possible samples of a given size considered in the first step and calculating the particular combination of the observations that if the hypothesis is true, will yield a known mathematical frequency distribution. To take two or three samples is logically equivalent to taking but one sample of greater size. Thus, even though the sampling distribution may change slightly, the logical process of testing hypotheses through statistical reasoning does not.

Exactly what particular combination of observations should be used is a mathematical problem which will not be discussed here. In practice, it turns out that there is a particular *test statistic* for which a formula can be written for each of the commonly used statistical hypotheses, just as there is a descriptive statistic for each of the major characteristics of a group of observations that needs to be described. The appropriate test statistics to use under a variety of circumstances are presented later in this chapter (Table 6.13) as part of a discussion that illustrates the logical steps of hypothesis testing with concrete examples.

[11] Actually, the procedure for obtaining such a distribution is straightforward. The problem is that a separate distribution would have to be calculated and tabled for each possible difference between the two groups—for 18, for 19, for 20, etc. Since it is not feasible to publish an infinite set of tables giving the distribution for all possible values, a single table showing the distribution for the assumption of no difference is used.

LOCATING THE OBSERVED TEST STATISTIC IN THE MATHEMATICAL FREQUENCY
DISTRIBUTION   Once the statistical hypothesis has been formulated, a sample
of observations taken, and the appropriate test statistic calculated, the third
step in testing hypotheses is that of locating the particular observed test statistic obtained in the mathematical frequency distribution.   Mathematically,
this is accomplished by using some form of the standard score—i.e., by subtracting the mean of the sampling distribution (the theoretical mathematical
frequency distribution) from the observed value and dividing the difference
by the standard deviation of the sampling distribution.   In practice, the
standard score form is already incorporated into the formula for many of the
test statistics, so that the operational procedure at this point is simply that of
comparing the observed test statistic with a tabled value.

MAKING A DECISION   The final logical step of testing hypotheses in the face
of uncertainty is that of making a decision to accept or reject the statistical
hypothesis.   If the observed test statistic could easily have come from the

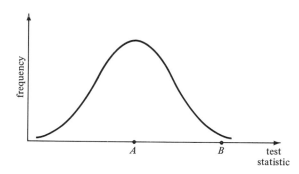

FIGURE 6.30   A mathematical frequency distribution obtained in repeated
sampling when the statistical hypothesis is true

mathematical frequency distribution (obtained if and only if the hypothesis
is true) the hypothesis will be accepted.   If, on the other hand, the value
found would occur only very rarely in the sampling distribution, then the
statistical hypothesis will be rejected.

For example, suppose the mathematical sampling distribution obtained
under the conditions of the statistical hypothesis (i.e., obtained when, in fact,
the statistical hypothesis *is* true) was that shown in Figure 6.30.   If the calculated test statistic fell at Point *A* in the sampling distribution, the statistical
hypothesis would be accepted because observed values like those obtained
occur quite frequently when the hypothesis is true.   On the other hand, if the
value of the test statistic obtained from the sample fell near Point *B*, the researcher would probably reject the hypothesis, because test statistics of size *B*

occur so seldom when the hypothesis is true that it is more likely that some alternative hypothesis is true.

Once the statistical hypothesis has been accepted or rejected, the answer to the original scientific question has been determined. It should be remembered that, if the statistical hypothesis was in the common null form, its rejection means the acceptance of the scientific hypothesis, and the acceptance of the null hypothesis represents the rejection of the scientific hypothesis. It should also be recalled that to ascertain the statistical significance of a result (i.e., to reject a null hypothesis) does not provide any information about the practical importance of the results. To reject the hypothesis that there is no difference between the performance of those in a treatment and those in a no-treatment group says nothing about whether the difference observed is large enough to be of any practical value—only that what difference was found could not be attributable to sampling fluctuations.

The Possible Errors of Statistical Decisions

TYPE I AND TYPE II ERRORS   The careful reader of the preceding section will have noted that a person who rejects the null hypothesis, even when the observed test statistic is in the tail of the sampling distribution, may be wrong. It is certainly possible that the investigator has experienced a rare event. The area under the curve to the right of Point B in Figure 6.30 represents the number of times a test statistic as large or larger than B can be obtained *when the hypothesis is true*. Why then did the investigator decide to reject the hypothesis? The answer is that while a test statistic of size B (or larger) may occur once in a thousand times when the hypothesis is true such a value may occur 682 times in a thousand when the null hypothesis is false and some alternative hypothesis is true. The research worker is better off taking a 682/1000 chance than a 1/1000 chance. Under the circumstances his best judgment would be to reject the null hypothesis, even though there is a slight chance of being wrong.

At first it might seem possible to avoid error in rejecting the hypothesis by simply setting a more stringent requirement on the test statistic—that is, requiring it to be further out in the tail. Unfortunately, most sampling distributions are asymptotic to the base line, thus they never quite touch the axis; and there will always be some possibility of making an error of this type (i.e., of rejecting the hypothesis when it is true). Logically, then, it is not possible to reject a hypothesis with complete certainty.[12]

If the research worker does not reject his null hypothesis, the only other

[12] On rare occasions, when the investigator is attempting to generalize only to a specific and restricted finite population, the sampling distribution may not be asymptotic, and thus complete certainty can be achieved. This can be accomplished, however, only by taking a considerable risk of making a second type of error to be described later. Thus, for all practical situations this statement is accurate.

alternatives are to accept it or to withhold a decision. If the latter is his choice, the investigator's behavior is the same as before he started the experiment and therefore, temporarily at least he is accepting it. Thus, for all practical purposes, it can be said that the only alternatives are to reject or to accept the hypothesis.

Since the experimenter is always faced with the possibility of error when he rejects the hypothesis, it might be asked whether he avoids error should he accept the hypothesis. Again the answer is no, for there is always the possibility of accepting a false hypothesis. There is always the possibility that some alternative phenomenon has produced the observed results, even though they also occur quite frequently under the conditions specified by the statistical hypothesis.

Investigator's Decision	State of Nature	
	Hypothesis is true	Hypothesis is false
Reject hypothesis	type I error	no error
Accept hypothesis	no error	type II error

FIGURE 6.31   The two types of errors that can occur when deciding to accept or reject a scientific hypothesis

In making a decision to accept or to reject a hypothesis, therefore, there are two types of errors which can be made: the rejection of a true hypothesis and the acceptance of a false hypothesis. As shown in Figure 6.31, rejecting a true hypothesis is called a Type I error and accepting a false hypothesis is called a Type II error.

These two types of errors place the research worker in a serious dilemma. For as it turns out, as the likelihood of making one of these types of errors is decreased, the likelihood of making the other automatically increases. That this is the case can easily be seen by considering an oversimplified problem of attempting to determine whether persons in a particular occupational group are average in scholastic ability (i.e., have an IQ of 100).

A research worker might decide that one way of answering this question would be to draw a sample of persons who are engaged in the particular occupation and administer to them a measure of scholastic ability scored in terms of IQ. It would be obvious to him that if the mean IQ for his sample were close to but not equal to 100, he would have no basis for rejecting the hypothesis that his group was average, for small deviations from IQ of 100 could be the result of chance fluctuations which occurred in the drawing of the sample. Similarly, it would be obvious to the investigator that if the observed IQ was very large, he would have evidence that his group was above average. The problem is that of determining the particular value at which he should change his mind from accepting the hypothesis of no difference from average to rejecting this hypothesis in favor of the alternative one that the occupational group is above average.

To help decide the answer to his question the investigator might obtain a sampling distribution for means; i.e., he might get the frequency distribution of all the means obtained by taking all possible samples of the size he had from a population where it is known that the true average IQ was 100. Such a sampling distribution would be quite similar to that shown in Figure 6.30 and indicates how often it is possible to get a particular observed value for the average IQ of a sample, even though, in the population, the true average was 100. Upon noting that in this sampling distribution of means an $\bar{X}$ of 105 occurs quite frequently, when, in fact, the true population mean is 100, the researcher might conclude that he should reject the hypothesis that his occupational group is average only if the observed value of the mean is very very large, say, when $\bar{X} = 185$ or higher. By doing this, he would almost never make the mistake of rejecting the hypothesis when it was true. Suppose, however, the average of the IQ's calculated for his group turned out to be 180. Since this value is not greater than the 185 he specified in order to avoid making a Type I error very often, he must accept the hypothesis that this group is only average. It is obvious that, if the investigator were to accept the hypothesis that the group was average, when the average of their IQ's was 180, he is very likely to be making a Type II error.

Similarly, suppose he decided to avoid the Type II error just described by accepting the hypothesis only when the observed average IQ was within one point of 100 (i.e., between 99 and 101). If the calculated IQ turned out to be 102, he would have to reject the hypothesis that the group was average. Yet, looking at the sampling distribution, the investigator would discover that sample mean IQ's of 102 occur almost (but not quite) as often when the true IQ of the population is 100 as do sample mean IQ's of 100. Under these circumstances the research worker is not likely to make a Type II error, but he is very likely to make a Type I error. Thus, if the researcher sets the decision point at which he changes his mind from accept to reject near Point A, he has a small chance of making a Type II error (accepting the hypothesis when it is false) but a large chance of making a Type I error (rejecting a true hypothesis). As the decision point is moved further and further toward Point B, the chance of making a Type I error is decreased, but the chances of making a Type II error are increased.

Faced with the dilemma described above, it has not been easy to establish a set of completely acceptable principles for selecting the critical value above which the researcher will reject the hypothesis and below which the researcher will accept the hypothesis. Up to the present time, three major different procedures have been suggested and followed. Historically, the earliest rule seems to be that of selecting a point three standard deviations above the mean of a sampling distribution (the critical ratio procedure). If the calculated critical ratio were three or higher, the hypothesis was to be rejected; if less than that, it was to be accepted. The use of this critical ratio procedure was simple and straightforward, and it minimized the chances of making a Type I error, that is, of rejecting the null hypothesis when it was true. As long as large samples were used, so that the sampling distributions were always approximately normal, no great problems arose. However, with the widespread use of sampling distributions such as the t distribution, the chi-square distribution, the F distribution, and others, in situations where they did not approximate the normal distribution too closely, problems arose. Under these latter circumstances, when the same critical ratio was used with all types of sampling distributions, the probability of making a Type I error varied from one sampling distribution to the next; and thus what appeared to be a common criterion was not so standard after all.

The next stage of development was that of specifying a particular probability of making a Type I error (the significance level) and using that as a standard no matter what the shape of the sampling distribution. During this stage, two significance levels (i.e., two probabilities of making a Type I error) came into common usage: the .01 level and the .05 level. A hypothesis rejected at the 1 percent level was said to be highly significant, and a hypothesis rejected at the 5 percent level was described as significant. In time researchers became more and more dissatisfied with the arbitrarily fixed significance levels of .01 and .05, and they became more and more concerned with Type II errors, which the significance level procedure ignored completely.

The most recent trend is toward a decision-theory approach which considers both types of errors. Basically, the decision-theory approach requires two things: (1) a calculation of the likelihood of making both types of errors; and (2) a value judgment as to how serious each type of error is likely to be. Then, some general strategy, such as minimizing the maximum loss or minimizing the overall loss, is applied to the information about the seriousness and likelihood of each type of error to arrive at a specific critical value.

In actual practice, the biggest problem faced by the research worker seems to be that of specifying the seriousness of the two types of errors. First, the seriousness of each kind of error is a value judgment to be made after considering the consequences of behaving as if a hypothesis were true, only to find out later it was false, as compared with the consequences of behaving as if the hypothesis were false, only to find out later that it was true. Not only are the consequences difficult to enumerate, or even imagine in the case of certain basic research problems, but each different individual also makes his own value judgment of the loss subsequently incurred.

Second, such value judgments must be made in specific, numerical terms—not just through broad, general, verbal statements. If decision theory is to work, the research worker cannot simply say that making a Type I error is a lot more serious than making a Type II error. Rather, he must say that a Type I error has a seriousness of degree 100 and a Type II error has a seriousness of degree 15—or at the very least say that a Type I error is seven times as bad as a Type II error under present conditions.[13]

Because of the difficulties in making explicit use of the decision-theory approach, most current investigators use it only on an informal basis. They carefully consider the consequences of each of the two types of errors in their particular circumstances and study the relationships between the two types of errors for the alternative hypotheses which are plausible before making their decision. Then, recognizing that the decision to accept or reject is in part a value judgment, they describe the location of their observed test statistic in the sampling distribution, so that other investigators, making different value judgments (because their situation is slightly different), can make their own intelligent decision as to whether to accept or reject the hypothesis under investigation.

The modern behavioral scientist, then, cannot rely upon the blind application of arbitrary standards such as the 5 percent or the 1 percent levels of significance. Rather, he must clearly see the relationship between the two logically possible errors he can make and how they change for each of the different alternative hypotheses which might be true. A more precise picture of how the Type I and Type II errors change as the critical decision point is shifted from the center of the sampling distribution toward the tail can be gained by careful study of Figure 6.32.

The decision situation represented by Figure 6.32 is essentially that which was discussed earlier, of attempting to determine whether a particular group of persons had some specified mean score. In statistical terms, the hypothesis under investigation is whether a population mean, μ, has some specific value, μ_0. The top half of the figure represents the sampling distribution of X's (that is, the relative frequency distribution of all the different $\overline{X}$'s obtained by taking all possible samples of a given size) obtained under the condition that the hypothesis is true. The top half of Figure 6.32 represents all the possibilities for the first column of Figure 6.31, showing the two types of error. Similarly, the bottom half of Figure 6.32 represents one of the set of many possibilities in which the second column of Figure 6.31 holds. That is, the bottom frequency distribution is the sampling distribution which would be

---

[13] Hills (1964), studying problems of college choice, has demonstrated that it is possible for even relatively naive people to make value judgments of a similar nature on a numerical scale.

obtained when one of the alternative hypotheses holds: namely, that μ equals μ_a instead of μ_0. Other possible alternative hypotheses would be represented by shifting the bottom frequency distribution to the right or left, depending upon how different the particular alternative hypothesis which held was from

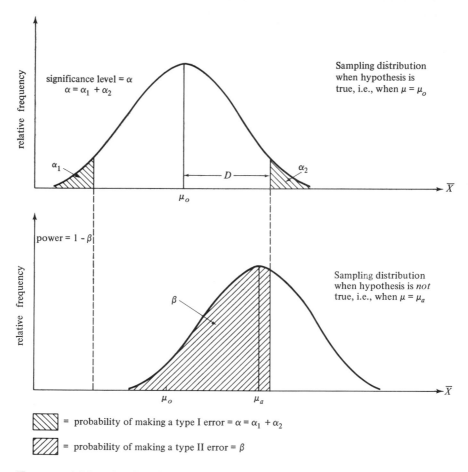

FIGURE 6.32   Application of a two-tailed critical region to hypothetical sampling distributions which occur when the hypothesis is and when it is not true

the original hypothesis specified. Thus, if $\mu_a - \mu_0$ were large (indicating that the postulated value was a long way off), the bottom distribution would be shifted to the right, and if the postulated value and the actual alternative value were close, the lower sampling distribution would be shifted to the left.

Assume that the research worker decided that if his observed mean ($\bar{X}$) fell more than a distance D from the hypothesized value μ_0, he would reject his hypothesis but that if it fell within the region $\mu_0 \pm D$, he would accept the hypothesis. Assuming that the hypothesis $\mu = \mu_0$ is true, the number of times in repeated sampling the research worker would make a Type I error is indicated by the shaded area in the upper curve. Thus, the significance level, $\alpha = \alpha_1 + \alpha_2$.

But what would happen if the investigator applied the same decision rule (reject if $\overline{X}$ fell beyond $\mu_0 \pm D$, accept if $\overline{X}$ fell within $\mu_0 \pm D$) when some alternative hypothesis $\mu = \mu_a$ was true? [14] In this case, the sampling distribution is that portrayed in the bottom half of Figure 6.32, and the error (Type II) is made when he *accepts* the hypothesis. Thus, the probability of making a Type II error is the shaded portion of the lower curve and is denoted by the symbol β.

Note that if the investigator wishes to reduce the probability of making a Type I error, he can do so by increasing the size of D. But this will increase the shaded area in the lower curve, thus increasing β, the probability of making a Type II error. Conversely, if the research worker were to reduce the chances of making a Type II error by decreasing the length of D, he would automatically increase the probability of making a Type I error (α).

Actually, the only possible way to decrease *both* types of errors at the same time is to increase the sample size, since a larger sample will result in a smaller standard deviation of both the upper and the lower sampling distributions. [15] Thus, in effect, the critical regions α_1 and α_2 would be, relatively, much further out in the tails of the curve, and the lower distribution would be shifted relatively to the right.

Also, it is apparent from Figure 6.32 that, for a given α, the magnitude of the Type II error will depend upon the difference between μ_0 and μ_a. For example, as the lower curve moves to the right (that is, the greater the positive difference between μ_0 and μ_a) β will become smaller; when $\mu_0 = \mu_a$, the Type II error will be at its maximum; and, as the difference between μ_0 and μ_a increases in a *negative* direction (i.e., for alternative hypotheses represented by a lower curve to the left of the top curve), the size of β will again decrease.

In summary, there are two types of errors. A Type I error is that of rejecting a hypothesis when it is true. The probability of making a Type I error is called the *significance level* and is designated by the symbol α. A Type II error is that of accepting a false hypothesis. The probability of making a Type II error is designated by the symbol β, and its converse, $1 - \beta$, is called the *power* of the significance test. In general, as α is decreased, β will increase, and as β is decreased, α will increase; but both α and β can be reduced by increasing the sample size. Finally, for a given α and sample size, the value

---

[14] It should be recalled that the problem under investigation is whether $\mu = \mu_0$ or $\mu = \mu_a$ is true.

[15] For example, in the case of estimating the mean, the standard deviation of the sampling distribution turns out to be $s_x/\sqrt{N}$, where s_x is the standard deviation of the original observations and N is the sample size.

of β will fluctuate inversely with the magnitude of the difference between the null and the alternative hypothesis as long as a two-tailed test is used.

TWO-TAILED AND ONE-TAILED TESTS   The statements made in the preceding paragraphs about the relationships between the two types of errors hold when the so-called *two-tailed* test portrayed in Figure 6.32 is made.   Sometimes it is not logically reasonable for the alternative hypotheses to deviate in both directions from the assumed null hypothesis.   For example, in an examination of the level of scholastic ability of a particular occupational group, it might not be reasonable to feel that members of the group could be below average. Under these circumstances, the question is not whether the group is average,

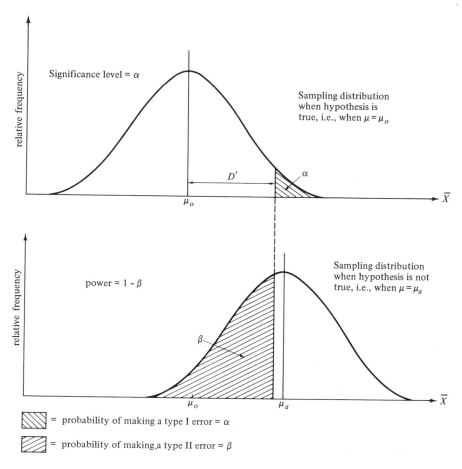

FIGURE 6.33   Application of a one-tailed critical region to hypothetical sampling distributions which occur when the hypothesis is and when it is not true

versus different from average, but rather whether the group is average or above average.

Whenever only one-sided alternatives are the reasonable ones, an increase in the power of a test (i.e., a reduction of the chances of making a Type II error) can be achieved while maintaining the same significance level by making a so-called *one-tailed* test of significance. In making a one-tailed test of significance, the entire critical region (that is, the region in which the null hypothesis will be rejected) is defined to be in one tail of the curve as shown in Figure 6.33. Careful comparison of Figures 6.33 and 6.32 will reveal that the total area of the shaded portion of the upper curve labeled α is identical in both cases. On the other hand, the shaded area in the lower curve, labeled β, is greatly reduced, even though the two frequency distributions themselves are identical in both figures. Thus, for a given α (the probability of making a Type I error), the β (the probability of making a Type II error) can be considerably reduced by defining the region of rejection to be in only one tail of the curve.

It should be remembered, however, that this approach to increasing the power while maintaining the same significance level is legitimate only when a restricted set of alternative hypotheses—a one-sided set—is logically possible. In the practical example given it will be recalled that the question was whether the average IQ for the particular group was equal to or greater than that of the general population and not merely whether it was different from that of the general population. In a practical sense, under these conditions the investigator has decided to reject the null hypothesis only if his observed $\bar{X}$ was greater than μ_0 by an amount D and to accept it whenever the obtained $\bar{X}$ was less than μ_0, even if it were less than μ_0 by an amount greater than D. Thus, any deviation from the hypothesis in the negative direction, no matter how great, would be considered by the researcher to be the result of a sampling error and not due to any real phenomenon.

Concrete Illustrations of the General Steps in Testing Hypotheses

Three basic problems which occur again and again in practice are those of (1) determining whether a mean of a group has a specific value, (2) determining whether there is an association between two characteristics, and (3) determining whether there is a difference among the means of two or more groups. The first practical problem has already been used as an illustration while describing the logic of testing hypotheses. To help fix this logic in mind, concrete illustrations of the latter two tasks will be provided in this section.

TESTING FOR AN ASSOCIATION BETWEEN TWO CHARACTERS   While the Pearson product-moment correlation coefficient or another appropriate index provides a measure of the degree of relationship between two characteristics in any observed sample, it is possible, through sampling peculiarities, to obtain a correlation coefficient of any magnitude, even when the population coefficient is zero. Thus, whenever a measure of relationship is obtained, it is essential to test it for significance if it is desired to make any inferences about persons other than those actually observed.

Suppose for purposes of illustration, that it was felt that dominant students earned better grades than did submissive students and that this possibility was taken as the scientific hypothesis to be tested. A straightforward way of testing this hypothesis would be to divide students into dominant and submissive groups, look up the grades of every student, and see if those classified as dominant did or did not average higher than those classified as submissive. In this case, the statistical hypothesis to be tested would be that there is no difference between the mean grade-point average of the two groups.

If, however, it is possible to describe students with respect to the *degree* of dominance rather than to just classify them as dominant or submissive, a more desirable approach can be used. Under these conditions, it is possible to test the scientific hypothesis by calculating the correlation coefficient between dominance and grades and test the statistical hypothesis that there is no relationship between the two variables.

The null hypothesis, it will be recalled, specifies a set of conditions about the *population* such that some combination of a sample of observations will have a particular mathematical frequency distribution. Using the product-moment correlation r as a convenient combination of observations, the question might be asked as to what value of r would be expected if the population correlation (between dominance and grades) were, in fact, equal to zero. Obviously, the expected value is zero, but it should be equally clear that, because of a chance combination of observations which appear in a particular sample, it is possible to get an observed correlation which has a value other than zero.

As an illustration of the fact that a calculated value of zero is not always obtained, even when the true correlation in the population is zero, consider the following situation. Suppose 10 poker chips are placed in each of two bowls, each chip being placed in a given bowl designated by a different number from 0 to 9. Now, since the two bowls are completely independent of one another, a situation has been created in which the true relationship between numbers obtained by drawing from one bowl and those obtained by drawing from the other is zero. That is, a situation has been created in which it is possible to obtain pairs of observations, just as is required for any correlation problem. In this instance, each draw from the two bowls is comparable to a subject, and the correlation under examination is that between the numbers drawn from Bowl A and the numbers drawn from Bowl B.

Now suppose that from this population in which the true relationship is zero a sample of size three were drawn. It could happen, by chance alone, that the results turned out as follows:

	Bowl A	Bowl B
Draw one	3	3
Draw two	8	8
Draw three	5	5

The value of r calculated on these particular observations would, of course, be 1.00, even though in the population the correlation between the numbers drawn from the two bowls is zero. Similarly, by chance alone, an observed correlation of any magnitude between and including -1.00 to $+1.00$ could be obtained, even though the population value is zero.

The actual probability of getting a correlation of any given size could be calculated. For example, if the drawing had been done with replacement of the chips selected each time, the probability of getting a three on the first draw from Bowl A *and* a three on the first draw from Bowl B would be $\frac{1}{10} \times \frac{1}{10} =$ .01; and the probability of getting 2 threes on the first draw *and* 2 eights on the second draw *and* 2 fives on the third would be $(.01)^3 = .000001$. If this value were then multiplied by the number of different combinations of 10 things taken three at a time, which would result in a perfect positive correlation $(10!/3!7! - 10)$, the probability of getting a perfect positive correlation when samples of size three are drawn from a population in which the true correlation is zero would be found to be .00011.

Without carrying out all the calculations, it should be obvious that the probability of getting a -1.00 correlation under the conditions of the null hypothesis in this situation would also be .00011; that the probability of getting an observed value of $r = .75$ is greater than that of getting a value of 1.00; that of getting a value of .20 greater than that of getting a value of .75; and so on, with the greatest probability (i.e., the most likely event when the true correlation is zero) being associated with an obtained value of $r =$ .00. If the entire set of calculated probabilities were then plotted against the various values of r, the result would be a sampling distribution similar to that shown by a solid line in Figure 6.34. An identical curve would be ob-

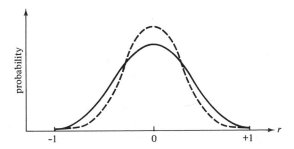

FIGURE 6.34 Sampling distributions for Pearson product-moment correlation coefficients when the population value is zero

tained if, instead of calculating the probabilities, we actually drew thousands of samples of size three and a frequency distribution of the resulting observed correlation coefficients were made.

Suppose that instead of a sample of size three (remember, in an actual experiment the research worker has only *one* sample of a size equal to that of his total number of observations) the researcher had been able to take a sample of size five. Now what would the sampling distribution look like when the null hypothesis (*H*: $\rho = 0$) is true? Reasoning as before, the probability of getting an observed correlation of $+1.00$ with a sample of size five when the population value is zero would be

$$(.01)^5 \left(\frac{10!}{5!5!} - 10 \right) = .0000000242$$

Thus, with a larger sample the probability of getting an observed correlation coefficient of $+1.00$ when the population value is, in fact, zero is greatly reduced. If similar calculations were to be carried out for each possible value of *r* and the results plotted as before, a curve similar to that shown by the broken line in Figure 6.34 would be obtained.

When the statistical hypothesis that there was no relationship between the two variables—dominance and grades—was set up, a condition about the population was specified such that a particular combination of the observations (in this case, the Pearson product-moment correlation coefficient) would come from (i.e., be one value shown in) a particular mathematical frequency distribution. The shape of the particular mathematical frequency distribution thus specified depends upon both the sample size and the particular combination of observations used.

The second logical step in testing a statistical hypothesis was that of making some actual observations. The research worker might find 18 students, administer to them a measure of dominance, and then look up their grade-point averages. Suppose he then calculated the observed correlation between the two measures for the 18 students and found it to be *r* = .50. The question is: Does this indicate that dominance and grades go together, or can a value of .50 arise quite often from samples of size 18 when, in fact, the true population value is zero?

To answer this question, the investigator must take the third logical step of testing statistical hypotheses, that of locating his particular observed value in the sampling distribution which would be obtained when the null hypothesis holds. If the entire theoretical frequency distribution were available, this task would be a straightforward and a simple matter. The distribution would be plotted as indicated in Figure 6.35 and the areas under the curve in the tails beyond $\pm.50$ determined. This area would be the significance level α and would indicate the probability of making the Type I error of rejecting the (null) hypothesis when in fact it is true.

Having seen the calculations necessary to plot just one point on the curve

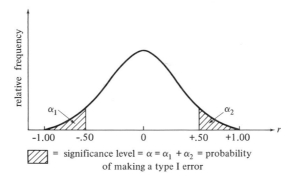

FIGURE 6.35   A hypothetical sampling distribution of correlation coefficients for samples of size 18 when the null hypothesis holds

for each of just two different sample sizes, the reader can imagine what a
horrendous task it would be to plot an entire frequency distribution for every
different possible sample size and how cumbersome graphs or tables showing
the results for each different possible value of r for each different possible
sample size would be.   In practice, tables showing only certain critical values
—values along the base line of the entire curve for various specified areas
under the curve—are used.   Table 6.11 shows the critical values for significance levels of .1, .05, .02, .01, and .001 for various sample sizes from
3 to 102.[16]

The critical values from this table which are of interest for the example at
hand are those found in the row for which $df = 18 - 2 = 16$.   From this
table it is possible for the investigator to visualize the location of his observed
value in the theoretical frequency distribution as that shown in Figure 6.36.
In this figure the areas in the tail are exactly half the values listed as column
headings in Table 6.11 because the column headings represent the α that
would be obtained with a typical two-tailed test rather than the α_1 shown in
the figure.

The final logical step in testing a statistical hypothesis is that of making
the decision to accept or reject the hypothesis.   It will be recalled, however,
that this final step cannot be taken without first making a value judgment as
to the relative seriousness of the Type I and Type II errors.   Because different
investigators are likely to assign different relative values to the two types of
errors and therefore differ in their willingness to accept a given risk of making
one or the other of them, this final step is a matter of personal judgment and
not one which can be prescribed for every situation and every research
worker in advance.   It is, however, necessary for each individual investigator to make his value judgment in advance of carrying out the study or

[16] Actually, the values are tabled according to the *degrees of freedom* (*df*) rather than
sample size.   Without going into this concept, we may say that in the case of correlation $df = N - 2$.

TABLE 6.11

Values of the Correlation Coefficient, r, for Various Levels
of Significance and Degrees of Freedom

df	.1	.05	Levels of Significance .02	.01	.001
1	.98769	.99692	.99507	.999877	.9999988
2	.90000	.95000	.98000	.990000	.99900
3	.8054	.8783	.93433	.95873	.99116
4	.7293	.8114	.8822	.91720	.97406
5	.6694	.7545	.8329	.8745	.95074
6	.6215	.7067	.7887	.8343	.92493
7	.5822	.6664	.7498	.7977	.8982
8	.5494	.6319	.7155	.7646	.8721
9	.5214	.6021	.6851	.7348	.8471
10	.4973	.5760	.6581	.7079	.8233
11	.4762	.5529	.6339	.6835	.8010
12	.4575	.5324	.6120	.6614	.7800
13	.4409	.5139	.5923	.6411	.7603
14	.4259	.4973	.5742	.6226	.7420
15	.4124	.4821	.5577	.6055	.7246
16	.4000	.4683	.5425	.5897	.7084
17	.3887	.4555	.5285	.5751	.6932
18	.3783	.4438	.5155	.5614	.6787
19	.3687	.4329	.5034	.5487	.6652
20	.3598	.4227	.4921	.5368	.6524
25	.3233	.3809	.4451	.4869	.5974
30	.2960	.3494	.4093	.4487	.5541
35	.2746	.3246	.3810	.4182	.5189
40	.2573	.3044	.3578	.3932	.4896
45	.2428	.2875	.3384	.3721	.4648
50	.2306	.2732	.3218	.3541	.4433
60	.2108	.2500	.2948	.3248	.4078
70	.1954	.2319	.2737	.3017	.3799
80	.1829	.2172	.2565	.2830	.3568
90	.1726	.2050	.2422	.2673	.3375
100	.1638	.1946	.2301	.2540	.3211

SOURCE: Table is taken from Table VII of Fisher, R. & Yates, F.: Statistical tables for biological, agricultural and medical research (6th ed.), published by Oliver & Boyd Ltd., Edinburgh, 1963, and by permission of the authors and publishers.

reading the results. Logically, the value judgments should not vary according to how the data turn out, and the researcher who makes his judgment after he makes the observations is likely to prejudice the scientific argument in his favor by capitalizing on the chance events of sampling.

For example, in the illustration at hand a research worker who had indi-

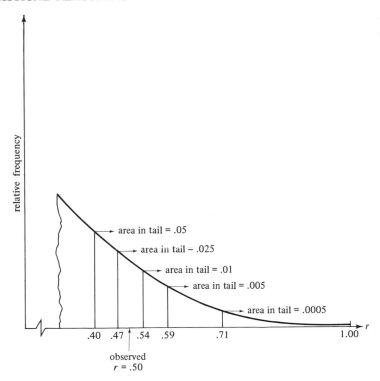

FIGURE 6.36 Location of an observed correlation coefficient in the tail of a sampling distribution

cated at the beginning of the study that he was willing to take a .05 risk of making a Type I error would now reject the null hypothesis, while an investigator who felt that this type of error was so serious that he would not take more than a .01 chance of making it would decide to accept the null hypothesis. The person who hoped to verify his hypothesis that the two variables of dominance and grades are related but who waited until after the data was in to make his value judgment is likely to decide, on the basis of the outcome rather than on the seriousness of the two types of errors, that a .02 risk of making a Type I error is acceptable and therefore make a decision to reject the null hypothesis that there is no relationship between dominance and grades. By making the judgment after he sees the results, such a person is putting himself in the same position as the "Monday morning quarterbacks" who now can tell you what should have been done to win the game and can't be proved wrong. While such a procedure may be salving to the ego, it most certainly is not scientifically acceptable, since it biases the case in favor of the investigator and reduces the extent to which his hypothesis is capable of refutation.

The final decision, then, as to whether to accept or reject the hypothesis will be in part determined by the investigator's *prior* judgment as to the willingness with which he will take a given risk of making a Type I error (which, in turn, depends upon the willingness with which he will take a risk of making a Type II error). All the statistical test shows is that, by chance alone, when samples of size 18 are drawn from a population in which there is no relationship between dominance and grades, an observed correlation of .5 will occur somewhat less than 5 percent and somewhat more than 2 percent of the time.

TESTING FOR A DIFFERENCE AMONG MEANS   One of the most frequently used types of studies in the behavioral sciences is that in which one or more equivalent groups are exposed to different actions or treatments and then comparisons are made among the groups after they have been exposed to the differing experiences.   The various basic designs needed to insure that the observed effects are not attributable to important variables other than the experimental one have already been described in Chapter 4.   In the language of Chapter 4, this section illustrates the logic of testing a statistical hypothesis as a way of eliminating so-called sampling fluctuations as the alternative explanation for any differences observed.

Suppose that each of four different theories of learning suggests a different approach to the organization and presentation of material in a high school biology class.   From each theory a particular method of instruction might be derived and tried on a group of students.   A straightforward design would be to divide the students randomly into four equal groups, then try each method (i.e., treatment) on one of the groups.   Following this, a common biology achievement test might be administered and the scores obtained by the different groups compared.

Obviously, no one would expect all students who were taught by one particular method to get identical scores.   Rather, the expected result would be some sort of frequency distribution of scores which might have a mean of $\bar{X}_1$ and a standard deviation of s_{x_1}.   Similarly, each of the other treatment groups would also yield frequency distributions, each with its own mean and its own standard deviation.

Now, if there are marked differences among the methods and if the score frequency distributions were plotted along the same base line, the result might be similar to that shown in Figure 6.37A.   If there were some differences in effectiveness among the ways of presenting materials, but not powerful ones, the result might be graphically represented by Figure 6.37B; and if there were absolutely no differences in the treatments and if randomization were perfect so that no differences occurred among the groups originally, the result might be that shown in Figure 6.37C.

In general, then, the less difference in the efficacy of the methods, the greater the overlap of the resulting frequency distributions, and the smaller the overlap, the greater the difference among the different treatments.   It is important

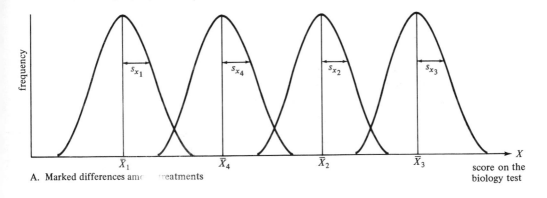

A. Marked differences among treatments

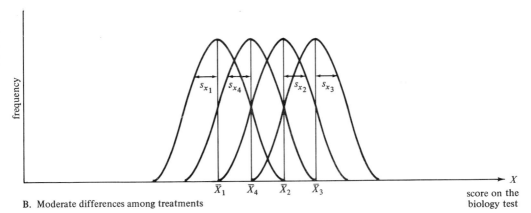

B. Moderate differences among treatments

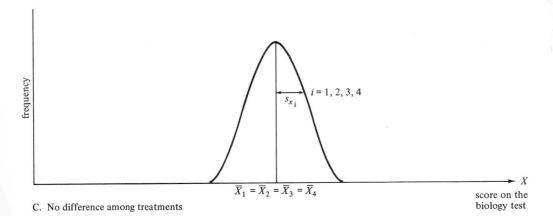

C. No difference among treatments

FIGURE 6.37 Hypothetical frequency distributions representing possible outcomes according to whether differences occur among instructional treatments

247

to note that the difference in overlap is dependent *both* upon the differences between the means (between variation) and the amount of variability within the different groups (within variation).

At this point, it should be intuitively reasonable that a sensible combination of observations to use as a test statistic is a comparison of the variation between the mean values with that of the average variation within the different groups. It is, however, instructive to examine the logic in greater detail. Consider a particular Individual i who was taught by a particular Method j. His score on the biology test following the instruction can be designated by X_{ij}, and it can be postulated that his performance, as indicated by the score, was influenced by three things which can be combined in an additive way. This conception can be represented algebraically by the expression

$$X_{ij} = \mu + \tau_j + e_{ij}$$

where μ represents that portion of the student's performance attributed to the fact that he is a member of the population sampled (that is, attributable to the fact that he is a biology student, which leads him to perform differently than he would if he were a member of some other age or grade group, such as a three-month-old child or a Ph.D. in biology)

  τ_j represents that portion of the student's performance attributable to the fact that he was given Treatment j and therefore might perform differently than if he were given Treatment k or l or m

  e_{ij} represents that portion of the student's performance which is attributable to the fact that he is, after all, a unique individual and therefore does not perform exactly like everybody else in his group, even though the others are also biology students and the material was presented to all of them in the same way (in experimental design, this component of the total score is often referred to as *error*, because it represents that portion of the individual's performance which has not yet been explained or accounted for in the study)

Graphically this conception can be represented as shown in Figure 6.38.

Because the only thing that can be observed is the X_{ij}, it is never possible to know μ, τ_j, or e_{ij} exactly. However, with a large group of individuals divided into four subgroups and given separate treatments as described at the beginning of this example, there is a way of estimating essential components. Thus, μ is estimated by taking the grand mean of all individuals regardless of treatment (and is designated $\overline{\overline{X}}$); each τ_j can be estimated by taking $\overline{X}_j - \overline{\overline{X}}$, the difference between the mean for those students given Treatment j and the grand mean which includes all students in all groups; and, finally, e_{ij} can be estimated by subtracting the group mean from the individual's score to get $X_{ij} - \overline{X}_j$. (See Figure 6.38.)

When testing a hypothesis about the differences among treatments, the re-

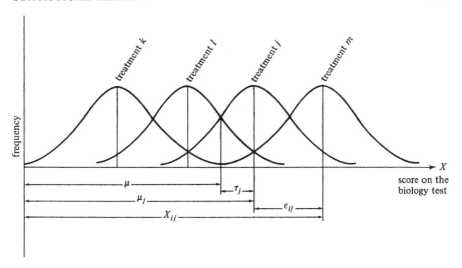

FIGURE 6.38   Frequency distributions and postulated components of a test score achieved by one individual who was part of an experiment in which different instructional treatments were tried.

searcher is not interested in the overall level of performance of the group but rather in the components representing the effect of the treatment and the uniqueness of the individual. (For if a treatment is to be effective, it must outweigh individual differences.) Thus, algebraically, the μ is subtracted from both sides of the original equation and then μ, τ_j, and ϵ_{ij} are replaced with the observed estimates of them, yielding the expression

$$X_{ij} - \bar{\bar{X}} = (\bar{X}_j - \bar{\bar{X}}) + (X_{ij} - \bar{X}_j)$$

which describes the situation for Individual i, who has been given Treatment j.

Because, however, the investigator is interested in generalizing his conclusions about the effect of the different treatments on other persons, it might seem reasonable for him to total these deviations over all persons tested to get an estimate of how much of the total performance of a number of persons is attributable to the treatment and how much is attributable to their uniqueness. But, if he summed the simple deviations from the average, he would (just as occurred earlier in the case of the average deviation) always get zero. If, as in the case of the standard deviation, the investigator does not really care about the direction of the deviation and is interested only in its magnitude and if he is willing to permit large deviations to count relatively more than small ones, he can overcome the difficulty by making use of the *squares* of the deviations rather than the simple differences.

Squaring both sides of the last expression, we have

$$(X_{ij} - \bar{\bar{X}})^2 = (\bar{X}_j - \bar{\bar{X}})^2 + 2(\bar{X}_j - \bar{\bar{X}})(X_{ij} - \bar{X}_j) + (X_{ij} - \bar{X}_j)^2$$

and adding over all *persons* (of which there are n in each group), it can be seen that for each group [17] (here Group j):

$$\sum_i (X_{ij} - \bar{\bar{X}})^2 = n(\bar{X}_j - \bar{\bar{X}})^2 + \sum_i (X_{ij} - \bar{X}_j)$$

Finally, adding across groups, we obtain the important relationship

$$\sum_j \sum_i (X_{ij} - \bar{\bar{X}})^2 = n \sum_j (\bar{\bar{X}}_j - \bar{\bar{X}})^2 + \sum_j \sum_i (X_{ij} - \bar{X}_j)^2$$

or

$$\text{SS}_{\text{total}} = \text{SS}_{\text{between}} + \text{SS}_{\text{within}}$$

which is read: Total sum of squares equals between sum of squares plus within sum of squares.

If only the sums are used, the magnitude of the various components of interest will be a function of the sample size and of the number of different treatment groups included. That is, the larger the sample and the larger the number of groups, the larger the values obtained. To obtain indexes that are useful regardless of the sample size and number of groups, it is necessary to divide each component by the number of independent contributions to it. The number of independent contributions is referred to as the *degrees of freedom* and is determined by taking the total number of elements added together and subtracting the number of theoretical values which have been replaced with values calculated from the observations.

For example, to obtain the total sum of squares, the scores of n individuals in each of k groups, or a total of nk contributions, were included. But $\bar{\bar{X}}$ was substituted for μ and thus one degree of freedom was lost. As a result, the degrees of freedom for the total sum of squares is $nk - 1$. Similarly, there was a total of nk differences added to get the *within* sum of squares. But, in obtaining these values, an $\bar{X}$ was substituted for the true mean for each of the k groups, thus losing k degrees of freedom and yielding $nk - k$ as the *within* degrees of freedom. In obtaining the *between* groups total, only k elements (one for each group) were added together. Also, in obtaining the *between* sum of squares, $\bar{\bar{X}}$ was substituted for μ, thus losing one degree of freedom. The resulting degrees of freedom for *between*, then, turns out to be $k - 1$. As a check on the logic used in deriving degrees of freedom for the two components, it can be noted that they, like the sum of squares, should add together to give the total degrees of freedom. In this instance the expression

$$nk - 1 = (nk - k) + (k - 1)$$

should turn out to be a correct identity.

When each sum of squares is divided by its respective degrees of freedom,

---

[17] Remember that $\Sigma(X_{ij} - \bar{X}_j) = 0$ and that the sum of the constant (with respect to i) $\bar{X}_j - \bar{\bar{X}}$ over n individuals will be n times the constant, or $n(\bar{X}_j - \bar{\bar{X}})$.

the mean squares (MS) which result, respectively, estimate that proportion of the population variance which is attributable to that component.[18]   Thus,

$$MS_{total} = \frac{SS_{total}}{nk - 1} = s_t^2$$

and estimates the extent to which persons in the entire group of biology students differ from one another with respect to performance in biology.

$$MS_{within} = \frac{SS_{within}}{nk - k} = s_w^2$$

and estimates the extent to which persons within a given treatment group differ from one another with respect to performance in biology and indicates the extent to which persons will still differ in biology even though they have been taught the same way.

$$MS_{between} = \frac{SS_{between}}{k - 1} = ns_b^2$$

and estimates the extent to which group averages differ from one another and indicates the extent to which people taught biology one way will differ from those taught biology another way with respect to their knowledge of biology.

Now, because the investigator is primarily concerned with the extent to which persons taught biology one way will differ from those taught another, it is of interest to note what happens to the $MS_{between}$ when his hypothesis holds and when his hypothesis does not hold.   First, if the treatments are effective (and the null hypothesis does *not* hold), it should be apparent that $MS_{between}$ will be quite large, and the more effective the treatments, the larger it will be.   On the other hand, if the treatments are *not* differentially effective (and the null hypothesis that there is no difference among the population means *does* hold), then the mean square *between* is likely to be close to, but not necessarily equal to, zero.   If the calculations were made with population values, the *between* mean square would, of course, be zero when the null hypothesis holds.   In practice, however, the investigator is always working with samples where each observed mean fluctuates about the true value.   Thus, variation among observed means will occur even when the hypothesis that the population means are equal holds.

By means of an important statistical principle called the *central limit theorem* and by recognizing that, under the null hypothesis, the best estimate of the total variation is the average of the variations within each group, we can show that

$$s_b^2 = \frac{s_w^2}{n}$$

A most reasonable test statistic, then, would be a comparison of the

[18] It should be noted that, *unlike* the sum of squares and the degrees of freedom, the $MS_{total} \neq MS_{within} + MS_{between}$.

$MS_{between}$ which is actually observed (and which becomes large if the treatments produce real differences) with the estimate of the $MS_{between}$ that will occur when the treatments have no differential effect, and the null hypothesis holds. If we remember that mean squares are variances and that the ratio of two variances has the theoretical frequency distribution called F (see Figure 6.15, page 198), it is most reasonable to use as a test statistic the ratio

$$\frac{n s_b{}^2}{n \dfrac{s_w{}^2}{n}} = \frac{MS_{between}}{MS_{within}}$$

Thus, with the development of the ratio given above, the first logical step in testing statistical hypotheses—that of finding a combination of the observation which has a known mathematical frequency distribution when the hypothesis holds—has been taken. The second step is that of making some observations and calculating the test statistic.

TABLE 6.12

Hypothetical Scores and Summary Calculations Resulting from a Biology Test Given to Four Groups of Three Students Each

Subject Number	Class 1	Class 2	Class 3	Class 4	Sum over Groups $\sum_{i} X_{ij}$
1	1	3	1	2	7
2	1	3	2	2	8
3	2	2	2	3	9
Sum over persons $\sum_{i} X_{ij}$	4	8	5	7	Grand Sum $\sum_{j}\sum_{i} X_{ij} = 24$
Group mean $\bar{X}_j = \dfrac{\sum_{i} X_{ij}}{n}$	1.3	2.7	1.7	2.3	Grand Mean $\bar{\bar{X}} = \dfrac{\sum_{i}\sum_{j} X_{ij}}{nk}$ $= \dfrac{24}{(3)(4)} = 2$

Suppose that the raw data for three different persons in each of the four different biology classes turned out to be that shown in Table 6.12.[19] Then, the numerator of the test statistic is

[19] To avoid complicating the illustration with unnecessarily awkward arithmetical calculations, a much smaller number of observations and less complicated hypothetical values than would be found in actual practice have been used.

$$MS_{between} = \frac{n \sum_j (\bar{X}_j - \bar{\bar{X}})^2}{k - 1}$$

$$= \frac{3[(1.3 - 2)^2 + (2.7 - 2)^2 + (1.7 - 2)^2 + (2.3 - 2)^2]}{4 - 1}$$

$$= 1.16$$

and the denominator is

$$MS_{within} = \left[\sum_j \sum_i \frac{(X_{ij} - \bar{X}_j)^2}{nk - k} = \frac{1}{k(n - 1)} \sum_j \sum_i (X_{ij} - \bar{X}_j)^2 \right]$$

$$= \frac{1}{4(3 - 1)} (1 - 1.3)^2 + (1 - 1.3)^2 + (2 - 1.3)^2 + (3 - 2.7)^2$$
$$+ (3 - 2.7)^2 + (2 - 2.7)^2 + (1 - 1.7)^2 + (2 - 1.7)^2$$
$$+ (2 - 1.7)^2 + (2 - 2.3)^2 + (2 - 2.3)^2 + (3 - 2.3)^2$$

$$= 0.335$$

The test statistic to be compared with values found in the F table thus becomes

$$\frac{1.16}{0.335} = 3.48$$

Examining an F table for $k - 1 = 3$ degrees of freedom (df) in the numerator (larger mean square) and for $k(n - 1) = 8$ df in the denominator (smaller mean square), we find the following critical values for the probabilities indicated:

Probability (α):	25	10	05	01
Critical F value:	1.67	2.92	4.07	7.59

Had the investigator elected to use the 5 percent level of significance for his critical value before he made his observations, he would have failed to reject the hypothesis that there is no difference among the group means and concluded that the treatments do not have an effect. On the other hand, had the research worker felt that a Type II error was more serious and, before he started the experiment, decided to use a significance level of 10 or 25 percent, his conclusion would have been the opposite, and he would have behaved as if the treatments do have an effect.

In this latter case, having rejected the hypothesis that the observed differences were produced by chance, the research worker would ask to what extent the differences were of scientific importance. From a theoretical point of view, the proportion of the variation in the criterion variable which is accounted for by the experimental variable can be determined by taking

$$\omega^2 = \frac{SS_{between} - (k - 1) MS_{within}}{SS_{total} + MS_{within}}$$

$$= \frac{3.48 - (4 - 1)(0.335)}{6.16 + (0.335)}$$

$$= 0.37$$

and from a practical point of view, it can be noted that the maximum difference between means for the different treatments is 1.4. Thus, while differences in teaching method account for 37 percent of the variation in performance on the biology test, the maximum difference produced in a typical class would be expected to be only about $1\frac{1}{2}$ raw-score points.

Before leaving this example, we should note that the statistical test made of the overall hypothesis of no difference provides no information about which particular treatments are producing such a difference. When the overall test illustrated above is significant, then and then only may the research worker proceed to carry out a *post hoc* analysis and make a series of additional statistical tests to compare various combinations of means.

If the investigator had in mind some specific comparisons of particular pairs or combinations of groups (hopefully based on theory or prior empirical findings) before he started collecting data, then a series of *a priori* tests, rather than the overall test and *post hoc* comparisons, could be made. Because the advantages and disadvantages of the *a priori* versus overall plus *post hoc* approaches are thoroughly discussed in most modern texts on statistics, they will not be included here. It suffices to say at this point that the careful research worker will consider both alternatives carefully before deciding which approach to use.

TESTING OTHER HYPOTHESES   Although the reader may be both astounded and distressed at the large number and seemingly endless variety of statistical tests available to him at the present time, he can take heart in noting two things.

First, almost all statistical tests are but direct extensions of those illustrated here, either to those situations involving more than one criterion variable or treatment variable or control variable or to those situations in which the observations are made at other levels of measurement than interval or ratio scales. In every instance, the same basic logic is involved. Thus, one who has understood the previous examples thoroughly should have no trouble in following the development of any new statistical test he might find useful in carrying out his research.

Second, the researcher applying statistical techniques to the problems in his particular field need not always logically derive an appropriate test statistic. Rather, his task will be that of translating verbally stated scientific problems into verbally stated statistical hypotheses such as those given in the first column of Table 6.13. Once this has been accomplished, the research worker can use such a table to determine what assumptions must be made, to find the formula for the appropriate test statistic to use, and to ascertain which of the tables of theoretical frequency distributions is applicable.

TABLE 6.13
Summary of Common Parametric Procedures for Testing Statistical Hypotheses

Problem	Assumptions	Test Statistic	Table to Use
Mean has a particular value, μ_0 Variance is known	observations are independent and come from a normal distribution	$\dfrac{\bar{X} - \mu_0}{\sigma_x / \sqrt{N}}$	normal
Mean has a particular value, μ_0 Variance is *not* known	observations are independent and come from a normal distribution	$\dfrac{\bar{X} - \mu_0}{s_x / \sqrt{N}}$	t_{N-1}
There is no difference between two means Both variances are known Independent groups	observations within each group are independent and come from a normal distribution	$\dfrac{\bar{X}_1 - \bar{X}_2}{\sqrt{\dfrac{\sigma_1^{\,2}}{N_1} + \dfrac{\sigma_2^{\,2}}{N_2}}}$	normal
There is no difference between two means *or* variances Independent groups	observations within each group are independent and come from a normal distribution Note: If it can be shown by an F test that the variances are equal, the test is for difference between means alone.	$\dfrac{\bar{X}_1 - \bar{X}_2}{\sqrt{\dfrac{(N_1 - 1)s_1^{\,2} + (N_2 - 1)s_2^{\,2}}{N_1 + N_2 - 2}\left(\dfrac{1}{N_1} + \dfrac{1}{N_2}\right)}}$	$t_{N_1 + N_2 - 2}$

TABLE 6.13 *(continued)*

Problem	Assumptions	Test Statistic	Table to Use
There is no difference between two means. Variances are not equal or known. Independent groups	observations within each group are independent and come from a normal distribution	If $N_1 = N_2 = N$, use: $$\frac{\bar{X}_1 - \bar{X}_2}{s_p}$$ where s_p is denominator of previous problem; if $N_1 \neq N_2$, use Behrens-Fisher exact test or approximations by Hartly or by Cochran-Cox	t_{N-1}
There is no difference between two means. Variances are not known. Paired groups	observations within each group are independent and come from a normal distribution. Let $d = x_1 - x_2$. N = number of *pairs*	$$\frac{\bar{d}}{s_d / \sqrt{N}} \quad \text{or} \quad \sqrt{\frac{\bar{x}_1 - \bar{x}_2}{\frac{s_1{}^2 + s_2{}^2 - 2r_{12}s_1s_2}{N(N-1)}}}$$ $$\frac{\Sigma d^2}{(\Sigma d)^2}$$	t_{N-1} $A_{N-1}*$
Variance has a specified value, $\sigma_0{}^2$	observations are independent and come from a normal distribution	$$\frac{(N-1)s_x{}^2}{\sigma_0{}^2}$$	$\chi^2{}_{N-1}$
there is no difference between two variances. Independent groups	observations within each group are independent and come from a normal distribution	$$\frac{s_1{}^2}{s_2{}^2}$$	$F_{N_1-1,\,N_2-1}$

Null hypothesis	Conditions	Test statistic	Distribution
There is no difference between two variances Paired groups	observations within each group are independent and come from a normal distribution N = number of pairs	$\dfrac{\dfrac{s_1^2}{s_2^2}\sqrt{N-2}}{\sqrt{4(1-r_{12})\dfrac{s_1^2}{s_2^2}}}$	t_{N-2}
There is no difference between two proportions	independent observations cell sampling error is normally distributed (can usually assume latter if all expected values are greater than 10)	$\dfrac{P_1-P_2}{\sqrt{PQ\left(\dfrac{1}{N_1}+\dfrac{1}{N_2}\right)}}$ where $P=\dfrac{P_1+P_2}{N_1+N_2}$ and $Q=1-P$	normal
There is no difference between an observed set of frequencies and an expected set of frequencies	independent observations cell sampling error is normally distributed (can usually assume latter if all expected values are greater than 10)	$\displaystyle\sum\frac{(o-e)^2}{e}$	$\chi^2_{(r-1)(c-1)}$ where r = number of rows c = number of columns
There is no relationship between two variables	observations are independent there is a linear relationship between the two variables N = number of pairs of observations	r $\dfrac{r\sqrt{N-2}}{\sqrt{1-r^2}}$	tabled directly for $(N-2)$ df t_{N-2}

TABLE 6.13 *(continued)*

Problem	Assumptions	Test Statistic	Table to Use
The relationship between two variables has a specified amount ρ_0 other than zero	observations are independent there is a linear relationship between the two variables N = number of pairs	$Z_i = \dfrac{1}{2}\ln\left(\dfrac{1+r_i}{1-r_i}\right)$ $\dfrac{Z_i - Z_{\rho_0}}{\sqrt{\dfrac{1}{N-3}}}$	Fisher's Z normal if N is greater than 30
There is no difference between two correlations Independent groups	observations are independent both relationships are linear Z_i is defined as in previous problem	$\dfrac{Z_1 - Z_2}{\sqrt{\dfrac{1}{N_1-3}+\dfrac{1}{N_2-3}}}$	normal
There is no difference between two correlations computed on the same persons	observations within the group are independent both relationships are linear N = number of triplets of observations	$\dfrac{(r_{y1} - r_{y2})^2 (N-3)(1+r_{12})}{2(1 - r_{12}^2 - r_{1y}^2 - r_{2y}^2 + 2r_{12}r_{1y}r_{2y})}$	$F_{1,\,N-3}$
Proportion has a particular value, π_0	independent observations sampling error is normally distributed (can usually assure latter if $N\pi_0 > 5$)	$\dfrac{P - \pi_0}{\sqrt{\dfrac{\pi_0(1-\pi_0)}{N}}}$	normal

* *British Journal of Psychology*, 1955, **46**, 225–226.

258

Bayesian Statistical Inference

The logic of testing hypotheses described in the previous section is essentially that followed by the Neyman-Pearson approach to decision procedures. Although this approach is currently the one most widely used by research workers, it is not the only one. For, as Turner (1967) points out,

Should we review the many applied texts and treatises of the past two decades, we might readily conjecture that statistical methodology is a finished product in which the only ostensible challenge to the writer is that of expository skill. This is especially true of the works written for the behavioral scientist. However, the literature on the foundations of statistics gives us quite another picture. Theoretical statisticians now as never before differ as to their interpretations of probability statements; they differ on the strategies and commitments of decision; and they differ as to what kinds of metaphysical attitudes are appropriate to the creative scientist.

Most prominent among the more recent statistical conceptions are those of personal probability and Bayesian statistical inference. The basic ideas are, at the risk of oversimplifying rather sophisticated mathematical reasoning, briefly described below. Those readers who wish further elaboration are invited to refer to the more thorough discussion of Edwards, Lindman, and Savage (1963) and to references contained in their bibliography.

The Neyman-Pearson approach added the concept of Type II errors to our knowledge, and this, through the development of Wald's (1950) decision theory, added considerable sophistication to the use of R. A. Fisher's concept of significance level in testing hypotheses. Similarly, the application of Bayes' theorem adds even more sophistication to the decision process by taking into consideration that information as to the veracity of a hypothesis which is available prior to an experimental test of the hypothesis. In those cases where Bayes' theorem is applicable, it now becomes possible to calculate a specific probability value (the posterior likelihood) that the hypothesis is true. This represents considerable advancement over procedures which left the research worker with only the probabilities of making the two types of errors, especially since one of these was a function of the unknown state of reality.

In its most simple form, Bayes' theorem makes direct use of simple laws of combining a sequence of mutually exclusive events and can be stated in terms of conditional probabilities as follows:

$$P(H/D) = \frac{P(H)P(D/H)}{P(D)}$$

where $P(H/D) =$ probability that the hypothesis H is true, given the data D of the experiment

$P(H) =$ probability that the hypothesis is true *prior* to gathering the data of the experiment

$P(D/H)$ = probability that the data observed will occur, given the truth of the hypothesis

$P(D)$ = probability that the observed data will occur regardless of what hypotheses are true

Because in most instances of the application of this theorem to scientific decision making the interest is in a particular hypothesis, say, H_1, out of all mutually exclusive hypotheses, H_i, which could possibly produce the data, the theorem can also be expressed as

$$P(H_1/D) = \frac{P(H_1)P(D/H_1)}{\Sigma_i P(H_i)P(D/H_i)}$$

Almost everyone would agree that when the necessary information is precisely available, computation of the posterior likelihood by means of Bayes' theorem represents the most appropriate procedure known for arriving at scientific decisions. There is a question, however, as to whether or not scientific applications, except at the most rudimentary level, permit determination of the required values.

The primary difficulty is in ascertaining the prior probabilities for the various alternative hypotheses, H_i. In general, three ways of obtaining the necessary estimates have been suggested. The first is the use of *personal probabilities*—the amount an ideally consistent person would bet that the hypothesis is true were someone to give him a unit return if, in fact, the hypothesis turned out to be true. Unfortunately, since different investigators have had different past experiences with respect to the given hypothesis, their personal probabilities, though internally consistent, may differ from one another. Even if the different research workers arrive at similar personal probabilities, there is no guarantee that the value thus specified approximates the actual situation. Because each different set of prior probabilities leads to a different posterior likelihood that the hypothesis is true, this approach is the least satisfactory of the three.

The second way of obtaining appropriate values for the prior probabilities is to adopt a simplifying assumption that all alternatives (in the face of ignorance about them) are equally likely. While this approach may be useful in the beginning stages of exploration into an area, it becomes less and less plausible as more and more data are gathered relevant to the hypotheses in question. Fortunately, for large samples of evidence the ultimate Bayesian decision functions seem to become insensitive to disagreements with respect to the prior probabilities. Thus, over a long period of time, most scientists will come to arrive at similar estimates of the posterior likelihood that a particular hypothesis is true, regardless of the prior values assigned.

The third solution to estimating prior probabilities is to make use of previously gathered empirical data. This is the most satisfactory solution to the problem and can lead rather quickly to precise determinations as to the veracity of a hypothesis with relatively small samples of evidence. The difficulty with this approach is the absence of the necessary information except in a few cases. Most notable among the situations in which data are often available are those in which diagnostic decisions are made about a particular case. When *base rates* for the diagnostic categories and *validity data* [20] for a diagnostic test are available, the Bayesian approach can be used without hesitancy.

Another disadvantage sometimes mentioned in connection with the Bayesian approach is the problem that arises from the fact that a given set of data may support many different hypotheses to different extents. Thus, even though the researcher now has a specific probability associated with each of the alternatives, he still must make a decision among them. That is, for the moment, the behavioral scientist must behave as if one and only one of the hypotheses is true. In these circumstances, the procedure to be followed comes very close to that used in the classical decision theory. The investigator first establishes the gain (losses are considered to be negative gains) for each possible outcome. Then, he computes the expectation (probability of the occurrence of the event multiplied by the gain summed over all possibilities) for each of the potential decision rules he might apply. Finally, he selects that decision rule which is optimal in the sense that it will maximize his expected gain, or minimize his expected loss. That is, he simply chooses the one which promises to provide the greatest return.

It should be recognized that not all scientists will arrive at the same decision with respect to the hypothesis. Given the same data and likelihoods, some will behave as if the hypothesis is true and others as if it is false because each makes his own value judgment as to the loss incurred if he is wrong and as to the gain incurred if he is right. Making a value judgment is a purely human enterprise which, in principle, is beyond the capabilities of science and mathematics, so that no ultimate agreement can be expected. All that can be asked is that all persons who would make the same value judgment be led to the same conclusion when given the same data. This objective is, in fact, achieved by a Bayesian approach when the prior probabilities can be precisely determined. Further, all this becomes inherently sensible when one recalls from the first chapter that the task of science is no longer conceived to be that of finding "truth" and eliminating "falsity" about the so-called real world but rather that of formulating conceptions and describing principles which are useful and discarding those, from whatever source, which are useless.

[20] Both the concept of base rate and ways of obtaining validity data are presented in Chapter 7.

7.
The Logic of Measurement

If the investigator in the behavioral sciences who wished to measure some particular trait could turn to a simple mechanical device like a ruler, a balance, or an ammeter or even to a handbook of currently acceptable standard measures, a chapter such as this would be unnecessary. Unfortunately, none of the behavioral sciences has yet reached the stage of development where this is possible, and those readers who are even slightly familiar with the history of the measurement of such a simple characteristic as that of distance (Jones, 1968), will recognize how long and involved the process of developing adequate standards of measurement is, in spite of modern communications and the systematic development of science.

Although Keats (1967) has already expressed the optimistic viewpoint that the *Kit of Reference Tests for Cognitive Measures* developed by French (1963) "might also be thought of as a first stage towards the establishment of standards for the accurate measurement of all important cognitive variables," most persons in the field would agree that the final stage is a long way off. In the meantime, research workers in the behavioral sciences will have to continue to depend upon current texts in the field and upon such basic references as Buros' *Mental Measurement Yearbooks* and the validity studies section of the journal *Educational and Psychological Measurement,* as well as scattered journal articles when they wish data and information about available instruments and will need to develop their own measures when working in a completely new area.

To accomplish either of these latter tasks, the research worker will need to be thoroughly familiar with the technical language of psychometrics and to have an understanding of the most important principles of psychological measurement. It is toward this end that the present chapter has been written and included in a text on research methods for the behavioral sciences. It is not intended that this material represent a complete theoretical or practical compendium of the state of knowledge in the field.

THE NATURE OF MEASUREMENT IN THE BEHAVIORAL SCIENCES

A Useful Definition

Lorge (1951) has indicated that the term *measure* is one of the thousand most frequently appearing words in printed English. He also points out that it was used in forty different ways. Thus, it is essential that a working definition of the term be developed for use in the context of this volume. Through the application of the operational approach to refining definitions which was suggested in Chapter 1, the writer has found that fewer misinterpretations are likely to be made, at least in the context of the behavioral sciences, if measurement is defined simply as *a process of obtaining a numerical description of the extent to which a person (or object) possesses some characteristic*. This definition is broad enough to include the entire spectrum of observational activity in which behavioral scientists become involved, from judging such things as individual creativity and group cohesiveness to determining the electrical potential of cortical reactions, and yet highlights those distinctive aspects which set measurement apart from the process of obtaining other types of observations such as preparing anecdotal records, recording case histories, and the like.

There are three facts about measurement that it is important to recognize. First of all, measurement is in essence numerical. That is, it is always quantitative in the full sense of the term as described in the last chapter and never qualitative. This condition remains whether precise instrumentation or loose human judgment is involved and whether numerical or verbal symbols are used to label the ultimate descriptive categories. Second, the word measurement implies not only an attribute of a person (or object) but an attribute which can be possessed to varying degrees. Thus, all measurement can, in theory at least, be thought of as providing a means for locating an individual along a continuum with respect to some particular characteristics. Finally, measurement is a purely *descriptive* process. In no sense should measurement be considered evaluative in nature. An evaluation may be made on the basis of a measurement, but there are important differences between measurements and evaluations. A great deal of the misuse and misapprehension of measurement which abounds in the behavioral sciences today results directly from a failure to note this distinction.

For all practical purposes in this context, an evaluation can be thought of as a process of drawing a conclusion or making a decision (i.e., making an inference) on the basis of descriptive information, either qualitative or quantitative. Thus, evaluation involves a value judgment which only a human being can make, and measurement represents a descriptive judgment of an empirical fact that might be made by a human being or by some instrument designed either to extend our senses, as do microscopes and telescopes, or to promote agreement among observers, as do rulers and thermometers. Further, an evaluation is usually specific to a particular situation, while a measurement generally describes an individual in a way which is, within the accuracy limitations of time and place, invariant across many situations. For example, the measurement of height describes the individual whether he intends to play basketball or to ride a horse in a race, but the evaluation as to how much it is worth to be a certain height will vary considerably depending upon which of the two situations is of concern. Similarly, how much it is worth for a person to be intelligent or creative or for a group to be dynamic or cohesive will depend upon the particular circumstances. On the other hand, the numerical description of the degree of intelligence, of creativity, or of group cohesiveness remains the same regardless of the situation in which the inference based upon the description will be used.

Clearly, the failure to distinguish between a human value judgment of worth and a judgmental description of empirical phenomena can lead the researcher into a great deal of trouble. Take, for example, the simple process of grading a set of themes written in a college English class. Different observers who read through the papers and directly record a grade (a value judgment as to how much the theme is worth) may have such different ideas as to the relative worth of correct mechanics (grammar, spelling, punctuation), of fluency of expression, of logical organization, and of creative thought that they produce results which seem so inconsistent as to be of little use to the researcher comparing methods of instruction. On the other hand, the same set of observers, given the task of successively rating the themes with respect to mechanics, then fluency, then organization, and finally, creativity, could display a great deal of consistency in their empirical description of these characteristics, even though they were based upon rather crude techniques of observation.

While any numerical description of the extent to which a person or thing possesses some characteristic constitutes a form of measurement, it is obvious that some such descriptions are likely to be more powerful than others. The different levels of measurement which can be achieved have already been described in the previous chapter and will not be repeated here. The reader, however, might find it worthwhile to review pages 178 to 180 at this point.

The Nature of Behavioral Traits [1]

In a very broad sense, any psychological test can be thought of as a way of obtaining a sample of human behavior under controlled conditions. This extremely general statement needs some clarification. When a test is administered, a sample of human behavior is obtained. Ideally this sample is taken with respect to some very specific characteristic or trait. When a scoring system is applied to the test, the observations made are quantified so as to resemble a measure of some existing, real, underlying variable which is often referred to as a mental trait. But just what is this thing called a mental trait—this thing which is being measured? It is not something that can be seen, heard, touched, smelled, or tasted. And if it is not something that can be known through one's senses, what justification is there for saying a mental trait—for example, that of intelligence—exists?

If a physicist were to be asked to explain the nature of gravity, he would probably either mention something about the force of attraction between two bodies or directly describe some empirical observations. Should the term *force* be used in describing the nature of gravity, it would be necessary to inquire as to what force is; and if the physicist were pushed far enough, he would ultimately retreat to the description of observable phenomena. Exactly the same situation is true in the measurement of behavioral characteristics. If a psychologist is to avoid specifying the nature of intelligence in terms which themselves need to be explained, he must ultimately resort to the description of certain observations. Thus, in the final analysis, a mental trait is nothing other than a convenient handle for specifying a particular set of observations; or if the psychologist wishes to go beyond a mere label and summarize a great mass of observed data, a theoretical concept. Such things as mechanical ability, musical talent, clerical aptitude, and even intelligence are considered to be postulated attributes of people—attributes which are inferred because of certain observed behaviors.

Although the original conception of some mental trait arises as an explanation for some particular set of data, the concept evolved is rarely restricted to one group of observations. The problem with which a behavioral scientist is faced in defining a mental trait, therefore, is not only that of developing a concept which accounts for present observables (that is, facts and empirical laws of which knowledge already exists) but also that of forming the concept in such a way that it provides implications for new observables which might be found. The latter is essential because the scientist is always interested in using his concepts in situations other than his

---

[1] The material of this section summarizes part of an important discussion of construct validity presented by Cronbach and Meehl (1955). Students who have a special interest in measurement per se would do well to refer to the original article.

laboratory. A counselor, for example, must rely on definitions of mental traits which have some generality. Otherwise, when sitting with a test score and a client before him, he would be unable to forecast behavior in diverse or even unique situations for which the relationship between test score and later behavior is not at present known.

Formally, a concept which meets the requirements of accounting for present knowledge and providing implications about new observables is known as a *construct*. Mental traits, as hypothetical constructs, always carry associated meanings with them. Thus, every time a test score which purportedly is a measure of some mental trait (that is, some construct) is interpreted, certain properties are added to this construct. For example, in the interpretation of a test score, it is implied that a person who possesses a given amount of this attribute will, with some specified probability, act in manner X when placed in situation Y. More concretely, when a test score is interpreted, assertions such as "a person with an I.Q. of 125 has a probability of 0.80 of getting a B in English at the state university," are made. When supported by evidence, this assertion and others like it give additional meaning to the original construct.

In the context of measurement, the definition of a mental trait—the specification of what it is that a test is measuring—must consider all the known relationships of test scores to other things *and* to that which is asserted about people who achieve certain test scores. When we formulate a concept of a mental trait, questions such as the following must be considered: Is the trait stable, or does it fluctuate from time to time within an individual? What is the distribution of the trait in the human population? To what extent is the trait influenced by heredity and to what extent by environment? What are the laws governing the development of the trait as the person matures? If the concept is to be accurate, all these must be answered.

Obviously, not all answers to these questions will be alike. One research worker might define a trait he calls intelligence in such a way that it is constant, then explain observed changes in test scores with age either as a result of changes in motivation or as the effects of a portion of the test that proves to be irrelevant because it measures a trait that is influenced by learning. A second investigator, however, might postulate a trait he calls intelligence as one which *does* change with maturity or environmental enrichment. Consequently, the early literature of mental testing is full of controversy as to whether this or that definition of some mental trait is correct. The modern point of view is that the hypothetical construct defining a mental trait is not to be thought of as right or wrong but as useful or useless for explaining present knowledge and as suggesting new relationships to be empirically verified.

Two important things for an investigator to realize when using the tools of measurement are:

1. It is not possible to have, until all the data about humans and their behavior are in, a completely satisfactory and universal definition of a mental trait such as intelligence.
2. Before a test designed to provide a measure of some psychological trait can be evaluated, it will be necessary not only to know something about the test and the author's concept of the trait but to subscribe to it as well.

Although no existing theoretical network suffices to account for all existing knowledge about any trait, sketches for many traits have been constructed. Otherwise it would not be possible to say anything intelligible about mental traits—only to list a series of observed empirical relationships. Behavioral scientists, however, are still in the process of discovering laws of human behavior, and many of their concepts are vague but often quite useful.

The importance of knowing the author's construct when evaluating or accepting a measurement of some trait can be illustrated by recalling the two possible concepts of intelligence mentioned above. An appropriate measure of intelligence for the researcher who postulates a constant trait would not vary with age if motivation could be held constant experimentally or corrected statistically, nor would it change with alterations in environmental enrichment. On the other hand, a measure which failed to change with age with motivation controlled or which failed to reflect changes in the learning environment would be the one which was considered inadequate if the second investigator's hypothetical construct of intelligence were accepted.

In summary, mental traits are to be thought of as hypothetical constructs formulated to varying degrees of precision on the basis of present knowledge of observable relationships. As such, the resulting traits may be somewhat vague in the beginning but often take form as the investigator develops and uses his measure. Thus, when we consider tests or other devices as instruments for measuring individuals with respect to these mental traits, it is essential not only to fully understand the particular construct as presently formed but also to examine the past research involving the use of the instrument as well.

Classification of Measuring Devices

At this point, it might be worthwhile to take a look at the various ways in which modern tests are classified. Not only will this provide an overview of the wide variety of tests now available, but it will also serve to familiarize the reader with a number of common terms used in describing tests. Before the different types of tests are discussed, it should be mentioned that classification systems per se are not right or wrong but useful or useless. Not every expert in the field of measurement would classify tests in the same way. In general, however, the classifications presented here have been useful for a number of people working in the area.

One major dimension along which tests have been classified is that of the nature of the trait it was designed to measure. Perhaps the broadest classification in this respect is that which divides tests into what Cronbach (1960) has called measures of *typical behavior* and measures of *maximum performance*. In trying to measure such things as attitudes, interests, and personality characteristics, an attempt is made to get some index of an individual's usual or typical behavior as he goes about his daily life. In such measures, the examinee is not urged to put his best foot forward but to report how he would normally behave in some situation. There are no right or wrong answers except as they are truly representative of the individual, and instead of one key, there may be several, each representative of different sets of typical behaviors found within a human population. In measures of maximum performance, on the other hand, an attempt is made to determine just how well a person can perform in a given situation. The researcher hopes that the individual will do his best, and the examinee's responses are compared with a key, prepared by experts, which distinguishes between correct and incorrect answers.

Traditionally, measures of maximum performance have been separated into three subclasses: tests of aptitude, of ability, and of achievement. As more has been learned about the correlates of and influences upon test performance, however, it has become increasingly difficult to ascertain the extent to which such devices measure "innate capacity" as contrasted with environmental influences. Thus, in the light of today's knowledge, it is inappropriate to think of tests of aptitude, of ability, and of achievement as discrete classes of tests distinguished by whether they measure innate ability, the influence of environment, or a combination of both. At the same time there seems to be a marked difference in the extent to which performance on different tests can be modified by experience. Aptitude tests are tests that measure functions that improve little with practice, ability tests are designed to show some relationship to general environmental enrichment, and achievement tests are designed specifically to measure the degree of accomplishment in some particular educational or training experience.

As is always the case when a classification system is based on a continuous rather than a discrete variable (in this case modifiability), there will be many tests that are difficult to place in one group rather than another. Also, there will always be some disagreement as to whether a particular test is aptitude or ability, or is ability or achievement. Nonetheless, there are some areas upon which almost universal agreement has been reached. For example, it is common practice to speak of musical aptitude and clerical aptitude, because performance on these tests changes little even with practice; of scholastic ability and mechanical ability, because scores on these tests can be improved to a limited extent; and classroom achievement tests, for these measure what has been learned. The basis for distinguishing among the classes is always the extent to which the trait measured is modifiable by environmental experience.

In addition to a classification of tests according to what kind of a trait they measure, a second major dimension of classification has been developed according to *how* the trait is measured. Thus tests are sometimes described as individual versus group, objective versus subjective, paper-and-pencil versus performance, language versus nonlanguage, and power versus speed.

Individual tests are those which must be given to only one person at a time. Such tests most commonly are those that require the manipulation of apparatus or in which the examiner seeks to make observations other than those easily recorded by the examinee as he responds to each question. Group tests, on the other hand, are presented in a format which permits each individual to record his own response and, of course, which is relatively inexpensive to produce in quantities. The classical example of an individual test is the famous Stanford revision of the Binet; any of the tests commonly used as entrance examinations to colleges and universities throughout the country, such as the College Entrance Examination Board Tests and the College Ability Test, serve as examples of group tests.

A classification of tests as objective or subjective depends upon the way in which the test is scored. If a test is set up in such a way that every person who scores the test, no matter when he scores it, will find the same score for a given individual, the test is completely objective. On the other hand, if some judgment in the evaluation of the response is left to the person doing the scoring, then the test is called subjective. It should be noted that the objectivity-subjectivity dimension for labeling tests is really a continuous one and not dichotomous as is sometimes assumed. A matching or multiple-choice test in which (1) the examinee selects from a list of possible answers the one he thinks is correct; and (2) for which a stencil key can be cut is (because of clerical errors in scoring) highly, but not completely, objective. A short-answer test in which the examinee must fill in a blank with a word or phrase or a mathematics test in which some credit is allowed for partially correct answers (for example, correct procedure but a minor arithmetical error) is somewhat more subjective. A test composed of general-discussion and essay questions represents an extreme of subjectivity.

The terms used in classifying tests as paper-and-pencil versus performance need no explanation. A typical apparatus test of mechanical ability might require the examinee to assemble certain objects such as a bicycle bell or a lock; a paper-and-pencil form of a mechanical ability test might be one in which tools are to be matched with the materials on which they are used.

Nonlanguage tests are those which, in contrast to most tests, use no written or spoken word in either the directions or the test questions themselves. All instructions are presented by demonstration and pantomime, and answers often involve performance on an apparatus, though paper-and-pencil tests are sometimes used. Such tests are used primarily for measuring the aptitudes or the abilities of illiterates or for those speaking foreign tongues.

In attempting to classify tests as speed versus power, it is necessary to think of the characteristic involved as really being continuous, with most tests falling near the middle of the scale rather than at either extreme. A pure speed test is one composed of items so easy that everyone who tries them will answer them correctly. Thus, the score obtained is entirely dependent upon how many items the examinee reaches in the time limit allowed. In a pure power test, on the other hand, every examinee is permitted to try every single item and his score depends entirely on how many questions he can answer or problems he can solve without regard to the rate at which he works. A classical example of a pure speed test is the Minnesota Vocational Test for Clerical Workers, in which the task is to examine a long list of pairs of names and pairs of numbers and to indicate which of the pairs contains identical numbers or names. Obviously, with sufficient time, everyone would be able to get every item correct. Thus, a severe time limit is imposed, and scores are almost entirely dependent upon how far an individual gets without making careless errors. On the other hand, a vocabulary test in which no time limit is imposed would represent a pure power test.

Finally, a third major basis for the classification of psychological tests results from the recent utility theory (Cronbach and Gleser, 1965) as contrasted with the more traditional measurement theory approach to testing. Considering the function of testing to provide information on the basis of which personnel decisions can be improved, it is reasonable to classify tests according to the use to which they are put—that is, by the type of personnel decision for which they provide the most useful information. Thus, more and more commonly, one hears of placement tests, classification tests, selection tests, readiness tests, mastery tests, diagnostic tests, etc. While at first such a system of describing tests seems somewhat artificial, it is most important from a practical point of view. For, although a test of mechanical ability might be used for any one of the three types of decisions, it is becoming more apparent to those in the field of psychometrics that different approaches to the construction and evaluation of tests are needed, depending upon the use to be made of the instrument. Thus, the same test which is extremely valuable in improving guidance or psychotherapy decisions (a classification situation) may not be the most desirable test where the problem is one of selection or placement.

Although other schemes for classification of psychological tests are possible (for example, tests can be grouped according to whether they are conventional, situational, or projective), the ways presented above are the ones most commonly used in describing tests at the present time and of greatest help in untangling the maze of labels used in naming published tests.

Finally, mention should be made of instruments which fall on the borderline between tests and nontesting devices for gathering descriptive information. Chief among these are rankings, rating scales, and checklists. Some writers tend to classify these instruments as nontest devices because they each require that a judgment be made by the person doing the observing during the time the data is collected, in contrast to tests in which judgments are made in the process of constructing the instrument and perhaps at the time of scoring the results but not while the subjects are responding or the observations of their products are being made. Most authors, however, would tend to think of rankings, ratings, and checklists in the same light as tests because all of these result in a numerical description of the extent to which a person possesses some trait.

Regardless of which way the reader prefers to classify them, he should recognize the differences between these techniques. Ranking procedures include any approach to getting the persons being measured into rank order with respect to the trait under consideration. Rating procedures, on the other hand, usually attempt to assign the individual to a certain position along a scale, the steps of which can be at least loosely characterized by verbal description. Checklists usually include long lists of relevant behaviors which either occur or do not occur; a score is obtained by counting (or making a weighted count of) the number of behaviors which do occur during the time of observations.

THE CRITERIA FOR CHOOSING A MEASURING DEVICE

It is obvious that both measurement specialists and research workers who develop their own measuring devices must be concerned with how to determine whether any instrument they prepare is a good one. But those research workers fortunate enough to find ready-made tests to measure psychological variables in which they are interested will also need to make decisions as to whether testing is appropriate for a particular situation and will then have to select from among those tests available the one most likely to provide the desired information. This and the next major section provide a basic framework for making intelligent judgments about the usefulness of tests by pointing out the kinds of things that need to be considered when selecting a test and by describing the technical criteria that have been developed to indicate whether or not it is a good measuring device.

Basic Considerations

It seems almost too obvious to mention that a measure of high-level scholastic ability is not appropriate as an index of the job capabilities of truck drivers or that a measuring instrument designed specifically for use with children cannot necessarily be used with adults. Yet, time after time, tests or other measures have been used which are completely inappropriate for the group involved or for the problem at hand. Thus, the initial consideration in choosing a test is the purpose for which it is to be used.

Because the research function of a measure is usually to provide the best possible information on the basis of which a decision about some problem can be made, it is apparent that the first step should be to specify carefully the research questions to be answered and to delineate clearly the group on whom the observations are to be made. Only when this has been done is it possible either to ascertain accurately the effectiveness of using a measuring device in contrast with gathering other kinds of descriptive information or to determine which of several alternative instruments will be most useful in the given situation.

A second basic consideration in choosing a measure is its feasibility. Although certain kinds of information might be extremely valuable in describing a particular trait, the cost of obtaining the data, either in dollars and cents or in terms of human values, may far exceed the cost of using a less accurate measure.

There are also many practical considerations. For example, purchase price is obviously important. Almost always the user of tests is operating within a budget, self-imposed or otherwise, and a highly expensive test must be worth the price in terms of yield. Sometimes it just is not possible to purchase the best instrument available because of price, and a less desirable test must be used. The time involved in taking the test is another important factor. A research worker must always consider how many man-hours are required to take tests; in school or military training situations where regular class meetings exist not only the total time but also the extent to which time limits on the test or its parts fit in with the classroom schedule becomes an important consideration.

The ease of administration and scoring, the possibility that the test content will offend some examinees, and the availability of comparable forms (this latter especially in research situations where it is necessary to be certain that those tested have not had previous experience with the items and where a measure both before and after the application of some experimental variable is desired) are all additional aspects which need to be given some thought when choosing a test.

One aspect of feasibility which is peculiar to certain research designs is the extent to which the particular measure selected is unobtrusive—that is, the extent to which the measurement can be obtained without changing the subjects observed. The discussion of reactive effects as a major source of invalidity in many experimental studies should have sensitized the reader to the importance, in many situations, of obtaining descriptive information in such a way that the subject is not even aware that a study is going on. A variety of such devices are described by Webb et al. (1966), and a researcher carrying out a study in which reactive effects are likely to occur should carefully consider the possibility of using unobtrusive measures similar to the ones they describe.

A Classification of Errors [2]

INTERPRETIVE ERRORS   It has already been noted that original measurements of behavioral characteristics lack both an absolute zero point and any guarantee that the units are equal throughout the range of the scale. Because of these conditions, the test score achieved by any one person has no meaning until it is interpreted in terms of the performance of other individuals. Unless the investigator has a clear understanding as to exactly which other individuals are used for this interpretation and precisely how the one person's score is related to the performance of the group, he is likely to attribute an inappropriate meaning to the score. Such misinterpretations are called *interpretive errors*.

Interpretive errors result from a misunderstanding of one of two things: first, with what sort of group the individual is being compared and, second, the way in which the comparison between the individual and the group performance is expressed. For example, it would make a considerable difference in the interpretation of the results if the score obtained by a high school senior is compared with those of high school freshmen rather than college freshmen. Similarly, the prediction made and the action taken would be quite different for a reported score of 70 if it were an I.Q. than would be the case if the number 70 were a ranking indicating that proportion of the others who took the test who got a lower score than the individual in question.

In testing, this problem of interpretive errors is taken care of through a process called *standardization*. Standardization means that the test has been given to a well-defined group (for example, college sophomores, female clerical workers, applicants for admission to medical school) and that careful records have been kept as to the scores the specified group or groups have made. These records are the norms. Norms may be provided for many groups even for one test and may be defined in such terms as occupation, geographical region, sex, age, school grade, or any combination of

[2] The classification of errors of measurement used in this section was suggested by Mursell (1947).

these, the idea being to provide data such that it is possible to make a comparison of an individual's score with that of an appropriate group.

There are two kinds of groups with which it is appropriate to compare an individual. The first is a group to which the individual already belongs. Certainly, no reader of this text would be proud to know that he had achieved the highest score among a group composed of 20 third-grade children and himself; nor would he be likely to be particularly discouraged because he was the lowest on an intelligence test given to himself, Galileo, Newton, Galton, and Einstein; nor would he be particularly disturbed to discover his scores on a personality rating were completely different from those of Australian bushmen. None of these comparisons is likely to be relevant to the interests of the college student.

Sometimes the most important comparison is not with a group to which an individual already belongs but rather with a group to which he aspires. For example, if a college sophomore is interested in becoming a physician, it is of greater significance to compare his scholastic ability test scores with those of successful medical students than it is to compare them with college sophomores as a whole (or even with applicants to medical school).

The final problem with respect to interpretive errors—that of expressing the relationship between an individual's score and those of the normative group—involves the translation of raw scores into mental age scores, intelligence quotients, percentile ranks, standard scores, or other types of derived scores. Procedures for the development and computation of such scores as well as the advantages and disadvantages of the various possibilities are discussed at length under the topic of standardization and therefore need only be mentioned here.

VARIABLE ERRORS   A second kind of error that may occur in psychological measurement is termed *variable error*. Variable errors arise from accidents and inaccuracies due to many causes. For example, if you were to measure the length of a table with a ruler today, tomorrow, and the next day, or if several different persons each were to measure the length of the table today, slightly different results would be obtained in each case. Exactly the same thing happens in measuring behavioral traits, only here the errors are likely to be much greater than normally occur in the measurement of physical quantities. During a timed test, a pencil breaks, a fire engine goes by outside the window, the test administrator gives incorrect directions, each causing those taking the test to receive slightly different scores for this testing from those they would receive under slightly different circumstances. All of these things result in chance inaccuracies called variable errors. These errors are referred to as variable errors because the amount of error varies from one person to the next and also because the amount of error is different for a given person each time he is measured.

In psychological measurement, the relative freedom from errors of this sort is the *degree of reliability*. As was the case with respect to relating the score obtained by an individual to that of a group, there are many approaches to the problem of estimating reliability, each with its own special advantages and precautions. These, together with suggestions for decreasing variable errors in testing, are presented in the next section.

PERSONAL ERRORS   When reading an automobile speedometer from his respective position in the car, each passenger is likely to come up with a slightly different result—even though the instrument itself is keeping a perfectly accurate record of the rate of travel. Similarly, any two persons observing exactly the same responses are likely to record different scores because they can see the performance only from their own position or bias. Or the same person examining the same responses on two different occasions is likely to vary somewhat in his reaction because he sees things differently each time.

Many studies have indicated that two readers of a given examination paper will often arrive at vastly different results. The same thing has been shown to be true even when the same person grades the same papers when the grading is done independently on two different occasions. Since such fluctuation in scores is directly attributable to the person who is doing the grading, they are called *personal errors*.

Because the personal bias of the person making the observations (that is, scoring the responses) fluctuates from time to time and from paper to paper, the resulting personal errors are a special class of variable errors. Personal errors are, however, of sufficient magnitude to require special attention when measuring behavioral characteristics and therefore deserve a special label. In psychometrics the term *objectivity* is used to designate that test characteristic related to personal errors. Just how personal errors are reduced and tests are evaluated by this criterion are discussed later in this chapter under that heading.

CONSTANT ERRORS   The final type of error to discuss here arises from the fact that most measurements of behavioral characteristics are indirect. It is neither possible nor desirable to open a person's skull, look inside, or put a chunk of gray matter on a balance and say that this is the amount of his mechanical ability. Rather, a measure is obtained on something (a test) which it is hoped is related to the trait or characteristic about which it is desired to have information. Indirect measurement is not unique to the assessment of behavioral characteristics. The same thing is done when one uses a thermometer. It is not the height of the mercury column per se which is desired. The height of the mercury column is useful only because it shows a very high degree of relationship to the amount of heat in whatever is being investigated. The major difference between this example and the problem in behavioral measurement is in the latter the relationship between the indirect index—the test score—and the underlying trait of interest is not nearly as perfect as it is with physical quantities.

It is not difficult to imagine that scores on a paper-and-pencil test which measures (indirectly) mechanical ability will depend to a certain extent upon one's accomplishment in reading. To the extent that the resulting measures reflect differences in reading ability rather than differences in mechanical ability, error is introduced. This error is called *constant error* (in contrast with the variable error previously discussed) because the error will be the same for every person who takes the test and the same for a given person no matter when or how many times the measurement is made. That is, if the test measures reading to a slight extent, it measures reading in this degree for everyone who takes the test and to this degree every time the test is taken.

In measurement, the problem of constant error is the problem of *validity*. It is always necessary to have some evidence that indicates the extent to which the indirect measurement is actually a valid indicator of the trait under investigation. It is necessary to know whether a test really measures what we think it does or, more precisely, whether we can make the kinds of inferences from the test scores which we think we can.

The Criteria

In the previous paragraphs it was noted that each of the four kinds of errors described was associated with a different characteristic of a measuring device. In turn, each of these characteristics represents a separate criterion for evaluating an instrument. Thus, to answer the question of whether a particular instrument is a good measuring device it is necessary to examine the following four things:

1. *standardization*—the quality of which determines the extent to which interpretive errors have been avoided
2. *reliability*—an indication of the relative freedom from variable error
3. *objectivity*—the degree of which reflects the extent to which personal errors have been avoided
4. *validity*—an indication that the measure describes what we think it does, and therefore is not influenced by constant error.

It is important to note that an instrument is not necessarily a good measuring device just because it is free from *one* of these types of errors. A test that is well standardized may still be highly unreliable, lacking in objectivity, and completely invalid. Similarly, a highly reliable test may not have been well standardized, or even if it were both well standardized and highly reliable, it could be completely useless for some specific purpose because of a lack of validity.

On the other hand, lack of objectivity will always be reflected in a lack of reliability. That is, a measure cannot be reliable unless it can be scored with a reasonable amount of objectivity, and validity requires some minimally satisfactory degree of objectivity, reliability, and standardization. If an instrument has been shown to be valid for a particular purpose (that is, for a particular way of making inferences from the results), it may be used in the way indicated without further question—although improvement with respect to the other characteristics would generally increase the validity (that is, make the instrument even more useful than it was). A measure which lacks validity, however, is completely useless no matter how objective, how reliable in other ways, or how well standardized it may be.

Ideally, then, a measuring device could be judged solely in terms of its validity. Unfortunately, no single bit of validity evidence tells the entire story (though lack of it may), and in many instances, for practical reasons, validity evidence is almost entirely lacking. In these circumstances, one evaluates the instrument with respect to the other characteristics and assumes (or just hopes) that it is also valid. Finally, a measure which shows some degree of validity in spite of a lack of objectivity, reliability, and adequate standardization is a highly promising one, for additional refinement with respect to these latter characteristics is likely to result in a substantial increase in validity.

ASSESSING A MEASURING INSTRUMENT

Standardization

In the discussion of interpretive errors, it was pointed out that the observations first recorded, the raw scores, whether they represent the number of items on a test which were correct, the time required to complete a given task, or whatever, indicate little of general significance until they are compared with the results obtained from some well-defined standardization group. Because raw scores do not represent an absolute scale with a zero point and equal units of measurement, they must often (but in research applications by no means always) be transformed to derived scores of some sort.

The two most common forms of derived scores are percentile ranks and standard scores as described in Chapter 6 in the section on locating a single observation in a group of scores. A third variety are the age and grade scores most often found in educational applications. Age scales relate the performance on a test to the chronological age of individuals in the standardization group, either by finding the average score obtained by persons at each age level to be included in the norms or by determining the average

age of persons receiving each of the possible different scores on the test. With either procedure, the result is a table through which raw scores on the measure may be converted to ages.

The primary advantage of such a procedure is that the results are immediately meaningful even to the person who is the most unsophisticated with respect to testing. This type of derived score is also very readily obtained, requiring only knowledge of the ages of the persons in the standardization group and the procedure for finding an arithmetical mean. On the other hand, such a procedure is completely meaningless unless the trait under consideration is highly related to age, at least within the range of scores under consideration. It would be meaningless, for example, to interpret a measure of cynicism on an age scale simply because one does not anticipate a regular increase in cynicism with age among most people. For this reason, age scales are usually used only with measures of general or scholastic ability or with achievement tests. Often in these situations, the age which is read out for any given score is called a *mental age,* and when such a derived score is divided by the individual's chronological age (and multiplied by 100), the result is frequently termed an *intelligence quotient.*

In many school situations, grade scales rather than age scales are used. Grade norms are obtained in exactly the same way that age norms are found—except that the child's grade level rather than his chronological age is used. To derive an accurate picture of how these scores are obtained, one need only reread the preceding two paragraphs, inserting the words school grade for chronological age.

In some special applications, for example, in certain factor-analytic techniques, another form of derived score, the *ipsative* score units are used.[3] According to Cattell (1952a), ipsative units are those "in which the raw scores have been expressed in standard scores with respect to the standard deviation of the population of occasions, i.e., of fluctuant measurements within the individual, instead of with respect to a population of persons, as in normative scores [percentile and standard scores]."

The basic concept of ipsative scoring is appealing in several respects. First, in the investigation of constructs such as drive, motivation, and interest, where the characteristics themselves imply a rank ordering of components within the individual, such a system of standardization would seem quite logical and natural. As Broverman (1962) points out, "an orderly inquiry into the nature of human behavior requires a stringent separation of the between-individual species parameters from the ipsative intraindividual organizational aspects of behavior in order that the separate relational networks of each realm may be established." Second, it is apparent that, except in forced-choice formats (see page 321), a score on an interest inventory is likely to be at least partly influenced by learning capacity,

---

[3] A third variety, *abative* scores, has been defined but thus far has rarely been used. See Cattell (1966).

breadth of past exposure, and other real but irrelevant characteristics. Thus, ipsative scoring would seem to be an ideal way to parcel out such contaminating influences. Finally, there are some "self" theorists in the field of personality measurement who seem to feel that direct contrasts of one individual with others are to be avoided and that all descriptive information should be related to the individual himself.

While those persons enamored with the idea of comparing subjects only with themselves and not with others may feel that ipsative measures represent an ideal form of derived scores, a great deal of caution should be exercised, at least at this stage of our knowledge. Keats (1967), after reviewing the literature on the efficacy of ipsative measures and noting the discouraging results, concludes, "If ipsative scoring is to be regarded as a serious alternative to normative scoring, there is considerable need for the development of a more adequate theoretical model in this area."

It should be emphasized that in many research applications standardization of the measures used is not necessary. It will be recalled that the function of standardization is to reduce interpretive errors, and where interpretive errors are not a problem, there is no need to convert to derived scores. If, for example, the only task is to determine whether two groups differ with respect to some characteristic, raw scores may be used directly, because all that is required is that the scores of the two groups be compared on the same scale. If, however, the research worker wishes to interpret any statistically significant difference found in some practical way, then some form of derived score may be used. Note especially that in such cases the derived scores are used after the analysis, not before.

In studies of the relationship among two or more variables, problems of the different units of measure do arise. However, most indexes of the degree of relationship include the necessary standardization in their formulas. (Remember that the product-moment correlation is the average of the products of the individual's standard scores!)

Objectivity

The objectivity of a measure, it will be recalled, refers to the extent to which the instrument is free from personal error—the personal bias of the observer. Just as a speedometer in an automobile could be designed (for example, by putting a mirror behind the indicator needle) to reduce the inaccuracies which result because each passenger reads the dial from his own position, a measure of a behavioral characteristic can be constructed to reduce the amount of personal error. For example, a test composed of questions asked in multiple-choice form is almost always more objective than one composed of free-response items.

An index measuring the degree of objectivity of any test could easily be developed by using something like Kendall's coefficient of concordance to indicate the degree of consistency obtained when several different persons score the same test.   However, a specific measure of this characteristic of a test is seldom used in practice,[4] simply because a lack of objectivity is directly reflected as a lack of test reliability.   Any test which has an adequate reliability as indicated by the measures discussed below may be assumed to possess sufficient objectivity for use.   On the other hand, a separate index of objectivity as described above may prove valuable to a test constructor by suggesting a specific cause of unreliability in an instrument under development.

Reliability

Reliability is an indication of the extent to which a measure contains variable errors—that is, errors which differed from person to person during any one testing and which varied from time to time for a given person measured twice by the same instrument.   To help clarify the concept of variable error, consider again the analogy of measuring the length of a table. Earlier it was noted that because of many and varied chance inaccuracies, two separate measurements of the same table might produce slightly different results.   The only difference between this situation and the measurement of behavioral characteristics is that in the latter case the size of these variable errors is much greater.

If it can be assumed that the length of the table does not change from time to time, then any differences in reported (that is, observed) table length can be regarded as error.   But which of the two measurements is correct?   Is there any justification for accepting one as a true length and rejecting the other as an erroneous observation?   If both measurements were made with equal care, there obviously is no way of determining whether one observation or the other or both are somewhat in error.

Since it is not possible with any one measurement to know the true length of the table independently of the error of measurement,[5] it seems reasonable to consider that every observation is composed of two components: (1) the true length of the table, and (2) an error which has occurred on this specific measurement occasion.   For example, if the length of the table is reported to be $61\frac{1}{2}$ inches long, it could be that the true length was

---

[4] On occasion, an interrater reliability (usually the correlation between the two sets of scores obtained when the responses from a single set of subjects are scored by two different individuals) is reported.   In the terminology used here this would be called an *index of objectivity.*

[5] If a sufficiently large number of measurements of a single object are taken and the errors are truly chance inaccuracies, it might be assumed that errors which lead to overestimates exactly balance the errors which lead to underestimates, and therefore the average of all the reported measures will be the true length.   This concept is used to derive the *standard error of measurement* discussed on page 290.

61¼ and that the measurement was ¼ inch too much. Perhaps, on the second measurement, the length was reported as 60¾ inches. If the true length is 61¼ inches, then the error component is −½ inch. Similarly, it could happen that Johnny knows the answer to 43 items but guesses the correct answer to 4 items he does not know, or he might have marked the wrong place on the answer sheet for one of the items even though he knew the correct response. In both instances, his true score on the test is 43, but in the first instance there is a positive error of 4, yielding an observed score of 47, and in the second case the error is −1, thus giving a score of 42. The person who administered the test to Johnny does not know what the true score is; all he knows is that on one occasion Johnny received a score of 47 and that when the test was given a second time, Johnny got a score of only 42. The problem is to find a way of estimating how much of Johnny's reported score is attributable to error and how much can be said to represent his true knowledge. While this cannot be done by making two measurements on just one person, if many people are measured twice with the same devices, it is possible to derive an index which will serve as an indication of the amount of variable error in that instrument.

DEFINITION OF RELIABILITY   Consider now that there are many tables to be measured. Assume for the moment that they are all exactly the same length—that is, assume that the true component of the observed measurement is the same for each object. Under these conditions, any variation in reported table length would be attributable to error. If the observed measures were very close together, we would assume that there was very little error in the measurement, while if these reported values differed by a great deal, it could be assumed that the error of measurement was large. Thus, when the true lengths of the tables are identical, the variance of the observed table lengths would provide a good index of the amount of error.

What if all the tables are not of the same length? (This is a much more realistic analogy, since it can seldom be assumed that a group of persons to whom a test has been given all have precisely the same amount of ability, knowledge, or whatever trait is being measured.) In this circumstance, the total variation in observed table lengths is partly due to true differences in table size and partly due to errors which vary from one measuring to the next. Thus, the total variation in the reported table lengths can no longer be used as an index of error. However, just as was the case when we considered a single score, it is possible to conceive of the total variance as involving an error component and a true component. Then, it seems reasonable to ask what proportion of the observed or measured differences in the table length is attributable to true, or actual, differences in length. If this proportion is large, then the measurements reflect true differences; on the other hand, if the proportion is small, a large part of what has been observed is error. This proportion of the amount of variation in true scores to the total variation has been given the name *reliability*. In the measurement of behavioral characteristics, reliability is defined as the ratio of the true-score variance to the variance in the scores as observed.

The concepts just described can be very easily expressed algebraically. To begin with, each person's observed score can be represented as

$$x_i = t_i + e_i$$

where x_i = score actually obtained by person i

t_i = true score for person i

e_i = amount of error which occurred for person i at the time the measurement was made

In the previous example, Johnny's first actual score, x_i, was 47; his true score, t_i, was 43, and the error at the time of the first measurement, e_i, was +4. The second time he was measured, x_i was 42; t_i (assuming Johnny did not change) was still 43; and the error (on this second occasion), e_i, was −1.

From a theorem of statistics, if two scores are normally and independently distributed, the sum of the scores will have a normal distribution such that the variance of the combination is the sum of the variances of the two components. Thus,

$$\sigma_x^2 = \sigma_t^2 + \sigma_e^2$$

where σ_x^2 = variance of observed scores

σ_t^2 = variance of true scores

σ_e^2 = variance of errors

Reliability, defined as the ratio of true-score variance to observed-score variance, can now be expressed as

$$\text{Reliability} = \frac{\sigma_t^2}{\sigma_x^2}$$

$$= \frac{\sigma_x^2 - \sigma_e^2}{\sigma_x^2}$$

From the latter expression it can be seen that if the measurement involves nothing but error (recall, for example, the situation where all tables were of the same length and thus any variation in observed length was entirely attributable to error), then $\sigma_x^2 = \sigma_e^2$ and the reliability is zero. On the other hand, when there is no variable error at all, $\sigma_e^2 = 0$, and the ratio defined as reliability becomes

$$\frac{\sigma_x^2}{\sigma_x^2} = 1$$

Thus, reliability, defined as the ratio of true-score variance to observed-score variance, is an index of the amount of variable error in a measure.

The reliability varies on a scale from zero to one, having the former value when the measurement involves nothing but error and reaching the latter value only when there is no variable error at all in the measurement.

PROCEDURES FOR ESTIMATING RELIABILITY   It is not possible ever to know directly an individual's true score independent of the amount of error which occurs on any particular measurement.   Thus, it is never possible to calculate exactly the values σ_t^2 or σ_e^2.   Consequently, the *true* reliability of an instrument can never be computed.   Rather, various experimental procedures have had to be devised for obtaining information from which the ratio σ_t^2/σ_x^2 may be estimated.   At the present time, there are four classic ways of estimating reliability.   Each of these procedures is basically different in that it defines what is meant by error in a slightly different way.

Test-retest reliability   One obvious way of defining a variable error is in terms of random fluctuations in performance from one testing session to another.   That is, error can be defined as anything which leads a person to get a different score on one testing than he obtained on another testing.   The kind of reliability which is obtained in thinking about errors in this way is commonly called *test-retest reliability*.   Because any fluctation in score from one time to another is called error by this procedure, such an index is sometimes referred to as the *coefficient of stability*.

Without going into the logical or mathematical details, we will simply note that it can be shown that

$$r_{xx'} = \frac{s_t^2}{s_x^2}$$

where $r_{xx'}$ = correlation between performance on the first testing, x, and performance on the second testing, x'

s_t^2 = estimated variance of the true scores

s_x^2 = calculated variance of the observed scores

The correlation between scores on the first testing and scores on the second testing provides an estimate of reliability defined as a ratio of the true variance to the observed variance.

Although at first this might seem to be a completely adequate solution to the problem of estimating test reliability, there is one important difficulty with the procedure.   Were the values obtained measures of the length of a desk or the weight of a coin, it would be completely reasonable to assume that the properties being examined did not change and that any difference in the observed length or weight was error.   This is not so, however, with human characteristics.   Many traits of personality, interest, and attitude are conceived of not as static but rather as continually in a state of flux.   It may, therefore, be inappropriate to consider any and all changes in score from one measurement in time to a second such measure as being error.

Even with measures of achievement, ability, and aptitude there are problems. For if a considerable time elapses between testings, because of some different experiences in the meantime, some subjects learn and others forget. Thus, many of the changes in score are not actually error, and to this extent reliability is underestimated. On the other hand, if retesting is administered immediately or after only a short period, the subjects, remembering their earlier responses, tend to answer the questions in the same way. The resulting effect is to produce a spurious increase in the estimated reliability. The test-retest procedure, then, may either overestimate or underestimate the true reliability of the test, and in many instances it is difficult to determine which has occurred.

Parallel-test reliability   One way of overcoming the problem of the recall of specific items (and thus a spurious overestimate of the reliability) is to administer not the same test twice but two tests composed of different items designed to measure exactly the same trait in the same way. Such tests are called *parallel tests,* or parallel forms of the same tests, and the estimate of the reliability obtained by computing the correlation between scores obtained by the same individuals on two such tests is known as parallel-test reliability.

With this procedure there is the problem of determining when the test constructor has developed two tests which are in fact parallel. Strictly speaking, two tests are parallel if and only if they sample the same content universe in the same way and result in scores (when both are administered to the same group of persons) such that the means, variances, and inter-item covariances are equal. While statistical tests have been developed (Gulliksen, 1950; Wilks, 1946) to determine whether the scores and items meet the latter condition, the checking with respect to content must be on a judgmental basis. If the test constructor has been careful in defining and classifying his content universe, and stratified sampling procedures are used in selecting items for the two parallel forms, it is possible to have considerable confidence that the two tests are actually parallel with respect to content. Then, and then only, if the statistical criteria are also met, can it be said that the two tests are in fact parallel.

The logic by which it can be shown that the computed correlation between scores obtained on two forms of a test provides an estimate of reliability defined as the ratio of true-score variance to observed-score variance is exactly the same as that for test-retest reliability. What is called error, however, is different in the parallel-form procedure from the test-retest procedure. It is obvious that anything which causes a person to receive a score on one of the parallel forms which is different from that he obtained on the other is termed error. Since it is impossible to administer two tests to the same individuals simultaneously, all the time-to-time fluctuations of the test-retest procedure are called error. Different scores on the two tests might also be obtained because the tests were not exactly equivalent. For example, since different items are used, one form may be slightly more difficult for one person and at the same time slightly easier for a second, or the items may not get at precisely the same trait. Thus, *both* time-to-time and form-to-form (sample-to-sample) fluctuations in performance are called error. For this reason, the parallel-form procedure yields what has been termed a measure of *equivalence and stability.*

Split-half reliability   Although parallel-form reliability eliminates the effects of remembering responses from one test to another, it does not overcome the difficulty of calling real fluctuation in the trait under consideration error. To do this, it would be necessary to administer both tests simultaneously to the same people. An approach which approximates this is to first administer a test and then, after the answers have been obtained, to divide the items into two equivalent parts, each scored separately. The correlation between the scores on one part of the test and those obtained on the other part may then represent a measure of form-to-form fluctuation only. Such an index is often called a *coefficient of equivalence,* or split-half reliability.

As was true with parallel-test reliability, there remains the problem of getting the two parts to be approximately equal. One could be very rigorous; it is possible to perform an item analysis on the results, pair items according to difficulty, content, discrimination, and so forth, and assign one item of each pair to each half. However, a much less laborious way, and one which in practice seems to work out very well, is simply to place all the even-numbered items in one half and all the odd-numbered items in the other. Once again, by a logic identical with the procedure for test-retest reliability, it can be shown that the correlation between the scores obtained on the two parts of the test is in fact an estimate of the reliability of a test.

There is one additional problem to be faced when using the split-half reliability that does not occur with the other procedures so far discussed. Test reliability is a function of the test length as measured by the number of items that comprise a test. (The reason for this will be discussed in a later section.) As the length of a test increases, so does its reliability. Thus, since the split-half procedure is based upon a correlation between scores obtained on only half the test, a correction is needed to determine the reliability of the entire test.

For this purpose, the Spearman-Brown prophecy formula is used. In completely general terms it is expressed as

$$r_{xx'} = \frac{mr'_{xx'}}{1 + (m-1)r'_{xx'}}$$

where $r'_{xx'}$ = reliability obtained from the original calculation

m = multiple of the original test length by which the test has been lengthened or shortened

$r_{xx'}$ = reliability of a test m times as long as the original

In the case of the split-half reliability, $m = 2$ because the whole test is twice as long as the half-test on which the original reliability was computed. Thus, when used to correct the correlation between scores on two halves of a test in determining split-half reliability, the Spearman-Brown formula becomes

$$r_{xx'} = \frac{2r'_{xx'}}{1 + r'_{xx'}}$$

When using this formula, we assume that the items added to make the test longer measure the same trait, and further that the variances of the two half-scores are equal (for example, that $\sigma^2_{odd} = \sigma^2_{even}$). If the division of the items into two parts is done carefully, both assumptions can readily be met. However, on occasions when the odd-even approach is used, the variances may not turn out to be equal. A second and more convenient formula which does not require this second assumption (though the first should still hold) has been developed by Guttman (1945). The formula

$$r_{xx'} = 2\left(1 - \frac{\sigma_{x_a}^2 + \sigma_{x_b}^2}{\sigma_x^2}\right)$$

where $\sigma_{x_a}^2$ = variance of the scores obtained on half a of the test
$\quad\quad \sigma_{x_b}^2$ = variance of the scores obtained on half b of the test
$\quad\quad \sigma_x^2$ = variance of the scores obtained on the entire test

may be used with the split-half procedure for estimating reliability.

Kuder-Richardson reliability   A fourth classical way of thinking about variable error is in terms of inconsistency of performance on the items within the measuring instrument. Ideally, when items are arranged in order of increasing difficulty, each person who takes the test should reach a point prior to which he has correctly answered all items in the test and beyond which he will be able to answer none. If such a perfect division as this occurred for each person who took the test (the break coming at different points for different individuals), the test would be perfectly reliable according to the conceptions of Kuder and Richardson (1937). To the extent that there is an area of overlapping where examinees get some of the more difficult items correct and the easier items wrong, error occurs and the test is unreliable.

While this view of variable error seems perfectly reasonable if the test is a relatively pure measure of a single trait such as arithmetic, vocabulary, or spelling (i.e., a unifactor test), such a definition is not acceptable where the test items lack complete homogeneity (i.e., measure different things). If a test measures both quickness in arithmetical computation and vocabulary, a person may miss some easy arithmetic items and get correct more difficult vocabulary items (or vice versa) not because of happenstance but because he has achieved more in one area than another. Because of this characteristic, the Kuder-Richardson reliabilities have sometimes been referred to as a measure of an entirely different characteristic of a test—homogeneity.

If a test is complex—if it measures more than one trait (not necessarily a difficult one!)—it is difficult to say to what extent the inconsistencies in performance result from error and to what extent they reflect intraindividual differences in the traits involved. In such a case, Kuder-Richardson reliability should not be used. However, when the test is obviously unifactor, this approach is perfectly acceptable.

The mathematical derivation of the Kuder-Richardson reliability formula is rather complex and will not be presented here. However, the formula for the index, frequently called K–R 20, is

$$r_{xx'} = \left(\frac{n}{n-1}\right)\left(\frac{\sigma_x^2 - \sum_{j=1}^{n} p_j q_j}{\sigma_x^2}\right)$$

where n = number of items in the test

σ_x^2 = variance of the observed test scores

p_j = proportion of persons who got item j correct

$q_j = 1 - p_j$

Hoyt reliability   Hoyt (1941) has presented a procedure for estimating reliability which defines a variable error in a slightly different way from other approaches presented so far. Though the results are identical with Kuder-Richardson reliability, it is instructive for understanding the concept of reliability to examine his conceptual approach. In Hoyt reliability, the final basic way of defining what is meant by variable error involves a slightly different breakdown of observed-score variance from what has been previously presented.

According to Hoyt's formulation, variation in the performance of an individual from item to item is not considered to be error at all. Rather, it is a real (nonerror) difference, an *intra*individual difference and one which should not be involved in the estimation of reliability. That is, total variation observed is conceived to be made up of three components: true *inter*individual differences, *intra*individual differences (measured by item variance), and error *inter*individual differences. In our previous notation, this concept can be expressed as

$$\sigma_x^2 = \sigma_t^2 + \sigma_i^2 + \sigma_e^2$$

where σ_i^2 = item variance

and the other terms are defined as before. Transposing the *intra*individual difference term, we get

$$\sigma_x^2 - \sigma_i^2 = \sigma_t^2 + \sigma_e^2$$

as the appropriate observed variance to be used. According to Hoyt, then, a better definition of reliability is

$$r_{xx'} = \frac{\sigma_t^2}{\sigma_x^2 - \sigma_i^2} = \frac{(\sigma_x^2 - \sigma_t^2) - \sigma_e^2}{\sigma_x^2 - \sigma_i^2}$$

By means of using a convenient analysis of variance procedure, this reliability can be estimated by

$$r_{xx'} = \frac{MS_{\text{individuals}} - MS_{\text{residuals}}}{MS_{\text{individuals}}}$$

where $MS_{\text{individuals}}$ = mean square of deviations from the individuals' means
$MS_{\text{residuals}}$ = mean square of deviations left over after individual and item variation has been removed

FACTORS INFLUENCING ESTIMATED RELIABILITY   *Procedure for estimating reliability*   Since each of the approaches to estimating reliability defines error in a slightly different way, it is not difficult to imagine that when all procedures are applied to the same test, each one produces slightly different results. It is thus essential for a person who is evaluating the reliability of a test to know exactly what procedure was used and also to be aware of which procedures yield higher and which procedures yield lower estimates of reliability.

First, it should be apparent that the parallel-form estimate of reliability, when computed for a given test on a given group of subjects, will result in a lower coefficient than will the test-retest procedure. This is so not only because parallel-test reliability includes form-to-form as well as time-to-time fluctuation in its definition of error but also because it eliminates the spurious increase in consistency of score which results from the fact that people remember from one time to the next how they responded to the question previously. Because it is a more conservative estimate, parallel-test reliability is the preferred measure. It is often considered a lower bound—that is, the true reliability is likely to be no lower than this estimate.

Split-half reliability, on the other hand, is usually felt to represent the upper bound. In other words, the true reliability is likely to be no higher than this estimate. While there is no reason to expect form-to-form fluctuation in general to be smaller than time-to-time fluctuation, it so happens that any single-trial method of estimating reliability (reliability estimates requiring only one administration of the test such as split-half, Kuder-Richardson, or Hoyt) will result in a serious overestimate if applied to tests having a large speed component. Exactly why this is so is discussed in a later section. For the present, one simply needs to remember that almost every test depends to some degree upon how fast the examinee works, and to that extent the split-half index will be an overestimate of the reliability. Thus, some instruments may appear highly acceptable with respect to reliability when in fact this is an illusion due to severe time limits on the test and the use of a split-half procedure to assess the reliability.

As has already been pointed out, the Kuder-Richardson procedure is not appropriate as a measure of reliability except with tests which are pure measures of some trait. To the extent that a test is complex (i.e., measures more than one characteristic), and as will be seen later, the best predictors today are complex measures, the K–R procedure will underestimate the true reliability. On the other hand, because the Kuder-Richardson is a single-trial estimate, it will overestimate the true reliability. Thus, no general statement can be made as to whether any given coefficient will be too large or too small.

Similarly, it is difficult to generalize about the Hoyt reliability coefficient. However, because of its sophisticated rationale and the fact that it can be used with weighted options (while the K–R cannot) as well as be conveniently computed by means of analysis of variance, this form of reliability is often preferred by researchers, especially those working in test theory.

Test length   A second major factor which has an influence upon test reliability is the length of the test. In the discussion of the split-half reliability, the Spearman-Brown prophecy formula was presented as a quantitative expression of this effect. It remains to indicate why such a relationship is reasonable.

Perhaps the easiest explanation will result from considering any set of items which are organized into a test as but a sample of all possible items which represent a given content universe. If the entire universe could be used, the test would be one of infinite length, and a person's score on it would be his true score. Because only a sample is taken in a practical situation, the score observed is only an estimate of the true score. From principles of sampling design, it is known that the larger the sample (and therefore the longer the test), the more precise the estimate and the smaller the error is likely to be on any particular testing. Thus, as a larger and larger sample is taken, the longer and more reliable the test becomes.

It is interesting to note that Lord (1955), approaching the entire problem of reliability from a sampling point of view, arrived at formulas equivalent to those of Kuder and Richardson.

Group heterogeneity   A third important influence upon the reliability, as estimated, is the range of abilities in the analysis group. This problem arises because by definition reliability, as the ratio of true-score variance to observed-score variance, is a relative measure. Suppose that the actual amount of error in the test remains the same, but the observed variation in score changes considerably (as might well happen if a scholastic ability test were administered first to a group of high school students and then to a population of college graduates). From the formula

$$r_{xx'} = 1 - \frac{\sigma_e^2}{\sigma_x^2}$$

it is apparent that the decrease in observed variance resulting from the restriction in range of ability would sharply increase the second term of the expression and reduce the reliability by a considerable amount.

To circumvent this problem, many test publishers are now reporting separate reliability coefficients for different subgroups of the entire analysis sample. Thus, a different reliability might be given for high school students, for college students, and for the general adult population.

A second way of overcoming this difficulty has become popular in recent years. This is to report an index which, while a function of reliability, is independent of the variability of the group on which it is computed. This index is the *standard error of measurement* and represents an estimate of the standard deviation of the errors obtained in repeated sampling.

Suppose it were possible to put in one group all persons having exactly the same degree of ability—i.e., having identical true scores (t). The scores actually observed on a test administered to them would not be the same because of errors which varied from person to person. That is, $\sigma_x^2 \neq 0$. If, then, a frequency distribution of the observed scores were made and the error components were, as seems reasonable, normally and independently distributed with a mean of zero, the mean of this distribution would be t and its variance σ_e^2 as seen in Figure 7.1 (i.e., its variance

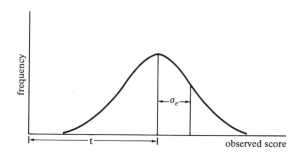

FIGURE 7.1 Frequency distribution of observed scores obtained by persons with a given true score (G. Helmstadter, *Principles of psychological measurement*. New York: Appleton-Century-Crofts, 1964, Fig. 7. P. 77.)

would be the error variance for persons of this level). Similarly, the frequency distribution of observed scores obtained from groups of other ability levels would have a mean equal to their true score and a variance which would be the error variance for persons of that ability level. If it occurred that the error variance was the same regardless of the ability level, the standard deviation of any one of these distributions would be the standard error of measurement. However, error variance does differ from one ability level to the next, and, thus, the standard error of measurement must be thought of as a kind of an average or overall estimate of the standard deviation of these distributions.

Because the standard error of measurement, like reliability, is defined in terms which can never be obtained in practice, it is necessary to estimate it from indexes obtained in an analysis group. Because the standard error of measurement is a function of reliability, the usual procedure is first to estimate the test reliability by one of the procedures already described and then use the test reliability to estimate the standard error of measurement. Thus, from the definition of reliability,

$$\rho_{xx'} = \frac{\sigma_x^2 - \sigma_e^2}{\sigma_x^2}$$

it is possible to obtain

$$\rho_{xx'}\sigma_x^2 = \sigma_x^2 - \sigma_e^2$$
$$\sigma_e^2 = \sigma_x^2 - \rho_{xx'}\sigma_x^2$$
$$\sigma_e = \sigma_x\sqrt{1 - \rho_{xx'}}$$

and the standard error measurement is estimated by taking

$$s_e = s_x\sqrt{1 - r_{xx'}}$$

where s_x is the computed standard deviation of the observed scores and $r_{xx'}$ is the estimated reliability.

Although the standard error of estimate gives an index of variable error which has been adjusted for by the homogeneity of the group on which the reliability is determined, it is a measure in terms of test score units. While the index will not fluctuate spuriously with the homogeneity of the analysis group, it is not possible to make direct comparisons from one test to another. It seems, then, that the choice between reliability and standard error of measurement as an index of the amount of variable errors may be "six of one and half a dozen of another." The main point is that before any evaluation of the amount of variable errors in a test can be made, it is necessary to know exactly what group was used for the analysis.

Speededness A fourth influence on the reliability of a test as estimated is the extent to which a test is affected by speed as contrasted with power. It was mentioned earlier that any single-trial estimate of reliability such as the split-half, the Kuder-Richardson, or Hoyt procedures results in an overestimate of the reliability of tests that have a large speed component. A test is referred to as a pure speed test if it is such that everyone who reaches an item gets it correct. For in this type of test, any differences among scores will depend entirely upon the rate at which the examinees work. An example of this kind of instrument is the Minnesota Vocational Test for Clerical Workers described earlier. Because the task is simply to check those pairs of names or numbers which are different, it is obvious that a person who had unlimited time would be able to attain a perfect score. With a time limit, every item reached is usually answered correctly, and thus, the score will depend almost entirely upon how many items are reached.

Contrasted with this, a pure power test is one in which unlimited time is available. Under these circumstances everyone is able to try all items and the score will depend entirely upon the number of items the examinee was able to answer correctly. For practical reasons, almost all tests have a time limit. A common practice is to set a time limit such that between 75 percent and 90 percent of the examinees on whom the test is tried are able to finish. Thus, almost every published test has at least a small component of speed.

The spurious effect of speededness on test reliability is most readily seen in the case where the odd-even form of split-half reliability is used with a pure speed test. Here the maximum difference between any person's score on the even items and his score on the odd items is one. For, if an examinee gets every item he tries correct, he must have the same number of odd and even items right if the last item worked is an even-numbered one and one more odd than even item correct if the last one attempted was odd-numbered.

Also because in a pure speed test no errors are made on the items reached, there are no inconsistencies in performance from item to item. Thus, estimates of reliability like Kuder-Richardson, which define error in terms of such item-score fluctuations, would also be increased spuriously.

Therefore, it is necessary to use a test-retest or parallel-form approach to reliability with highly speeded tests. One of the best and simplest procedures is to break the items into two parts or sections *before* the test is administered. Then, each half can be separately timed and scored. The reliability for the total test can then be properly estimated with Guttman's formula (see page 286) or by computing the correlation between the scores obtained in the two parts and using the Spearman-Brown prophecy formula (see page 285) to correct to a result for a test twice as long.

Even with such a procedure, speeded tests will generally be found to have higher reliability than power tests. This is not a mathematical artifact, however, but seems to reflect the fact that in actual behavior a great consistency exists in rate of work on a relatively homogeneous set of tasks.

Construction and administration of the test A final set of factors or conditions which can affect the reliability of a test relate to ways in which items are written and the test administered. Knowing what is meant by variable error and bearing in mind that by and large reliability relates to consistency of score (from time-to-time, form-to-form, or item-to-item), you should easily be able to list many things that might be done to improve the usefulness of a test in this respect. No attempt will be made here to present a complete list. Rather, the factors mentioned should serve as examples.

First, there are many things within the test itself. For example, the arrangement of items can sometimes make a difference. If there is a wide range of difficulty among the items, it is usually best to place the easier items near the beginning of the test. This prevents the examinee from wasting time on items beyond his ability and not reaching items he might be able to do. Interdependent or nearly identical items will reduce the reliability. If the ability to answer one item depends on whether or not an examinee has correctly responded to a previous question, or if two items are essentially the same question asked in two different ways, the test is, in effect, shortened. Such things as "catch" questions or emotionally loaded items will also reduce reliability because on one occasion the examinee may see through the "gimmick" or overcome his emotional response, while in a second situation, by chance, the circumstances may prevent him from doing so.

Another important influence is the form of the item. To the extent that the correct response can be obtained by chance, the test will be less reliable. Thus, a true-false item form is not as desirable as a five-answer multiple-choice item. The problem of guessing is often a serious one, and procedures for correcting for it (cf. Helmstadter, 1964) should be employed where appropriate. One final important influence within the test itself is the appropriateness of the difficulty level of the test. A test that is too easy or too difficult for the group contains many items which do not discriminate and thus serve no purpose. This, in effect, shortens the test. In addition, an overly hard test leads to considerable guessing.

Also, some factors which lower the reliability are attributable to the person taking the test. Lack of familiarity with the type of question is one which in the early days of objective testing was quite prevalent. For this reason, many early tests contained several practice problems. It has been shown that the first time a person takes a new type of test such things as multiple-choice items and separate answer sheets may be bothersome. After one experience with such tests, however, sufficient familiarity is acquired so that future performances are not likely to be affected. Since nowadays almost every schoolchild has taken a variety of such tests, practice sessions and overly elaborate directions (except in tests for very young children) are seldom used.

Another characteristic of the person taking the test which may influence reliability is his general attitude. This may be manifest as a set to respond positively or negatively, a tendency to guess, a motivation to fake the results, and so forth. To the extent that such feelings as these vary from time to time, the test results may be inconsistent. In any case, it is usually assumed that this factor can be sufficiently controlled by establishing rapport in the test situation and by using adequate standard directions in the test administration.

No mention has been made of the examinee's physical well-being. Contrary to expectation, it has been found that persons who do not feel well, have headaches, are sick to their stomach, etc., do no more poorly on a test under these conditions than they do when they think they are at their best physically. It is the personal subjective feeling of how well one performs that is lowered, not the test score. Obviously, when an examinee is so violently ill that he actually cannot see or must interrupt the test, the above generalization does not hold. In most instances when an examinee claims he received a low score because he did not feel well when he took the test, it might be a good idea for public relations purposes to give it to him again. But it is not likely that the score will change beyond normally expected fluctuations.

The final set of factors in this group are those resulting from the person giving the test. Failure to establish rapport, to communicate the importance of responding honestly and to the best of one's ability permits the personal attitudes just described to multiply in their effect. It is also obvious that insufficient or varying instructions, a misread stopwatch, a kindly attitude of, "Oh, let's let him have a few extra minutes to finish," or a special hint in answering a question can reduce the reliability of a test. This is why it is so important that persons administering the test read the directions verbatim and follow explicitly the other instructions for test administration.

MINIMUM DESIRABLE RELIABILITY TEST   One final word about reliability concerns the question as to how reliable a test should be before it is useful. This is an extremely difficult question to answer. It has already been mentioned that the reported reliability may vary considerably depending upon the procedure used to estimate it and the homogeneity of the analysis group. Of course, reliability varies too with the degree of speededness, the test length, the item construction, and the directions for test administration. But these latter are traits which in part comprise the quality of the measuring instrument itself and therefore must not be partialed out or ignored when it is evaluated. There are, however, some additional considerations when one is attempting to determine the adequacy of a test with respect to its freedom from variable errors.

One of these is the purpose for which the test is to be used. Many years ago Kelley (1927) devised a classic guide to be used with achievement tests. Assuming that a test must make discriminations of a difference as small as 0.26 times (i.e., approximately one-fourth of) the standard deviation of a grade group with a chance of 5 to 1 of being correct, the following represents minimum reliabilities for different purposes:

1. to evaluate level of *group* accomplishment, .50
2. to evaluate differences in level of group accomplishment in two or more performances, .90
3. to evaluate level of individual accomplishment, .94

4. to evaluate differences in level of individual accomplishment on two or more performances, .98.

Although these requirements are quite stringent and seldom adhered to today, they amply illustrate that the needed degree of reliability varies considerably with the purpose for which the test is to be used.

Similar to this is a statement often heard in test circles that the maximum possible validity (in this case, the correlation between a test and some independent measure of performance) is the square root of the reliability. Actually, this relationship is derived from Spearman's famous correction for attenuation, which is usually given as follows:

$$r_{XY} = \frac{r_{xy}}{\sqrt{r_{xx'}}\sqrt{r_{yy'}}}$$

where r_{XY} = relationship between two traits measured with perfect reliability

r_{xy} = relationship between two traits as measured

$r_{xx'}$ = reliability of the measure of one trait

$r_{yy'}$ = reliability of the measure of the second trait

Considering the test measure to be represented by the symbol x and the independent measure or criterion by y and multiplying both sides of the expression by the denominator of the right-hand term,

$$r_{xy} = r_{XY}\sqrt{r_{xx'}}\sqrt{r_{yy'}}$$

we may then conceive of the maximum validity as occurring when the true relationship between the test and the independent, or criterion, measures is perfect (i.e., when $r_{XY} = 1.00$).

Thus, the maximum observed correlation between test and criterion is

$$r_{xy} = \sqrt{r_{xx'}}\sqrt{r_{yy'}}$$

If it is further assumed that the criterion is measured without error (i.e., that $r_{yy'} = 1.00$), then

$$r_{xy} = \sqrt{r_{xx'}}$$

and it can be stated that the maximum test criterion correlation is the square root of the reliability of the test.

In addition to the purpose for which a test is to be used, it is necessary to consider the content of the test when evaluating the adequacy of its reliability. In the discussion of test-retest reliability, it was hinted that measures of certain trait areas would tend to be less reliable than those of others. As it turns out, generally speaking, aptitude and ability tests will have slightly lower reliabilities than achievement tests, and measures of typical performance have reliabilities much lower than tests of maximum performance. For example, by simply recording reported reliabilities for well-known tests in each of several areas, the author obtained the medians and ranges shown in Table 7.1.

TABLE 7.1

Range and Median Values of Reliabilities Reported
for Various Types of Measures

Type of Test	Number of Reliabilities	Value of Reported Reliabilities		
		Low	Median	High
Achievement batteries	32	.66	.92	.98
Scholastic ability	63	.56	.90	.97
Aptitude batteries	22	.26	.88	.96
Objective personality	35	.46	.85	.97
Interest inventories	13	.42	.84	.93
Attitude scales	18	.47	.79	.98

SOURCE: G. Helmstadter, *Principles of psychologica measurement.* New York Appleton-Century-Crofts, 1964, Table 8. P. 85.

Closely related to the above, the final consideration before deciding whether a particular reliability is adequate is the general run of coefficients reported for other measures of the same trait. In some instances, a reliability which is far from perfect may be the best yet, much better than impressionistic judgment, or better than simply ignoring the trait because no measuring device is available.

In summary, a reliability coefficient must be interpreted in terms of the procedure used and the homogeneity of the analysis group and is to be evaluated in the light of the purpose for which the test is to be used, the content area measured, and the success with which other similar instruments have met in eliminating variable errors.

Validity

It will be recalled that the problem of validity arises because psychological measurement is indirect. Under such circumstances, it is never possible to be completely certain that a test measures the precise characteristic for which it was designed. Thus, it is always necessary to gather some sort of evidence which provides confidence that a test score really represents what it appears to represent.

As in the case with reliability and variable errors, determination of the extent to which a test is affected by constant errors (errors which are the same for every person who takes the test and a given person each time he is measured) involves a variety of experimental procedures. These many different approaches may be conceived as representing three basic kinds of validity, each primarily concerned with a different aspect of the total testing situation as represented in Figure 7.2. This total testing situation for each individual can be thought of as involving three major components: the test-

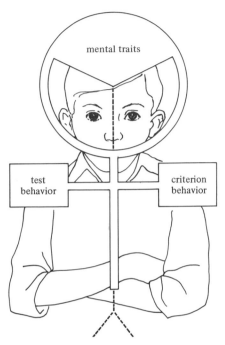

FIGURE 7.2   Schematic representation of the total testing situation for an individual (G. Helmstadter, *Principles of psychological measurement.* New York: Appleton-Century-Crofts, 1964, Fig. 8.   P. 88.)

taking behavior, the mental traits which supposedly determine behavior, and behavior in some external (nontest-taking), or criterion, situation.

One way of gathering evidence which will support the idea that a test measures certain characteristics is to make a careful examination of the test-taking situation and the test behavior in and of itself.   When this is the primary emphasis of the study, the concern is for what is known as *content validity*.   Contrasted with this, the evidence used to indicate that a test measures what it is designed to measure might be entirely restricted to the relationship between the test behavior and the criterion behavior. This kind of evidence is called *empirical validity*.   Finally, when the evidence gathered implies or depends upon the existence of some mental trait (seen earlier as a hypothetical construct), it is referred to as *construct validity*.   Each of these three basic types of validity—content, empirical, and construct—includes several kinds of evidence and has special value under certain conditions.   Thus, each type is discussed at some length below.

CONTENT VALIDITY   *Face validity*   The most common variety of content validity (or of any type of validity, for that matter) is face validity.   Face validity does *not* refer to what an instrument actually measures but to what

it appears, on the basis of a subjective evaluation, to measure. Face validity is the least justifiable of all the concepts of validity. Obviously, reading
over the items of a test to see if the items look satisfactory and judging
whether the content appears to be appropriate is not a very scientific form
of evidence. Yet, time and time again, casual examination of the items by
a prospective test user rather than inspection of data reported in a test
manual has determined whether or not a particular test was used.

Even though face validity is never to be regarded as a substitute for more
objective kinds of evidence, it does have a place in testing. First, in the
original writing of items, face validity is about all there is to rely upon. It
is difficult to believe that anyone would create test items which did not appear (either ostensibly or because of some empirically observed or hypothetical relationship) as if they would work. But, once items have been
written, face validity in test construction is not at all important, for there
are objective ways of determining whether an item is doing a good or a
poor job for the specific purpose for which the test was conceived.

A second way in which face validity has some importance is in gaining
rapport and maintaining good public relations. Particularly when tests are
used in industry, in military situations, or in connection with civil service
examinations, it is of some importance that the items and the test as a
whole appear to be plausible and relevant to the stated purpose. If they
are not, those taking the test are likely to exhibit negativism, and a public
which is uninformed as to the better and objective criteria for evaluating
the worth of a test may be severely critical of both the specific agency involved and the use of tests in general. Fortunately, it is almost always
possible to develop tests which combine face validity with other types of
validity. If a choice is unavoidable, however, the test which has been
found valid by some procedure other than face validity is the one to be
preferred.

Logical, or sampling, validity The second variety of content validity
has been variously termed logical validity, validity by definition, content validity proper, and sampling validity. Actually, it is the last term which
comes closest to describing what is meant. Here, the primary concern is
whether a specifically defined universe of behavior is adequately sampled
by the test in question.

Although logical validity, like face validity, depends upon the judgment
of an expert in the field, it involves far more than merely looking at the
items to see if they appear to do the job. First, it requires a careful definition in behavioral terms of the trait or content area to be measured. Second, it involves a breakdown of the total area defined into categories which
represent all major aspects of the area. Finally, it involves a judgment as
to whether there is in each of the categories a sufficient number of items
which do in fact discriminate between those persons who have the particular characteristics or possess the knowledge or trait and those who do not.

It should be pointed out that logical validity properly finds its greatest use in measures of achievement and in measures of newly defined characteristics, where no direct criterion external to the measure itself seems available. Whenever independent criteria do exist, they should be used instead of (or at least along with) logical validity.

Factorial validity Probably the most sophisticated form of content validity makes use of the technique called *factor analysis* to determine to what extent a given test measures various content areas. Because a factor analysis involves gathering empirical data on test performance for a variety of measures, some writers classify factorial validity as a type of empirical validity. However, because most such studies include only test behaviors and because their primary purpose is to analyze test content, it logically fits into the scheme presented here as content validity. In those few studies which include both other test behaviors and some external or criterion measure, the factor analysis would seem to provide one way of gathering evidence for construct validity. The term *empirical validity,* as earlier determined, is restricted to those studies concerned only with the relationship between a test and a criterion measure.

To understand fully the meaning of factorial validity, it is necessary to know some of the basic tenets of factor analysis. These principles are given in some detail in the following chapter and will not be repeated here. For now, it is sufficient to note that, starting with a table of intercorrelations expressing the observed relationships among many measures, factor analysis provides a means by which first one "new" trait or factor is postulated and then another, each in turn accounting for as much as possible of the "common performance" observed among the measures that remain after the effects of the preceding factors have been removed. The result is a *factor matrix,* or table of factor loadings. These factor loadings provide an index of the extent to which the given test measures each of the traits or content areas involved and thus of the factorial validity of each instrument included in the original correlation matrix.

It is not difficult to see how factor analysis fits in with the idea of content validity. Suppose, for example, the researcher wished to ascertain the validity of a paper-and-pencil test of mechanical ability. One approach would be to ask about the extent to which the test content depends upon (or perhaps more accurately, is related to) such things as spatial perception, a knowledge of "barnyard physics," tool familiarity, manual dexterity, and other traits which seem logically related to mechanical ability, rather than upon such things as reading achievement and general scholastic ability, which should not be too highly related to mechanical ability but which must come into play to a certain extent whenever a paper-and-pencil test is used.

Instead of merely making a subjective judgment after looking over the instrument, one can administer this test along with two or three separate measures of each of the more or less pure traits mentioned above. Then, a factor analysis is likely to yield a separate factor for each of the major different types of tests included in the battery, and the factor loadings of the test for mechanical ability will provide an indication of the extent to which that test measures scholastic ability, reading, tool familiarity, "barn-yard physics," spatial perception, and so forth. These factor loadings represent the factorial validities of the test. While it is obvious that, with this procedure, no factor can come out of the analysis which does not go in with the tests selected for inclusion, such a procedure will quickly reveal important content lacks and point out the extent to which scores are likely to be dependent upon some obviously irrelevant characteristics.

EXPRESSING EMPIRICAL VALIDITY   Earlier in this section it was noted that empirical validity provides the evidence that a test score can be interpreted in a particular way by showing that a relationship exists between the test performance on the one hand and, on the other, behavior in some second (criterion) activity. This relationship between test and criterion perform-ance can be expressed in several ways.

Because it represents a measure of association between two continuous variables, the Pearson product-moment correlation coefficient is the most common index of empirical validity. Thus, a measure of scholastic ability is validated by correlating test scores with subsequent grade-point averages, a test of mechanical ability is assessed for validity by means of the correla-tion between scores on the measure and ratings of performance on the job, and so forth. If either the criterion or the test or both variables are not measurable on an interval scale or are not linearly related, then some other form of correlation such as rank-order, biserial, tetrachoric, or the correla-tion ratio may be used.

Sometimes direct measurement of the criterion behavior is expensive, un-reliable, or nearly impossible to obtain. Under these circumstances, other ways of describing the relationship between the two behaviors must be found. One possibility is that of noting the mean difference in performance among readily recognized groups. For example, evidence of the empirical validity of a measure of art aptitude might be expressed in terms of the differences in mean scores obtained by people in general, by art students, and by professional artists. If the test is empirically valid, scores should increase considerably from the first group to the last. Similarly, a test of scholastic ability might be empirically validated by showing that the aver-age of the scores obtained on the test increases as it is administered to per-sons at successively higher levels of education.

Another somewhat different approach is to express the relationship be-tween test and criterion performance in terms of the percentage of individ-uals who would be correctly classified by the test according to their known group membership. Thus, an interest measure which was designed as an aid in occupational guidance might be empirically validated by showing that a high proportion of persons presently on the job could be correctly classified according to their occupation from the test scores alone.

When empirical validity is expressed, as it usually is, in terms of the correlation between test scores and performance on some criterion, the further question arises as to how high the validity coefficient should be for the test to be useful. In general, this question can be answered in two ways: first, it is possible to determine the amount of error which would be made if the test were used to predict an individual criterion score; second, it is possible to compare the number and kind of selection errors made when using a test for screening purposes with those errors made without the use of the test. Each of these answers to the question will be discussed in turn.

Predicting an individual criterion score [6]   Consider the problem of attempting to predict the success of a boy who is about to enter college. Since grade-point average at the end of the first year is the index used to determine whether the boy will be allowed to return to school the next year, assume that it is the criterion score which is to be predicted.

Without any information at all about this boy, except that he hopes to enter a particular college, it is still possible to make a prediction about what his grade-point will be. Logically, the best guess as to his grade-point would be that typically received by entering freshmen. That is, if the average grade-point earned by freshmen at this particular institution was 1.76, then, in the absence of other relevant information, the best guess as to this new entering freshman's performance would be 1.76. Suppose, however, some information were available as to this entering student's performance on an entrance test known to be related to grade-point. No longer is the best estimate as to his future grade-point the average of that achieved by all freshmen. Rather, from the basic logic of prediction as described previously, the best guess is now the grade-point typically achieved by those students who received the same score on the entrance test as did this new applicant.

Just how such a prediction would be made can be seen from the schematic scatterplot between entrance test scores and grade-points as shown in Figure 7.3. The curve to the left of the Y axis can be thought of as representing the frequency distribution of grade-points achieved by all freshmen, and the curve to the left of the vertical line at point X can be thought of as representing the frequency distribution of the grade-points achieved by those freshmen who received a score of X_0 on the entrance test. The line

---

[6] It should be recognized that for most practical situations it is not actually necessary to predict exact criterion scores but only to assign the individual to broad categories like *pass–fail, satisfied–unsatisfied, likely to profit from treatment–not likely to profit from treatment.* Nonetheless, the logic of predicting an individual score represents an important theoretical notion and does provide a way for interpreting validity coefficients in the absence of information about the base and validity rates described in the next section.

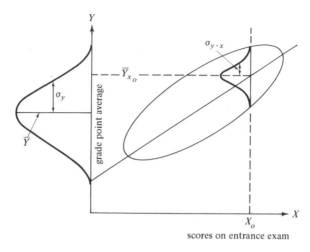

FIGURE 7.3   Errors of predicting an individual performance with and without test information (G. Helmstadter, *Principles of psychological measurement.*   New York: Appleton-Century-Crofts, 1964, Fig. 18.   P. 116.)

$Y = a + bX$ represents the regression line for predicting Y from X; and, as
usual, the thickness of the ellipse which circumscribes the scatterpoints representing the individual students can be used to judge the degree of relationship
between the two variables.   In this figure, then, $\overline{Y}$ represents the best estimate
of grade-point when no test information is available and the value $\overline{Y}_{x_0}$ represents the best estimate of grade-point for an applicant who received a
score of X_0 on the entrance test.

Next, it is necessary to consider how accurate the estimate of grade-point
would be, first without and then with the test-score information.   If every
entering freshman received exactly the same grade-point, then there would
be no error whatsoever in the estimate of grade-point.   At the other extreme, if the grade-points of freshmen varied all the way from 0.00 to 4.00
(where 4.00 represented a straight-A average), the estimate of 1.76 (the
average of the grade-points achieved by all freshmen) could be as much as
1.76 above and 2.24 below the actual achievement of the new applicant.
Within these extremes, it is easy to see that the larger the spread of freshmen
grade-point averages, the worse the estimate of 1.76 might be, and the smaller
the spread, the less likely the value 1.76 will deviate from the grade-point
actually achieved by a significant amount.   It is reasonable that the variance
of the grade-points achieved by all freshmen can be used as an index of how far
off the estimate is likely to be when *no* test information is available.   Similarly,
it is reasonable that the variance of the grade-points achieved by freshmen
who received an entrance score of X_0 can be used as an index of how far off
the estimate is likely to be when we predict the grade-point of an applicant
who gets a score of X_0 on the entrance test.   Thus, the amount of error

anticipated when estimating a grade-point without any test information is represented in Figure 7.3 by the value σ_y^2, and the amount of error anticipated when estimating a grade-point with the test information is represented by the value $\sigma_{y \cdot x}^2$.

There is a direct mathematical relationship among the values ρ_{xy} (the correlation between the test and the criterion measure) and the values σ_y^2 and $\sigma_{y \cdot x}^2$ as defined above. This relationship can be expressed as

$$\rho_{xy}^2 = \frac{\sigma_y^2 - \sigma_{y \cdot x}^2}{\sigma_y^2}$$

Three different indexes, each making use of this relationship, have been used to provide more direct information as to the usefulness of the test for predicting a criterion score than is given by the validity coefficient itself. These indexes are the standard error of estimate, the coefficient of alienation, and the relative reduction of error variance.

(a) The Standard Error of Estimate   This index is a kind of average of the standard deviations of grade-points calculated separately for those freshmen who received each of the different possible scores on the entrance test. The value $\sigma_{y \cdot x}^2$ really represents a kind of average of the values $\sigma_{y \cdot x_1}^2$, $\sigma_{y \cdot x_2}^2$, $\sigma_{y \cdot x_3}^2$, and so forth, where x_1, x_2, x_3, and so forth represent the various possible scores on the entrance test.

The standard error of estimate can be computed by means of a formula obtained by solving the equation given above for $\sigma_{y \cdot x}$. Thus,

$$\sigma_{y \cdot x} = \sigma_y \sqrt{1 - \rho_{xy}^2}$$

This standard error of estimate can then be used to set confidence limits about an estimated criterion score in exactly the same way that the standard error of measurement was used in determining the confidence limits of a true score. Suppose that an applicant to college achieved a score of 119 on an entrance test known to have a correlation of .60 with the grade-point average at that institution. If the average of the grade-points achieved by past freshmen who got a score of 119 was 2.9 and the standard deviation of the grade-points achieved by all freshmen was 0.5, then the 95 percent confidence limits would be determined by taking: $2.9 \pm 1.96\, s_{y \cdot x}$. The value $s_{y \cdot x}$ would be calculated as follows:

$$\begin{aligned} s_{y \cdot x} &= s_y \sqrt{1 - r_{xy}^2} \\ &= 0.5\sqrt{1 - (.60)^2} \\ &= 0.4 \end{aligned}$$

Thus, confidence limits become $2.9 \pm 1.96(0.4)$, and it would be anticipated, with 95 percent confidence, that the grade-point achieved by the applicant, were he to be admitted, would be somewhere between 2.1 and 3.7.

(b) The Coefficient of Alienation   While the standard error of estimate provides an excellent practical measure of the amount of error when estimating a criterion score, it is always expressed in the same units as is the criterion measure. When the criterion is measured with large numbers, the standard error of estimate will be large, and when the criterion is measured in terms of small numbers, the standard error of estimate will also be small in absolute magnitude. Thus, the actual size of the standard error is always a function of the size of the standard deviation of the criterion distribution.

This bothersome problem of having an index of error which is affected by the units of the criterion measure can be overcome by the use of a relative index. One such index is the coefficient of alienation, which can be expressed as the ratio of the standard error of estimate to the standard deviation of the criterion scores. That is,

$$\text{Coefficient of alienation} = \frac{\sigma_{y \cdot x}}{\sigma_y} = \sqrt{1 - \rho_{xy}^2}$$

When the standard error of estimate is small in relation to the standard deviation of the criterion distribution, the efficiency of predicting an individual score is high and the coefficient of alienation is low. As the standard error of estimate approaches the criterion standard deviation, the efficiency of prediction becomes less and less and the coefficient of alienation is an inverse measure of the effectiveness with which a prediction can be made from a test.

(c) The Relative Reduction in Error   A much simpler and more direct relative measure of the efficiency of predicting a criterion score can be obtained by simply squaring the correlation between the test and the criterion measure. It has already been noted that

$$\rho_{xy}^2 = \frac{\sigma_y^2 - \sigma_{y \cdot x}^2}{\sigma_y^2}$$

Since $\sigma_{y \cdot x}^2$ represents the amount of error with the use of the test and σ_y^2 represents the amount of error when estimating the criterion score without the use of the test, the difference $\sigma_y^2 - \sigma_{y \cdot x}^2$ represents the reduction in error which results from use of the test. Dividing this difference by the original amount of error gives the relative reduction in error achieved through the use of the test.

Thus, if the correlation between a test and a criterion were .30, the relative reduction in error would be only .09, while if the correlation between a test and criterion were as high as .70, we would be .49, or nearly 50 percent, more accurate in estimating the criterion scores with the test than without it.

Using tests to improve decisions   Those readers who are aware that with the present state of knowledge the obtained correlations in predicting success in college centers around .60 may be quite shocked to realize that the reduction in error over pure chance (i.e., over guessing the mean grade-point average of all freshmen for every new student) when predicting a specific grade-point average by the use of a test is only slightly more than one third. Fortunately, except for individual counseling purposes, it is seldom necessary to predict an individual's exact criterion score. In most situations, tests are used for screening or selection purposes, and the determination of the extent to which a test is useful in these circumstances takes a different form from that just described.

A typical screening situation has been represented graphically in Figure 7.4. In this figure, the ellipse represents the scatterplot indicative of the

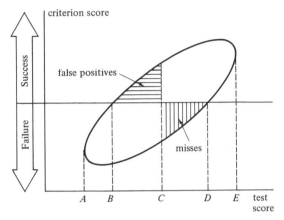

FIGURE 7.4   Schematic representation of the effectiveness of a test in a selection situation (G. Helmstadter, *Principles of psychological measurement.* New York: Appleton-Century-Crofts, 1964, Fig. 19.   P. 120.)

degree of relationship between the test scores and the criterion scores. At some point along the *Y* axis is a place at which, administratively or otherwise, quality of performance is considered to be entirely unsatisfactory. All measures of performance exceeding this value lead to the decision *successful,* and all persons performing less well would be termed *failures* (they would be dismissed from school, fail to receive a degree, be fired from a job, and so forth). Any one of the possible cutting scores on the test, such as those represented by points *A, B, C, D,* and *E,* is a score to be selected as representing the test performance which must be achieved by a person in order to be accepted (admitted to school, hired for a job, given a license, and so forth).

With the cutting score on the test somewhere near the middle of the score range, say, at point *C,* the ellipse, containing all individuals, will be divided into four sections. In the lower left quadrant will be persons who would not be acceptable if the cutting score were used and who would have failed had they been given the chance. In the upper right quadrant are points representing persons who would have been selected for the task and who would have succeeded. Thus, the decision based on the arbitrary cutting score to accept or reject would have been correct for every person falling in these quadrants. Not so individuals whose test and criterion scores place them in the upper left or lower right quadrants. In both of these latter instances, an error would have been made had the cutting score C, as pictured, been selected. Persons falling in the upper left portion of the ellipse are those who would not have been accepted by their test performance but who would have succeeded had they been given an opportunity; those in the lower right are persons who would have been accepted but who would have failed at the task. The former are designated *false positives* and the latter *misses*.[7]

To evaluate the effectiveness of a test in a screening situation, two conditions other than the size of the correlation (which is represented in the figure by the narrowness of the ellipse) between test and criterion scores must be known. The first of these is the cutting score itself. The second is the *base rate of error,* that is, the proportion of persons who failed prior to the use of the test. The base rate represents the proportion of incorrect decisions which are made when selecting individuals without the use of the particular test under evaluation. In effect, when individuals are all given an opportunity to try out, a prediction is made for each person that he will succeed. To evaluate the effectiveness of a test in a particular situation, then, the proportion of incorrect decisions made when the test is used must be determined and compared with this base rate of error.

SPECIAL PROBLEMS IN EVALUATING TESTS BY MEANS OF VALIDITY COEFFICIENTS   It would be ideal if it were possible when evaluating tests by means of empirical validity coefficients simply to choose that test which had the highest reported validity coefficient. Although it is generally true that the higher the validity coefficient, the more useful the test for predicting an individual criterion score or for screening purposes, two specific situations arise in which the validity coefficient is not truly representative of the effectiveness of the test. In one case, the value of the test may be underestimated; in the other, it will be exaggerated. The user of tests, therefore, needs to be aware of what these circumstances are and the way in which they operate spuriously to affect the validity coefficient.

Concurrent validity   In almost all the previous discussion of empirical validity coefficients, it has been assumed that the test data were gathered first and then at some later time, by means of a follow-up study, the crite-

---

[7] This terminology may seem backward to those interested in employee selection who might ordinarily think of persons hired who later failed as false positives and persons not hired who could have done the job as misses. The notations, however, derive from medicine, where a false-positive test implies that disease was indicated when it did not exist, and the person who has the disease but is not detected is called a miss.

rion data were gathered. This approach to gathering empirical validity results in information often referred to as *predictive* validity.

On the other hand, it is sometimes expensive, inconvenient, ethically undesirable, or otherwise nearly impossible from a practical point of view to obtain data in this way. Rather, it is necessary to obtain criterion data at the same time or even prior to securing the test information. For example, it may not be possible to administer a test to hundreds of children and then to wait five or ten years to follow them up to see how many have become successful mechanics. It is obviously much less costly simply to search out mechanics who are presently on the job and administer to them the test at the same time that ratings or other criterion information are gathered from their employers. In contrast to the predictive validity described earlier, empirical validity data gathered in this latter way would provide information referred to as *concurrent* validity.

Although such a time-wise distinction may seem pedantic and even superficial at first, it is of considerable importance when we attempt to assess the usefulness of a test in a particular practical situation, because test results if they are to be useful (as contrasted with just interesting) must, in the final analysis, be predictive. Thus, immediately, the student will suspect that predictive validity is a much more valuable type of evidence than concurrent validity. Beyond this, however, there is a very serious limitation of concurrent validity: a restriction in range (on both test and criterion scores) as a result of preselection.

The usual procedure in obtaining concurrent validity is to administer a battery of tests to a group of employees already on the job or to students while they are in school. At the same time, supervisor ratings, productivity indexes, grade-point averages, or other criterion data are gathered. Then, the correlation between test results and criterion scores is computed and reported as the validity evidence. The restriction in range occurs because such a study omits one extremely important group. It does not include persons who, either through failure or as a result of their own selfselection, have already left the situation. It is obvious that the effect of this preselection will be to reduce the computed relationship between the two variables. The danger is that such an effect is greatest on those very characteristics which are the most important and useful as far as prediction of success is concerned. Thus, a crucial variable may be overlooked or discarded.

To take an extreme example, it is conceivable that the most important single factor in determining success or failure as a musician is whether a person is tone-deaf. If this were the case and a battery of tests were administered to professional musicians, little relationship would be found between a measure of tone-deafness and ratings of performance, salaries, or other criteria. Thus, simply because no person on the job as a musician is tone-deaf, it might be erroneously concluded from the empirical study alone that a measure of this trait is of little importance. Yet, for guidance work and for early identification of the musically talented, it would be perhaps the most important characteristic of all.

Cross-validation   The failure to consider the effects of the restriction in range when it is necessary to gather empirical data by the process of concurrent validation results in underestimating the usefulness of a test. On the other hand, neglecting to gather new information as to the effectiveness of the test *after* the prediction or selection system has been worked out (i.e., failure to cross-validate) can lead to exaggerated claims as to the effectiveness of the prediction or selection.

Whenever a test is used either for prediction of a specific criterion score or for screening purposes, the resulting prediction equation or cutting score is determined in such a way that error is minimized for the specific data at hand. In this way, many of the chance fluctuations occurring in the particular observations obtained are used to advantage. This advantage tends to spuriously increase the estimated accuracy of prediction over that which can actually be accomplished when the findings are applied to new observations. Therefore, to properly evaluate the usefulness of a test, the prediction equation, or cutting score, must be derived from one sample of information and validated on a second sample of subjects from the same universe. If this has been done, the test is said to be cross-validated for that universe.

A person who attempts to apply the test, even to a second sample of the same universe, without cross-validation should anticipate a reduction in the test-criterion correlation found in practice as compared with that calculated in the original analysis. In general, when a single test is used, the smaller the size of the original sample, the greater the shrinkage of the validity coefficient in cross-validation. If more than one measure is used in the prediction or selection system, the amount of shrinkage will also be a function of the number of variables tried out: the larger the number of original predictors used and the smaller the proportion of variables retained, the greater the reduction in actual validity from that found with the original sample.

In many instances, a potential user of a test examines validity coefficients reported in the literature in the hope of determining whether the test would be useful in his own situation. Judgments of this sort require inferences beyond the original universe, and thus the actual validity in the new situation can be expected to be smaller than the reported coefficient, even if the latter were cross-validated on a second sample in the original situation.

It may be necessary for the potential user of a test to carry out additional cross-validation studies to assess accurately the usefulness of the test in a new situation. For example, the research workers may wish to check the effectiveness of the test on a population slightly different than that used in the original validation study. If this is done by the same criterion as in the original study, it is called *validity generalization*. Or the potential user of a test may wish to assess its usefulness as a predictor of a slightly different criterion as well as on a slightly different population. This latter type of cross-validation is referred to as *validity extension*. Other variations of cross-validation studies which may be useful in special circumstances have been described by Mosier (1951).

Cross-validation is especially important in the selection of items for a test and in discovering so-called *psychometric signs* (score characteristics, empirically derived, which distinguish between two or more groups). For example, suppose an attempt were being made to develop a system for distinguishing between clinically diagnosed groups of psychopathic deviates and schizoids. Further, suppose that scores are available for each patient on ten personality variables. If it were felt that the relevant information was to be found in score differences rather than the scores themselves, there could be different indexes which might be tried. Suppose that upon testing the significance of differences between mean index values for the two groups one found 3 of the 45 possible indexes to be significant at the 5 percent level. Could it be said, from this evidence alone, that the 3 significant indexes were psychometric signs which could be used for distinguishing between the two clinical groups studied?

The answer is no. By the very meaning of the 5 percent level of significance, one should expect to find differences this large or larger 5 times in 100 even though the null hypothesis (i.e., no difference) was true. Roughly, $(45)(0.05)$, or between two and three significant differences might be expected, even though the null hypothesis holds in every case.

While no one with any statistical sophistication at all would fail to determine the significance of any observed correlation (or multiple correlation), too many researchers have failed to compare the observation of psychometric signs with a chance distribution. The best answer to the question of how to tell if the "significant" psychometric signs represent real differences or expected chance occurrences is to cross-validate by taking a new sample and seeing if the same psychometric signs appear. If they do, the researcher can have a fair degree of confidence that his finding will hold up in subsequent studies.

The person who is selecting items for a test or developing a system for distinguishing between two or more groups on the basis of psychometric signs must be careful, however, not to confuse successive refinements of the instrument with cross-validation. Once he has identified a number of test items or signs which significantly distinguish between the criterion groups obtained in one sampling of the two universes, the investigator may wish to try them out on a second sample. If he then further refines the instrument by retaining only those items which turned out to be significant on both trials, the final measure cannot be considered to have been cross-validated, for at no time has the predictor been tried out exactly as it will be used on a new sample. Proper cross-validation begins only after all refinements of the procedure have been completed and requires that the selection or prediction system be applied to a new situation *unchanged* from the previous trial.

In summary, cross-validation provides more accurate information about the usefulness of a test in a particular situation than can be obtained from a validity coefficient calculated on the original group of subjects used to develop the prediction or screening system. Cross-validation is accomplished by trying out a previously developed and refined test (or series of psychometric signs) on a completely new group as close as possible to that for which the test will ultimately be used. To the extent that the original sample used for the test development was small (or different), to the extent that a large number of predictors was tried and only a small proportion ultimately retained, there is likely to be considerable shrinkage in the cross-validation validity coefficient from that obtained with the original analysis group.

CONSTRUCT VALIDITY   Construct validity is the most recent addition to the conceptual ideas concerning the kinds of evidence required before a test user can feel justified in interpreting test scores in certain ways. Suggestions for its use first appeared in two reports of an APA Committee on Psychological Tests (1952, 1954). More recently, Cronbach and Meehl (1955) have elaborated and clarified the concept. Most of the ideas and even some of the examples discussed in this section have been taken from this latter article.

In an earlier section it was pointed out that human characteristics such as mechanical ability, musical talent, clerical aptitude, intelligence, and in fact all mental traits (including attitude, interest, and personality) which one might attempt to measure with tests, scales, and inventories are hypothetical constructs, each carrying with it a number of associated meanings relating how a person who possessed the specified traits would behave in certain situations. The process of establishing the construct validity of a test is no simple one. Every validation study becomes an evaluation not of the test alone but also of the theory and concept of the trait as well.

As Cronbach and Meehl describe it, the logical process of construct validation requires: first, setting forth the proposition that this test measures Trait A; second, inserting this proposition into present theory of Trait A; third, working through the theory to predict behavior characteristics which should be related to test scores and those which should show *no* relation to test scores if the test truly measures Trait A as presently conceived; and, finally, securing data which will empirically or experimentally confirm or reject the hypothesis.

If the anticipated relationships are found, all is well. For the moment the test is considered valid, and the hypothetical trait with its associated meanings is a useful construct. On the other hand, as Cronbach and Meehl point out, if the predictions (positive or negative) do not hold up, there are three possibilities:

1. The test does not measure the construct variable.
2. The theoretical network which generated the hypothesis is incorrect.
3. The experimental design failed to test the hypothesis properly.

A decision must be made as to which of these three conditions has occurred. A great many of the claims and counterclaims about tests and their interpretation stem from disagreement as to which of the three possibilities is the culprit. The practical test user or the theory builder is likely to say, "That was a nice try, but your test just didn't work out." The test constructor, on the other hand, will reply, "If you had used the appropriate statistical technique or controlled on such and such, you would have obtained the expected results," or, if he can find nothing wrong with the experimental design, will say, "So much the worse for your theory."

Sometimes it is relatively easy to tell what has happened. A well-trained research worker with adequate knowledge of the subject matter involved, through an examination of the procedure followed, would be able to determine whether the design of the study itself was adequate. In some cases, a theory, through much other evidence, is already so well confirmed that a particular validity study is relevant only to the usefulness of the test. Once in a while, when a test has already successfully predicted a great many and a wide variety of criterion behaviors, it may be that in a specific situation where predictions fail to hold up, it is appropriate to reject a part of the theory or some of the associated meanings of the postulated trait.

Perhaps the best way to clarify the nature of construct validation is to point out several features of the process which need special emphasis. First, it should be noted that a specific criterion used in the early stages of the development of a test may be later rejected as less valid than the test itself. According to Cronbach and Meehl (1955), "We start with a vague concept which we associate with certain observations. We then discover empirically that these observations covary with some other observation which possesses greater reliability or is more intimately correlated with relevant experimental changes than is the original measure, or both." These authors then cite as examples the measurement of temperature with a mercury thermometer and scholastic ability with the Binet scale:

For example, the notion of temperature arises because some objects feel hotter to the touch than others. The expansion of a mercury column does not have face validity as an index of hotness. But it turns out that (*a*) there is a statistical relation between expansion and sensed temperature; (*b*) observers employ the mercury method with good interobserver agreement; (*c*) the regularity of observed relations is increased by using the thermometer (for example, melting points of samples of the same material vary little on the thermometer; we obtain nearly linear relations between mercury measures and pressure of a gas). Finally, (*d*) a theoretical structure involving unobservable micro-events—the kinetic theory—is worked out which explains the relation of mercury expansion to heat. This whole process of conceptual enrichment begins with what in retrospect we see as an extremely fallible "criterion"—the human temperature sense. The original criterion has now been relegated to a peripheral position. We have lifted ourselves by our bootstraps, but in a legitimate and fruitful way.

Similarly, the Binet scale was first valued because children's scores tended to agree with judgments by school teachers. If it had not shown this agreement, it would have been discarded along with reaction time and the other measures of ability previously tried. Teacher judgments once constituted the criterion against which the individual intelligence test was validated. But if today a child's I.Q. is 135 and three of his teachers complain about how stupid he is, we do not conclude that the test has failed. Quite to the contrary, if no error in test procedure can be argued, we treat the test score as a valid statement about an important quality, and define our task as that of finding out what other variables—personality, study skills, and so forth—modify achievement or distort teacher judgment.

Second, a consumer of tests needs to know not only the test itself but also the theory behind the test and the evidence which supports the theory. That is, it is absolutely essential that a test user know what interpretations of a test are theoretically possible and which of these have been empirically verified. As Cronbach and Meehl have pointed out, unless essentially the same theory is accepted by all test users, no general scientific validation is possible. A person who does not accept the test author's theory must validate the test for himself in his own situation following his own conception of the trait involved.

Third, scientists can properly evaluate a claim supporting the usefulness of a test and the associated theory of the trait it measures only if the evidence is made public. It is worth noting that failure to meet this latter qualification—the refusal to make evidence available to others—has resulted in severe criticism of a number of test authors and publishers by the American Psychological Association's committee on ethics, as well as suspicion on the part of many psychologists that the tests involved have not really been validated. Excuses that no really adequate criterion for validation purposes exists are not acceptable, and rationalizations about a trait which fail to result in observable consequents cannot be considered construct validation.

Fourth, it should be perfectly clear that each positive study results in greater and greater confidence that a test is a valid measure of a certain construct. On the other hand, in spite of hundreds of prior successes, one well-established negative finding can completely destroy any belief in the absolute reality of the trait measured. Such a pronouncement may seem harsh and actually contrary to what happens in practice, for very few workers would as a result of one contrary finding stop using the test in those situations where positive results had been repeatedly obtained. This apparent conflict can readily be resolved by conceiving of any mental trait (and for that matter any other hypothetical construct which appears any-where in science) not as representing or failing to represent underlying Truth (with a capital T) but as being a relatively useful or useless concep-tion in certain practical or theoretical situations. While one solid negative finding does destroy the logical necessity of the trait as representing the truth, it only sets a boundary on the usefulness of the construct and its measure.

Finally, it should be apparent that it is naive to ask whether a test is valid. As Cronbach and Meehl point out, a test is never really "validated" at all. Rather, a principle for making certain kinds of inferences about persons who obtain given test scores is verified or refuted. If a test yields many types of inferences, some may be valid and others not. The question should not be, Is the test valid? but, Is the test valid for such and such?

From the preceding it might well be anticipated that no single numerical estimate of the degree of construct validity will be found. Rather, a wide variety of approaches and evidences may be used to support claims about what a test measures (and consequently the ways in which it can be used). Cronbach and Meehl list five types of evidence which might be appropri-ate. In reviewing these, the reader will note that procedures previously suggested in assessing content and empirical validity reappear. Although some writers have expressed a fear that construct validity allows test au-thors and publishers to neglect crucial validity studies, what it actually does is to increase the types of evidence required for adequate validation. No longer will a single study in one specific situation involving one particular criterion measure be acceptable as complete evidence that a test measures what its authors claim.

Group differences The first general type of evidence which might lend support to a claim of construct validity is group differences. Many traits are postulated in such a way that persons in different groups are conceived to possess different amounts of the characteristics involved. Thus, men as a group would be expected to perform differently from women as a group in any valid test of mechanical or clerical ability; persons of different age groups (at least through the early years) would be expected to perform differently on any valid test of intellectual development; persons who have had specific training in an area should do better on any valid measure of achievement in that area than persons not having such training; and over-achievers should be different from underachievers (as distinguished in some manner independent of the test under consideration) with respect to a valid measure of scholastic information. Some overlap would be anticipated, and in many circumstances a positive finding would not add greatly to the degree of confidence in the test; but a finding of no difference at all would certainly lead to real doubt about the validity of the test in question.

Changes in performance Somewhat similar to this kind of evidence are changes in performance over occasions. In some respects, this kind of data differs from the former in the same way that a longitudinal study differs from a cross-sectional one. Rather than making comparisons among groups of different individuals, the same persons are studied upon two or more occasions. Whether or not any observed changes in score add to or detract from the confidence in the test will depend upon the conception of the trait it measures. If such traits as musical talent or scholastic aptitude are postulated as constant with age, observed changes in score over a period of time would be discouraging. Similarly, a measure of elation which resulted in an identical score for the same person on all occasions would not be very satisfying.

More convincing than either general stability or fluctuation in score over time is evidence that the introduction of specific variables results in predictable changes (or lack of change) in score. Performance on an aptitude measure should remain the same in spite of the introduction of a training program, while performance on an achievement test in the same situation should increase. Similarly, an increase in scores on a measure of frustration administered immediately following an experimentally induced humiliation over what was found prior to the experiment might be anticipated and a scale measuring authoritarianism should produce the same result whether the questions are stated positively or negatively.

Correlations Another type of evidence which can shed light on construct validity is correlational. Certainly, two measures of the same trait (whether the one is considered a criterion or simply another measure of the same characteristic) should correlate highly. On the other hand, to the extent that a measure correlates with an obviously irrelevant variable, it may be thought of as lacking validity. Student evaluations of classroom teaching which correlate very highly with the grades received would generally not be considered as satisfactory a measure of teaching competence as a scale of opinions which resulted in a somewhat lower relationship between these two characteristics.

While a single correlation between a test and a criterion is generally not considered sufficient evidence in and of itself to establish construct validity, an appropriately designed factor analytic study may. If a trait is conceived such that its function is somewhere in between two others and is completely unrelated to a third, the measure of it might be included in a battery of tests designed to establish these other factors. Then a factor analysis would indicate whether the measure in question had the predicted interrelationships. It should be noted that such a procedure need not imply that the factors found are the true underlying dimensions of the mind. Rather, they are best thought of as reference points set up specifically for an experimental test of certain predictions about the measure under examination. Such a form of reference is more appropriately viewed as being useful or useless for describing and summarizing certain observed phenomena and for predicting new relationships (e.g., Eysenck, 1950).

More recently, Campbell and Fiske (1959) have suggested a way of systematically studying correlational evidence for purposes of inferring construct validity which does not involve a factor analysis. First they point out that a test is always a trait-method unit. That is, a trait cannot be measured independently of some method. Thus, some of the observed-score variance on any test is attributable to the particular method used rather than to just the trait involved. While this method variance is of no particular problem in a purely empirical situation, where the object is to predict some practical criterion, it can be misleading when we attempt to determine whether a test measures some specific trait. Conceivably two separate tests might correlate highly simply because the same method of measurement was used and not because the same trait was involved.

Second, Campbell and Fiske emphasize the importance of the idea, mentioned by Cronbach and Meehl, that any measure is clearly described only by means of a joint method of similarities and differences. It is necessary to tell both what a test measures and what it does not. Evidence of the construct validity of a test must therefore make use both of a convergent principle, which suggests that two measures of the same trait should correlate highly with one another even though they represent different methods, and a discriminant principle, which suggests that two measures should not correlate highly with one another if they measure different traits even though a similar method is used.

As a result of these considerations, Campbell and Fiske advocate a validation process which requires the computation of intercorrelations among tests which represent at least two traits, each measured by at least two different methods. To illustrate the technique, these authors prepared the fictitious multitrait-multimethod matrix presented as Table 7.2. The major components of this table are the following:

1. three *reliability diagonals,* each containing three reliability coefficients in parentheses representing the degree of relationship between the same trait measured in the same way on different occasions
2. three *validity diagonals,* each containing three validity coefficients in brackets representing the degree of relationship between the same trait measured by different methods
3. three *heterotrait-monomethod triangles,* each containing three correlation coefficients representing the degree of relationship between measures of different traits using the same method
4. six *heterotrait-heteromethod triangles,* each containing three correlations representing the degree of relationship between measures of different traits using different methods.

According to Campbell and Fiske, evidence of convergent validity occurs when the entries in the validity diagonal are significantly different from zero and high enough to encourage further investigation. Discriminant validity is suggested when (1) values in the validity diagonal are higher than the values in the heterotrait-heteromethod triangle adjacent to it;

TABLE 7.2

A Synthetic Multitrait-Multimethod Matrix

	Traits	Method 1			Method 2			Method 3		
		A_1	B_1	C_1	A_2	B_2	C_2	A_3	B_3	C_3
Method 1	A_1	(.89)								
	B_1	.51	(.89)							
	C_1	.38	.37	(.76)						
Method 2	A_2	[.57]	.22	.09	(.93)					
	B_2	.22	[.57]	.10	.68	(.94)				
	C_2	.11	.11	[.46]	.59	.58	(.84)			
Method 3	A_3	[.56]	.22	.11	[.67]	.42	.33	(.94)		
	B_3	.23	[.58]	.12	.43	[.66]	.34	.67	(.92)	
	C_3	.11	.11	[.45]	.34	.32	[.58]	.58	.60	(.85)

SOURCE: After D. Campbell & D. Fiske. Convergent and discriminant validation by the multitrait-multimethod *Psychological Bulletin*, 1959, **56**, 81–105.
( ) = reliability coefficients in three reliability diagnoses
[ ] = validity coefficients in three validity diagnoses
    ▭ = heterotrait-monomethod triangle
    ▭ = heterotrait-heteromethod triangle

(2) the validity diagonal values are higher than those found in heterotrait-monomethod triangles (so that the trait variance is larger than the method variance); and (3) the same *pattern* (regardless of the size of the coefficients) is found in all heterotrait (both monomethod and heteromethod) triangles.

The use of the multitrait-multimethod matrix as suggested by Campbell and Fiske does not provide a system which will automatically determine whether a test has or does not have construct validity. Indeed, the very concept of construct validity prohibits this possibility. Such an arrangement of validity information does, however, facilitate the meaningful interpretation of crucial information and, perhaps even more important, provides a means for suggesting steps which might be taken to further improve the measurement of a particular trait.

Internal consistency A fourth type of evidence useful in determining the construct validity of a test is that which comes from studies of its internal consistency. Again, whether high or low internal consistency is encouraging as far as the usefulness of the measure is concerned will depend upon whether the concept of the trait requires a pure or a complex measure. As in the case of factor analysis, the study should involve more than just applying a specific mathematical technique to a set of data which has been gathered in a convenient way. In both cases, a careful, logical analysis of the trait and its relationship to other variables and to special characteristics of the measuring device should lead to specific predictions as to what to expect in terms of observables if the trait concept is appropriately formulated and if the test devised to measure it is adequately designed.

Study of the test-taking process A final kind of evidence which provides information by which a test may be evaluated as a measure of a construct is that which comes from a study of the process which the subject undergoes when taking the test. Informally, one of the best ways to judge what accounts for variability in the scores is to take the test oneself, listing the activities required to answer the items.

To be completely acceptable as validity evidence, however, a more formal procedure should be followed. The listing of the activity types might be done by a group of judges or by observers watching subjects perform, and the list might then be used for the construction of special measures for the purpose of gathering correlational evidence. Sometimes a simple count of the frequency with which various "distractors" are marked on an examination, or an analysis of scratch paper, or an interview with persons who have taken the test may be very revealing. Lucas (1953), for example, by such a procedure showed that the Navy Relative Movement Test actually involved two different abilities: spatial visualization and mathematical reasoning. In addition, an analysis of the scoring procedures (Helmstadter, 1957) may reveal such things as the influence of response sets.

Actually there are no set procedures which can be spelled out and recommended for the analysis of the mental processes required to take a test. It can only be pointed out that with ingenuity rigorous studies of the test-taking process can be made which will produce excellent evidence about the construct validity of a test. Once again this illustrates the point made at the beginning of this section that no single index or even study will in and of itself be adequate evidence of construct validity. Rather, a diverse attack, much as is expected for the verification of any psychological theory, will be required before any measure and its corresponding trait, the construct, will be accepted.

SPECIAL PROBLEMS IN INTERPRETING TEST RESULTS Because it is the principle for making inferences from scores and not the test itself which is validated, all the special problems faced when interpreting test results are directly related to construct validity. This final section discusses three areas of special concern—the criterion problem, guessing and faking, and response sets.

The criterion The criterion problem refers to the fact that in many cases it is extremely difficult to obtain adequate evidence for the validity of a test, simply because no criterion appears to be completely satisfactory. The concept of construct validity and the resulting idea that many varieties of evidence may legitimately support test validity has alleviated the situation somewhat. Nevertheless, on many occasions, even in a practical prediction situation, where empirical validity is of prime importance, a satisfactory criterion will be far from simple to obtain. Yet one must be found if the test is to have any usefulness at all. Thus, it is worthwhile to discuss the general nature of criteria.

Generally speaking, as a measure of success, a criterion might include either a standard of performance set up independently of the person evaluated or an indication of the satisfaction which the individual derives from the activity or both. No matter which of these aspects constitutes the major proportion of the criterion, difficulties arise. For an adequate measure of satisfaction, it is necessary to consider life from the viewpoint of the subject involved. To what extent does he value money, prestige, living in a particular geographical area? What are some of the pressures exerted on him by his family, his community? If an attempt is made to avoid some of this indirection by simply asking the person about the extent to which he is satisfied, additional difficulties are encountered. For example, inferences based on verbal reports are usually less satisfactory than observation or measurement of other overt behaviors; what a person *says* and what he *does* are often two different things. In any case, there will also be a problem resulting from natural selection. All those persons remaining on the job are to a certain extent satisfied. Persons who were sufficiently unhappy to overcome the pressures (or inertia) to stay will have left the job or occupation. Such individuals are practically impossible to trace for inclusion in the analysis sample. If the selection has been severe, the resulting restriction in range may make it impossible to develop an adequate measure.

If the primary concern is that of establishing performance standards, the difficulty is one of accounting for all sorts of specific situational factors which may operate entirely independently of the individual to raise or lower his apparent level of performance. For example, if an attempt is made to use something like the dollar volume on individual sales in a given period, there is the problem of equating different sales territories. A person selling a minimum in one area may be doing better than another who sells twice as much in a region richer in prospects.

Whatever criterion is developed, there are several qualities by which its value may be judged. The one absolutely essential characteristic is that the criterion be *relevant* to the purpose for which the test is used. This statement may at first seem of no consequence yet time and again attempts have been made to validate tests against criteria which are of little ultimate importance. At the start of World War II, tests designed to predict success in gunnery were validated against grades in a training situation. The ultimate goal was success in hitting the prescribed target in combat. As it turned out, grades in training courses were largely dependent upon the student's ability to memorize nomenclature and related only slightly to the ultimate criterion. Once this fact became apparent the content of the gunnery school course was changed, but all the selection tests then had to be reevaluated. Thus, it can and all too often does happen that an immediately available criterion is not always relevant. This is particularly true when success in a training or educational program is involved.

The criterion should also be free of variable errors. If the criterion is a continuous measure, this means it must have reliability; and if it is a discrete variable, it means the same people should always fall into the same category upon repeated classification. Relative freedom from variable errors is a necessary but not a sufficient quality of a good criterion. A certain degree of reliability is necessary in order that it contain some relevant variance, but a high degree of reliability does not guarantee that the criterion has relevance.

Similarly, it is important that the criterion be relatively free from *constant errors*. Lack of relevancy of the criterion represents one form of constant error. Another, not so apparent, arises when a population is divided into subgroups, and then scores obtained by the two or more groups on the test to be analyzed are contrasted in order to obtain evidence of validity. If the procedure used to select subjects for the study produces biased samples, the difference between mean scores obtained by the two groups may be either over or underestimated, depending upon the direction of the bias. Thus, to take an extreme example, suppose an attempt were being made to validate a scale designed to measure social maturity by comparing scores made by freshmen, sophomores, juniors, and seniors in high school. If the sampling included students from schools located in very high and very low socioeconomic areas, the natural attrition (i.e., student dropout) might result in a biased sampling of groups which could effect the results. If social maturity were a trait related in a positive direction to socioeconomic level, and the dropout rate in high school were higher (as it seems to be) for students from lower socioeconomic backgrounds than for those at the upper end of the scale, differences between freshmen and seniors might not be as large as they would be had an unbiased sample of persons from the age groups involved been obtained.

Before we turn to other areas, a word of caution should be given about a remark all too often made by certain test authors or publishers to the effect that "no suitable criterion was possible to obtain." Usually such a statement is intended to excuse the test author from the responsibility of providing any validity data at all. The test publisher just assumes that the test will work and leaves the burden of gathering the evidence upon the user. Most of the time a criterion *can* be found if careful consideration is given to the reasons why the test is to be used. If, after spelling out exactly what it is that the test is expected to do, no criterion becomes apparent, then the user has no business in using the test for this particular purpose (unless, of course, there is considerable evidence that the test is a measure of a particular construct and that the theory which suggests that the trait measured is related to the desired but unmeasurable criterion is well established on an empirical and/or experimental basis).

The person who uses a test without such evidence is only misleading himself when he interprets the scores without evidence that the interpretation is legitimate. Worse than this, such a person is hiding his ignorance behind something which has the appearance of being rigorous. To most professionals in the area of testing, the use of tests under such circumstances is completely unethical, both because the client (either the person whose score is being interpreted or the person for whom the test is interpreted) is likely to make an incorrect decision or otherwise be adversely affected and because such a use can lead to distrust of test results even when the interpretation is well supported by good, solid evidence.

Faking   The second major problem in interpretation of test results is faking.   Faking is the term used any time an examinee deliberately attempts to alter the results in some specific way.   Whether the measure is one of maximum performance or of typical behavior, such deceit is possible.

If the measure is one of aptitude, ability, or achievement (i.e., one of maximum performance) there is usually little opportunity to increase the score.   This can be done by guessing or through cheating during the test— copying, marking more than one answer on a machine-graded test, using concealed notes, and so forth—or through special coaching on specific items in the test (which may momentarily raise the score without a concomitant long-term increase in knowledge or performance).   With formulas which correct for guessing, with adequate safeguards to keep the tests secure, with sufficient supervision during the examination period, and with simple checks when scoring the papers, these types of faking can be practically eliminated.

On the other hand, deliberate attempts to *reduce* scores on measures of maximum performance are much more difficult to prevent and practically impossible to detect.   This kind of deceit seems to occur because an individual feels that if he receives a high score, too much will be expected of him.   He may be afraid, for example, that he will be placed in a higher section in some college course and therefore be graded more stiffly or that in a military situation he will be sent for special training in some area in which he thinks he is not interested.   About the only means of prevention in such cases is to emphasize in the test directions the advantages of obtaining the best score possible.   In most selection situations, the user of the results can console himself with the realization that a person who fakes in this way is probably not well motivated in the desired direction anyway, and a prediction of his likely success in a training program or future activity in the area of the test might even be improved as a result of his having deliberately obtained a low score.   For general counseling, however, the results can be quite misleading.   Fortunately, though, in a counseling situation, there is greater opportunity for convincing the examinee that it is to his own benefit to do his best and to find out whether the subject did attempt to fake the test results.

The problem of faking is infinitely more important when it comes to the measurement of typical performance.   Faking is much easier to do with interest, attitude, and personality measures and much more difficult to prevent.   As a result, it occurs far more frequently, and it has been in this area of measurement that the most attention has been devoted to the problem. It is in this context that some of the current solutions to the problem are described.

Theoretically, one should be able to prevent faking by convincing the examinee that it is to his own advantage to obtain the truest picture possible of his interests, attitudes, and personality. In many situations, however, this is just not possible. Sometimes the subjects lack sufficient foresight to see the advantages, sometimes their motivation to fake—for example, in the case of job applicants who want to make a good impression—is so strong that they cannot be so convinced, and sometimes people act on the basis of family and other social pressures of which they themselves are not entirely aware.

A number of devices have been developed to help discourage faking. Perhaps the simplest is to include in the directions instructions to "work rapidly." While very few measures of typical behavior have time limits, if the subject can be cajoled into making quick, spontaneous judgments, it seems reasonable to assume that he will not have time to think of all the implications of his responses and is less likely to be influenced by some of the subtle pressures of which he is not fully aware.

A second approach to this problem has been an attempt to disguise the purpose of the test. Usually this amounts to giving the test or scale an ambiguous or misleading name—such as calling a measure of cynicism a measure of criticalness—but this usually does not fool anyone except the most naive, who probably would not be able to do a good job of faking anyway.

Another way of discouraging faking is to use item forms such that the weighting or implication of the responses is not clear to the casual observer, which the subject certainly is if he is working through the instrument as rapidly as possible. Perhaps the best example of this approach is the development of a forced-choice scale in which either of the responses is equally popular, but one has been shown empirically to be indicative of one of the traits under consideration and the other either not indicative or a measure of some second trait. A typical item from a scale of this sort is shown in Figure 8.9. While the original studies using such a scale held tremendous promise, later investigation indicated that the results were not so outstanding as had at first been supposed and suggest that the important thing that brought about what improvement did occur may have been the care in construction of the scale rather than the particular format in which it was presented.

A different technique, which has become more and more popular recently, has been the development of what are called *faking, lie,* or *validity* keys. A study is made of responses given under conditions in which it is very unlikely that faking has occurred, and these responses are compared with those given when faking has occurred (usually upon the explicit instructions from the experimenter). Knowing how responses change when an individual is attempting to fake, a test constructor can develop a key which yields a score indicating the extent to which a person has responded as do malingerers. Thus, the results obtained with a person who scores high on the "validity" key are held in doubt. A recent example of the use of this principle can be seen in data presented in the manual of the Kuder Preference Record, Form D. These are reproduced in Figure 7.5.

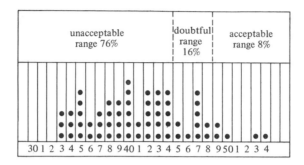

FIGURE 7.5   Distribution of V scores of 62 college students attempting to conceal the fact that they were faking (*Kuder preference record manual for occupational form D,* 5th ed. Chicago: Science Research Associates, p. 14.)

While this technique was originally developed in the area of personality measurement to identify those who tried to show themselves in a good light, it can be used in aptitude measurement to identify those who are purposely trying to appear dull. A key which compares fakers with truly retarded persons could be readily developed. Perhaps, more simply, a study could be made of individual responses in relation to the item difficulty. Item difficulty is often hard to judge, and if an individual is found to have correctly answered difficult items while missing many easier items, he may be suspected of faking.

Before leaving this topic we should note that faking is not a problem in a strictly empirically oriented test—at least for the particular situations in which the test was developed. Here, the test user is not so much interested in what the examinee does as what he *says* he does. If an item asks, "Do you have headaches often?" the interest is not to place persons in order on a scale in terms of the number of headaches they do have but rather in order on a scale with respect to whether they *feel* the number of headaches they have is large or small. Similarly, if a test has been developed to select salesmen on the basis of their interests and if the key has been derived by administering the tests to job applicants and noting the differences in responses made by those who later were successful and those who later failed, then one need not worry about attempts to fake *when the test is administered in similar selection situations.* In a sense, the *lie* key is already built in.

As is true with all empirically constructed tests, however, the extent to which they can be generalized to other situations is limited. If the test is given in a counseling or other nonselection situation where faking was not likely to occur, the results may be rather peculiar. At least the user should be aware that without additional evidence he has no right to attempt to interpret the scores in the same way in the two situations.

Response set Some years ago, Cronbach (1946) called attention to the fact that a score received on a test was sometimes a function of the way in which the items happened to be presented rather than (or, at least, as well as) the trait being measured. For example, if interest is measured by having the respondent simply check on a list each of those items which represents a thing that he likes to do, the tendency to like a great many or a few things will have a marked effect on the result. Had the individual been asked to check exactly half of the items, indicating those he liked best, quite different results probably would have been obtained. This important source of methods variance in test scores has been labeled *response set*.

Specifically defined by Cronbach as "any tendency causing a person to give different responses to test items than he would when the same content is presented in different form," response sets have been increasingly recognized as important influences on scores obtained on tests of all types. Thus, Metfessel and Sax (1958) found that one-third of the fifteen well-known standardized measures of aptitude and achievement they reviewed were keyed in such a way that persons with a set to select a particular alternative (for example, the first, the last, the true, or the false choices) could be spuriously helped or hindered in obtaining high scores; Barnes (1956) concludes, "that response sets . . . play a larger part in personality testing than has been suspected"; and Loevinger (1959) has cautioned that, "Proliferation of tests of high sounding psychological constructs in disregard of response bias is a conspicuous waste of research." Although some writers (see Rorer, 1965) feel that the concern over response sets far exceeds their actual occurrence, a sufficient number of psychological measures seem to have been affected by them for any researcher to use caution in the area. Best known among the rather wide variety of response sets supposedly identified are those which represent a tendency to guess, a tendency to acquiesce (to respond "yes" regardless of the content of the statement), a tendency to be critical (i.e., to deny or disagree with any assertion), a tendency to check or list many adjectives, a tendency to take an extreme position, and a tendency always to describe oneself as socially desirable.

Response sets like those just listed are known to occur primarily when tests or inventories have but two or three alternatives for each item. Further, this effect is most likely to be greatest when a decision among the alternatives presented is extremely difficult for the subject to make. If a person knows the answer on an aptitude or achievement test, or if he has a strong preference with respect to the content of the item on an interest or personality inventory, his tendency to guess or select more "likes" than "dislikes" will not appear.

When response sets do occur, either they may represent an undesirable influence which needs to be eliminated or they may reflect a real and important dimension of human differences which is potentially useful for making predictions about behavior. As Broen and Wirt (1958) point out in a discussion of the results of their factor analysis of eleven different response sets, such effects should be eliminated "only in those cases where there is no correlation between the response set itself and the criterion for which prediction is being attempted. If there is a correlation between a response set and a criterion, then either the suppression of that set or the neglect to use tests in which that response set can operate may lead to lower validities."

To be able to capitalize upon the effect of response set when it is useful and to eliminate it when it is undesirable, some procedure is necessary for obtaining the separate set and content components of a test score. Helmstadter (1957), Webster (1958), and Jackson and Messick (1958) have presented ways of accomplishing this.

It should be emphasized that the user of any system for obtaining separate set and content components of a test must not assume that the resulting scores will automatically be reliable and valid. Additional studies will be needed to ascertain whether the set, as identified, is consistent from testing to testing and whether the corrected content score or the new set score, or both, are valid measures of human characteristics.

In the final analysis, the criterion problem, faking, and response sets are all most adequately handled through careful construct validity studies. Such studies must not merely relate test scores to a readily available criterion measure (which everybody admits is inadequate) but rather must consider the form in which the items are written, the various circumstances under which they are administered, the alternative ways of deriving scores from the responses, and the specific kinds of inferences it is hoped can be made from such results.

8.

Special Methods and Techniques

In addition to knowledge of information centers, an understanding of the logic of statistical reasoning, and familiarity with the basic ideas of psychological measurement, all of which will be used by every scientific researcher engaged in the study of the individual or group behavior of organisms, there are a number of broad general methods and techniques which originally developed in special fields but which seem to be tools that can be used in many areas of work. For example, sample design is especially important to those in social psychology and sociology but has import for those in education and those doing experimental field studies; factor analysis was developed by those who were primarily interested in the organization of human abilities but has now been applied to many cultural studies; psychometric scaling is an outgrowth of the psychophysical laboratory but is now widely used in sociological studies; and sociometry, which comes from the field of sociology, is now used in many psychological and educational studies.

While every research worker in the behavioral sciences may not use the methods and techniques described in this chapter, it is important that he be sufficiently familiar with them to sensibly interpret studies which have used them and that he understand them sufficiently to know when they might be applicable to a problem with which he is concerned even though they have never been used in that way before. These special methods include *sampling design, factor analysis, scales and scaling, sociometry,* and several other techniques which, while widely useful, have not yet been developed into the beginnings of distinct areas of specialization.

325

PLANNING AND DRAWING ADEQUATE SAMPLES

The Sampling Problem

A major portion of Chapter 6 was concerned with the problem of statistical inference, a problem which arises because the scientist wishes to generalize from the results he obtains on a particular set of observations to a larger group—a population of which he considers his small set of observations a sample. The discussion in this section now turns to the prior question of exactly what procedures should be followed in arriving at an appropriate sample. To answer this, we must know both the logical criteria by which a sampling plan is evaluated and the advantages and disadvantages of the major alternative sampling plans which are currently available to the modern investigator.

THE UNIVERSE AND THE POPULATION   The entire set of elements (things or people) to which the researcher wishes to generalize his conclusions is referred to as the *universe*. When it is said that a person is "overgeneralizing," he is being accused of applying the results of his observations to a different universe from the one from which his observations came. Thus, in any research study it is absolutely essential that the investigator carefully and clearly define his universe. Otherwise, misguided attempts may be made on the part of those who read the results to draw conclusions or to apply the resulting principles in situations to which no rigorous inferences can legitimately be made. It could happen that the results will apply to other universes, but those who overgeneralize should recognize that they are making assumptions that have not yet been put to test—that they have only a hypothesis that their conclusions or applications will work in the new situation and not scientific evidence to that effect.

While the universe represents the entire set of elements of concern, a *population* is defined as the entire set of values which results from the measurement of some characteristic of all the elements of the universe. If "all second-graders in the United States attending public school on a particular day" is defined as a universe, then the list of all ages of such second-graders is considered to be a population. Similarly, the list of all heights of such second-graders is considered to be another population of that universe, and the entire set of I.Q. scores obtained on these second-graders would be considered to be a third population taken from the same universe of children.

In many situations, the distinction between a universe (the things themselves) and a population (a measurement of some characteristic of the things) is unimportant, and the two terms are used synonymously. This, however, is not the case in the area of sampling design. Here it is important to recognize that there are many populations for each universe because in some sampling plans knowledge of one population of characteristics can be used to obtain a more fully adequate sample of elements of the universe to get information on a second and unknown set of population values.

THE SAMPLE By definition, a sample is any subset of elements from the universe or one of its populations. A subset is any size combination of elements which does not include the entire set of elements that have been defined to be the universe. A sample may be one element, all but one element, or any of the possibilities in between.

When a sample is defined simply as a subset of elements, it is immediately obvious that some samples will be more "representative" of the population as a whole than will others. But what exactly is meant by representative? Actually, representativeness is an ideal goal which may never be quite achieved (even if it is, there is often no way of knowing it for sure) but toward which investigators strive when using various sampling plans. By definition, a sample is said to be representative if the measurement or analysis made on its elements produces results equivalent to those which would be obtained had the entire population been used.

The most frequently used type of sample is labeled a *sample of convenience*. This sample is obtained when the researcher elects or is forced, through practical considerations, to make use of whatever subjects are conveniently available to him. It is apparent that to label such a sample as representative of some poorly defined larger group has little merit, and this practice is to be discouraged as much as possible. In reality, using a sample of convenience is often the only alternative the researcher has. Under these circumstances the careful worker will describe his sample as precisely as possible with respect to as many relevant characteristics as he can think of so that others who read the report of his study can, perhaps, visualize a population of which this sample might be representative, or at least they can determine whether the group to which they had hoped to generalize the results of the study differs in specific ways from the sample which was used.

A second type of sample, which is found all too frequently in the research literature of the behavioral sciences, is a *judgment sample*. The elements in this type of sample are selected subjectively by the investigator in an attempt to get a set which appears to him to be representative of the population. Thus, the chance that some particular element will be selected for the sample depends upon the subjective impression of the person doing the choosing. Because it is impossible to determine exactly why each different investigator thinks each element he chooses will help make the sample more representative, it is impossible with a judgment sample to determine the likelihood that any specific element will be included in the sample.

When the elements of a sample are selected in such a way that it is not possible to determine their likelihood of getting into the sample, it is also impossible to determine from the observations themselves just how far off the sample estimates of the population characteristics are likely to be. From a scientific point of view, this latter is inadequate, for, in terms of making either a practical application or a sound theoretical judgment, it is far better to be somewhat inaccurate but know how much error is likely to occur than it is to have no idea how close to an accurate answer a given estimate is.

A third type of sample, and one which is more acceptable, is called a *probability sample*. A probability sample is one that has been selected in such a way that every element chosen has a known probability of being included.

A classic example of the difference between judgment samples and probability samples occurs in the field of election polling. Some political prognosticators pick "barometer" election precincts, while others randomly draw precincts from a specifically defined universe of precincts. Those who choose the former approach select those precincts, which, on the basis of their prior election experiences, are representative of what will happen in the nation as a whole. These individuals can make predictions about the outcome of an election, but they cannot tell how far off their predictions are likely to be. On the other hand, those pollsters who use a random process for selecting sample precincts on the basis of which to make predictions will not only be able to make predictions but will be able to state, in terms of probability, how close their predictions are likely to be.

Studies such as those carried out by R. J. Jessen (1950), who used stone weights as the characteristic under examination and who sampled from known populations, suggest that only under rather unusual conditions will the research worker be likely to make more accurate estimates when he uses judgment samples than he will when he uses some sort of probability sample. In general, the only circumstances in which a judgment sample might pay off are those in which (1) the entire set of elements (i.e., the entire universe) can be viewed at the same time; (2) the person doing the judging has demonstrated his capability in making accurate judgments of the characteristic under examination; (3) the sample size is very small (say, less than 10); (4) the population is homogeneous; and (5) the population splits as it had in earlier studies.

Since a judgment sample does not permit rigorous ways of estimating the degree of accuracy of estimates of population characteristics and, further, can produce more accurate results only under highly restricted circumstances, judgment samples are not generally to be recommended for research work. While the selection and description of barometer precincts may result in more entertaining newspaper reading, it seldom if ever produces more accurate results.

THE SAMPLING DISTRIBUTION   Perhaps the most important of all concepts in the area of sample design is *sampling distribution*. This term was used in connection with the specific examples in the chapter on statistical reasoning. It can now be defined in a more general sense as the frequency distribution of estimates of a population characteristic made up of (containing) estimates from *all possible* samples of a given size.

The sampling distribution is important, for it includes *every single possibility* that can occur and thus tells the investigator his maximum error in estimating a population characteristic. It further provides the investigator with knowledge about his chances of being within certain limits of the true value. Finally, it is in terms of a sampling distribution that the most useful concepts of *bias* and *precision* have been formulated.

Bias is defined to be the difference between the mean of the sampling distribution and the population value which is being estimated. For example, if the investigator is trying to estimate the population mean of characteristic X, the bias of his estimate can be expressed as $\mu_{\bar{x}} - \mu_x$, where $\mu_{\bar{x}}$ represents the mean of the sampling distribution as shown in Figure 8.1.

It is important to note, then, that when it is said that a sample is unbiased,

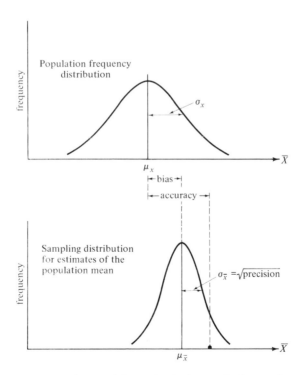

FIGURE 8.1   A comparison of hypothetical population and sampling distributions

this does *not* mean that it is without error. Rather, since unbiased simply means that $\mu_{\bar{x}} - \mu_x = 0$, the term refers to the fact that out of the possibilities the expected sample estimate is one without error. If the sampling distribution is symmetrical, unbiased also implies that the most frequently occurring sample is one without error and that samples drawn in this way will yield estimates which fall above the true population values as often as below it.

If lack of bias does not imply lack of error, then it is not difficult to imagine that an index, in addition to that of bias, will be needed to evaluate the effectiveness of various sampling plans. For example, consider that two alternative sampling plans (i.e., procedures for drawing a sample), Plans A and B, have been suggested for obtaining a sample from which to estimate some population characteristic, such as the mean reading speed of second-graders in School District No. 214. Suppose that each of the two plans resulted in a different sampling distribution, as shown in Figure 8.2. And, further, suppose that the population value (which is never known in a real study, or it would not be necessary to do the study) was that indicated by the arrow.

Even though Plan A has the least bias, most researchers would prefer to use Plan B because even though, on the average, the estimate would come closer to the true value with Plan A, there is a substantial chance (a high frequency among all possible samples) that the estimate of the mean value will be much further off with Plan A than it ever could possibly be were Plan B to be used. Most investigators would always prefer to be off by a small amount in their estimate than to take the rather substantial chance of being considerably off in order to maintain the small possibility of being without any error.

The most obvious characteristic, other than their means, which distinguishes the sampling distributions for sampling Plan A and sampling Plan B in Figure 8.2, is their variance. In the context of sampling design, the variance of a sampling distribution is referred to as the *reliability,* or the

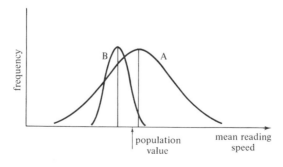

FIGURE 8.2   Sampling distribution for hypothetical sampling Plan A and Plan B

precision, of the sample. Since the word reliability already has a very special meaning in the context of psychological measurement, the term precision will be used throughout this text to represent this characteristic of a sample. It is also important to note that the variance of a sampling distribution, when used as an index of the precision of a sample, is an inverse measure. That is, the larger the variance, the less precise the sample. In Figure 8.2, Plan B was preferred to Plan A because it was more precise, even though Plan A had the least bias.

One final term needs to be defined before it is possible to consider the question of how samples should be drawn in order to obtain adequate estimates of population characteristics. The term is *accuracy.* This is what the research worker is really concerned with and is defined as the difference between the particular sample estimate obtained and the value he is trying to estimate. However, unlike the bias and the precision of the sample, which can be calculated from the observations (provided a probability sample was taken), accuracy can never be determined in a real study, because the population value is always unknown.

Obtaining Accurate Estimates

Even though it is impossible for an investigator to know the accuracy of his results precisely, it is usually possible, by control of the bias and precision of the sample, for him to be confident (with a specified degree of probability) that the accuracy will be within certain specified limits.

REDUCING BIAS The first step toward obtaining accurate estimates is that of carefully defining the universe to be sampled. Failure to do this may lead the researcher to draw a sample (perhaps even an excellent one) of a population other than the one to which he wishes to generalize. When this occurs, the resulting estimates will be biased because the mean of the sampling distribution will fall at the mean of the population actually sampled rather than at the mean of the population the research worker intended to sample.

The classic example of this type of mistake is that made in the *Literary Digest* election poll of 1936. Prior to the election of that year, the *Digest* poll mailed out over 10 million straw ballots to persons selected largely from telephone lists and car registrations—the largest sample that pollsters had taken to that date. Based upon the returns of over 2,300,000 respondents, an election prediction was made which missed the percentage of votes cast for the winning candidate by 19.8 percent. This was in direct contrast to the *Fortune* magazine poll, which with some 4500 straw ballots predicted the outcome within 1 percent. Apparently, the *Digest* editors ignored a public warning, by the American Institute of Public Opinion, as to what was happening some four months before the election and based their prediction on a sample which came largely from the upper income level (Katz & Cantril, 1937; Parten, 1950). Unfortunately for the *Literary Digest,* voting in that election was largely along economic lines, and thus the fact that they had sampled (probably quite accurately) only one segment of the voting population led to a disastrous prediction.

A second way of increasing the accuracy of sample results by reducing bias is through the proper handling of nonrespondents. Strictly speaking, a researcher who makes use of a survey never has a sample of the population he originally defines but only of those members of that universe who are willing to respond. Persons who respond to questionnaires or to interviewers are often quite different in essential respects from those persons who either cannot be contacted or who refuse to reply if they are. To the extent that certain elements of the universe are unobservable (i.e., are nonrespondents in a survey), the results will be biased, and the larger this group, the larger will be the resulting bias.

In general, there are three ways of handling nonrespondents—that is, of reducing the effects of the resulting bias. Usually these techniques are applied in the order discussed. The first technique is that of making repeated contacts of those who failed to respond the first time. This is a relatively inexpensive technique and, if the nonrespondent group is fairly large on the first contact, will usually produce substantial gains. In fact, some investigators have found that approximately the same percentage of returns is obtained on each successive contact. For example, a research worker who obtained 60 percent return on the first contact might expect 60 percent of the remaining 40 percent (or 24 additional out of every 100 originally contacted) to respond to the first follow-up and then 60 percent of the remaining 16 percent on the second follow-up.

When additional follow-up contacts of every nonrespondent reach the point of sufficiently diminishing returns to be too expensive to continue, the investigator can turn to the second technique—that of taking a subsample of the nonrespondents. He will consider his nonrespondents a new universe and, instead of trying to obtain a census from this restricted group, will draw a sample from it and make every effort to obtain results from this subsample of the original population. Because he will be working with a much smaller number of persons at this point, the investigator can afford to spend more money, time, and effort in contacting and in convincing the subject of the importance of providing the desired information. Often, at this stage, the total amount of time required of the respondent may be greatly reduced by asking only for absolutely essential information. This may include some questions not asked of the original group but which have been included to help note the difference between this group and those who responded to the original or the early follow-up contacts.

Even after a subsampling procedure has been employed, there will be a residue of so-called hard-core nonrespondents—members of the subsample who could not be located or who, when found, absolutely refused to provide the information sought. At this point, the research worker may simply use the technique of assuming the extremes. That is, the investigator first assumes that all hard-core nonrespondents would have reacted one way and calculates the results he would have obtained had this been the case; next, the investigator assumes that all those subjects for whom no results are available would have reacted in the opposite way (or successively in each alternative way) and then calculates his results under this assumption. If the hard-core nonrespondent group is not too large (and it shouldn't be if the researcher was skillful in using the other two techniques for handling nonrespondents), the two calculations will set rather narrow boundaries within which the true result should fall.

A final technique for handling possible bias in results obtained from a sampling procedure concentrates not on the universe sampled but rather on the index used to estimate the population characteristic. As it turns out, there are certain estimators which can be used that have known biases. A research worker who uses one of these (rather than some other index which may have an unknown amount of bias) can make a correction for the bias when his calculations are finished. If he has carefully defined his universe and properly handled his nonrespondents, the investigator can be assured that his result will contain very little if any bias. As a matter of fact, to gain other ends, an investigator will sometimes consciously select a technique he knows results in biased estimates, recognizing that later he can overcome the weakness of this estimator by making a proper correction.

INCREASING PRECISION   In addition to reducing bias, the investigator can gain some control over the ultimate accuracy of his results by increasing the precision of his sample. Increasing precision, it may be recalled, amounts to reducing the variance of the sampling distribution. From the previous discussion of the sampling distribution in connection with the testing of hypotheses, the reader may remember that the simplest way to reduce the variance of the sampling distribution is to increase the sample size. Thus, the most effective way of gaining precision is to increase the sample size.

Unfortunately, increasing the sample size does *not* ordinarily have a similarly desirable effect on the bias.[1] In fact, failure to note that increasing sample size increases precision but has no effect on bias often leads to misplaced confidence in the results obtained. For example, when the *Literary Digest* poll cited earlier used the largest sample any polling agency had obtained up to that time, the result was an estimate which was precise but

---

[1] The only time that bias is affected by sample size in a desirable way is when the estimator uses results in a bias which is an inverse function of the sample size. An example of this situation is the use of $\Sigma(X_i - \overline{X})^2/N$ to estimate σ_x^2.

wrong. The effect of the fact that increasing the sample size will increase the precision and not necessarily influence the bias can be portrayed graphically, as has been done in Figure 8.3. In this illustration, the top frequency distribution shows results that might be obtained from following a particular sampling plan and using a particular procedure for estimating the mean. The second sampling distribution shows what is likely to occur if the same plan and estimator is used but the sample size is increased. The bottom sampling distribution represents all the possible outcomes if, in addition to increasing the sample size, an unbiased estimator of the mean were substituted for the original.

In addition to increasing the sample size, the precision of a sampling dis-

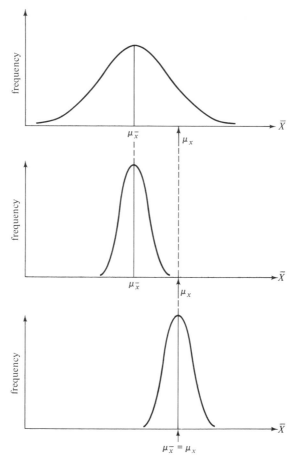

FIGURE 8.3   Hypothetical sampling distributions depicting the effects of increasing sample size and using an unbiased estimator (Adapted from M. Hansen, W. Hurwitz, and W. Madow. *Sample survey methods and theory.* New York: Wiley, 1953, Fig. 4. P. 35.)

tribution can be increased by using information about other populations (of the same universe) than that being estimated, either to design special estimators or to devise special sampling plans. For example, if a study is intended to estimate the average amount of schooling of parents of children in a particular school district, a sampling plan can be devised which will produce much more precise results if the fathers' occupations are known than if this additional information about a second population of the same universe is not known. Exactly how this is accomplished will be seen later in the discussion of basic sampling plans.

In summary, accurate sample estimates are obtained by reducing bias and by increasing the precision of the sampling distribution. Bias is reduced by carefully defining the universe from which the sample is taken, by proper handling of nonrespondents, and by using either unbiased estimators or estimators for which the bias is known and therefore can be corrected. On the other hand, precision is increased by increasing the sample size and by using additional information about other populations of the same universe to devise special estimators or special sampling plans.

Some Basic Sampling Plans

Before we turn to specific sampling plans, it is necessary to note the criteria that are usually employed for deciding what sampling plan to follow. First and foremost, any sampling plan which is to produce results useful for scientific purposes must be one which enables the researcher to determine the precision of his sample estimate from the observations he makes. Thus, some sort of probability sample is always required. Second, the sampling plan selected must be administratively feasible in the situation in which the study is being carried out. There are many theoretically fine sampling plans which are impossible to put into effect in certain circumstances. Even worse, a research worker who has not carefully thought through all the requirements of the plan may discover halfway through the project that he is not going to be able to get that information which is essential to make the sampling plan useful.

Finally, from among those sampling plans which meet the first two requirements, the design which maximizes the precision per unit cost will be chosen. Sometimes this maximum efficiency is accomplished by greatly reducing the cost for a small loss of precision; sometimes it is accomplished by greatly increasing the precision for only a small additional cost. Obviously, if a person has a fixed amount of funds, he selects that plan which yields the greatest precision for the amount of money available; or, if the problem demands a fixed amount of precision if its solution is to make a contribution, the investigator can determine the least amount of money he must have if the study is to yield results which will be of any value.

In the sections that follow, each of five basic sampling plans are described, and their advantages and disadvantages are pointed out. Even though these plans are discussed separately, the reader should be aware that in practice these basic approaches can be combined into rather complex multistage sampling designs which can utilize the advantages and minimize the disadvantages of each plan used alone. The reader who ultimately finds himself involved in studies requiring careful samples would do well to consult Hansen, Hurwitz, and Madow (1953) or other texts devoted entirely to sample designs before carrying out his study.

To help make each of the designs described more meaningful we shall apply them, in turn, to a concrete problem. For example, suppose that a research worker wanted to estimate the social maturity of all secondary school students in the state in which he resides. Further suppose that he feels the best way to accomplish this would be to determine the average score the universe of students would obtain on a test of social maturity.

The first question that arises is whether he should administer the test to every secondary school student in the state or whether he should select a sample of students and see the results obtained from them to get information about the entire population of social maturity scores. Obviously, the advantage of a complete census is that the entire problem of sampling error and the task of making rigorous inferences from sample to population could be avoided. On the other hand, the advantage of drawing a sample is that it will be far less expensive and will probably take a lot less time. Not so obvious an advantage of the sample approach is that the magnitude of clerical errors may be reduced tremendously because a much smaller amount of data is handled. While modern computers are sufficiently accurate to make this less of a problem today, it has been suggested in the past that the size of clerical errors in a complete census may be larger than the size of the sampling errors plus clerical errors on a smaller amount of data and thus that the sample may turn out to be even more accurate than the census.

Finally, suppose that the investigator has considered the arguments above and has decided that a sample will be more efficient than a complete census. Now the question arises as to exactly how to go about drawing a sample that will produce representative results. Should the research worker use a purposive sample, a simple random sample, a stratified sample, a cluster sample, a systematic sample, or some combination of these? To answer this question, each of the basic types of sampling plans mentioned is described.

PURPOSIVE SAMPLE   The purposive sample is a type of judgment sample in which the person doing the selecting tries to insure representativeness by requiring the sample to match the universe in known characteristics. The assumption is that if the sample is representative with respect to known population characteristics, it will also be representative with respect to the unknown characteristics which are under investigation. It should be recognized that the fact that a sample matches the population with respect to several known characteristics in no way guarantees that the sample will be at all representative in other respects. In the past, many persons have assumed that it does, and this assumption has led them into trouble.

A classic example of this type of sample is the quota sample often used by some election pollsters. The procedure is simply that of sending out interviewers with instructions to get results from a specified number of persons in each of several categories. An interviewer might be required to poll a certain number of men, a certain number of women, a certain number within each of several age brackets, a certain number of each party affiliation, etc. The required numbers are determined in the office ahead of time according to known counts of persons in various categories of sex, age, religion, and political affiliation. In estimating the social maturity of high school students, the researcher might first determine from school enrollment lists the total number of students of each sex and each age level. Then the investigator might select a few typical schools and in each school interview so many boys, so many girls, and so many from each age group until he had a sample which was proportionate in each of these respects to the total school enrollment.

The difficulty which arises in making the assumption is that the individuals who are providing data usually include only those persons within each category who are most readily available. Usually, persons (or other types of sample elements) who are readily available are quite different from those who cannot be found. To avoid this problem, the person gathering the data is required to make judgments about which of the subjects who fit in his categories are typical. As has already been noted, the conditions under which a judgment sample can produce more accurate results than a probability sample are very restrictive and certainly not likely to be met when a purposive sample is taken. The use of any type of judgment sample also precludes the calculation of estimates of the likely range of error, and thus is not acceptable for scientific work.

SIMPLE RANDOM SAMPLE The most straightforward procedure for obtaining a probability sample is that which leads to the simple random sample. By definition, a simple random sample is one in which each element of the population has an equal *and* an independent chance of being included in the sample.[2] To get such a sample from the universe of high school students, the investigator would first need a list of every secondary student in the state. Then, he might assign each student a different code number, each containing the same number of digits as the number representing the universe size (i.e., representing the total number of elements in the universe).

[2] Another way of saying the same thing is that all possible combinations of a given sample size have an equal chance of being selected as the sample.

Next, numbers would be drawn from a table of random numbers until the appropriate sample size was reached, and each child whose number was drawn would then be included.

The major advantage of the simple random sample is its extreme simplicity. Unfortunately, it is often not feasible in practice, because it requires a list of every single element in the universe. While such is likely to be available in the example cited here, the reader can imagine the difficulties he would run into should he attempt to obtain a list of all persons in the United States who were between 16 and 25 years old.

Nonetheless, the simple random sample is very important in sample design. First, almost all theoretical work in statistics assumes this type of sample. Second, the simple random sample has been used as a prototype sample for the derivation of the concepts of bias, precision, accuracy, etc. Finally, the simple random sample serves as a standard base for comparison of the more complex sampling plans with respect to cost, precision, and other characteristics.

STRATIFIED SAMPLE   The investigator who uses a stratified sample seeks to increase precision by using supplementary information about other populations of the same universe. Superficially, it is similar to the purposive sample in that it divides the universe into groups on the basis of classificatory information such as sex, age, and occupation. Unlike the purposive sample the selection of elements from within groups is made by using a simple random sampling procedure rather than depending upon the judgment of the person actually collecting the data. Further, in the stratified sample the number of elements selected from each of the categories is not always proportional to the population counts for the different groups.

The object in dividing the universe into groups is to create homogeneous categories with respect to the particular characteristic under investigation. That is, persons within a group should be more like one another than persons selected from different categories. To the extent that this is accomplished the precision of the estimate will increase because, now that some elements are drawn from each category, those sample possibilities that included only persons from one extreme or the other have been eliminated. The appropriate characteristic to use for purposes of stratification, therefore, is one which is correlated with the trait being examined and yet is readily known. Note that it is in the selection of an appropriate stratification variable that the skill and judgment of the researcher should come into play, not in trying to select certain "typical" elements.

Although several different characteristics might be used for dividing the high school universe into homogeneous categories with respect to social maturity, one which is likely to be readily available (and thus not too costly) and still reasonably related to social maturity is high school class. The research worker might first break down the list of all high school students in the state into separate lists for freshmen, sophomores, juniors, and seniors. Then, using each list as a separate universe he would follow the procedures outlined in the previous section and obtain a simple random sample from within each of the four strata. The final sample, then, would be that which combined all those persons selected from within each category.

As suggested previously, the number selected from each stratum need not correspond proportionately with the total number of students enrolled in each of the classes in the universe. As a matter of fact, it might occur that the research worker would take an equal number of students from each of the four classes, thus yielding a *disproportionate* sample, even though he recognized that there were many more freshmen than seniors. Without going into the details as to why it is so, it will suffice to say at this point that disproportionate sampling will lead to even greater precision than proportionate sampling.[3] An illustration of this using a numerical example that also may clarify the concepts of bias, precision, and accuracy is presented in the Appendix.

The major advantage of a stratified sample is that it can lead to a large increase in the reliability (or precision) of the sample at very little extra cost. The obvious disadvantages are two: (1) extra effort is required to obtain the additional information needed for purposes of stratification; and (2) like a simple random sample, a list of every element in the universe is required. Whenever such a list is available and when a simple stratification variable which is likely to be highly related to the characteristic under study can be found, the investigator has very little, if anything, to lose by using a stratified sample. It should be recognized, however, that if the stratification variable and the criterion variable turn out to be uncorrelated, there will be no gain in precision for the extra effort expended.

CLUSTER SAMPLE In some respects the cluster sample represents a sampling design at the opposite end of the pole from a stratified sample. The purpose of a cluster sample is not to increase precision but to reduce costs; the universe is divided into groups which are heterogeneous rather than homogeneous, and the final elements are obtained by taking a sample *of* groups and not *from within* groups. The cluster sample seeks to maximize the precision per unit cost by reducing the costs as much as possible, while engendering only a small loss in precision.

This goal is most likely to be accomplished when already existing natural groupings are used, provided that these natural groupings are not too homogeneous. For example, counties, school districts, voting districts, city blocks, natural geographic boundaries, and the like might be used. Once again, this is a place (i.e., in selecting heterogeneous clusters containing

When a disproportionate sampling procedure is followed, weighted averages (according to universe stratum size) must be used rather than the simple mean; otherwise, a biased estimate of the population characteristic will result.

easily accessible elements) where the judgmental skill of the researcher should be used rather than in choosing what appears to him to be representative elements.

In trying to estimate the social maturity of secondary school students, the investigator might obtain a list of all the school districts that contain high schools in the state. Each such district would then serve as a cluster of students, and each cluster would be assigned a number. Finally, the researcher would take a simple random sample of school districts and then administer the measure of social maturity to every secondary student in the district so selected.

At this point it is quite obvious that a multistage sampling procedure which combines a cluster and a stratified sample might be used. The research worker could start with a cluster sample so as to avoid traveling to every school district in the state to get just a few students from each. Then, once a limited number of school districts have been selected, he can recoup some loss in precision incurred at the first sampling stage (because school districts are somewhat homogeneous) by stratifying by class within each school district selected. The result could be a sample which is both less expensive and more precise than a simple random sample.

The cluster sample, like the simple random sample and the stratified sample, is a probability sample. It permits accurate determination of the precision of the estimate from the sample itself. Unlike either the simple random sample or the stratified sample, however, the cluster sample does *not* require a list containing every single element in the universe. A cluster sample can be used in many situations where it is simply impossible to obtain other types of samples. Consider, for example, the task of obtaining a sample of persons between the ages of 16 and 25. While no list of such persons exists, the investigator can first divide the country into limited geographical areas. Then, after drawing a sample of these areas, he can canvass each one selected and very likely locate all those persons within the age range sought who live in the clusters chosen.

The major disadvantage of a cluster sample is its loss of precision, although this loss will be small if the individual elements within the cluster are sufficiently heterogeneous to represent the entire range of the population characteristic under study. Because the cost per element is so greatly reduced for the cluster sample (e.g., it would be much less expensive to test a large group of students in a few schools rather than a few students from every school in the state), it is almost always possible to take a larger sample and regain any precision that has been lost.

In this connection it might be mentioned that as a minor disadvantage the investigator has no tight control over sample size. Rather, he must estimate what the total number of subjects is likely to be from the average cluster size and the number of clusters he will choose. Fortunately, unlike experimental studies where a relatively small number of cases are used so that sample size is extremely important, most situations in which a cluster sample is appropriate do not require precise specification in advance of the total number of elements to be included.

SYSTEMATIC SAMPLE   The systematic sample represents a sampling plan which is frequently used in practice and which is often confused with a simple random sample.   Thus, it is important that the investigator note the differences between these two sample designs.   The systematic sample first requires that each element of the universe (or some surrogate symbol for it) be arranged in an orderly fashion.   Then, instead of assigning code numbers to the elements and drawing these at random, the research worker decides upon a *sampling fraction* or percentage of the population which is to be included in the final sample.   The sampling fraction is next translated into an indication of the number of elements along the list which are to be included in a series of groups from each of which the research worker will select but one element for his sample.

For example, if the sampling fraction were 10 percent, then one element in ten is needed; if the sampling fraction were 20 percent, then one element in every five is to be chosen.   In general, suppose 1 element in k is needed. Then the investigator randomly draws a number between 1 and k.   If this number turned out to be p, he would start with the pth person and use every kth element in order.

Suppose that the research worker investigating the level of social maturity of high school students in his state decided he needed a 25 percent sample.   This means he should take one in every four.   If, upon drawing a number between 1 and 4 from a table of random numbers, he should happen to select 3, then he would start with the third person and select every fourth one.   That is, he would take the third, seventh, eleventh, fifteenth, and so on, until he had worked through the entire arrangement of the universe of elements.

At this point it is important to note that even though each element has an equal chance of being included in the sample, as is true of simple random samples, each element does *not* have an independent chance of being selected.   No sample containing both 2 and 4 or containing 9 and 16 is possible; and, similarly, a sample which contains element number 1 *must* contain number 13, 17, etc.

Actually, the systematic sample is a special case of a cluster sample. Here there are four clusters, one containing elements 1, 5, 9, 13, 17, etc., one containing 2, 6, 10, 14, etc., one containing 3, 7, 11, 15, etc., and one containing 4, 8, 12, 16, etc.; and only *one* of the possible clusters has been selected.

Because the systematic sample is a cluster sample, the reader will recognize that it is a probability sample and might anticipate that it is possible to obtain an estimate of the sample precision from the sample values themselves. Unfortunately, the formula for estimating the precision in this special case where only one cluster is selected becomes indeterminant. At the present time, exact mathematical procedures for estimating the precision of the systematic sample do not seem to be available. Approximate procedures for estimating the precision of systematic samples, however, suggest that, under certain conditions and with large samples, the results will be similar to or even better than those results for proportionate stratified sampling.

The conditions under which the systematic sample yields the greatest precision are those under which there is a high correlation in the characteristic being measured between adjacent units on the list and in which this correlation decreases as the interval between the units becomes larger. When elements adjacent to each other on the list are quite similar with respect to the trait under study, and elements at some distance from one another on the list are dissimilar, the systematic sample can result in a surprisingly large increase in precision over the simple random sample.

Another important advantage of the systematic sample is the simplicity with which it can be obtained in some circumstances. For example, in attempting to get a sample of licensed drivers in a particular state it would be an arduous task to make a list of every license on file, randomly draw from this list, and then hunt for and pull each license so selected to get the information from it. On the other hand, if the total length of file space occupied by such licenses is known and the sampling fraction specified, it is a simple matter to pull out that license which appears every so many inches in the file drawers.

There is one important disadvantage to the systematic sample. Should it happen that there is a periodic fluctuation in the characteristic under examination in relation to the order in which the items appear on the list and should that period, or some multiple of it, correspond to the interval between elements selected, the result will be a tremendous increase in sampling variance. Thus, just as there are conditions under which the investigator may achieve a considerable gain in precision, there are also conditions under which he may suffer a considerable loss.

Data of interest to the behavioral and social scientist are often such as to be related to the order in which lists available for use with systematic samples are prepared. Lists of persons arranged either by street address or alphabetically could display either periodicity or decreasing serial correlations. Therefore, in practice it is safe for the behavioral scientist to make use of the systematic sample only in situations in which he is sufficiently acquainted with the data to be able to determine which, if either, of the conditions described above actually exists. No matter how feasible, from a practical point of view the research worker should avoid using the systematic sample when exploring an unfamiliar area.

FACTOR ANALYSIS

Strictly speaking factor analysis represents a mathematical approach to the solution of certain problems of interest to behavioral scientists in general and to psychologists in particular. As such, factor analysis is similar in function to some statistical techniques and makes use of certain formulations and concepts of statistical analysis. As was the case with statistics, it is not the intention of this section to teach factor analysis per se but rather to provide the investigator with an overview of the purposes and basic concepts of factor analysis, to suggest some of the types of problems for which factor analysis may be useful, and, finally, to enable the reader to be sufficiently acquainted with the terminology of factor analysis to be able to read factor-analytic studies intelligently when they are encountered in the research literature. The reader who wishes to go into the subject in greater detail might want to start with Henrysson's (1957) excellent monograph and then continue with one of the more complete basic texts in the field, such as Thurstone (1947), Cattell (1952), Fruchter (1954), Harman (1960), and Horst (1965).

The Aims of Factor Analysis

Eysenck (1953) points out that factor analysis has three basic aims: description, suggesting hypotheses, and testing hypotheses. Although a given study may involve all three aims, each is sufficiently distinct to make separate comment worth while.

DESCRIPTIVE FACTOR ANALYSIS   Whatever else factor analysis may be, it is a procedure that leads to the description of a relatively large number of observed relationships with relatively few concepts. Typically, the research worker starts with an entire table or matrix of intercorrelations and asks the question of how few variables need to be postulated in order to describe these observations. As Henrysson (1957) put it, "Factor Analysis supplies methods for reducing a large number of observed variables to a lesser number, in some way more fundamental variables or, as they are usually called, factors."

One of the best examples of this use is work done in the area of interest measurement. In one study reported by Guilford et al. (1954), 95 different measures of interest were obtained on over 700 men and the resulting 4465 possible intercorrelations were computed. When factor analysis was applied, it was found that practically all of the covariation among the measures could be explained in terms of 23 factors. The economy of describing a set of observed relationships in terms of 23 rather than 95 variables can hardly be denied.

It is important to note that there is no implication in the purely descriptive use of factor analysis that the resultant mathematically efficient variables are scientifically meaningful. Nor, as will become apparent later, can it even be said that a particular factor-analytic result represents the only way that the observed relationships can be effectively described in terms of a fewer number of variables. All that is obtained as a result of factor analysis is *one* relatively rigorous summary description.

Exactly how useful the resulting description will be, either in practical situations or in gaining further knowledge, must be determined *outside* the technique itself. As Henrysson (1957) says,

A factor analysis of a set of data may be regarded as a deductive procedure. . . . The factor loadings obtained are deduced from the observed values. This procedure, in itself, only gives the factors descriptive properties. If, besides this, they are also to have an explanatory meaning, then the analytical method or the further steps which follow must be so constituted that the factors obtain also some new characteristics typical of explanatory concepts.

This immediately suggests one very important point about the results of factor analysis, namely, that the factors with which the research worker ultimately describes the observed relationships in no way can be considered ultimate entities or statements of what nature is like, *really*. Most scientists today—or at least philosophers of science—would immediately point out that any scientific law in any field is not a part of nature but a way of comprehending nature. Again, it is important to note that any theory or law or description should be thought of, not as true or false, but as useful (in a theoretical as well as a practical sense) or useless.

EXPLANATORY FACTOR ANALYSIS I: SUGGESTING HYPOTHESES   It has been noted that the description resulting from factor analysis is neither unique nor always scientifically meaningful. This latter statement might properly be amended by adding the phrase, "in the light of present concepts." Sometimes, though not always, the description *will* make sense—very real sense—if present concepts of the variables involved or of the relationships among them are modified. When this happens, then factor analysis has suggested some new hypothesis which the researcher will go on to test experimentally on new data (i.e., on new observations which did not suggest the hypothesis). Factors which suggest or take on content beyond that present in the original matrix are often labeled *explanatory factors.* Such explanatory factors can be considered to be useful hypothetical constructs and, after considerable additional work, may even become what Rozeboom (1956) prefers to call *mediation variables.*

As Henrysson (1957) suggests, such an application of factor analysis is most likely to be useful to research workers in exploring a new field where there is but little knowledge and few, if any, theoretical formulations. It should be recognized, though, that these resulting hypothetical constructs or explanatory variables are likely to be of special value, since they represent concepts arrived at by a rigorous description of observations rather than by pure armchair speculations or by casual observations as is done in many case studies.

EXPLANATORY FACTOR ANALYSIS II: TESTING HYPOTHESES   In addition to suggesting new variables and relationships, factor analysis can be used in a logical sense to gather specific evidence for the support or refutation of a particular scientific hypothesis. It is here that factor analysis is weakest and fraught with the most dangers, for by its nature factor analysis cannot be considered to be a mathematically rigorous hypothetical-deductive process. The problem arises because of several subjective decisions which must be made if factor analysis is to serve other than a purely descriptive function (where it is, indeed, possible to transpose mathematically one set of variables for another and to make appropriate statistical tests). While somewhat arbitrary decisions are no real handicap in suggesting hypotheses, they represent major concerns when attempting to test a hypothesis.

Among the choices which the factor analyst must make that can have an important influence on his conclusions with respect to a particular hypothesis are the following: (1) What variables should be included in the analysis? (It just is not possible to get anything out of an analysis that has not somehow been included in it in the first place.) (2) When should the process of extracting factors cease? (3) What kind of estimates should be used for the communalities? [4] (4) What kind of rotation, if any, is appropriate? While the different answers an investigator gives to each of these questions will have an effect on the results he obtains, there are a number of hypotheses, especially those concerned with mental structure and organization or with the construct validation of behavioral measures, which are exceedingly difficult, if not impossible, to support or refute by nonfactorial techniques. While it is impossible to arrive at a rigorously deterministic solution by means of factor analysis, it is possible to draw useful conclusions by providing sensible answers to the questions raised in the analysis. Thus, the results of factor analysis can be of tremendous help to the research worker in gaining confidence about certain hypotheses and in questioning certain others. This is as much as any scientific technique can do outside of the purely descriptive realm.

[4] A definition of the term *communality* is given on page 354.

As an example of the possible use of factor analysis to test a scientific hypothesis, consider the question of how important motivation is for academic achievement at the college level. Although the study of covert participation by Stern, Stein, and Bloom (1956) suggests that a great deal of variance in scholastic performance might be accounted for by differences in motivation, investigators up to the present time have met with little success in improving the prediction of grade-point average by including a measure of motivation beyond the improvement now obtainable from a combination of scholastic ability score and past accomplishment in high school. This latter observation could be due to one of several different possibilities: perhaps motivation is so closely tied to particular situations that it cannot be described as a general trait of individuals, perhaps motivation is currently taken care of in the index of past performance in high school, perhaps no adequate measure of motivation has as yet been devised, or perhaps grades are not an adequate measure of scholastic performance.

Keeping these alternatives in mind, it is possible to set up a factor-analytic study which includes as its original input variables several measures of scholastic aptitude, several indexes of high school achievement, several measures of motivation as now constituted, and examination scores as well as the currently acceptable measure of college achievement (i.e., the one used in practice for admissions, retentions, and promotion decisions). Then, if no motivational factor appeared, the third alternative might be suspected as a major contributor to the observed phenomenon, for at the least, current measures of motivation showed little in common. On the other hand, if a motivational factor did appear but the measures of college achievement were not loaded on it, then the first possibility would be a reasonable alternative, for it could be that most persons who are spending time and money attending college are sufficiently motivated and thus this variable becomes relatively unimportant in contrast to differences in scholastic capability. Should a motivational factor appear and the several measures of high school achievement be as highly loaded on it as are the specific measures of motivation, then one might have more confidence that the second alternative is most reasonable. Finally, if examination scores are much more highly loaded on factors of aptitude and motivation than are grades, then the last of the four possible alternatives should be investigated further.

From this example, it should be amply clear that the use of factor analysis to test hypotheses is not so mathematically rigorous as the statistical techniques described in Chapter 6. At the same time it should be equally clear that the procedure follows the same logical pattern as is found in any use of the scientific method where the investigator asks himself, "What will happen if my hypothesis is true (that will not happen if it is not) that can be observed?"

Types of Problems for Which Factor Analysis Is Suited

THE COVARIATION CHART   R. B. Cattell (1952b) has portrayed the logically different possible factor-analytic research designs with his covariation chart (see Figure 8.4) and suggested as well some of the types of problems for which the factor-analytic technique would be appropriate. As suggested by this figure, each scientific observation would seem to provide a description of a particular person (or object) with respect to a particular attribute (or variable) obtained on a particular occasion (representing a particular

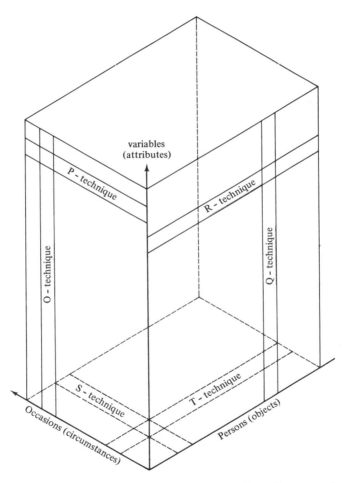

FIGURE 8.4.   The covariation chart (After R. Cattell.   The three basic factor-analytic research designs, *P-, R-,* and *T-techniques,* and their derivatives.   *Psychological Bulletin,* 1952, **49,** Fig. 1.   P. 501.)

set of circumstances). Each face of the chart represents a mathematically transposable pair of the six possible factor-analytical techniques labeled *O, P, Q, R, S,* and *T.*

The *R* technique represents the most common factor-analytic approach. Here correlations are obtained between attributes (by summing cross products of standard scores over people) as measured on one occasion. When the matrix of all possible pairs of such correlations is factor analyzed, the result is clusters or groups of variables (the factors) on which persons performed alike on the one occasion or set of circumstances under which observations were made. Both of the studies so far described in the discussion of factor analysis are of this type. Because Cattell has estimated that 95 percent of the factor analyses performed represent an application of the *R* technique, the reader will have no difficulty in locating many examples on his own.

In contrast with the *R* technique, the *Q* technique, given popularity by Stephenson (1936), starts with correlations between persons (summed over tests) and ends up with clusters or groups of persons who performed alike on a battery of tests administered on a particular occasion. Although the *Q* technique is sometimes referred to as inverted, or obverse, factor analysis, it is more appropriately recognized as the *transpose* of the *R* technique, just as *S* is the transpose of the *T* technique and *O* is the transpose of the *P* technique (and vice versa). Further, as Cattell (1952a) points out, "If the correlation of ability tests yields . . . a factor of mechanical aptitude, then correlation of persons will yield a corresponding factor of 'mechanically apt persons,' the only difference being that in R-technique we point to a highly loaded *test* as exemplifying the factor, whereas in Q-technique we point to a highly loaded *person.*"

While transpose techniques such as *R* and *Q* may produce mathematically equivalent results when the same metric is used, there are some differences with respect to the scaling of the variables (which will not be discussed here) and some differences in the practicability of obtaining sufficient data. For example, correlations used in factor analysis should be based on a large number of elements over which the cross products are summed. Thus, while observations on 50 persons (as required for Lawley's method—see Lawley 1940 and 1943—when applied to the *R* technique) may not seem like many, obtaining observations on a minimum of 50 tests (for the *Q* and *O* techniques) or on 50 different occasions (for the *S* and *P* techniques) is another matter.

In the *P* technique, correlations are obtained between pairs of attributes as observed over a series of occasions in one person. The resulting factors represent clusters of traits which, in the person studied, seem to change in the same way with time and circumstance. If the different occasions over which the observations are made represent distinctly different systematically varied stimulus situations, it is possible to study specific influences on change. For example, if the different occasions represent different stages of therapy, the clinician can sort characteristics of the individual into groups of traits which fluctuate similarly throughout the therapy sequence.

Published studies which illustrate the use of the P technique include one concerned with ascertaining the combinations of psychological and physiological traits which vary concomitantly (Cattell, Cattell, & Rhymer, 1947), one concerned with the dimensions along which the cultural patterns of different nations can be described (Cattell, 1949), and one which is concerned with social change in the United States (Cattell & Adelson, 1951).

As the transpose of the P technique, the O technique starts with correlations between occasions summed over a series of attributes as measured in one individual. Although both P and Q techniques are concerned with just one individual and are thus peculiarly suited to counseling and clinical psychology, Q technique seems to be the less widely applicable and the less manageable of the two from a practical point of view.

Because the O technique results in clusters of occasions on which the subject shows similar attributes, it seems ideal for studying the types of circumstances under which the individual will play different roles. Cattell (1952a) also recommends this technique for "longitudinal studies of nations or societies, whereby the pattern of culture on one occasion can be compared with that on another, thus establishing the degree of reality to be attached to concepts of era, epoch, historical phase, business cycle phase, etc."

The T technique represents a second approach to arriving at clusters or groups of occasions. In this instance, however, the interest is in a single attribute as observed in a number of different persons. For example, a research worker might note the different occasions on which people responded to an opinion poll question in a similar way. As Cattell points out, the usefulness of this technique will depend upon the researcher's ability to record the distinctive characteristics of each occasion. If this is done, the T technique would provide a sort of thermometer of social climate which would suggest what and how many different atmospheres affect people's responses.

According to Cattell (1952b), S technique "is par excellence the method for social psychology." This approach starts with correlations between pairs of persons observed in a variety of occasions with respect to one particular trait. It results in clusters or groups of persons who showed similar responses on the various occasions. The obvious use of the S technique is, therefore, that of detecting and defining social roles. It also might be used for determining the internal structure of a group or institution. Because it correlates similar responses to a single issue over many occasions, it defines functional subgroups within the total organization. A series of studies over many issues might suggest the way in which subgroupings change with respect to different issues.

STANDARD APPLICATIONS   Even though Cattell's complete covariation chart outlines the logically different possible applications of factor analysis, it would seem worthwhile to mention briefly several of the more or less standard types of problems for which a factor analysis is useful. It has already been noted that the primary application of factor analysis is in the reduction of the number of descriptive concepts required to describe some phenomenon. All the examples of this cited so far have started with measures previously and independently constructed for other purposes. Yet the greatest reduction may occur when the investigator starts with an extensive everyday vocabulary (such as the 18,000 English words describing normal characteristics compiled by Allport and Odbert, 1936) and seeks to organize these into clusters which seem to represent relatively independent attributes.

Very close to this is the use of factor analysis to study item responses during the construction of scales, questionnaire inventories, and other types of psychometric instruments. The object here is either to group items into empirically meaningful subtests or to purify a scale by eliminating those items which do not load heavily on that which the total scale measures. When used in this way, factor analysis is closely related to certain problems of scaling and test homogeneity.

Another fairly standard application of factor analysis is in studies of the shift in the structure of tasks when the individuals are given more practice or simply grow older. As a classical example of this use of factor analysis, Henrysson (1957) cites a study done by Fleishman and Hempel (1954) of the effect of training on performance in a complex psychomotor test.

In the areas of industrial and counseling psychology, factor analysis has been found extremely useful in applied problems related to the task of predicting successful future behavior. Besides data reduction and test construction as described above, factor analysis can be used in both job classification—grouping into job families those jobs which require persons with similar traits (Coombs & Satter, 1949), and job analysis—the study of task performances to discover what particular traits are required for success in each activity (McQuitty et al., 1954).

Finally, as Henrysson (1957) points out, "Factor analysis has made important contributions to the behavioral sciences both directly and indirectly by emphasizing and defining more strictly the concept of dimensionality." Essentially, the problem of dimensionality refers to the task of finding the appropriate number of independent dimensions required to adequately describe some phenomenon. For example, How many different ways of classifying smells must be used in order to account for all the different olfactory sensations people experience? or, How many different ways of classifying abstract artistic designs must be used to account for observed differences in preference? or, How many different aspects of a set of materials used in a learning task must be examined in order to categorize it completely with respect to instructional requirements? Factor-analyzing intercorrelations can provide a sensible answer to all of these questions within the limits of the observations included in the analysis. In this connection, factor-analysis methods seem to have spawned the closely related techniques of multi-dimensional scaling (Torgerson, 1958) and latent-structure analysis (Lazarsfeld, 1944).

A Word of Caution

A word of caution is in order before turning from the uses of factor analysis to an examination of its basic tenets and its primary methods of solution. To the uninformed reader the factor-analytic technique may seem to come close to being a panacea for almost all of his research problems. Indeed, it is a powerful technique which has contributed a great deal to the understanding of many behavioral phenomena. Factor analysis is not, however, an end in itself but rather a tool which can be helpful in many situations in enabling scientists to achieve a better understanding of the empirical world. Unfortunately, some investigators have been so taken with the method that they tend to see all problems in factor-analytic terms and attempt to apply the technique to whatever data is at hand. Thus, before getting deeply involved in a factor-analytic study, the reader should carefully review Guilford's (1952) article entitled "When Not to Factor Analyze." [5]

Finally, the reader should be aware that, in spite of all the fine logical promise that factor analysis would provide a limited number of conceptually pure and completely general characteristics which can be combined in different ways to predict behavior in any specific situation, this hope simply has not worked out empirically. Thus, Henrysson (1957) concludes: "Even if it can be maintained that tests based on factor analysis constitute theoretically, a rational solution of many prediction problems, the practical result hitherto obtained in the form of statistically reported validities are not particularly numerous or convincing." It would seem most profitable at the present time to use factor analysis in an exploratory sense to help formulate theoretical concepts about the structure of phenomena rather than try to solve practical prediction problems.

---

[5] Since many of Guilford's ten common faults in using factor analysis require an understanding of factor analysis procedures well beyond that presented in this book, they will not be included here.

The Basic Tenets of Factor Analysis

Because of the large number of equations which would otherwise be required, much of the theory and method of factor analysis has been written in matrix notation, and the reader who wishes a full understanding of the logic and procedure involved will need to learn at least the rudiments of matrix algebra. In the following discussion matrix notation has been kept to a minimum and described graphically whenever possible. Nonetheless, readers unfamiliar with matrix algebra will on occasion need to accept algebraic statements on faith and concentrate on the verbal statements that are made.

Because factor analysis developed largely in the context of psychological testing and more readers are likely to be familiar with testing than other forms of measurement, the discussion makes use of testing terminology. For example, the original intercorrelated variables are labeled *tests,* the individual objects are referred to as *persons,* and the measurements of these objects are called *scores.* Those who are not familiar with some of the notions of psychometrics which are used may wish to review at certain points concepts presented in the chapter on measurement; all should recognize that factor analysis as a method is *not* limited in its application to the area of psychological testing.

THE NATURE OF INDIVIDUAL DIFFERENCES   A major postulate of factor analysis is that the differences among people that appear in performances on a large number of tests can be described as additive functions of individual differences in a limited number of fundamental variables. For a single individual this postulate can be algebraically expressed as

$$Z_{ji} = a_{j1}X_{1j} + a_{j2}X_{2i} + \cdots + a_{jq}X_{qi} + \cdots$$

where Z_{ji} = *standard score* of individual i on test j

X_{qi} = amount (in standard score scale) of fundamental variable Q (i.e., the factor) which is possessed by person i

a_{jq} = factor loading, or square root of the *proportion* of the total variance in test j which is attributable to the factor q

Because factor analysis is concerned with more than one person, with more than one test, and with several factors, not just one such equation, but rather a whole set of equations, is involved. (For example, in the study mentioned earlier in which 95 measures were administered to 700 individuals, a total of 700×95 or 66,500 such equations would be required.)

In matrix notation, this large number of individual equations can be very simply expressed as $FP = Z$, with a graphic interpretation of this notation as follows:

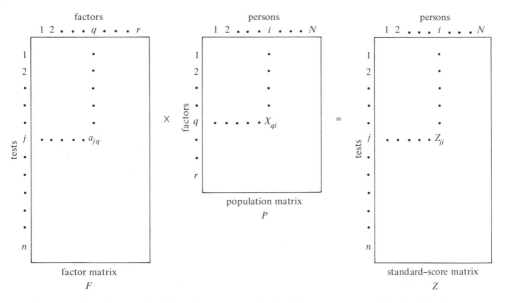

In practice, the Z, that is, the scores obtained by a group of individuals on the set of tests represented by j, are observed. Then, by means of factor analysis, the F is determined. It is possible to solve the expression $FP = Z$ for the values in P to determine the extent to which different persons possess the different factor traits.

THE STRUCTURE OF THE FACTOR MATRIX   A second basic postulate of multiple factor analysis [6] specifies the nature of the factor matrix itself. Essentially, the model assumes that the total observed variance of any test j can be thought of as arising from three basic sources which can be combined in an additive fashion. The sources are:

1. *common variance*—variation resulting from true differences in the amount of traits possessed by individuals in the sample and common to two or more tests included in the battery
2. *specific variance*—variation resulting from real differences in the amount of those traits measured only by test j
3. *error variance*—variation resulting from fortuitous fluctuations in test scores.

In terms of symbols, this can be expressed as

$$\sigma_j{}^2 = \sigma_{j1}{}^2 + \sigma_{j2}{}^2 + \cdots + \sigma_{jq}{}^2 + \cdots + \sigma_{jr}{}^2 + \sigma_{js_1}{}^2 + \sigma_{js_2}{}^2 + \cdots + \sigma_e{}^2$$

$$\underset{\substack{\text{total}\\\text{variance}}}{} = \underset{\text{common variance}}{} + \underset{\text{specific variance}}{} + \underset{\substack{\text{error}\\\text{variance}}}{}$$

---

[6] Some methods of factor analysis start with a slightly different model at this point. However, since multiple factor analysis represents the most common model used in this country, it will be presented here. Some of the differences in other models are described beginning on page 358.

Dividing both sides by the total observed variance we can obtain the following equation, which expresses the postulate in terms of the proportion of the total variation which is accounted for by the various components:

$$1 = \frac{\sigma_{j1}^2}{\sigma_j^2} + \frac{\sigma_{j2}^2}{\sigma_j^2} + \cdots + \frac{\sigma_{jq}^2}{\sigma_j^2} + \cdots + \frac{\sigma_{jr}^2}{\sigma_j^2} + \frac{\sigma_{js_1}^2}{\sigma_j^2} + \frac{\sigma_{js_2}^2}{\sigma_j^2} + \cdots + \frac{\sigma_e^2}{\sigma_j^2}$$

Now it is possible to define a number of the technical terms which are used in the literature in describing factor-analytic studies. First, it will be recalled that a factor loading has been defined to be the square root of the proportion of the total test variance which is attributable to that factor. In the notation used here,

$$a_{jq}^2 = \frac{\sigma_{jq}^2}{\sigma_j^2}$$

Thus, the basic postulate can now be written in terms of factor loadings as

$$1 = a_{j1}^2 + a_{j2}^2 + \cdots + a_{jq}^2 + \cdots + a_{jr}^2 + s_j^2 + e_j^2$$

where s_j^2 = proportion of variance specific to test
e_j^2 = proportion of error variance in test

Next, because test reliability has been defined as the ratio of true-score variance to total-score variance, reliability can be seen as equal to the sum of the squares of common and specific factor loadings. That is,

$$\text{Reliability} = \frac{\sigma_{\text{true}}^2}{\sigma_j^2} = \frac{\sigma_{j1}^2 + \sigma_{j2}^2 + \sigma_{iq}^2 + \cdots + \sigma_{jr}^2 + \sigma_{js_1}^2 + \sigma_{js_2}^2 + \cdots}{\sigma_j^2}$$
$$= a_{j1}^2 + a_{j2}^2 + \cdots + a_{jq}^2 + \cdots + a_{jr}^2 + s_j^2$$
$$= 1 - e_j^2$$

The *communality* of a test, h_j^2, is the proportion of the test variance attributable to factors which the test has in common with other tests and thus is the sum of the squares of factor loadings. In symbols,

$$h_j^2 = a_{ji}^2 + a_{j2}^2 + \cdots + a_{jq}^2 + \cdots + a_{jr}^2$$
$$= \sum_{q=1}^{r} a_{jq}^2$$

Specificity is the proportion of the variance attributable to traits specific to that test and not found in any of the other tests included in the battery under analysis. Since several different traits might be specific to a particular test, the specificity can be thought of as having several subcomponents and therefore is denoted as

$$s_j^2 = \frac{\sigma_{js_1}^2 + \sigma_{js_2}^2 + \cdots}{\sigma_j^2}$$

Finally, the *uniqueness* of a test is that part of the total test variance which is not shared with other tests. Because by definition the fortuitous fluctuations defined as error variance are independent from one test to the next, the uniqueness includes both the specificity of the test and the error associated with it. Algebraically,

$$u_j^2 = s_j^2 + e_j^2$$

In summary, the second basic tenet of factor analysis postulates a complete factor matrix F_1 which can be illustrated diagrammatically as follows:

F_1

Further, the postulate suggested a number of concepts which, along with some interesting relationships among them, can be expressed algebraically as follows:

Total variance for test j $\quad = \sigma_j^2 = \sigma_{j1}^2 + \sigma_{j2}^2 + \cdots + \sigma_{jq}^2 + \sigma_{jr}^2$
$\qquad\qquad\qquad\qquad\qquad\qquad + \sigma_{s_1}^2 + \sigma_{s_2}^2 + \cdots + \sigma_e^2$

Proportion of total variance $= 1 = h_j^2 + s_j^2 + e_j^2 = h_j^2 + u_j^2$

Factor loading $\qquad\qquad = a_{jq} = \sqrt{\dfrac{\sigma_{jq}^2}{\sigma_j^2}}$

Reliability $\qquad\qquad\quad = r_{jj} = h_j^2 + s_j^2 = 1 - e_j^2$

Communality $\qquad\qquad = h_j^2 = 1 - u_j^2 = r_{jj} - s_j^2$

$$\text{Specificity} \quad = s_j^2 = s_{1j}^2 + s_{2j}^2 + \cdots$$
$$\text{Uniqueness} \quad = u_j^2 = s_j^2 + e^2 = 1 - h_j^2$$
$$\text{Error variance} = e_j^2 = 1 - r_{jj}$$

TENABILITY OF THE ASSUMPTIONS   The sophisticated reader will readily recognize that, if the model described above is to be useful in working with empirical data obtained from the real world, certain of its assumptions should be approximately fulfilled.   The ultimate test as to whether the assumptions are sufficiently fulfilled is whether or not the results of factor analysis, both theoretical and practical, enable science to increase its understanding and control of human behavior.

An excellent discussion of all the assumptions made in applying a factor analysis can be found in Wolfle (1940).   As Henrysson (1957, p. 30) points out, however, no scientist who has worked very long in the area of psychometrics doubts the usefulness, at least for theoretical and conceptual purposes, of considering human differences in performance on a wide variety of tasks as resulting from a smaller number of more or less basic traits; nor would he deny the usefulness of attempting to classify various human tasks according to the extent to which they require the basic traits.   The major question that arises is whether or not the relationships among basic traits and specific performances can be legitimately expressed by means of an additive linear function.   While there seems to be no great body of evidence specifically designed to bear upon this question, Thorndike (1949) pointed out some years ago that: "The possibility of encountering a significantly non-linear relationship should always be borne in mind.   However, one should not count on finding such relationships.   For example, in the study of many different tests for several different job criteria in the A.A.F. no convincing evidence was found for the existence of non-linear relationships."   In any case, the problems of additive combinations and linearity represent empirical questions which can be answered in each specific situation.   Even though past studies have generally found the model as postulated to be adequate, increasing knowledge in a field demands increasing rigor.   Thus, future studies may require a model which goes beyond that presently used.

The Basic Procedure of Factor Analysis

Taken together the two basic tenets of factor analysis have provided a model which can be mathematically expressed in matrix notation by the fundamental equation,

$$F_1 P = Z$$

The matrix Z represents a set of observations and, therefore, of known values. Both F_1 and P, however, represent unknown values. Thus, the basic expression cannot be solved without another equation relating one of these matrices to a set of observable values.

THE LOGICAL SOLUTION   In an attempt to find the additional observable phenomena needed, it certainly is not too unreasonable to speculate that observable relationships among test performances would provide some useful information. If two or more tests depend upon the same basic traits, then it is reasonable that they should be highly correlated; and to the extent to which a set of tests require unique abilities, the observed correlations should approach zero.

Starting with this notion, the reader may recall that the Pearson product-moment correlation between any two tests is simply the average of the products of the standard scores. Thus, the correlation between Test j and Test k can be written in the notation used earlier to express the first basic tenet of factor analysis as

$$r_{jk} = \sum_{i=1}^{N} Z_{ji}Z_{ki}$$

where r_{jk} = correlation between the two tests
Z_{ji} = standard score of person i on test j
Z_{ki} = standard score of person i on test k
N = number of persons given both tests

It also should be noted that the correlation of any test with itself can be expressed as

$$r_{jj} = \frac{\Sigma Z_{ji}Z_{ki}}{N} = \frac{\Sigma Z_{ji}^2}{N}$$

But, since Z_{ji} is a standard score,

$$\frac{\Sigma Z_{ji}^2}{N} = 1$$

The two equations above represent the correlation between just two tests, namely, j and k. But, in factor analysis, the correlation between all possible pairs of tests must be considered. Thus, once again turning to matrix notation to express the entire set of relationships, it can be said that

$$R_1 = \frac{1}{N}ZZ'$$

where R_1 = matrix of observed correlations with the value 1 in the diagonal
$\quad\quad Z$ = standard score matrix defined previously
$\quad\quad Z'$ = transpose of Matrix Z (i.e., the Matrix Z written with the rows and columns interchanged)
$\quad\quad N$ = number of individuals to whom the entire battery of tests was given

Diagrammatically, this relationship is represented as follows:

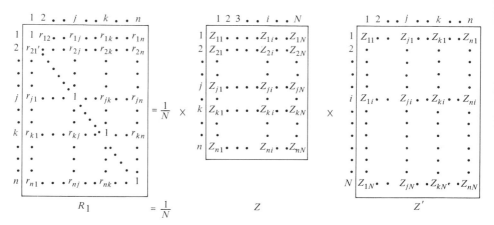

But because $Z = F_1P$ (the basic postulate again), it can be seen that

$$R_1 = \frac{1}{N}(F_1P)(F_1P)'$$

Applying the transpose law of matrix combination, we have

$$R_1 = \frac{1}{N}(F_1PP'F_1')$$

Then, just as it was shown that $R_1 = ZZ'$, so it can be shown that $R_f = XX'$, where R_f is the matrix of intercorrelations of factors, where X represents the matrix of individual scores on factors, and where X' is the transpose of X. If an orthogonal set of factors is now assumed (i.e., it is accepted that the more basic traits into which it is desired to translate the original variables are uncorrelated), it can be shown that R_1 equals I (a matrix with diagonal elements all equal to one, and off-diagonal elements equal to zero), and thus that $PP' = NI$.

Finally, substituting NI for PP' in the basic equation and noting that multiplying by I in matrix algebra is like multiplying by one, we see that

$$R_1 = F_1F_1'$$

This last expression, then, represents the logical solution to the problem raised. Diagrammatically, the solution is as follows:

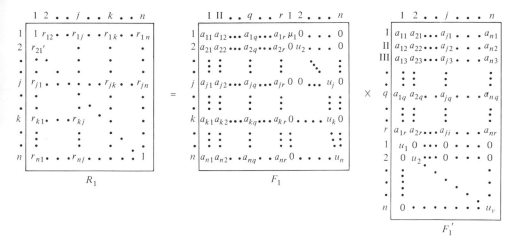

Examination of the off-diagonal elements of this expression indicates that

$$r_{jk} = \sum_{i=1}^{N} a_{ji} a_{ki}$$

That is, the correlation between any two tests is the sum of the cross-products of their respective factor loadings. The diagonals tell us that

$$1 = \sum_{i=1}^{N} a_{ji}^2 + u_j^2 = h_j^2 + a_j^2$$

as was indicated on page 355, where it was shown that the proportion of total variance was equal to the sum of the communality and the uniqueness.

SOME WORKING METHODS   While the matrix expression $R_1 = F_1 F_1'$ represents a logical solution to the problem, it does not provide a unique procedure for obtaining a factor matrix F_1 such that $F_1 F_1' = R_1$. Thus, a variety of different procedures have been suggested and used. While the modern research worker does not need to know the details of these approaches, he should be familiar with the basic idea and some of the advantages and disadvantages of each.

The *principal-components* procedure, suggested by Hotelling (1935) and modified by Kelley (1935), represents a least-square treatment [7] which results in a mathematically unique and statistically rigorous solution. Because in this method each factor extracted in turn takes out the maximum remaining variance (thus minimizing the residuals), it results in the minimum number of orthogonal factors which account for the complete correlation matrix. Because each test included in the battery is likely to contain

---

[7] It will be recalled from the earlier discussion that a least-squares treatment is one in which the sum of the squares of the errors is minimized.

some specific variance, a principal-components solution ends up with as many factors as tests and, further, is more dependent than other solutions upon what particular tests have been included in the battery. Finally, while the principal-components solution permits completely accurate reproduction of the individual's test scores from the factors, the resulting factors are often not very meaningful from a psychological or scientific point of view.

In contrast to the principal-components solution, the *centroid* method, as advocated and used extensively in this country by Thurstone (1947) and his followers, gives up some statistical rigor for (1) a reduction of the number of resulting common factors; (2) factors which are psychologically and scientifically meaningful; and (3) results which vary less as particular tests in the battery under analysis are changed.

Whereas the principal-components approach makes no distinction between common and specific factors and thus analyzes the complete matrix, the centroid method analyzes only the common factor portion of the complete matrix and therefore uses communalities rather than unity in the diagonal of the intercorrelation matrix. This leads to the problem of finding an appropriate estimate of the communalities and to the fact that a mathematically unique solution is not possible. Because there are a number of incomplete (i.e., common) factor matrices F such that $FF' = R$, where R is the intercorrelation matrix with communalities in the diagonal (as contrasted with R_1, which has unity in the diagonal), those using the centroid method have had to introduce additional, more subjective concepts, such as *positive manifold* and *simple structure* and the techniques of *rotation,* in attempts to obtain relatively unique solutions.

Another statistically rigorous approach is *Lawley's maximum likelihood method* (Lawley 1940; 1943). Assuming that all test and factor scores are stochastic and have a normal distribution in the population, this method guesses at the number of factors and proceeds to estimate that orthogonal factor matrix for which the likelihood of the actually observed correlation matrix occurring is a maximum in the course of random sampling. When the factors have been extracted, a test of significance is made to determine whether the residuals can be considered to be only random sampling fluctuations. If they are, the process is stopped; if they are not, it is repeated, using a new guess as to the number of factors based upon the analysis just completed.

In addition to being statistically rigorous, Lawley's method is robust in large samples with respect to the normality assumptions and seems to work well with sample sizes as small as 50. On the other hand, the maximum likelihood approach is computationally laborious; and if the original estimate of the trial factor loadings is not near the solution, the convergence with successive approximations may make it awkward, even with modern computers.

Because of the latter problem, some factor analysts have suggested that the centroid method be used to obtain the first approximation to the factor loadings. Indeed, Lawley himself seems to feel that the centroid method is much more efficient than is generally believed and points out that the centroid method often produces results quite similar to those obtained by his maximum likelihood approach (Lawley, 1955).

The *bifactor method* developed by Holzinger (Holzinger & Harman, 1941) and used primarily in England has about the same advantages and disadvantages as the centroid method already described. The major difference between the two is that the bifactor approach requires that each test be loaded on a *G,* or general ability, factor and, beyond that, on one and only one group factor. Since, as Cattell (1952a) has pointed out, the results are similar in form to a principal-components solution but contain the same degree of subjectivity as the centroid method, this approach has not found favor with many persons in the United States.

A final working method that might be mentioned is *cluster analysis,* which has been most fully developed by Tryon (1939). Although sometimes referred to as a "poor man's factor analysis," this technique is not a true factor-analytic method at all. Rather than breaking the test variance down into components and arriving at factors, cluster analysis groups whole tests into clusters which have high intercorrelations within groups but low average correlations between groups. As a relatively simple technique, cluster analysis can be used as a preliminary to other approaches or in situations where a very small sample size or the involved computations of regular factor-analytic methods seem too much work for the rough results needed. If the tests included in the battery are relatively pure measures (i.e., tend to measure only one factor), the results will approximate those obtained with more complex methods. Otherwise, cluster analysis should be used for classifying test variables rather than for seeking more basic factors.

SCALES AND SCALING

The Psychometric Scaling Procedures

Modern psychometric scaling procedures have their roots in the psychophysical methods of such early psychologists as G. T. Fechner, G. E. Muller, and E. H. Weber (Boring, 1956). As they originally conceived it, their task was that of finding relationships between mind and body. Thus, the original methods sought to determine the magnitude of some physical stimulus required to reach the threshold of sensory experience and, beyond this, to find the relationship between the actual physical scale of magnitude and a psychological scale of magnitude of the resulting sensation. While modern psychophysics has extended this task to include the development of full-scale mathematical models for the description of behavioral phenomena, most research workers outside the field find the greatest application remaining in the development of psychometric scales.

UNIDIMENSIONAL SCALING   Most psychometric scaling procedures as described by Guilford (1954), and Edwards (1957), and Torgerson (1958) represent techniques for placing a set of stimuli along a single unidimensional scale, seeking in every instance to reach the highest level of measurement possible under the conditions imposed. While the stimuli of concern often remain the classical ones of the early sensory studies, they have been extended by modern investigators to include such things as color photographs, artistic designs, cafeteria desserts, odors, other people, and attitudinal statements to be used as items in developing a scale to measure attitudes.

The most frequently used procedures for assigning scale values to a set of stimuli are the methods of pair comparisons, rank order, equal-appearing intervals, and successive categories. While these methods represent quite different ways of obtaining the basic raw data, all are logically only special applications of Thurstone's law of comparative judgment. Because the details of each of the various scaling methods can readily be found in any of the references cited above, only the central idea of comparative judgments will be presented here.

Since the purpose of any scaling procedure is to locate some stimulus object i along a psychological continuum, it is convenient to designate the true position of this object on the continuum as S_i. Next, suppose it were possible to have a group of persons make judgments about the absolute location of Stimulus i on the scale (as might be done in guessing the length

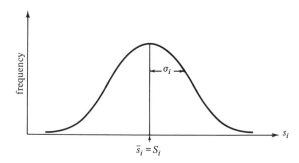

FIGURE 8.5   Frequency distribution of judgments of the position of a stimulus object along a scale

of a table). Let each judgment made be designated s_i. Now it is reasonable to assume that if a frequency distribution were made of a very large number of judgments, s_i, the result would be a normal curve centered on the true value with a variance on σ_i^2, as shown in Figure 8.5.

In symbols, this can be expressed as

$$s_i \overset{d}{=} \mathfrak{N}(S_i, \sigma_i^2)$$

where the symbol $\overset{d}{=}$ can be read "is distributed as," where $\mathfrak{N}$ indicates the normal distribution, and where s_i, S_i, and σ_i^2 are as defined above. For a second stimulus object j, it could be similarly said that

$$s_j \overset{d}{=} \mathfrak{N}(S_j, \sigma_j^2)$$

If it were possible to judge stimulus objects directly with respect to their position along an established continuum, the values $\bar{s}_i$ and $\bar{s}_j$ could be used as the estimate of their scale positions.[8] For many attributes, however, it is not possible to make meaningful judgments as to the absolute position of the stimulus object. For example, how could the reader or anyone else directly judge the creativity of a child to be 45, the cynicism of an adult to be 108, or a sample odor as falling at 23? Or how could anyone judge the degree of preference for a dessert or an attitudinal statement about some social practice in such a way?

Even though absolute judgments in such instances are meaningless, it frequently is both possible and sensible to make statements that Person A is more creative (or less cynical) than Person B, that the first bottle contained an odor that was more pungent than that in the second, that pie is preferred to cake, and that this statement about religion is more favorable than that. In general, it is almost always possible to make comparative judgments of the sort that $s_i > s_j$ or $s_i = s_j$ or $s_i < s_j$. Judgments of this sort are, in effect, judgments of differences in stimulus position, that is, of $s_i - s_j$. And, where

$$s_i \overset{d}{=} \mathfrak{N}(S_i, \sigma_i^2)$$

and

$$s_j \overset{d}{=} \mathfrak{N}(S_j, \sigma_j^2)$$

it can be shown that

[8] Such a possibility seldom if ever occurs, except in those situations where more exact forms of measurement can occur and therefore where scaling procedures as described here are unnecessary.

$$s_i - s_j \overset{d}{=} \mathfrak{N}(S_i - S_j, \sigma_i^2 + \sigma_j^2 - 2P_{ij}\sigma_i\sigma_j)$$

the graphic representation of which is given in Figure 8.6.

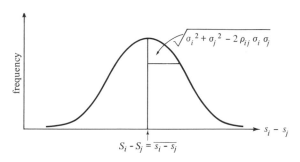

FIGURE 8.6   Frequency distribution of judgments comparing two stimulus objects

From Figure 8.6 it can be seen that if there were a way of locating a zero point on the scale, it would be possible to know the value $S_i - S_j$. That is, it would be possible to obtain a numerical value representing the scale separation of the two stimulus objects. In Chapter 6 it was noted that the most useful way of locating any point in a frequency distribution was to calculate the standard score

$$Z_i = \frac{X_i - \mu_x}{\sigma_x}$$

In the distribution of comparative judgment shown in Figure 8.6, this becomes

$$Z_{ij} = \frac{s_i - s_j - (S_i - S_j)}{\sqrt{\sigma_i^2 + \sigma_j^2 - 2P_{ij}\sigma_i\sigma_j}}$$

The zero point on this scale, then, is that place where $s_i = s_j$ and therefore where $s_i - s_j = 0$ and thus where

$$Z_{ij} = \frac{0 - (S_i - S_j)}{\sqrt{\sigma_i^2 + \sigma_j^2 - 2P_{ij}\sigma_i\sigma_j}}$$

Solving this latter equation for the true difference in stimulus positions, we obtain Thurstone's law of comparative judgment, which states that:

$$S_j - S_i = Z_{ij}\sqrt{\sigma_i^2 + \sigma_j^2 - 2P_{ij}\sigma_i\sigma_j}$$

While, as will be seen later, the value Z_{ij} can be determined experimentally, σ_i^2, σ_j^2, and P_{ij} remain unknowns which can be eliminated only by making additional assumptions. The different set of assumptions made to eliminate the latter three values represents the different "cases" of the law of comparative judgment (Thurstone, 1927). The most famous of these, Case V, makes the reasonable assumptions that all $\sigma_i = \sigma_j = \sigma$ and that all $P_{ij} = P$. That is, it assumes that the variance of judgments is the same for all stimuli and that the correlation between the judgments of any pair of stimuli is the same for all possible pairs. With these assumptions the Law of Comparative Judgment becomes

$$S_j - S_i = Z_{ij}\sigma\sqrt{2(1 - P)}$$

And, since the scale unit is arbitrary, it is most convenient from a practical point of view to set it equal to the constant $\sigma\sqrt{2(1 - P)}$. Thus,

$$S_j - S_i = Z_{ij}$$

This expression indicates that, under the assumptions, the true scale separation of two stimuli is equal to the normal deviate corresponding to the proportion of times that one stimulus is judged greater than the other.

The inherent reasonableness and the elegant simplicity of this notion can be even more fully appreciated from a study of Figure 8.7. It is not difficult to imagine that if two stimulus objects i and j are far enough apart on the scale, all judges would agree that $s_i < s_j$ or that $s_i > s_j$, depending upon whether $S_i < S_j$ (and thus $S_j - S_i > 0$), as in Curve A, or whether the reverse was true, as in Curve E. If j was higher on the scale than i, but the scale separation was not too great, as in Curve B, it might be expected that some of the judgments will turn out to be that $s_i > s_j$ even though most of the judgments made would still be that $s_i < s_j$. When this occurs, the proportion of judgments that j was higher than i, $P_{j>i}$, would be between 50 and 100. The farther the scale separation, the larger this proportion would be, and the smaller the scale separation, the smaller the proportion of such judgments would be. If the two stimuli fell on exactly the same place on the scale, and the judges were not permitted to declare them equal, it would be expected that exactly half the judges would state that $s_i < s_j$, while the other half would state that $s_i > s_j$, and thus $P_{j>i}$ would equal 50 percent. Similarly, to the extent that j was lower on the scale than i, it would be anticipated that fewer and fewer judges would state that $s_j > s_i$ (thus yielding $P_{j>i}$ between 0 and 50) until the separation was large enough that once again all judges would agree, and no one would perceive j as greater than i.

By having a number of judges compare all possible pairs of stimuli, we can note the proportion of times Stimulus j is judged greater than Stimulus i, look this proportion up in a table of the normal curve, and read out the normal deviate as an estimate of the scale separation of the two stimuli. Finally, by compiling the results from all possible pairs of stimuli, we can determine the location of each of the stimulus objects along a unidimensional interval scale.

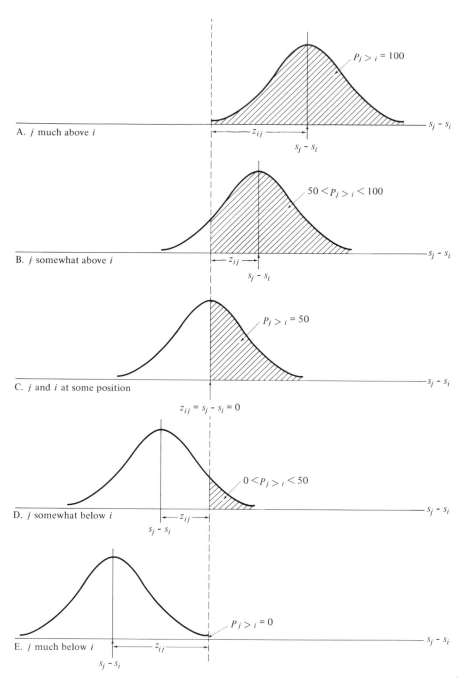

FIGURE 8.7 Frequency distributions of comparative judgment made for stimulus objects having different amounts of scale separation (Adapted from A. Edwards, *Techniques of attitude scale construction.* New York: Appleton-Century-Crofts, 1959, Fig. 2.2. P. 26.)

MULTIDIMENSIONAL SCALING   In the process of obtaining pair-comparison data, research workers soon began to note that many of their observers seemed to be making inconsistent judgments, particularly when working with some of the more esoteric stimulus objects.   For example, a judge viewing artistic Design i might prefer it to Design j, and when viewing Designs i and k, choose j over k.   But, when making a comparative judgment between i and k, the same judge would select k in preference to i.

At first, such apparent inconsistencies were considered to be errors, and the tendency to make such errors was thought to be a personality characteristic of the particular judge.   The number of inconsistent triads (such as $i > j, j > k, k < i$) were often counted and correlated with other measures of individual differences.   While such an interpretation is plausible when the stimulus objects are simple ones and the judgments are made with respect to well-known physical dimensions, another possibility is more reasonable when the stimuli are complicated and the qualities judged have no known relationship to some corresponding physical dimension.

This second interpretation recognizes that the triad of comparative judgments given above is inconsistent only if a single unidimensional continuum is assumed.   If the three stimulus objects i, j, and k are located in two-dimensional spaces as shown in Figure 8.8, then the triad $i > j, j > k, k < i$ is perfectly reasonable.   All that has happened is that the judge compared i with j and j with k with respect to one attribute (dimension A), but when he made the comparison of i and k, he did so on a different basis (dimension B).

It is with this latter interpretation, then, that multidimensional scaling is

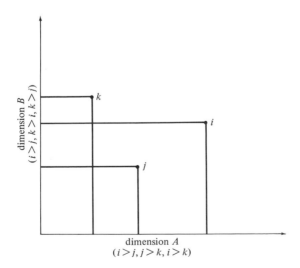

FIGURE 8.8   A pattern of three stimulus objects in two-dimensional space which might lead to inconsistent pair-comparison judgments

concerned.   The task is first to find the smallest number of dimensions required to explain the apparent judgmental inconsistencies found when many judges compare a number of stimulus objects and then to locate the stimuli in the resulting judgment space.   The analytic procedures, fully described in Torgerson (1958), are quite complex and will not be presented here.   The reader should note that these methods have much in common with factor-analytic techniques, which also seek to ascertain underlying attributes.   However, rather than starting with explicit dimensions along which people are already measured and seeking to reduce them as does factor analysis, multidimensional scaling starts with simple judgments of less than or greater than and seeks to determine the implicit bases along which such judgments are being made.

Rating Scales

Although classical rating scales can be thought of as representing the logical application of the psychometric scaling method of successive categories in which each of the stimuli is placed into one of a limited number of intervals, the resulting devices are so varied and the problems associated with their use so great that they deserve special attention.

A GENERAL EVALUATION   Rating scales and inventories (which are actually just self-rating scales and therefore need no special treatment) are among the most popular of techniques for describing human characteristics.   Because of the many distorting factors described below, rating scales would not appear to be so rigorous as the more formal testing techniques discussed earlier.   On the other hand, unstructured ratings, projective techniques, situational tests, and the like are subject to all the faults of rating scales, plus some additional ones, and thus would seem to be far less satisfactory than those techniques presented in this chapter.   Then, too, if the intent is to determine the way in which others react to the individual in question, a rating scale in one of its various forms provides the most direct measure possible.   In this situation, rating scales would seem to be valid by definition, the resulting measurements being limited only in terms of interpretive and variable errors.

Among the many practical advantages cited in favor of a rating approach are the facts that it takes less time, can be used with a large number of subjects, and seems to work well even with relatively naive judges (or raters). The major logical objection to the rating scale form of the successive-interval approach is that ratings are often based only on broad impressions about the person being rated and are usually recorded some time after the original observations have been made.   The problem with impressionistic judgments of broadly defined "traits," especially when recorded some time after the observations are made, is that such ratings do not often reflect actual behavior. Rating scales which do not in some way relate to relevant observable behaviors may be interesting but are not useful either to an investigator or to a worker in an applied field.

Empirical evidence as to the general efficacy of rating scales is difficult, if not impossible, to obtain. In the first place, rating scales are often constructed and used in those situations where other measurement approaches are exceedingly difficult to apply. Criterion data against which to compare the results of rating scales are often not readily available. In the second place, whether or not a particular rating scale will be valid depends (much more than is the case with a more formal testing approach) on the particular behavior observed, on the opportunity the raters have had to make the observations, and on the care with which the scale has been constructed. It is instructive to note the results of some of the studies that have been executed because they suggest ways that evidence might be gathered that is helpful in determining whether a particular rating scale is a useful measuring device.

In an early study, Marsh and Perrin (1925) compared three types of five-point scales which were used to rate a number of different characteristics with respect to both the degree of agreement among five independent raters and the correlations between ratings and other measures of the same characteristics. There were marked differences in the effectiveness of the ratings of the various characteristics, although the results for the three scale formats were similar. For example, rater agreement was highest for ratings of size of head and least for leadership, poise, and control. At the same time, the correlation between the ratings of head size and actual physical measurement of this characteristic was .76, while ratings of leadership correlated .50 with the irrelevant but more readily observed characteristic of physical attractiveness. Other, more recent studies also illustrate that ratings of specifically defined characteristics obtained on carefully developed scales can have validity, while judgments of broadly defined traits are often subject to irrelevant influences. For example, Gebhart and Hoyt (1958) found that overachievers scored significantly higher than underachievers on a self-report, forced-choice scale designed to measure achievement needs and scored significantly lower than underachievers on a scale (of the same instrument) designed to measure need for affiliation. On the other hand, Guilford (1959) describes an unpublished study of the ratings of a large group of military officers in which a factor analysis revealed that, no matter what the trait, the resulting ratings could be interpreted to reflect differences in "expressional fluency, an ability to produce connected verbal discourse." Guilford also describes some experimental studies by Thornton (1943; 1944), in which judgments were made with and without certain irrelevant clues. In these studies, persons wearing glasses were judged to be higher in intelligence, dependability, and industriousness than when not wearing them, and persons whose photographs showed them smiling were judged higher in sense of humor, kindliness, and honesty than they were when their photographs pictured a more serious face.

In conclusion, it would appear that because of their many practical advantages and their clear, logical superiority over less structured techniques, rating scales will continue to be one of the most widely used ways of obtaining measures of human behavior. The careful worker will, however, take pains to see that his scale is well constructed, and the wise user of such devices will always obtain validity information on the effectiveness of the ratings in the specific situation in which they are employed by showing that the numerical ratings do, in fact, correspond to relevant and observable behavioral differences.

TYPES OF RATING SCALES   In the broadest sense, there are two major varieties of rating scales: the Thurstone type and the Likert type of scale. In the Thurstone type of scale, each of the items is first used as a stimulus and scaled by a special panel of judges by means of one of the psychometric scaling procedures mentioned earlier. Once the items have been scaled, a respondent is asked to check those statements with which he agrees (or a rater checks those statements which are descriptive of the person or object being rated). The individual's scale position is then determined by some index of the central tendency of the items selected.[9]

In contrast to this, a Likert-type scale presents the respondent with a set of unscaled items and requests him to indicate the extent to which he agrees or disagrees with the statement. (Or a rater may be asked to indicate the extent to which each item applies to the individual being rated.) The individual's total score is then obtained by summation of the ratings. Refinement of the Likert scale can then be carried out by means of traditional item-analysis techniques, as is done in the construction of aptitude and achievement measures, or by applying Guttman's scalogram analysis (Guttman, 1944) to insure that a unidimensional scale has been achieved.

While Thurstone-type scales are generally considered to be based upon much firmer logical grounds than Likert scales, the latter seem to produce highly satisfactory results if carefully developed (Edwards, 1957). The main thing that is lacking in the Likert approach is the ability to interpret scores independently of the normative group. But this is true of almost all measurement of behavioral characteristics and certainly is of no consequence when the researcher is interested in the amount of change, rather than in an absolute position on a defined scale. The Likert scale is the most widely used today, because it is usually more easily constructed than the Thurstone scale.

There is almost a limitless variety of formats into which the instruments

---

[9] Whenever the only information required is the relative position of the individuals rated, the sum of the scale values is sufficient.

themselves might be cast within the framework of the two types of scales described above. Certain types, however, have been so commonly used and seem sufficiently distinct to be worth briefly describing.

Numerical scales One of the simplest scales to construct and easiest to use is the numerical rating scale. This type of instrument usually consists of several items each of which names or describes the behavior to be rated and then offers as alternative responses a series of numbers representing points along the scale. For example, one item from a scale designed to present a description of a student's behavior in a classroom situation might be:

Which of the following best describes this student's verbal participation in class?
1. avoids expressing himself even when asked
2. will express himself only when asked
3. freely expresses himself on some things but avoids comment on others
4. freely expresses himself on almost every topic
5. insists on expressing himself on every topic even when discussion is not called for.

Such scales do not always provide a verbal description for every point along the scale, and in some instances the numbers that may be used in the analysis of the results are not actually printed on the scale where the rater can see them. In the latter instance, the scales are sometimes referred to simply as multiple-choice ratings.

The simple numerical scale does have face validity and therefore seems to be widely accepted. Nevertheless, many more sophisticated workers prefer other types of scales when the practical situation permits a more elaborate development. There is some evidence that this simple numerical format is more subject to the errors and biases that occur in ratings than are other types, probably because such a format encourages evaluations and inferences beyond a simple recording of the behavior observed.

Graphic scales If the format of the rating scale is such that the characteristic to be rated is represented as a straight line along which are placed some verbal guides, the instrument is referred to as a graphic rating scale.

Because it appears so easy to construct, the graphic scale seems to be the most widely used of all the specific types of rating scales to be described. This practice is unfortunate because such quickly formulated scales usually fail to yield dependable measures. By representing the characteristic under consideration along a line, the graphic scale format invites the raters to make judgments about an underlying trait rather than simply to provide a record of what was observed.

Standard scales In the standard-scale approach, an attempt is made to provide the rater with more than verbal cues to describe various scale points. Ideally, several samples of the objects to be rated are included, each with a given scale value that has been determined in experimental studies prior to the use of the scale.   When products of human endeavor are the objects to be rated and the samples can be made readily available to the raters, this technique has much to recommend it.   While the value of the final instrument would obviously depend upon the care used in establishing the scale values of the products, there is no logical or methodological reason that highly useful standard scales cannot be developed for measuring such things as handwriting, business letters, and certain aspects of commercial drawing.

When attempting to measure human characteristics which do not result in observable products, the use of the standard-scale approach becomes more complex.   It is apparent that it is not possible to have different persons available as samples for the raters to use in describing others.   It is possible, however, to list the names of persons to represent the various points along the scale for each characteristic to be rated.   The major difficulty arises in attempting to find a common group of persons with whom all of the raters are familiar and whose names can be used to define the desired points along the scale.   While theoretically it is not necessary for all raters to be acquainted with all persons listed on such a scale, it is essential that each judge know at least one person listed at each of the major scale steps and that the person constructing the scale have some way of establishing appropriate scale values by comparing all persons whose names will be used on a common basis.

One interesting attempt to develop a standard scale for use in measuring human traits is the Man-to-Man scale which Guilford (1954) attributes to W. D. Scott.   According to Guilford, this scale was developed for military use and required the rater to write down the names of 12 to 25 persons whom he knew well.   Next, the rater was required to put the names in rank order on each of five traits.   For each trait, then, the first and last men on the list were used to represent the top and bottom points on the scale, the middle person was placed at a third position on the ultimate five-point scale, and the two men halfway between the extremes and the center position were taken as representing the second and fourth position on the final scale.   Because this approach requires an assumption which is difficult to justify (namely, that each rater knows individuals who vary throughout the entire range on every trait to be rated), it is not generally recommended. The Man-to-Man scale, however, does illustrate an ingenious attempt to build an appropriate standard scale for use in rating human characteristics that do not result in a tangible product.   Also, it might be used in conjunction with other techniques to produce a type of scale which combines the advantages of several approaches.   It has been suggested [10] that the actual job behavior of the so-called standard men be examined to obtain a list of critical behaviors which could then be scaled and ultimately cast into the checklist format described in the next section.

[10] By Marvin D. Dunnette in personal correspondence.

In conclusion, when the standard-scale approach is used under appropriate circumstances and when extreme care is taken to develop accurate scale values for the standards used, the resulting instrument is likely to be one of the best possible rating scales. It is not likely, however, that most users of ratings will be willing to put forth the effort required, and thus this approach will probably find its greatest use as a criterion for other more practical techniques.

Checklists An approach that is widely popular because it is simple to administer and still permits wide coverage in a short time is the behavior checklist. Usually this instrument contains a long list of specific behaviors which represent important individual differences, and the rater simply checks whether the item applies. A person's position on the scale which represents the behavior index is obtained by counting the number of items which have been checked by the rater. On more elaborate scales, each item may have been weighted, and the rating is obtained by cumulating the points given to those items which have been checked.

In addition to the practical advantages, the checklist technique avoids the problem of having inexperienced raters make complex judgments and, if properly developed, forces the rater to adhere to observed behaviors rather than general impressions. Ideally, in all rating procedures (as in formal tests), judgment should occur only when hypotheses are being formulated about what behaviors are likely to be both readily detectable and relevant to the future situation of concern. Subsequent item analysis (similar to that used with tests) of data gathered in an actual tryout of the materials should identify those particular behavior descriptions which should be retained as items on the checklist.

The only problem with this approach is the response set of the rater, which may lead him to check many or only a few characteristics for any one individual. This difficulty can be minimized by asking each rater to check some specified number of items or by requiring that every item be marked as "applicable," "not applicable," or "don't know." Although even the latter format is still subject to some response set (the tendency to mark "don't know"), it is less likely to be resisted by raters who generally dislike being forced to list a given number of items when they may feel that fewer or more are really applicable.

Forced-choice scales One of the more recent innovations in the rating scale area has been the development of a forced-choice technique which has been specifically designed to overcome some of the major difficulties encountered with most of the other approaches. In a forced-choice rating, the rater is required to consider not only one attribute but also several characteristics all at one time. Assuming that a relevant item is difficult for a rater to distinguish from one which is not predictive if both are equally favorable to the person, the format requires that only a few of several behaviors listed in each item be selected as applicable. In the original form in Figure 8.9, two favorable and two unfavorable statements were presented in each item, and the rater was asked to select the one most and the one least descriptive of the individual being rated.   More recent studies by Highland and Berkshire (1951) have indicated that the most effective format was one in which four favorable characteristics were listed and the rater asked to select the two which were most descriptive of the ratee.

	a. Insists upon his subordinates being precise and exact.
1	b. Stimulates associates to be interested in their work.
	a. Allows himself to become burdened with detail.
2	b. Does not point out when work is poorly done.

FIGURE 8.9   Sample item from a forced-choice rating scale designed to measure supervisory performance (From L. Huttner, and R. Katzell. Developing a yardstick of supervisory performance. *Personnel,* 1957, **33,** 373.)

In general, the forced-choice technique does seem to overcome some of the most serious rating errors.   The results, however, are not as spectacular as the theory behind it would imply, and there is not much evidence to suggest that what improvement is obtained is other than the result of the far more than usual care in construction and validation of the devices.   Also, raters are sometimes sufficiently antagonistic toward this type of format to make its use impractical.   That this latter need not be the case has been demonstrated by Huttner and Katzell (1957).   These workers supplemented the conventional forced-choice approach by having the rater indicate, on a separate scale, the extent to which the behavior checked applied to the person rated.   According to Huttner and Katzell, this modified format "seems to have encountered no noteworthy degree of resistance from those who use it; indeed, widespread acceptance of this procedure has been evidenced throughout company management."

Ranking methods   In some situations, it does not seem reasonable (or the user is unwilling) to make the assumption that the person preparing the scale or the rater can accurately judge equivalent distances at various points along the scale.   Under these circumstances a ranking procedure which requires only that the subjects who are being rated be placed in order on each trait can be used.[11]   On some occasions this system can be modified by simply having the raters divide the subjects into large groups as top 5 percent, next 20 percent, middle 50 percent, and so forth.   This latter approach seems useful primarily when large numbers of persons are to be rated and tends to approximate the multiple-choice rating procedure described earlier.

[11] With appropriate scaling techniques, the pair-comparison form of ranking can be converted to interval scales (Guilford, 1954).

Although some writers refer to the ranking approach as a completely separate psychometric scaling technique, and thus not appropriate for discussion along with other rating procedures which are varieties of the successive-category approach, ranking is used sufficiently often in judging human beings that it still seems desirable to include a description of it in this chapter. The ranking approach seems most desirable when but one rater is to describe an entire group of ratees. If several judges are ranking different sets of ratees to obtain a combined set of results for an entire group of subjects, it is necessary to assume that each set of ratees is essentially equivalent. If it is possible to start with a complete pool of subjects and draw equivalent samples from it, assigning one sample to each judge, this assumption is not bothersome. Under the usual situation, however, where each rater ranks only the persons he happens to know, there is no guarantee that the assumption can be satisfied.

In general, the ranking approach has the advantage of forcing the judges to make definite discriminations among the ratees and, in addition, eliminates differences from judge to judge with respect to leniency. On the other hand, if the number of subjects is very large, the ranking task becomes an extremely difficult one—though raters generally show less antagonism to rankings than they do toward forced-choice scales. Another disadvantage of the ranking procedure is that the size of groups ranked must be uniform or special procedures used to correct for this when results are combined. Finally, because the ordinal steps do not represent equal units of measure, it is inappropriate to use the mean as a measure of central tendency for obtaining composite ratings. Although the median might be used, problems still arise if it becomes necessary to interpolate between ranks. Guilford (1954) indicates that the simple sum of rank values will provide the best indication of an overall rank position when the results from several judges are to be combined.

Q sort   Another relative rating technique is the Q sort, developed by Stephenson (1953). In contrast to the ranking procedure described above, the judgment in this technique is among various behavior descriptions for a single individual rather than among several individuals for a given behavior. In this sense, the Q sort is like the forced-choice approach. The rater is given a series of cards on each of which a single statement describing the behavior is written. Following a successive-category procedure, the rater is then required to sort the cards into a series of piles according to the extent to which the statements are descriptive of the person being rated. Usually, but not always, eleven piles ranging from most to least applicable are used, and the statements have been weighted by a prior scaling procedure like that of Thurstone (Thurstone & Chave, 1929). Each subject's score is then obtained as the summation of the products of the statement weight and the scale position.

When properly carried out, the Q sort would seem to be a most useful approach to obtaining a comprehensive description of one individual. Because this technique does require considerable effort in the original scale preparation as well as raters who will give careful consideration to a long list of behaviors for each person to be rated, the Q sort has not yet been widely adopted. With modern computers, however, a Q sort deck can be distilled in such a way that a great deal can now be accomplished with a relatively small number of items. Because it does provide a standardized description, it is possible that the Q sort will become more widely used as a way of rating persons in research situations where it is desired to obtain comprehensive measures of changes either over a period of time or as a result of the introduction of some experimental variable.

OBTAINING SOUND RATINGS   Just any quickly devised rating scale cannot be depended upon to provide accurate descriptions of the extent to which a person possesses some trait. As a matter of fact, a great many of the faults of rating scales can be attributed to the illusion that such devices are simple to construct. The user of rating scales should therefore be aware of several of the special problems that arise in the application of rating procedures and should know some of the major techniques that have been developed to help overcome these difficulties.

Special problems in using ratings   When ratings are used, errors arise which may be attributable either to the particular behavior under consideration or to the person who is doing the rating. Both are considered below.

(*a*) Errors Resulting from Rater Characteristics   Each rater will have his own unique biases which will influence his particular ratings. This type of error need be of no great concern to the careful user of rating scales. Appropriately motivated raters can be helped to overcome such specific biases, and these biases, because they are different for each rater, tend to cancel out when separately obtained individual ratings are pooled. The most bothersome errors are those which are constant, in the sense that they seem to be similar for all or almost all raters. Failure to take appropriate measures to reduce these types of errors can lead to ratings which are of little value in spite of fairly high interrater reliability.

Perhaps the most widely observed constant error is *leniency*—a tendency of almost all raters in this country to be overly generous in their descriptions. Whether this arises because of a humane unwillingness to make unfavorable remarks about one's fellow man or because of an identification with the ratee such that a rater feels it is a reflection upon himself to give low ratings, scores on a rating scale of any format tend to pile up at the upper end of the scale. This error is so marked as to seriously reduce the discrimination power of rating scales at any place but the lower end, where even an average rating may signify a person who is quite low on the scale.

Another widely observed error is a tendency on the part of raters to obscure intraindividual differences by rating a given individual in the same way on all behaviors whether the characteristics tend to go together or not. This type of error has been detected by noting relatively high intercorrelations among ratings which by other measures seem to be relatively independent. This *halo effect* is usually attributed to the fact that many raters allow an overall impression of the subject to influence their description of his specific behaviors. One of the important results of the halo error is to displace the ratings on each of a person's behaviors toward the average rating received on all of his behaviors.

Somewhat akin to the halo error are the *proximity* and *logical* errors. Proximity errors arise because of a judge's tendency to describe behaviors which appear close together on the printed rating sheet as more nearly alike than he would behaviors which are physically separated by some distance. The logical error is a tendency for raters to rate a person similarly on characteristics that the rater feels should go together.

All of us tend to perceive other individuals in relationship to ourselves. This tendency leads to a habit of raters to place others on a scale in contrast to their own characteristics. A generally optimistic individual tends to see others as more pessimistic than he is, and a generally pessimistic judge would displace the ratings toward the optimistic end of the scale. Whether this *contrast error* represents a reaction formation or whether it simply reflects different standards held by the various judges is not clear. However, such a behavior-rater interaction effect can be serious if all of the raters happen to be persons who themselves lie at one general position on the scale.

One additional error which should be noted because it is typical of almost all raters is that referred to as the *error of central tendency*. Raters seem to avoid using the extreme positions on a rating scale regardless of the descriptive phrases used. The effect of this error is to reduce the variability of the ratings and thus to make adequate discrimination among those rated more difficult to obtain.

In addition to those errors described above, there are several types still attributable to the rater which usually will be reflected in a lack of consistency from judge to judge (i.e., a low interrater reliability). First there are the errors that arise when a judge may have made only a limited contact with the person he is to rate or perhaps is unwilling to take the trouble to do the kind of job that is required. The effect of lack of information (or refusal to use it) is generally to allow irrelevant or chance effects to influence the scale positions and to produce a wide variation in scores assigned to a given individual by several judges or even the same judge on two different occasions.

Even when the rater has had adequate opportunity to observe the person he is to rate, there is a possibility of variable errors. Each rater may hold a slightly different conception of the behavior under consideration, or each different rater may be basing his ratings on somewhat different standards.

In either case there may be marked consistency from time to time when the same judges are used but wide differences at all times among the ratings given to the same individual by different judges.

(b) Errors Resulting from the Behavior Selected   It is perfectly reasonable to anticipate that some characteristics can be more dependably rated than others.   It is not difficult to see that broadly defined general "traits" like good citizenship, kindliness, and adaptability might mean quite different things to different people or that a person's kindliness, adaptability, and good citizenship might vary markedly from one specific situation to the next. Similarly, it would be expected that such things as loneliness and sensitivity, which refer to one's inner feelings and can be inferred only indirectly from certain observables, would be more difficult to describe than more overt characteristics such as talkativeness and perseverance.   In fact, it might be said that traits are never really rated—only that behavior is described and scaled.   The fact that some characteristics are more readily rated than others has been adequately verified by a number of empirical studies of the interrater consistency with which various behaviors can be observed.   Rather than attempting to compile a list of characteristics which can and cannot be rated with a reasonable degree of reliability, it is sufficient to point out that the interobserver agreement is highest for those characteristics that are specific entities rather than composites and for those characteristics that are directly descriptive of one's behavior rather than those derived indirectly by evaluation or by interpretations from different behaviors.

Techniques for the improvement of ratings   Despite the many special problems outlined in the last paragraphs, ratings can be obtained that are both reliable and highly useful in a wide variety of situations.   By restricting the use of ratings to particular behaviors, by following certain suggestions in the construction of the scales, by carefully selecting and training the raters, and by appropriately analyzing the raw data gathered, the conscientious worker will be able to achieve measurements which are entirely satisfactory for most situations, both applied and research.   The specific techniques by which each of these general approaches to the improvement of ratings can be carried out are described in the following sections.

(a) Selecting the Proper Behaviors   The first rule in deciding whether to obtain ratings of a particular behavior is to eliminate those which can be measured by the more rigorous forms of testing.   Next, the characteristic selected must be one which has a readily discernible and highly consistent meaning for a wide variety of judges.   Any behavior which is to be appraised by means of rating scales should also be relatively specific.   Highly complex behaviors are best handled by being analyzed into specific components, so that the raters can observe each specific behavior separately.   Finally, attempts to assess future promise should be avoided in favor of ratings of past or present accomplishments.

In general, the further the characteristic is from a specific, readily observed behavior, the less satisfactory the ratings will be. Any inferences to be made from the behaviors either as to traits or as to future performances should be left to later analysis and not required of the judges at the time of observation.

(*b*) Building the Scales   The most dependable means for assuring adequate ratings is through the careful preparation of the rating scale itself. Many elaborate techniques have been devised to help overcome some of the errors involved in using ratings. However, rating schemes which become too complex often result in sufficient rater resistance to add errors of a different type large enough to make the scale useless. The object is to be able to develop the right kind of scale for the particular conditions of rater sophistication, time, information available, and ultimate use at hand.

One of the most important aspects of scale development is the selection of behavior labels short enough to fit on the scale yet sufficiently unambiguous to result in general uniformity of meaning for all potential raters. Usually, labels alone are satisfactory. Thus, it is almost always desirable to include a concise description and, if possible, a few examples along with each behavior label. Some writers have suggested that the label and description be replaced entirely by the specific examples which a rater can simply check as present or absent. Although this will bring about the desired uniformity of meaning, such a listing makes the scale more complex, and if many behaviors are to be described, will almost always result in careless marking on the part of the raters. Therefore, it is generally recommended that short but precise descriptions be used.

Once a clear understanding of the individual behaviors has been accomplished, the next task is that of deciding how many steps should be used. It would seem reasonable, as studies by Champney and Marshall (1939) verify, that there will be an optimal number of steps above and below which it does not pay to proceed. If possible it would seem best to determine what this number is empirically in each specific situation. Early studies by Symonds (1924) indicated that 7 would be sufficient for most purposes, and that even fewer would produce as much accuracy as could be obtained when complex behaviors or naive, unmotivated raters were used. Guilford (1954), however, now feels that 7 is usually lower than optimal and suggests that under some conditions as many as 25 steps should be used. Nonetheless, most popularly used rating scales still contain somewhere between 5 and 11 steps.

In addition to a decision on the number of steps, it is usually necessary to provide the rater with reference points at various positions along the scales. The use of general terms like "average," "excellent," and "very poor" should be avoided, if possible, because they mean different things to different raters. The more specific the cues, the better. At the same time, extreme words are likely to be avoided by raters and therefore contribute to the central tendency error. Words like "never" and "always" should not

be used as cues. Champney (1941) provides an excellent list of characteristics of useful cues. It is possible further to reduce the piling up of scores
on one end and to obtain some degree of uniformity of standards by indicating the percentages of a group likely to be found at each level.

When the individual behavior scales have been adequately developed, it
is necessary to organize them into a complete rating instrument. The way
in which the behaviors are listed can be of some help in reducing certain of
the types of errors described earlier. Ideally, the best way to eliminate
both proximity and halo errors would be to have each scale placed on a
separate card and to have the judges rate one behavior, and then wait a
period of time sufficient to obliterate their recollection of the way in which
the previous characteristic was rated before turning to the next. Because
such a procedure can be followed only under the most unusual of circumstances, various compromise suggestions have been made. For example, it
has been suggested that proximity errors can be considerably reduced simply by placing behaviors which are judged to logically go together as far
from one another as possible in the physical makeup of the scale. Similarly, it has been suggested that halo errors can be reduced by alternating
the direction of the high end of the trait scales. Although this latter approach would seem to reduce the halo effect, at least one writer (Guilford,
1954) has contended that such a format is so confusing to inexperienced
raters that enough clerical errors are likely to be made to offset any advantage that such a format may have in other respects. Thus, for naive raters,
it is recommended that all scales be set up with the high end of the scale at
the top or toward the left.

Perhaps the best practical suggestion is to have each judge rate all subjects on a given behavior before he turns to the next. A format which lists
each behavior on a separate page, say across the top, and places the persons
to be rated following it will facilitate this approach. When trained judges
are used (so that the unusual format is not disturbing), the listing of the
names across the top and placing the descriptions of the various forms the
behavior can take on vertical rather than horizontal scales has the advantages of permitting longer cues to be used and of pinpointing the cues more
precisely along the continuum. Both formats have the additional advantage
of encouraging a more stable standard for a given judge from one ratee to
the next.

(c) Selecting and Training the Raters   No matter how well constructed
the rating scale might be, if it is misused by those doing the rating, the results will be unsatisfactory. One of the most effective ways of insuring adequate results from this approach to measurement is the careful selection
and training of those who will do the rating.

Obviously, it is impossible for a person who has had inadequate opportunity to observe the subjects to provide accurate descriptions even with the
best of scales. Thus, the first rule in selecting raters is to choose only those

who have or can be provided with the opportunity to make the necessary observations of the subject and to make them in pertinent situations. Next, it is important to try to secure raters who are willing to provide the necessary information without distortion. This latter task may prove somewhat difficult because it is not always possible to detect those who seem to derive pleasure out of faking the results. However, some simple common sense suggestions can be helpful in this respect. Persons who seem to delight in criticizing everybody and everything, persons who through family ties, social friendships, or employment relationships may be ego involved in the outcome, and persons who may have to face the person rated with his ratings are not likely to be able to provide unbiased ratings no matter how conscientious they are. Finally, in the selection of raters, it would appear that the contrast error can be reduced if care is taken to use judges who themselves represent the entire range of the scale being used.

Perhaps the first task in training raters to use a scale appropriately is to convince them of the value of honest and accurate ratings. If this can be accomplished with properly selected judges, the greatest difficulty in obtaining good ratings will have been overcome. Next, pointing out the types of errors raters are likely to make and providing some suggestions for avoiding them can be a great deal of help. A simple awareness of the existence of halo errors and an understanding as to why one should rate all subjects on one trait, then all subjects on the second trait, and so on, proves extremely valuable in eliminating this bothersome error. If, in addition merely to telling the raters about the errors, it is possible to have them obtain some practice with the specific instrument they are to use and on persons similar to those for whom the ratings are desired, much more can be accomplished. Practice, of course, is valuable only if knowledge of the results can be secured. It is desirable that the pilot use of the instrument be executed under supervision, and it is essential that the results of these practice ratings be discussed. Not only will the viewing and discussion of the results illustrate the types of errors that occur, but the results will also be helpful in clarifying the meaning of the descriptions used along the scale positions and in developing a uniform standard among all the judges.

(*d*) Analyzing and Using the Results   A final opportunity to make ratings the most accurate descriptions possible under the circumstances arises from combining and analyzing the results. The reliability of ratings can be greatly improved by a pooling of the results from several judges who have made their ratings independently. When such a procedure is followed, the individual errors and biases tend to cancel out, and the lack of information on the part of one rater may be compensated for by the results from the others. Studies have indicated that the combining of ratings in this way has an effect similar to that of lengthening a test. In fact, the Spearman-Brown formula presented earlier can be used to predict the increase in reliability that can be obtained by pooling the results of a given number of judges.

It is important to note that the value of pooling judgments is greatest when the individual ratings have been obtained independently. Having all raters sit down together to arrive at a joint rating would seem to provide a description that is influenced greatly by the personality interactions of the judges. For example, a dominant, or a highly persuasive, or a socially prestigious person may have far greater influence on the joint result than is desirable.

If the ratings are obtained in a situation in which it is imperative that the results be as accurate as possible without consideration of time or expense for additional analysis, further modifications can be made. Guilford (1954), for example, has developed a rationale for errors of rating and presents techniques for making adjustments to eliminate the effects of leniency, halo, and rater-trait interaction errors. Also, many of the standard psychometric techniques presented in more advanced books can be used to raise the level of measurement from ordinal to at least an interval scale. If sufficient care and trouble are taken, rating scales can be used to obtain highly satisfactory quantitative descriptions of many behaviors which cannot be studied by other measuring devices.

SOCIOMETRY

According to Moreno (1960, p. viii), who is the recognized founder of the field, "Sociometry is the mathematical study of psychological properties of populations, the experimental technique of and the results obtained by application of quantitative methods." This definition includes a wide variety of methodologies, and the reader who is interested in obtaining a complete overview of the field should read Nehnevajsa (1960) and consult Moreno (1953). In this discussion the term *sociometry* is used in the more restricted sense to refer to graphic representations, analytic procedures, and numerical indexes developed to summarize the dyadic relationships observed in a specified group of individuals.

The Nature of Sociometric Data

The primary information in sociometric studies is a statement from each individual in a group as to his preference either for working or for otherwise interacting with each other member of the group in some specific situation. For example, a group of research workers might be asked to name from among a prescribed list of individuals those persons with whom they would like to work and those persons with whom they would not like to work on an interdisciplinary study of the cause of riots.

There are three possible choices—select, ignore, reject—which each individual can make; therefore, every dyadic relationship (i.e., the relationship between every pair of persons) can be expressed as one of the following six combinations of responses:

1. A selects B and B selects A
2. A selects B and B ignores A
3. A selects B and B rejects A
4. A ignores B and B ignores A
5. A ignores B and B rejects A
6. A rejects B and B rejects A.

This list assumes that the *kind* of response rather than *who made* the choice is the only important information. Thus, A choosing B and B ignoring A would be considered to be exactly the same as B choosing A and A ignoring B. The six different combinations of responses are then considered to fall at different points along a bipolar continuum moving toward strong social aversion in one direction and toward strong social ties in the other as indicated in Figure 8.10.

For certain kinds of analysis, it is convenient to record the choices in the form of a matrix, as shown in Figure 8.11. In this matrix, each column and corresponding row represents one individual. Each row gives the outgoing choices, and each column indicates the choices received. When represented in this format, a +1 indicates a selection and a −1 indicates a rejection, while a blank indicates that the individual indicated by the row heading ignored the person indicated by the column heading. If the values in corresponding cells (e.g., row 3, column 5, plus column 5, row 3) are added, then values are assigned the possible choice combinations along the bipolar continuum which range from a −2 for reject-reject to a +2 for select-select.

The Analysis of Sociometric Data

SOCIOGRAM   The basic graphic representation of sociometric data is the *sociogram*. In this chart each individual is traditionally represented as a circle, and the distance between individuals is made proportional to values assigned to the choice combination along the continuum of dyadic relationships of Figure 8.10. Arrows between the pairs of persons indicate which person made which kind of choice. A typical sociogram, representing the choices from the matrix of Figure 8.11, is given in Figure 8.12.

While the sociogram presents all the data in one glance, there remains some degree of arbitrariness in the pattern of the location of the individuals. Interpretation of the sociogram is subjective and most certainly must be made only in the light of knowledge about the individuals who made the choices, knowledge which comes from beyond the choice questionnaire alone. For example, the interpretation of an *isolate* (a person not chosen by others in the group) might be quite different if the group pictured were

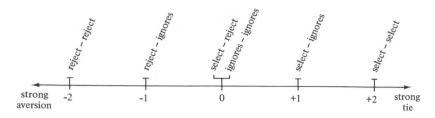

FIGURE 8.10   The continuum of dyadic relationships

a class of third-graders in school than it would be if the group were composed of the owner and the employees of a small company. Similarly, the
sociogram might be interpreted quite differently if the choice made were
related to a social activity than if it were related to accomplishing some
group task such as carrying out a research project.

MATRIX ANALYSIS   Although a direct analysis of the choice matrix does not
overcome the difficulty of having to interpret the results in the light of the
context in which the information was gathered, it does provide a means by
which all research workers applying the same technique of analysis can arrive at the same results. A variety of different methods for accomplishing
the analysis, which seeks to map the various subgroups, or cliques, has been

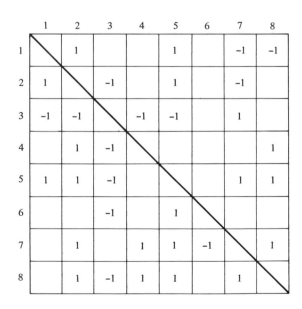

FIGURE 8.11   Sample matrix of the sociometric choices of eight individuals

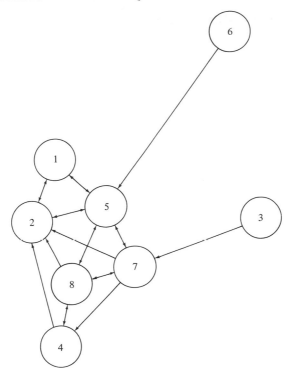

FIGURE 8.12   Sociogram of the dyadic choice of eight individuals

suggested, and while it is beyond the scope of this book to outline the logic and mathematical techniques employed in them all, a brief note about the major ones is in order.

A classic technique, first developed by Forsyth and Katz (1946), has the effect of shifting the rows and columns of the matrix about until the −1's fall away from the diagonal and the +1's cluster along it. From this analysis, the investigator can detect both the subgroups and their general order with respect to acceptance in the population as a whole and an idea of leadership patterns as well. Although tedious by hand calculation, modern computers have rendered this method as feasible as any.

A different approach, suggested by Luce and Perry (1949) and extended by Festinger (1949), ignores the rejection possibility and thus seems limited to applications in the analysis of communication networks (such as tracing rumors) or others where the rejection alternative as described earlier has no meaning.

The use of factor-analytic techniques to study the choice matrix seems to have been first suggested by Cervinka (1948) but developed more fully by MacRae (1960). Following an empirical comparison of several such methods of analysis, Nosanchuk (1963) concluded that "factor analysis, although little used in the analysis of sociometric data, gives in many cases, a far more useful output than do the other techniques."

Since Nosanchuk's study, Hubbell (1965) has developed a new approach which seems to have definite advantages over both the traditional approaches and the factor-analytic rationale, Beaton (1966) has provided an interbattery factor-analytic approach, and Riffenburgh (1966) has suggested the possibility of using a multiple-discriminant function. While these latter techniques have not yet been widely enough applied to be appraised fully, the investigator working with sociometric data should give them careful consideration.

SPECIAL INDEXES   In addition to analyzing the entire choice matrix to obtain information about the structure of subgroups, we can make use of information in specific columns and rows (i.e., for specific individuals) to develop special numerical indexes of individual, of group, and of subgroup characteristics. For example, each individual can be described according to his *selection status* by noting the proportion of times he was selected, according to his *rejection status* by noting the proportion of times he was rejected, and according to his *positive expansiveness* by noting the proportion of possible selection choices which he made. Similarly, *group expansiveness* has been defined as the total number of choices made by the members of the group divided by the number in the group, *group cohesion* as the ratio of the number of mutual pairs to the possible number of pairs, *group coherence* as the ratio of the number of mutual choices to the number of unreciprocated choices, and *group integration* as the reciprocal of the number of isolates. Finally, there are a number of indexes which can be applied to subgroups identified by a previous matrix analysis, such as those of ingroup preference, ingroup cleavage, ingroup cohesion, and ingroup climate. The reader who is interested in the conceptual and computational details of the many different sociometric indexes should consult Proctor and Loomis (1951), Moreno (1953), and Nehnevajsa (1955).

OTHER TECHNIQUES

Sample design, factor analysis, psychometric scaling, and sociometry all represent special research methods of sufficiently broad usage to have engendered many full-blown college courses and, in some instances, both special research journals and the beginnings of a distinct field of specialization. In addition, there are a number of other special techniques which do not nearly approach this level of development but which nonetheless are of sufficient importance to be of interest to many researchers in the behavioral sciences. Three such techniques will be briefly described here. The reader who is interested in pursuing these and other highly specialized techniques in greater detail should see the *Handbook of Multivariate Experimental Psychology* (Cattell, 1966); the *Handbook of Social Psychology, Vol. I: Theory and Method* (Lindzey, 1954); *Sociological Studies in Scale Analysis* (Riley, Riley, & Toby, 1954); and *Measurement and Prediction* (Stouffer et al., 1950).

The Semantic-Differential Technique

Developed largely by C. E. Osgood and his associates (Osgood, 1952; Osgood, Suci, & Tannenbaum, 1957; Miron & Osgood, 1966), the semantic-differential technique is based on the central theme that man, as a verbal being, reveals a great deal about himself through his language. Essentially, the technique attempts to get objective information as to the connotation of concept words by having a sample of persons rate them on a series of bipolar continuums anchored at each end by descriptive words. For example, the concept word PACIFIST might be judged on continuums like the following:

good	bad
kind	cruel
hard	soft
straight	twisted
warm	cool
weak	strong
fresh	stale

etc.

Using the same set of attribute terms with the same population of individuals permits an analysis of how concepts differ; using similar concepts and attribute terms with different individuals or groups of individuals provides information about how different people view specific aspects of the world about them. Thus, the technique appears to have a great deal of potential for studying the classical problems of individual differences, for noting subtle changes as a result of intervening historical, therapeutic, or educational experiences, for investigating cross-cultural communication problems, and for studying the general structure of the language.

The thoughtful reader will immediately recognize that the major methodological problem of concern in using the semantic-differential technique is whether the set of attribute terms remains sufficiently invariant across different concepts and different samples of subjects. A number of studies reviewed by Miron and Osgood (1966) have led them to the conclusion that

"The same three dimensions—Evaluation, Potency, and Activity—account for the largest proportions of variance and usually in that order. This system overrides variations in subject populations, in the nature of the task, and in methods of analysis—but it does *not* override variations in concept populations." The shifting-attribute scale structure (as revealed by factor analysis) seems, however, to be somewhat predictable and related to whether literal or metaphorical meanings of the concept word are being rated. It is the metaphorical interpretation of concepts which seems to be of greatest interest to research workers in the behavioral sciences, and where the concern is only with connotations, the desired invariance does seem to occur.

Latent-Structure Analysis

Lazarsfeld (1950) has developed a very general model for studying human attributes that is intimately related to both factor analysis (Green, 1952) and Guttman's scalogram analysis (Guttman, 1944; 1950). Operationally, any behavioral attribute can be considered to be a syndrome of consistent responses to a set of stimuli (such as a set of items on an attitude scale). To the extent that there are response consistencies, the different items will be intercorrelated. *Latent-structure analysis* reverses this reasoning by holding that whenever one observes intercorrelation among questionnaire items, there must be an underlying variable which produces this effect.

When the latent-structure analysis is applied to a set of continuous manifest variables, it leads to multiple factor analysis as a special case. However, when the model is applied to stimulus elements or to items to which an all-or-none response is made, the result is *latent-class analysis*. In latent-class analysis, the research worker starts with the observed sets of intercorrelations among items and asks how many and what kinds of sub-groupings of the respondents could have produced the observed effects. Then, on the basis of the subject's item responses, the probability that each individual belongs to a particular latent class can be determined and a classification made by placing each respondent in that class for which the probability is a maximum.

A special case of latent-class analysis leads to the *latent-distance scale* and provides a probability model for Guttman's scalogram analysis. In effect, Guttman's scalogram approach represents a test for the unidimensionality of a set of attitude or other questionnaire items. The criterion for unidimensionality is that the rank order of persons on the total scale must be preserved for each item. That is, if Person A shows a more favorable attitude on the total scale than Person B, then Person A must give a response to each item which shows him to have a stronger favorable (or weaker negative) attitude than the response to that item made by Person B. Because an empirically observed set of observations seldom meets the criterion described above perfectly, the criterion for achieving a Guttman scale has been reduced to 90 percent reproduceability plus some other conditions.

The use of multiple criteria makes the Guttman approach cumbersome, and Clark and Kriedt (1949) have further indicated that the resultant scales are, in fact, less reliable than those produced through the use of a traditional item analysis. In the latent-distance scale, this many criteria become unnecessary, for as a probability model, it is possible to determine directly whether the model fits the data within the limits of sampling fluctuation. Furthermore, not only can the error in each item be determined by comparing it with the total scale, but the scale parameters themselves can be determined from summary statistics.

Projective Techniques

Traditional forms of psychological measurement present the subject with a standard set of stimuli and then seek to make inferences about his characteristics from responses, often restricted to a few predetermined categories. Persons advocating the use of projective techniques have felt that a great deal of useful information about an individual is lost by this procedure, particularly because disguising one's true feelings is so easy when direct and unambiguous questions are asked.

The basic idea of projective techniques, therefore, is to present the subject with an ambiguous stimulus and to permit a free response to it. The hope is that what the respondent sees, or projects into this ambiguous stimulus situation, represents his true feelings and that reduction of the free responses into meaningful categories can be made by the skilled examiner at some later time. For example, the Rorschach Test presents subjects with meaningless inkblots and categorizes their responses to the query as to what they see in the stimulus card according to the total number of responses, the percentage of responses which use only part of the blot, the percentage of responses which refer to animals, and so on. Similarly, the Thematic Apperception Test requires the respondent to make up a story about each of a set of pictures, and the examiner interprets the results in terms of the story's hero, the specific needs of the hero, the pressures on the hero, and the outcome of the story. Other projective tests, some involving auditory rather than visual stimuli, follow the same procedures.

While the use of projective techniques is favored among psychologists primarily concerned with helping their fellow man through therapy, it has not been widely accepted among research workers who wish to employ rigorous methods of numerical description to their study of human behavior. While there is evidence that the reliability of some scoring procedures used with certain projective techniques reaches a level comparable to personality measures using the more traditional approach, only meager evidence of validity has as yet been found with any of the projective devices. While Cronbach and Gleser (1965) point out the usefulness of measures with low validity coefficients in some applied work, where a "broad bandwidth" of information rather than "high fidelity" is important, this is not usually the case in basic research, which generally seeks to find variables that can be related to other phenomena and where precision is important.

As useful as projective tests seem to be (judging from their popularity) for providing clinicians with insights about their patients, such devices have not yet fulfilled their promise in research. An investigator who feels that the use of some projective technique is essential to his problem should recognize that he is much less likely to obtain findings which reach a satisfactory level of statistical significance with such devices and that these instruments are likely to be most productive in exploratory work, where the formulation of new hypotheses is considered to be a more important outcome than the rigorous testing of ideas.

IV.

Results
of Research

9.

The Communication and Implementation of Research

Just to carry out a research study is not enough. If society is to obtain a return for the investment it makes in research activity, the results of every sound, scientific investigation, even negative ones, must be added to the body of knowledge; and where the results have obvious implications for practice, they should be implemented.

While investigators have almost always accepted the task of describing the results of their endeavors to their colleagues, either through presentations at professional meetings or publication in a scholarly journal, they have traditionally left the wider dissemination and the implementation of their findings to others—notably to the popular writers and the practitioners. It was the belief of many early professional research workers that publication in traditional channels of communication was adequate dissemination for their discoveries to bring about changes automatically in the course of time. It has gradually become clear that this belief is not well founded.

Realization of this has led to the founding of such organizations as the Society for the Psychological Study of Social Issues which maintains as one of its purposes, "making available to citizens outside the psychological profession conclusions drawn from the scientific study of human behavior," and which publishes yearbooks to "report new researches, summarize existing knowledge on the given topics and, so far as justified, submit conclusions and recommendations in the form of plans of action" (Murphy, 1945). It has also led to the formulation of the concept of action research by Collier (1945) who stated: "Since the findings of research must be carried into effect by the administrator and the layman, and must be criticized by them through their experience, the administrator and the layman must themselves participate creatively in the research, impelled as it is from their own area of need"; to the publication of semipopular articles concerned with the application of findings by such eminent basic researchers as B. F. Skinner (Skinner, 1954; 1961); to the founding in 1961 of the American Psychological Association's Project on Scientific Information Exchange in Psychology (Brayfield, 1966); to the holding of symposia on the dissemination and implementation of research in education (Goldhammer & Elam, 1962) and the preparation of entire books concerned with the problem of bringing about innovation (Evans, 1967; Miles, 1964). In almost all areas of the behavioral sciences, investigators themselves are becoming more and more involved in the communication and implementation of their findings.

COMMUNICATION OF RESEARCH RESULTS

In practice, the communication of research findings involves two somewhat distinct phases. The first is the preparation of the research report and the second is the dissemination of the report to the appropriate persons. Since most of what is to be said about the dissemination of research materials has already been mentioned in the discussion of the modern electronic information systems and the types of publications available contained in Chapter 5, this section of the present chapter will be devoted exclusively to scientific report writing.

The Characteristics of Scientific Writing

Because scientific writing has a special function to perform, it differs in many respects from the essays and themes most students are required to prepare in high school, in college freshman English classes, and in preparing for a senior English exam. The successful writer of a research report must keep these special characteristics in mind as he records the results of his investigation.

First of all, it should be remembered that the sole purpose of scientific writing is to *inform*. It is not designed to entertain nor to persuade in the usual sense of the term. To be sure, some popular articles translating the findings of science for the general public are both entertaining and informative, but reports of original research are rarely, if ever, designed to tickle the aesthetic sense with colorful description or to create strong emotional responses simply for the purpose of having the experience.

Similarly, while some research reports may seem to be persuasive in the sense that they confirm or reject some favored hypothesis or theory, strong words are not needed when the data tell the story unequivocally. Rather, the object is simply to provide the reader with enough information about both the procedures and the findings of the study so that he can draw his own conclusions and compare them with those of the investigator.

Because it seeks to be informative, the research report is accurate and truthful without exaggeration; it is factual rather than expressive of opinions; it is written in a disinterested third person and in the passive voice; and it rarely contains humor. Further, because the study has already been completed when the writing occurs, the report is usually written in the past tense, although the present tense may be used for those statements of continuing or general applicability. Deviation from these stylistic traditions is permitted, but only when the result is more efficiently accomplishing the sole function of informing.

Just as the function of a research report is to inform rather than to entertain or to persuade, the basic organization of the report is logical and systematic rather than psychological or spontaneous. This characteristic is likely to become even more important in the future than it has been in the past, for even the most modern of electronic literature search-and-abstracting equipment is likely to be highly inefficient if a series of unconnected pieces of information is fed into it in a nonsequential or a random order.

To insist that the research report be logical and systematic is *not* to say that the organization of the report must follow some particular form. Research problems themselves are far too varied to be fitted into a single mold without loss of information, and there is nothing sadder than the lack of communication which results when an otherwise well-done study of a unique problem is reported in a stylistic straitjacket. That is to say, in the final analysis the specific organization to be used is determined by both the kind of subject matter involved and the nature of the particular problem under investigation.

Finally, it is a characteristic of research reports that the standards of mechanics are purely practical. Rules of capitalization and punctuation, procedures for footnoting, forms for citation of references, and the like are all determined in such a way as to simplify the preparation and to facilitate the use of the report, rather than to achieve an elegance of expression. While at the present time this purely pragmatic approach has led different scholarly journals and different publishers of scientific information to formulate their own style, the move toward massive information centers as described in Chapter 5 should ultimately produce a highly efficient and generally standardized set of writing mechanics to be followed.

A Useful Pattern of Organization

While the reader should keep in mind the fact that a unique problem may require that the research report be organized in a unique way, he should also recognize that past experience in writing research reports has resulted in a generally useful pattern of presentation, which should be violated only when the writer can justify his departure explicitly by the increased understanding that he will achieve by so doing. The following outline is presented as a general guide and a checklist of things which should be included when writing the results of a typical research investigation.

STATEMENT OF THE PROBLEM   The statement of the problem should present, as concisely as possible, the questions asked and the practical or theoretical reasons for asking them. It should then state, in formal terms, the specific hypotheses to be tested and should describe the logic by which the author predicted these particular outcomes rather than alternative ones. This latter will often entail a review of the findings and arguments reported in the scientific literature. If the literature in the field is extensive and there is no published review of this previous work which can be cited, it may be necessary to set up a special section at this point for this part of the report.

DESCRIPTION OF THE METHOD   The procedures followed should be described in sufficient detail so that the reader could, if he wished, duplicate the study in his own laboratory or field situation. Although it may include justification for the use of any completely unique or highly specialized tools used, the methods section usually contains only a detailed description of steps followed to carry out the study. Often the methods section of the report is divided into subtopics to include as many of the following items as are relevant to the investigation.

1. *Design*   This subsection describes the overall logic of the attack on the problem. If a standard, descriptive, experimental, or sampling design is used, it should be named. In any case, the variables involved should be labeled as independent, experimental, control, dependent, criterion, or whatever is appropriate for the study. When relevant, the design may also present the relationship between the empirical data gathered and the theoretical propositions of concern.

2. *Subjects*   The subjects actually used in the study should be described with respect to all characteristics which make them unique as a group and which might have had an effect on the outcome. When appropriate, the population from which the subjects were sampled and to which the conclusions can be legitimately generalized should be identified.

3. *Instrumentation*   This includes naming (and, where necessary, describing) any instruments or apparatus used to collect the observations, to produce an experimental effect, or to maintain an experimental control. Where special devices have had to be constructed for the study, this section will also include a report of the evidence gathered to indicate that the instrument is valid, reliable, objective, and otherwise dependable.

RESULTS   This major section of the report includes the presentation of all data gathered which are relevant to the problem.   It must include enough information to justify the conclusions regardless of whether they support or refute the hypotheses under examination.   Whenever possible, the results should be presented in graphic or tabular form and should include enough descriptive information (for example, averages should never be reported without indicating the standard deviation and the sample size) so that the reader can make intelligent inferences of his own.   In this section, the results of any statistical tests are usually presented, but without any logical or scientific interpretation.

DISCUSSION AND CONCLUSIONS   It is in this section that the scientific interpretation of the data and of the statistical tests described in the previous section is presented.   This often includes a formal statement or listing of the conclusions supported by data *of this study*.   It also includes an accurate statement of the limitations of the study (though not an alibi for a weak study or for unexpected negative conclusions), an indication of the point of agreement and of disagreement between the results of the study and others which have been done, and finally, it includes the implications of the results of the study for both theory and practice.

SUMMARY   In many reports of research, the summary has been replaced by the abstract which is now required by many publications and granting agencies and which is often printed at the beginning rather than at the end of the article.   Once again, the increasing use of electronic information processing devices is exerting a strong influence in this direction.   There are still some instances where the restrictions on the abstract (in terms of both number of words and format) are so great, and the study reported is so complex, that an intermediate statement between the full description and the abstract is desirable.   In those situations where an abstract is used and the discussion section is long and involved, this last section of the research report may consist only in a final, formal statement of the investigator's conclusions.

Some Helps in the Mechanics of Writing

In scientific writing, as in all writing, there exists the basic requirement of adherence to elementary rules of grammar and good English usage.   Those who are a little unsure of troublesome points (for example, in deciding between "effect" and "affect" or in deciding whether a particular clause should or should not be set off by commas) will find such references as Perrin's *Writer's Guide and Index to English* (1959), Bryant's *Current American Usage* (1962), and Copperud's *A Dictionary of Usage and Style* (1964) highly useful.

Persons who are experienced in general writing, but who are somewhat unfamiliar with the special form and style of technical writing, may find Reisman's *A Style Manual for Technical Writers and Editors* (1962), Morris' *Principles of Scientific and Technical Writing* and similar books quite helpful. In addition, special references on the preparation of charts and graphs (cf. Rogers, 1961; Schmid, 1954; Spear, 1952) and on the preparation of tables (cf. U.S. Government Printing Office, 1967; Walker & Durost, 1936) are available to the novice technical writer.

One rule which any writer should follow is to examine previous reports prepared for or published by the agency or journal to which his manuscript will be sent for special style and form requirements. In the field of psychology, this is simplified by the common requirements for all journals published by the American Psychological Association. A basic reference in psychology is the latest edition of the *Publication Manual of the American Psychological Association* (A.P.A. Council of Editors, 1967). In education, Campbell's *Form and Style in Thesis Writing* (1954) is often followed, and in sociology many publications follow the style and form used for *The American Sociological Review* and described on page xii of the index to Volume 30 (1965). Sometimes, however, special requirements are maintained (e.g., Rules for preparation of manuscripts for Psychometrika, *Psychometrika,* 1967, **32,** 113–114; *Style Manual* (Rev. ed.), U.S. Government Printing Office, 1967). It is always best to review any special advice available from the journal editors themselves (American Psychological Association, Council of Editors, 1965) and to make a final check of form and style against the latest issue of the publication which the writer has in mind for the dissemination of his research findings. In this connection, the reader may be interested in noting Table 9.1 which represents a tabulation of reasons for rejecting articles submitted for publication in the *Journal of Abnormal and Social Psychology* in 1949 and in the *Journal of Consulting Psychology* in 1966.

As an additional aid to the research worker in reporting the results of his study, the list of common faults described in the *Publication Manual* of the American Psychological Association (1967) is presented here.[1]

1. *Long, awkward sentences* A clumsy sentence can be improved and often shortened by removing nonfunctional words, by restoring a logical order, and sometimes by dividing it in two.
2. *Short, choppy sentences* A reduction of sentence length is not a universal remedy for incomprehensible writing. Sentences can be too short and poorly integrated.
3. *The indefinite "this"* The topic sentence of a paragraph should be comprehensible in itself, even at the cost of repeating a name or a concept. The use of the pronoun "this" should almost always be avoided within a paragraph.

---

[1] This list has been adapted from paragraph 2.2, pages 15–17 of this publication, and does not include the many other helpful examples presented in that manual.

4. *Strings of modifiers*   An awkward and often ambiguous construction results when a long string of modifiers is placed before the noun modified, especially when the modifiers are themselves nouns used as adjectives.
5. *Faulty words*   The best word, of course, is the one which conveys the exact meaning desired. Technical words must be chosen with care and must be used consistently. Nontechnical words offer a wider choice and a greater hazard.

TABLE 9.1

Reasons Given by Journal Editors for the Rejection of Manuscripts

Reasons Given for Rejection	*Journal of Consulting Psychology* (1966)	*Psychological Review* (1966)	*Journal of Comparative and Physiological Psychology* (1966)	*Journal of Abnormal and Social Psychology* (1949)
	% of reasons given	% of reasons given	% with the fault [a]	% with the fault [a]
Inadequate		72		
Insufficient contribution (not important or premature)	51		75	55
Faulty conception, design, or conclusion	28			52
Poor presentation (unclear)	8			49
Overwritten (too long)			60	46
Failure to follow manuscript rules (papers not rejected for this reason alone) [b]			very common	96
Inappropriate (outside content emphasis of the journal to which submitted)	7	28	10	48
Other	6			

The data from the *Journal of Abnormal and Social Psychology* were obtained from Table 12, p. 186 of Daniels, R., & Louttit, C., *Professional Problems in Psychology*. New York: Prentice-Hall, 1957; and for the other journals through personal communication with the editors.

[a] These percentages represent the subjective judgment of the editor.
[b] The editors indicate that manuscripts are not rejected for this reason alone.

Always to be avoided are: (*a*) pseudosophisticated words; (*b*) words warped from one part of speech to another; (*c*) colloquial expressions; and (*d*) coined words.

It is this latter problem which has led nonscientists to hurl charges of gobbledygook at technical writers and led the latter to write articles expressing concern about the readability of their own reports (e.g., Hebb & Bindra, 1952; Stevens, 1950; Williamson, 1947). Particularly helpful in this context is Halpin's (1962) distinction between "profane" and "sacred" jargon. According to Halpin, "profane jargon is composed of cliches, half-formulated concepts, slogans, loaded words, and parades of abstract terms for which there are no referents." He points out that: "Jargon of this kind usually results from the infrangible fact that the author's ideas are not clear; because his ideas are not clear he covers his bed of imprecise ideas with a blanket to match—a patch quilt of fuzzy language." Halpin goes on to say, however, "Jargon may also mean the technical language of a science. Because science must be conceived, in large part, as a special language, and because the syntax of science is as important as its content, we cannot eliminate the use of special language and special concepts in scientific writing. This jargon results not from fuzzily conceived ideas but from ideas that have been defined operationally and usually with devastating clarity." The latter type of jargon is that which Halpin labels "sacred," and which is to be encouraged, since it increases the precision of expression rather than hides unclear ideas.

THE IMPLEMENTATION OF RESEARCH RESULTS

It has already been noted that modern day research workers seem less and less inclined to be satisfied just to add to the body of knowledge and to be more and more interested in seeing to it that the results of their efforts are put into practice. In a broad sense they have always been unhappy when changes do not occur as a result of their findings and theories. For example, von Helmholtz complained that his ideas were not being accepted, and Max Planck, in turn, complained that von Helmholtz would not accept his newer ideas (Barber, 1961). In this broad sense, the problem of the implementation of research results can be seen as not just that of getting teachers to apply the findings of educational research, getting industrial and clinical psychologists to apply the findings of the research psychologists, and getting social service administrators to apply the principles and ideas of sociology; nor can it even be seen as just getting the lay public of parents, neighbors, and statesmen to apply the findings of all the behavioral sciences. It must include, as well, the task of getting the scientists themselves to accept even the most basic scientific discoveries and theories of their colleagues.

The Resistance to Scientific Discoveries

Although at least one person [2] (speaking in the context of educational re-search) has expressed the view that in a free society the implementation of research results is taken care of in the natural process of competition of ideas, others would point out that educational enterprises are not competitive in the ordinary sense, and most (e.g., Barber, 1961; Corey, 1953; Gold-hammer & Elam, 1962; Taylor et al., 1962) writers feel that implementa-tion is a very real problem. It is not difficult to imagine that in the long run, a society which finds a stockpile of unused research and which is pressed for many social needs may turn its financial resources elsewhere.

Foremost among the reasons cited as a cause of the failure to imple-ment research findings is a purported lack of interest on the part of the research community itself. This, it is said, results in both poor communi-cation and in inadequate dissemination. (Campbell, 1962, reports, "I have found that many of the teachers do not use research findings because they do not always understand the language they are written in.") Most re-search workers turn to other things once their findings have been published in a professional journal though that journal may not be immediately avail-able to the practitioner.

But lack of interest is not a one-way street and also seems to be dis-played by many consumers who do not see research as vital to their practice or relevant to their everyday living. As a result, such persons simply do not (or are not permitted to by their employers) take the time or make the effort required to search through scattered and (to them) obscure journals for the information which would keep them up to date.

Just why many practitioners feel that research is of no concern to them is difficult to say, but several suggestions have been made. First, as a re-sult of a survey of research consumers, Campbell (1962) concludes that many practitioners simply do not understand the basic nature of research. They seem to confuse it with popular fads of the times; they see it as a highly technical exercise engaged in purely for the pleasure or the ag-grandizement of the researcher; they expect the results of all research to be immediately applicable to everyday problems; and they feel that research will tell them what they *should* do (i.e., they expect research to make a value judgment for them, rather than to indicate what is likely to happen if they do such and such). Second, since many consumers of research are not in a profit-loss situation where failure to achieve a goal affects them di-rectly, they simply do not care about deficient or weak procedures. Third, where the consumer *is* altruistically concerned about the outcome of his actions, the feedback of results is either absent or so remote that he never

[2] See the discussion following a presentation of a paper on the dissemination and im-plementation of educational research by Gange (1962).

really has any indication as to the efficacy of his present procedures. Finally, in some fields, as Barton and Wilder (1964) found as a result of their study of the implementation of research on reading, the persons doing the research themselves were largely untrained, were doing part-time, one-shot research, and seemed to have little contact with other disciplines. The resulting research is voluminous, but of poor quality and noncumulative—hardly the kind to inspire belief by practitioners in the efficacy of the results of scientific research efforts.

The lack of interest by either the research worker, or the consumer of research, or both, is not the sole reason for the lack of implementation of the findings in the behavioral sciences. For, as Clark (1962) points out, the practitioner is not merely passive, but often is actively resistive of new research results; and Barber (1961) has clearly documented the negative attitude many members of the scientific community itself take against findings which challenge their prior beliefs. Even when new findings are adequately disseminated and well understood, there is, though often denied by the practitioners themselves, a natural resistance to change.

While many writers have commented on the general resistance to change with which all mankind is afflicted, few have taken the next step and described why the resistance occurs. Several reasons are apparent. First, there are the built-in aversive properties of any new findings. Any new idea or new practice, almost by definition, implies that the old idea was wrong and that the practitioner's current methods are ineffective or at least inadequate. Not even the most open-minded scientist nor the most conscientious practitioner likes to be told he is wrong or that he has been wasting his time. In addition to the aversion to being told one is wrong, anyone who accepts new findings and their implications for practices faces the arduous task of unlearning old ways of responding and of acquiring a newly organized repertory of behaviors.

A second major resistance to the acceptance of new scientific findings stems from the conflict between these findings and religious beliefs or other extraprofessional attitudes and values. Readers familiar with the history of science or the history of medicine will have no trouble in recalling many examples of the terrible persecution suffered by many early day physical scientists and physicians at the hands of religious leaders or of public officials in the name of religion. Almost everyone recognizes that such persecution no longer seems to exist in the physical sciences and that it has been largely, but not entirely, overcome in the biological sciences. The major hostility today is concentrated on the behavioral scientists, or at least on the suggested practice based on their findings; both scientists and practice are often labeled "idiotic," "immoral," "godless," or "communistic."

A third reason for the general resistance to change can be seen by examining what Barber (1961) calls the patterns of social interaction among scientists. Among these patterns are those of professional standing and seniority.   Those scientists who have already established themselves and have high professional standing are the ones who hold positions of power in scientific and professional organizations.   Such persons often tend to ignore, look down upon, or even ridicule the ideas of younger, less well-established colleagues.   This particular pattern of social interaction is especially devastating to the rapid acceptance and implementation of new scientific findings because the most creative contributions of many scientists come at a relatively early age (Lehman, 1953).

Other patterns of social interaction which contribute to the resistance to new research results are those which stem from professional specialization and from the development of schools of thought within a given field.   Persons within a particular field of specialization tend to resist findings of persons in related areas even though they have a direct bearing on the given area of professional specialization.   For example, modern findings by geneticists and physiological psychologists may be completely rejected, or at least ignored, by those in social psychology, and findings by the learning theorists in the animal laboratory are ignored by those concerned with the teaching of children.   All this occurs at the same time that evidence for the environmental modification of behavior and the results of studies of human learning are disparaged by those working with lower organisms.   Similarly, the disciples of cognitive learning theory and the disciples of association learning theory both tend, indiscriminately, to disbelieve or circumscribe, rather than expand or integrate, the findings of the opposite camp.   Likewise, the phenomenologically oriented and the behavioristically oriented therapists seem to prefer to mutually ridicule each other's practices rather than to search the opposite view for new suggestions which might be helpful to them in working with their patients.   Recognition of this kind of dissension is supposed to have led T. H. Huxley (Barber, 1961) to say: " 'Authorities,' 'disciples' and 'schools' are the curse of science; and do more to interfere with the work of the scientific spirit than all its enemies."

Our modern society has produced one additional major barrier to the implementation of research results—even when basic apathy and natural resistance to change have been overcome.   There is a mounting fear that the results of research might be subverted and used for undesirable purposes. Many physical scientists have been deeply concerned about the consequences of their discoveries ever since the development of the atom bomb. As Oppenheimer (1956) noted in an address presented to the American Psychological Association, someday the biological and behavioral scientists are likely to unleash a power over man far beyond any that could be developed by the physical scientists.   As a result of this, many philosophers and even some behavioral scientists are urging that certain research results be held back until society is sufficiently stable that they can be assured that the findings in this area will always be used for the benefit rather than the destruction of mankind.   While the value system of scientists (see Chapter 1) leads them to hope that all of their efforts will ultimately lead to the betterment of mankind, they well recognize that knowledge leading to the prediction and control of human behavior is a double-edged sword.

Overcoming Resistance to Using Scientific Results

Just being aware of the nature of some of the barriers to the implementation of research results is a first step toward overcoming them. With the comments of the previous section in mind, the investigator can take sufficient pains to make certain that his findings are clearly communicated and widely disseminated to those practitioners who can use them. Administrators of appropriate agencies can create a more receptive climate by encouraging and rewarding efforts to try new things and at the same time provide both the release time necessary to keep up with the research literature and the financial resources required to adopt new practices. Just this alone is not likely to go very far in decreasing the tremendous lag which seems to occur between the report of a research finding and its application in practice. Those most concerned with implementation have made numerous specific suggestions which are summarized below under the headings of education, involvement, and special promotion.

EDUCATION   One major group of suggestions for overcoming the barriers to using research results amounts to increasing efforts to educate for research. This includes both creating an audience of practitioners and laymen who understand and appreciate research and training research workers themselves more thoroughly.

Increased training of both the practitioner and consumer has been most strongly urged by Halpin (1962) who, speaking with particular reference to the field of education, says: "If we are to disseminate research findings . . . we first must produce a wide audience that understands the structure of scientic thought." F. J. Rummel (Goldhammer & Elam, 1962) remarked: "I think that until we get a body of consumers at the level of implementation . . . who understand some of the techniques of research and are able to analyze research and say, 'this is valid or not valid, or more valid, if possible, than another piece,' we can't do much in the way of implementation." To a large extent, an appropriate attitude on the part of the consumer can be created by all professors in the behavioral sciences regardless of their area of specialization, if they will but accept their role as a scholar as well as a teacher, and when in the classroom, base more of their teachings on research results rather than on "knowledge" which comes from intuition, personal experience, and reasoning alone. All consumers should have a crystal clear concept of the nature of research. Campbell (1962), after conducting a survey to determine the major causes of the failure of practitioners to put research results to use lists concept confusion, "in the concept of what research is, in the concept of the process involved in going from investigation to application, and in the concept of what research can and cannot do," as the most significant single barrier to the implementation of research results in the field of education.

In addition to creating appropriate attitudes toward and clear concepts of research in all consumers, efforts will be needed to increase the in-service training of practitioners in all the behavioral sciences. While some of this is now done in the field of education, both psychology and sociology seem to have lagged in this respect, and few persons in the behavioral sciences seem to have recognized the extent to which this approach to insuring the implementation of new findings is used in other fields of applied science. To take just one example, Jacobson (Goldhammer & Elam, 1962) reports, "the dean of our Medical School tells me that they spend more man-hours and money on the in-service training than on the initial training of physicians in the medical schools."

In the behavioral sciences, a great deal more needs to be done with respect to the training of the research workers. As a result of their findings of the poor training of research workers working in the area of reading (as reported in the previous section) Barton and Wilder (1964) point to the history of medicine in the United States as an appropriate analogy when they say:

During the nineteenth century and the earlier part of this one, medical research showed very similar patterns to those we now find in education and in reading research. The same physicians who taught at medical schools also had private practices, did part-time research, ran professional organizations, and sometimes even had their own hospitals. The Renaissance-man physician is now a thing of the past. Knowledge is too vast and specialties are too complex for any single man to play all of these roles adequately. In response to this problem, the leading medical schools have recently made policy statements to the effect that their primary goal is to make contributions to medical knowledge through research. There is clear recognition that this can only be done by providing facilities and rewards for full time research activities at medical schools; with this goal in mind, new positions have been created and organizational changes made at most major medical schools.

It would seem that the sooner the applied fields of the behavioral sciences followed the lead of the engineering and the medical sciences in this respect, the sooner they are likely to find the results of research in the behavioral sciences put to the fullest use possible.

INVOLVEMENT   In direct contrast to the recommendations given above, Corey (1963) seems to completely reject the idea that implementation of research will occur when the practitioner asks the professional investigator to study the problem and to suggest solutions. Corey argues, "the professional investigator can never study individual problems in any strict sense," and, "even when the recommendations are sound, it is difficult to incorporate them into the behavior of the practitioner," and therefore strongly advocates an approach which has become known as *action research*. According to Corey, action research "is research undertaken by practitioners in order that they may improve their practices."

The basic idea represents an attempt to make use of the sound learning principle that behavioral changes occur only when the learner himself becomes actively involved. The advocates of action research would contend that the only way to change the behavior of practitioners is to get them involved in carrying out research studies on problems which are of concern to themselves.

Although action research has been widely acclaimed in education and in certain areas of sociology as an ideal solution to the problem of implementation, many investigators are somewhat skeptical. Campbell (1962), in reporting his finding that confusion about the basic nature of research was a major factor inhibiting the application of research results, has complained that "recent emphasis on action research has probably contributed to this confusion." Similarly, A. G. Clark (Goldhammer & Elam, 1962) points out that a study by Brickell (1961) shows that "there seemed to be relatively little difference in the reaction of teachers to change that had been effected in the school district by an administrator and change that had grown out of teachers' participation." As Blackwell (1961) puts it in her review of action research—its promise and its problems: "Action research is assumed to be an instrument for improving educational practice and a more potent instrument than professional research. Common sense supports this assumption. Educational practice supports it. The empirical evidence is sparse."

SPECIAL PROMOTION   At opposite poles from the advocates of action research are those who contend that research must be done by professionals and then promoted among consumers by means of a special agent or agency. These individuals feel that the methodology of research in the behavioral sciences has now developed well beyond the stage where it can be carried out adequately by laymen, even under the guidance of a professional. They also accept the findings of the study by Brickell (1961) which suggest that the major agent of change in the public schools of New York was the school administrator and that the only system for accomplishing change which worked with the teachers was that of demonstrating the new technique in other schools. It is their contention that the appropriate solution to the problem of implementing research findings is not the involvement of the practitioner but the establishment of an agency to promote the application of the findings. As Gange (1962) puts it: "As I read history, the great movements and major changes in the development of mankind have come about as a consequence of the driving force of an idea or two led by a powerful group who asserted leadership in a particular direction."

It has been suggested that the private foundations should promote change even though, traditionally, such organizations have considered their task completed once the research they have supported has been completed and the findings widely disseminated. On the other hand, it has been pointed out that private foundations often seem to have a special axe to grind or a special view to promote, and are not likely to be willing to support new findings that may have unfavorable financial implications for them. Also, a foundation that is dependent upon voluntary contributions, no matter how unbiased in its policies, cannot long support unpopular causes—which many of the findings in the behavioral sciences often turn out to be when they are first announced. Those who have taken the latter position feel that all that is required is to appoint a special person in the agency producing the original research who will see to it that the practitioners in the field are told specifically which findings of the research studies completed have implications for their work.

Simply asking either a private foundation or a person within the research agency to promote the implementation of new research findings greatly underestimates the magnitude of the task of moving from basic research to meaningful applications. Examples from agriculture, engineering, medicine, and the military all suggest that implementation is a multistage process which includes the following major steps:

1. a review of basic research findings for potential applications
2. a feasibility study to determine whether the new application is likely to bring about an increase in efficiency of sufficient magnitude to offset the cost of making the change
3. the developmental testing and tryout of all new equipment, materials and procedures
4. final evaluation study of the entire new system as it operates in the natural setting
5. demonstration of the new application to other operating units or practitioners.

Once the stages listed above have been recognized, it becomes apparent that the size of the investment in terms of funds, time, and human effort now devoted to the task will need to be vastly increased if it is to be expected that basic research findings in the behavioral sciences will be implemented on a regular basis.

Just how this additional effort should be deployed to best accomplish the goal of rapid implementation of research findings is not yet settled, but at least two distinct possibilities are currently apparent. One is that of strengthening the development sections of research agencies now in existence, such as has been done in business and industry generally, but most notably in concerns involved in the manufacture of aircraft, electronics equipment, and drugs. The other approach is that of following the example of agriculture, with its experimental stations, extension services, and county agents.

Although both approaches will likely be followed, with the addition of development sections to current research units on the local scene probably occurring first, a major thrust with respect to the second possibility has already been made in the field of education with the establishment, by the U.S. Office of Education, of major research and development centers and companion regional laboratories. Similar developments are likely to follow in both sociology and psychology as the recognition of the problem of implementation and the desire of a beleaguered society for a solution to its human problems increase.

COMMUNICATION OF THE VALUES OF RESEARCH AND THE PROBLEM OF EXPERIMENTATION WITH HUMANS

The Conflict in Rights

In addition to the task of helping practitioners keep up to date with the latest research findings, the scientific community today is faced with an even more important communications problem. This is the task of conveying to the general public some notion of the tremendous value that research—particularly basic research on human behavior—can have for mankind, and of convincing those outside the field that behavioral scientists are ethical and moral persons who have a great respect for the individual and his rights.

To a great extent the need for this type of communication arises because the success of behavioral research has attracted sufficient public interest that its methods, techniques, and devices are no longer inconspicuous. One of the results of this new-found attention has been to bring into focus a basic conflict between the rights of individuals to safety and privacy on the one hand and on the other hand, the right of the society to know and of the investigator to inquire. Only with a great deal of understanding of the nature of behavioral research and its approaches on the part of the public and with a feeling for humanity on the part of the scientists themselves will a sensible compromise be possible.

In the case of conflict, there are strong advocates on both sides of the question. There are those who feel that using human beings for purposes of scientific experimentation is unjustified under any circumstances. These persons feel that enough unethical practices have already occurred to lead us to Freund's (1967, p. 399) conclusion that: "In the end, we may have to accept the fact that some limits do exist in the search for knowledge."

On the other hand, there are some research workers who feel quite strongly that continued expansion of knowledge in the behavioral sciences is absolutely essential to the continued advancement of mankind. They might argue that without a greater understanding of human behavior, mankind will soon destroy itself, and they would agree with Bennett (1967) that the moral imperative is often on the side of the surrender of minor individual rights.

Others would attempt to effect a compromise between the extremes by suggesting that limits are reasonable for basic research but not for applied work which has a clear and direct benefit to man, or that limits might be imposed on the research techniques to be used but not on the choice of subject matter to be investigated.

APPLYING RULES OF CONDUCT   It would seem that the conflict in rights described above could be easily resolved if only the investigator would but follow a few generally accepted informal guidelines. Among those rules most often suggested are the cautions that every possible safety measure be incorporated into the techniques used; that the investigator treat the subject as he would like to be treated if he were the subject of an experiment; that before proceeding, every subject should give his informed consent to participating and be granted the right to discontinue at any time during the study at which he might change his mind; that all information gathered be kept confidential; and that the complete anonymity of the subjects must be preserved at all times.

But the situation is not so simple. Both Lovell (1967) and Katz (1967) point out that misuses of psychology, which are quite real and very serious, do occur, and Katz (p. 360) claims that: "Unethical practices . . . occur more frequently and are more serious in nature than any rational thinking, ethical investigator has any reason to suspect." Even if the informal rules were incorporated into a formal code of ethics to be rigidly enforced through the professional disciplines themselves, problems would arise. Consider, for example, the principle of consent. First, there are limits even when consent is given. The law does not accept consent when given by children nor does it accept consent of the victim in homicide cases. Second, it is sometimes difficult to ascertain whether the consent of the subject has been freely given or whether some coercion was felt. This is particularly true in such cases as those of college students in psychology who may feel that their future grades in the area might suffer if they fail to volunteer for an experiment being carried out by their instructor. Third, it is simply not always possible to completely inform the subject about the nature of the experiment before consent is obtained. Sometimes the complexity of the experiment is so great as to make it impossible to explain adequately to a person who is not trained in the field and sometimes deception is required to preserve the validity of the results. Finally, there is always the possibility that information which was freely and intelligently given for one purpose might at some later time be used for purposes not intended by the investigator nor consented to by the subject.

The difficulties arise when an investigator attempts to apply the concept of anonymity. If the study design does not require that an individual respondent be identified with a particular response for later analysis, anonymity can generally be preserved. Sometimes relationships between responses and other personal characteristics need to be obtained, and in such situations some identifying records must be maintained at least until all data have been gathered. As Ruebhausen and Brim (1966) point out, research data are clearly subject to subpoena. In spite of his best intentions, an investigator carrying out a longitudinal study simply cannot guarantee his subjects confidentiality of the information gathered. Further, even in the case of short-term studies or investigations where identification for correlational purposes is not required, the behavioral scientist may find himself in an ethical dilemma if he has promised his subject anonymity and then the subject reveals strong antisocial tendencies which could be dangerous to others who may come in contact with the subject.

In spite of these difficulties, some solution to the problem must be found. There is a great deal of pressure being exerted through Congress and in institutions where research is carried on to impose arbitrary limits on research methods. If scientists do not develop an adequate set of procedures to follow which guarantees as much protection to the subjects of experimentation as possible, and if the importance of advancing knowledge in the behavioral sciences is not communicated to the public, then some melodramatic case not well understood by lay people could well lead to excessive government restraints.

According to Conrad (1967), one such rigid rule (which in effect says that any "objectionable" test item which appears in an instrument used in a research project be "deleted, modified or replaced by another item that is more acceptable") is already being applied by the Bureau of Research in the U.S. Office of Education. A plethora of such regulations which show little insight into the subtleties of the problem and which may be blindly applied by persons who have little knowledge of, training in, or sympathy for the behavioral sciences could well prevent the very protection of individuals which such policy has as its goal.

For example, such regulations could halt important developmental studies of children which are just beginning to provide the information necessary to stop the rather capricious and sometimes harsh fashions in child-rearing practices. Severe restrictions designed to protect the right to privacy by requiring parental consent in studies using children as subjects could well eliminate important investigations of the effects of parental cruelty on the child and subsequent adult behavior. Conceivably, certain restrictions as to areas of study and techniques of research employed could prevent investigations which seek to question so-called standard practices which are widely used even though little evidence as to their effectiveness or possible side effects has ever been gathered.   Finally, blind and insensitive restrictive regulations could spiral a conflict between the scientific community and the general public to such proportions that the latter will not accept well-established findings (such as the effectiveness of mass inoculations for the prevention of some cruel disease), even though application of the findings would be a tremendous benefit to humanity.

OTHER SOLUTIONS   If rigid rules which give the research worker complete license or which severely restrict either the content he can explore or the methods he uses to explore it are intolerable, the question arises as to what other possibilities exist for solving this basic conflict between community and individual rights.   From a legal point of view, the ideal solution is one which provides some inner check or built-in reciprocity.   (When the person who divides the cake in two has second choice of the pieces, the result is likely to be as fair a compromise as is humanly possible.)   One such safeguard, suggested by Freund (1967), is to require that all research results be published whether the findings are positive or negative.   This, Freund feels, would lead scientists to carry out fewer "little" studies for the purpose of gaining recognition, and to carry out only those studies for which there was a good chance of success.   In turn, such a requirement might also lead to more thorough development of theory before going to the laboratory and to more imaginative research designs which might avoid some of the conflicts now faced.

Such an inner check as that suggested will not be completely adequate, and without a stronger built-in reciprocity, additional safeguards will be needed.   One such safeguard is to insist that every experimental project involving human beings as subjects be reviewed and given approval by someone other than the experimenter himself.   But who should have the responsibility for the review and approval?   Should it be a government agent acting as a broker between the scientist and the people?   Or should it be a group of persons?   If it is a group, should the group be composed of professional colleagues or laymen or both?   Should the members of the group be local persons who know the researcher well and the local feelings in the community, or should they be persons from outside who are better able to arrive at fair judgments because they are not personally involved with either the researcher or the community?

Even if agreement can be reached as to the nature of the reviewer or reviewing group, problems will arise as to what should be considered in making the decision to approve or reject a particular research study. Among those items that have been suggested as of importance are the general community consensus of feelings about such studies as those proposed; whether the researcher has a conflict of interest which prevents his giving full consideration to the welfare of his human subjects; whether the anticipated outcome of the experiment will be of sufficient benefit to mankind to make some minor discomforts and risks reasonable; how serious the invasion of privacy is and how great the personal risk to the subjects is; the skill and competency of the investigator; and the adequacy of the research design to permit drawing valid conclusions from the results.

Other safeguards suggested are the development of a strong code of ethics to be enforced by the academic disciplines, and the development of legal mechanisms of due process which will both permit socially useful risks to be sanctioned and at the same time protect individual rights to privacy and safety. Some steps along these lines have already been taken. In 1966 the House Subcommittee on Science Research and Development suggested that a "technology assessment board" be set up to study possible harmful effects of technological innovations and serve the public as an early warning system. In that same year the U.S. Office of Science and Technology appointed a panel to "examine the issues and propose guidelines for those who are engaged in behavioral research or associated with its support." Finally, in February and June of 1966, the Surgeon General of the U.S. Public Health Service issued some directives to be effective 1 November of that year which set up a decentralized system of review of proposals for research which involved human beings as subjects and which receive financial support from the U.S. Public Health Service.

Ultimately, the ideal solution will come from a public understanding and trust of the behavioral scientist. This in turn can come only with effective communication of the results of experimental scientific investigation. As Ruebhausen and Brim (1966) point out, when such understanding and trust have been accomplished, society will not only support but will insist on a decent accommodation between the conflicting values of complete individual human rights and the right of society to the benefits of behavioral research.

Appendix

AN ILLUSTRATION OF THE EFFICACY OF DISPROPORTIONATE STRATIFIED SAMPLES

a. Use as population: 1, 1, 2, 2, 3, 5, thus: $\mu = 2.33$.
b. Draw sample of size 2.
c. For proportionate $(1, 1, 2 \mid 2, 3, 5)$

Sample	$\overline{X}$	$(\overline{X})^2$
1, 2	1.5	2.25
1, 3	2	4
1, 5	3	9
1, 2	1.5	2.25
1, 3	2	4
1, 5	3	9
2, 2	2	4
2, 3	2.5	6.25
2, 5	3.5	12.25
Σ	21.0	53.00

$$\mu_{\overline{x}} = \tfrac{21}{9} = 2.33$$

$$\frac{\Sigma(\overline{X})^2}{N} = \frac{53}{9} = 5.89$$

$$(\mu_{\overline{x}})^2 = (2.33)^2 = \underline{5.43}$$

$$\text{diff} = .46$$

Correction:

$$\frac{N}{N-1} = \frac{9}{8} = 1.125$$

$$\left(\frac{N}{N-1}\right)(.46) = \sigma_{\overline{x}}^2 = .52$$

d. For disproportionate $(1, 1, 2, 2 \mid 3, 5)$

	Unweighted		Weighted	
Sample	$\overline{X}_u$	$(\overline{X}_u)^2$	$\overline{X}_w$	$(\overline{X}_w)^2$
1, 3	2	4	$\frac{1}{6}(4)(1) + (2)(3) = \frac{10}{6} = 1.67$	2.79
1, 5	3	9	$\frac{1}{6}(4)(1) + (2)(5) = \frac{14}{6} = 2.33$	5.43
1, 3	2	4	$\frac{1}{6}(4)(1) + (2)(3) = \frac{10}{6} = 1.67$	2.79
1, 5	3	9	$\frac{1}{6}(4)(1) + (2)(5) = \frac{14}{6} = 2.33$	5.43
2, 3	2.5	6.25	$\frac{1}{6}(4)(2) + (2)(3) = \frac{14}{6} = 2.33$	5.43
2, 5	3.5	12.25	$\frac{1}{6}(4)(2) + (2)(5) = \frac{18}{6} = 3.00$	9.00
2, 3	2.5	6.25	$\frac{1}{6}(4)(2) + (2)(3) = \frac{14}{6} = 2.33$	5.43
2, 5	3.5	12.25	$\frac{1}{6}(4)(2) + (2)(5) = \frac{18}{6} = 3.00$	9.00
	22.0	63.00	18.67	45.30

$$\mu_{\overline{x}_u} = \frac{22}{8} = 2.75 \qquad\qquad \mu_{\overline{x}_w} = \frac{18.67}{8} = 2.33$$

$$\frac{\Sigma(\overline{X}_u)^2}{N} = \frac{63}{8} = 7.875 \qquad\qquad \frac{\Sigma(\overline{X}_w)^2}{N} = \frac{45.3}{8} = 5.68$$

$$(\mu_{\overline{x}_u})^2 = (2.75)^2 = 7.562 \qquad\qquad (\mu_{\overline{x}_w})^2 = 5.43$$

Uncorrected $\sigma_{\overline{x}}^2 = .313$ Uncorrected $\sigma_{\overline{x}}^2 = .25$

Corrected $\sigma_{\overline{x}}^2 = .36$ Corrected $\sigma_{\overline{x}}^2 = .28$

Correction: $\frac{N}{N-1} = \frac{8}{7} = 1.14$

References

Allen, E. Why are research grant applications disapproved? *Science,* 1960, **132,** 1532–1534.

Allport, G., & Odbert, H. Trait-names: A psycholo-lexical study. *Psychological Monograph,* 1936, No. 211.

American Library Association. *Glossary of library terms.* Chicago: American Library Association, 1943.

American Library Association. *The library and information networks of the future.* Report prepared for the Rome Air Development Center, April, 1963.

American Psychological Association Committee on Psychological Tests. Technical recommendations for psychological tests and diagnostic techniques. *Psychological Bulletin Supplement,* 1954, **51**(2), part 2, 1–38.

American Psychological Association Committee on Psychological Tests. Technical recommendations for psychological tests and diagnostic techniques: Preliminary proposal. *American Psychologist,* 1952, **7,** 461–476.

American Psychological Association, Council of Editors. *Publication manual of the American Psychological Association* (1967 Revision). Washington, D.C.: American Psychological Association, 1967.

American Psychological Association, Council of Editors. Publication in APA journals: advice from the editors. *American Psychologist,* 1965, **20,** 711–720.

American Sociological Association. *The American Sociological Review,* 1965, **30,** index, p. xii.

Ames, A. *Visual perception and the rotating trapezoidal window.* Washington, D.C.: American Psychological Association, 1951.

Anderson, R., & Bancroft, T. *Statistical theory in research.* New York: McGraw-Hill, 1952.

Bachrach, A. *Psychological research: An introduction.* (2nd ed.) New York: Random House, 1965.

Bales, R. *Interaction process analysis.* Reading, Mass.: Addison-Wesley, 1950.

Bancroft, Gertrude, & Welch, E. Recent experience with problems of labor force measurement. *Journal of the American Statistical Association,* 1946, **41,** 303–312.

Barber, B.   Resistance by scientists to scientific discovery. *Science*, 1961, **134,** 596–602.

Barnes, E.   Response bias and the MMPI. *Journal of Consulting Psychology,* 1956, **20,** 371–374.

Bartlett, F.   *Remembering.*   Cambridge: Cambridge University Press, 1932.

Barton, A., & Wilder, D.   Research and practice in the teaching of reading: A progress report. Chapter 16 in M. Miles (Ed.), *Innovation in Education.* The Horace Mann–Lincoln Institute of School Experimentation. New York: Bureau of Publications, Teachers College, Columbia University, 1964.

Barzun, J., & Graff, H.   *The modern researcher.*   New York: Harcourt, Brace & World, 1957.

Baxendale, P.   Machine-made index for technical literature—an experiment. *IBM Journal of Research and Development,* 1958, **2,** 354–361.

Beaton, A.   An inter-battery factor analytic approach to clique analysis. *Sociometry,* 1966, **29,** 135–145.

Becker, J.   The sorcerer's apprentice. *National Society of Programmed Instruction Journal,* 1964, **3**(7), 15.

Becker, J., & Hayes, R.   *Information storage and retrieval: tools, elements, theories.*   New York: Wiley, 1964.

Bennett, C.   What price privacy. *American Psychologist,* 1967, **22,** 371–376.

Berelson, B.   *Content analysis in communication research.*   Glencoe, Ill.: The Free Press, 1952.

Beshers, J. (Ed.)   *Computer methods in the analysis of large-scale social systems.*   Cambridge, Mass.: Joint Center for Urban Studies of the Massachusetts Institute of Technology and Harvard University, 1965.

Blackwell, S.   Action research—its promise and problems. *American Vocational Journal,* 1961, **36**(1), 14–19.

Blum, M., & Balinski, B.   *Counseling and psychology.*   Englewood Cliffs, N.J.: Prentice-Hall, 1951.

Boring, E. A.   *A history of experimental psychology.*   (2nd ed.)   New York: Appleton-Century-Crofts, 1956.

Borlco, H.   *The construction of an empirically based mathematically derived classification system.*   Report SP-585, October, 1961, Systems Development Corporation, Santa Monica, California.

Borko, H. (Ed.)   *Computer applications in the behavioral sciences.*   Englewood Cliffs, N.J.: Prentice-Hall, 1962.

Brayfield, A.   Foreword. *American Psychologist,* 1966, **21,** 997–998.

Brickell, H.   *Organizing New York State educational change.*   Albany, New York: State Education Department, 1961.

Broen, W., & Wirt, R.   Varieties of response sets. *Journal of Consulting Psychology,* 1958, **22,** 237–240.

Broverman, D.   Normative and ipsative measurement in psychology. *Psychological Review,* 1962, **69,** 295–305.

Bruner, J., & Goodman, C.   Value and need as organizing factors in perception. *Journal of Abnormal and Social Psychology,* 1947, **42,** 33–44.

Bryant, Margaret (Ed.)   *Current American Usage.*   New York: Funk and Wagnalls, 1962.

Burt, C.   The inheritance of mental ability.   *American Psychologist*, 1958, **13,** 1–15.

Bush, Vannevar.   As we may think.   *Atlantic Monthly*, 1945, **75,** 101–108.

Cahn, J.   *A system of systems*.   Paper presented at the Fourth American University Institute for Information Retrieval, 1962, Washington, D.C.

Campbell, D., & Fiske, D.   Convergent and discriminant validation by the multitrait multimethod matrix.   *Psychological Bulletin*, 1959, **56,** 81–105.

Campbell, D., & Stanley, J.   *Experimental and quasi-experimental designs for research*.   Chicago: Rand McNally, 1963.

Campbell, R.   The role of school study councils and local school districts in the dissemination and implementation of educational research.   Chapter III in K. Goldhammer, & S. Elam (Eds.), Dissemination and implementation to the Gange reference.   Third Annual Phi Delta Kappa Symposium on Educational Research.   Bloomington, Ind.: Phi Delta Kappa, 1962.

Campbell, W.   *Form and style in thesis writing*.   Boston: Houghton Mifflin, 1954.

Cattell, R.   The dimensions of culture pattern by factorization of national characters.   *Journal of Abnormal and Social Psychology*, 1949, **49,** 443–469.

Cattell, R.   *Factor analysis*.   New York: Harper and Brothers, 1952(a).

Cattell, R.   The three basic factor analytic designs P- R- and T-techniques—and their derivations.   *Psychological Bulletin*, 1952b, **49,** 499–520.

Cattell, R. (Ed.)   *Handbook of multivariate experimental psychology*.   Chicago: Rand McNally, 1966.

Cattell, R.   The data box: its ordering of total resources in terms of possible relational systems.   Chapter 3 in Cattell (Ed.), *Handbook of multivariate experimental psychology*.   Chicago: Rand McNally, 1966.

Cattell, R., & Adelson, M.   The dimensions of social change in the U.S.A. as determined by P-technique.   *Social Forces*, 1951, **30,** 190–201.

Cattell, R., Cattell, A., & Rhymer, R.   P-technique demonstrated in determining psycho-physiological source traits in normal individuals.   *Psychometrika*, 1947, **12,** 267–288.

Cervinka, V.   A dimensional theory of groups.   *Sociometry*, 1948, **11,** 100–107.

Chamberlain, T.   The method of multiple working hypotheses.   *Science*, 1965, **148,** 754–759.

Champney, H.   The measurement of parent behavior.   *Child Development*, 1941, **12,** 131–166.

Champney, H., & Marshall, H.   Optimal refinement of the rating scale.   *Journal of Applied Psychology*, 1939, **23,** 323–331.

Chapin, F.   *Experimental designs in sociological research*.   New York: Harper, 1947.

Chassen, J.   Statistical inferences and the single case in clinical design.   *Psychiatry*, 1960, **23,** 173–184.

Clark, D.   The function of the United States Office of Education and the State Departments of Education in the Dissemination and Implementation of Educational Research.   Chapter IV in K. Goldhammer, & S. Elam (Eds.), Dissemination and implementation to the Gange reference.   Third Annual Phi Delta Kappa Symposium on Educational Research.   Bloomington, Indiana: Phi Delta Kappa, 1962.

Clark, K., & Kreidt, P.   An application of Guttman's new scaling technique to an attitude questionnaire.   *Educational and Psychological Measurement,* 1948, **8,** 215–224.

Collier, J.   United States Indian Administration as a laboratory of ethnic relations.   *Social Research,* 1945, **12,** 265–303.

Conrad, H.   Clearance of questionnaires with respect to "invasion of privacy," public sensitivities, ethical standards, etc.   *American Psychologist,* 1967, **22,** 356–359.

Coombs, C., & Satter, G.   A factorial approach to job families.   *Psychometrika,* 1949, **14,** 33–42.

Copperud, R.   *A dictionary of usage and style.*   New York: Hawthorne Books, 1964.

Corey, S.   *Action research to improve school practices.*   New York: Bureau of Publications, Teachers College, Columbia University, 1953.

Cox, D.   *Planning of experiments.*   New York: Wiley, 1958.

Cronbach, L.   *Essentials of psychological testing.*   New York: Harper & Row, 1960.

Cronbach, L.   Response sets and test validity.   *Educational and Psychological Measurement,* 1946, **6,** 475–494.

Cronbach, L.   The two disciplines of scientific psychology.   *American Psychologist,* 1957, **18,** 671–685.

Cronbach, L., & Gleser, G.   *Psychological tests and personnel decisions.*   (2nd ed.) Urbana, Ill.: University of Illinois Press, 1965.

Cronbach, L., & Meehl, P.   Construct validity in psychological tests.   *Psychological Bulletin,* 1955, **52,** 281–302.

Daniel, R., & Louttit, C.   *Professional problems in psychology.*   Englewood Cliffs, N.J.: Prentice-Hall, 1953.

Doyle, L.   Semantic road maps for literature searchers.   *Journal of the Association for Computing Machinery,* 1961, **8,** 553–578.

Dunnette, M.   Fads, fashions and folderol in psychology.   *American Psychologist,* 1966, **21,** 343–352.

Edwards, A.   *Techniques of attitude scale construction.*   New York: Appleton-Century-Crofts, 1957.

Edwards, W., Lindman, H., & Savage, J.   Baysian statistical inference for psychological research.   *Psychological Review,* 1963, **70,** 193–242.

Evans, R.   *Resistance to innovation in higher education.*   San Francisco: Jossey-Bass, Inc., 1967.

Eysenck, H.   Criterion-analysis—an application of the hypothetical deductive method in factor analysis.   *Psychological Review,* 1950, **57,** 38–53.

Eysenck, H.   The logical basis of factor analysis.   *American Psychologist,* 1953, **8,** 105–114.

Feigenbaum, E., & Feldman, J. (Eds.)   *Computers and thought.*   New York: McGraw-Hill, 1963.

Ferster, C., & Skinner, B.   *Schedules of reinforcement.*   New York: Appleton-Century-Crofts, 1957.

Festinger, L.   The analysis of sociograms using matrix algebra.   *Human Relations,* 1949, **2**(2), 153–158.

Fisher, R. *Statistical method, and scientific inference.* Edinburgh: Oliver and Boyd, 1956, 1959.

Fisher, R., & Yates, F. *Statistical tables for biological, agricultural, and medical research.* (6th ed.) New York: Hafner Publishing Company, 1963.

Fisher, S., & Fisher, R. Relationship between personal insecurity and attitude toward psychological methodology. *American Psychologist,* 1955, **10,** 538–540.

Fiske, D. A study of relationships to somatotype. *Journal of Applied Psychology,* 1944, **28,** 504–519.

Flanagan, J. Critical requirements: a new approach to employee evaluation. *Personnel Psychology,* 1949, **2,** 419–425.

Fleishman, E., & Hampel, W. Changes in factor structure of a complex psychomotor test as a function of practice. *Psychometrika,* 1954, **19,** 239–252.

Forer, B. The fallacy of personal validation: a classroom demonstration of gullibility. *Journal of Abnormal and Social Psychology,* 1949, **44,** 118–123.

Forsyth, E., & Katz, L. A matrix approach to the analysis of sociometric data: preliminary report. *Sociometry,* 1946, **9**(4), 340–349.

French, J. *Kit of reference tests for cognitive factors.* Princeton, N.J.: Educational Testing Service, 1963.

Freund, P. Is the law ready for human experimentation? *American Psychologist,* 1967, **22,** 394–399.

Fruchter, B. *Introduction to factor analysis.* New York: Van Nostrand, 1954.

Gange, J. The role of private philanthropy in the dissemination and implementation of educational research. Chapter II in K. Goldhammer, & S. Elam (Eds.), Dissemination and implementation to the Gange reference. Third Annual Phi Delta Kappa Symposium on Educational Research. Bloomington, Ind.: Phi Delta Kappa, 1962.

Gebhart, G., & Hoyt, D. Personality needs of under and over achievers. *Journal of Applied Psychology,* 1958, **42,** 125–128.

Geis, G. L. Programmed instruction—a means rather than an end. *NSPI Journal,* 1964, **3**(7), 6–7.

Goldhammer, K., & Elam, S. (Eds.) Dissemination and implementation to the Gange reference. Third Annual Phi Delta Kappa Symposium on Educational Research. Bloomington, Ind.: Phi Delta Kappa, 1962.

Green, B. Latent structure analysis and its relation to factor analysis. *Journal of the American Statistical Association,* 1952, **47,** 71–76.

Guilford, J. When not to factor analyze. *Psychological Bulletin,* 1952, **49,** 26–37.

Guilford, J. *Psychometric methods.* (2nd ed.) New York: McGraw-Hill, 1954.

Guilford, J. *Personality.* New York: McGraw-Hill, 1959.

Guilford, J., Christensen, P., Bond, N., & Sutlan, M. A factor analysis of human interests. *Psychological Monographs,* 1954, **68**(4).

Gullahorn, J., & Gullahorn, Jeanne. A computer model of elementary social behavior. In E. Feigenbaum, & J. Feldman (Eds.), *Computers and thought.* New York: McGraw-Hill, 1963. Pp. 375–386.

Gulliksen, H. *Theory of mental tests.* New York: Wiley, 1950.

Guttman, L. A basis for scaling qualitative data. *American Sociological Review,* 1944, **9,** 139–150.

Guttman, L. A basis for analyzing test reliability. *Psychometrika,* 1945, **10,** 255–282.

Guttman, L. The basis for scalogram analysis. Chapter 3 in S. Stouffer, *et al. Measurement and prediction.* Studies in Social Psychology in World War II, Vol. IV. Princeton, N.J.: Princeton University Press, 1950.

Halpin, A. Problems in the use of communication media in the dissemination and implementation of educational research. Chapter VI in K. Goldhammer, & S. Elam (Eds.), Dissemination and implementation to the Gange reference. Third Annual Phi Delta Kappa Symposium on Educational Research. Bloomington, Ind.: Phi Delta Kappa, 1962.

Hansen, M., Hurwitz, W., & Madow, W. *Sample survey methods and theory.* New York: Wiley, 1953.

Harman, H. *Modern factor analysis.* Chicago: University of Chicago Press, 1960.

Hays, W. *Statistics for psychologists.* New York: Holt, Rinehart and Winston, 1963.

Hebb, D., & Bindra, D. Scientific writing and the general problem of communication. *American Psychologist,* 1952, **7,** 569–573.

Helmstadter, G. Procedures for obtaining separate set and content components of a test score. *Psychometrika,* 1957, **22,** 381–393.

Helmstadter, G. *Principles of psychological measurement.* New York: Appleton-Century-Crofts, 1964.

Henrysson, S. *Applicability of factor analysis in the behavioral sciences.* Stockholm, Sweden: University of Stockholm, Almquist and Wiksell, 1957.

Highland, R., & Berkshire, J. A methodological study of forced-choice performance ratings, V. *Research Bulletin,* 51-9 H.R.R.C., San Antonio, Texas, 1951.

Hilgard, E. A perspective on the relationship between learning theory and educational practices. In E. Hilgard (Ed), *Theories of learning and instruction.* Sixty-third Yearbook of the National Society for the Study of Education. Chicago: University of Chicago Press, 1964.

Hills, J. Decision theory and college choice. *Personnel and guidance journal,* 1964, **43,** 17–22.

Hoggatt, A., & Balderston, F. *Symposium on simulation models: methodology and applications to the behavioral sciences.* Cincinnati, Ohio: Southwestern Publishing Company, 1963.

Holzinger, K., & Harman, H. *Factor analysis.* Chicago: University of Chicago Press, 1941.

Horst, P. *Factor analysis of data matrices.* New York: Holt, Rinehart and Winston, 1965.

Hotelling, H. Simplified calculation of principal components. *Psychometrika,* 1935, **1,** 27–35.

Hovland, C. Two new social science research units in industrial settings. *American Psychologist,* 1961, **16,** 87–91.

Hovland, C., & Hunt, E. Computer simulation of concept attainment. *Behavioral Science*, 1960, **5**, 265–267.

Hoyt, C. Test reliability estimated by analysis of variance. *Psychometrika*, 1941, **6**, 153–160.

Hubbell, C. An input-output approach to clique identification. *Sociometry*, 1965, **28**, 377–399.

Huff, D. Parlez-vous statistics? *Think*, 1963, **29**, 25–28.

Huttner, L., & Katzell, R. Developing a yardstick of supervisory performance. *Personnel*, 1957, **33**, 371–378.

Jackson, D., & Messick, S. Content and style in personality assessment. *Psychological Bulletin*, 1958, **55**, 243–252.

Jahoda, M., Deutsch, M., & Cook, S. *Research methods in social relations, part 2: selected techniques.* New York: Dryden Press, 1951.

Jessen, R. *Statistical survey techniques.* Ames, Iowa: (ditto notes), 1950.

Jones, L. The nature of measurement. In R. Thorndike, *Educational measurement* (2nd ed.), Chapter 14. Washington, D.C.: American Council on Education, 1968 (in press).

Katz, D., & Cantril, H. Public opinion polls. *Sociometry*, 1937, **1**, 155–179.

Katz, M. Ethical issues in the use of human subjects in psychopharmacologic research. *American Psychologist*, 1967, **22**, 360–363.

Keats, J. Test theory. *Annual Review of Psychology*, 1967, **18**, 217–238.

Kelley, T. *Interpretation of educational measurement.* New York: World Book Company, 1927.

Kelley, T. *Essential traits of mental life.* Cambridge, Mass.: Harvard University Press, 1935.

Kimble, G. *Hilgard and Marquis' conditioning and learning.* New York: Appleton-Century-Crofts, 1961.

Kintz, B., Delprato, D., Mettee, D., Persons, C., & Schappe, R. The experimenter effect. *Psychological Bulletin*, 1965, **63**, 223–232.

Kuder, G., & Richardson, M. The theory of estimation of test reliability. *Psychometrika*, 1937, **2**, 151–160.

Lawley, D. The estimation of factor loadings by the method of maximum likelihood. *Proceedings of the Royal Society of Edinburgh*, 1940, **60**, 64–82.

Lawley, D. The application of the maximum likelihood method to factor analysis. *British Journal of Psychology*, 1943, **33**, 172–175.

Lawley, D. A statistical examination of the centroid method. *Proceedings of the Royal Society of Edinburgh Section A*, 1955, **64**(2), 175–189.

Lazarsfeld, P. The logical and mathematical foundation of latent structure analysis. Chapter 10 in S. Stouffer, *et al., Measurement and prediction,* Studies in Social Psychology in World War II, Vol. IV. Princeton, N.J.: Princeton University Press, 1950.

Lehman, H. *Age and achievement.* Princeton, N.J.: Princeton University Press, 1953.

Lewis, D. *Quantitative methods in psychology.* New York: McGraw-Hill, 1960.

Licklider, J. Discussion of papers by Fleisher, A. and by Greenberger, M. In

H. Besher, *Computer methods in the analysis of large-scale social systems.* Cambridge, Mass.: Joint Center for Urban Studies of the Massachusetts Institute of Technology and Harvard University, 1965.

Lindzey, G. (Ed.) *Handbook of social psychology,* Vol. I, *Theory and method.* Reading, Mass.: Addison-Wesley, 1954.

Loehlin, J. "Interpersonal" experiments with a computer model of personality. *Journal of Personality and Social Psychology,* 1965, **2,** 580–584.

Loevinger, J. Theory and techniques of assessment. *Annual Review of Psychology,* 1959, 287–318.

Lord, F. Sampling fluctuations resulting from the sampling of test items. *Psychometrika,* 1955, **20,** 1–22.

Lorge, I. The fundamental nature of measurement. In E. Lindquist (Ed.), *Educational measurement.* (1st ed.) Washington, D.C.: American Council on Measurement, 1951.

Lorge, I., Tuckman, J., Aikman, L., Spiefel, J., & Moss, G. Problem solving by teams and by individuals in a field setting. *Journal of Educational Psychology,* 1955, **46,** 160–166.

Lovell, V. The human use of personality tests: a dissenting view. *American Psychologist,* 1967, **27,** 383–393.

Lucas, C. Analysis of the relative moment test by a method of individual interviews. *Bureau of Naval Personnel Research Report,* Contract Nonr-694, 00NR151-13 ETS, March, 1953.

Luce, R., & Perry, A. A method of matrix analysis of group structure. *Psychometrika,* 1949, **14,** 95–116.

Luhn, H. Automatic creation of literature abstracts. *IBM Journal of Research and Development,* 1928, **2,** 159–165.

Luhn, H. Keyword-in-context index for technical literature. *American Documentation,* 1960, **11,** 288–295.

Lyons, J. *A primer of experimental psychology.* New York: Harper & Row, 1965.

MacRae, D. Direct factor analysis of sociometric data. *Sociometry,* 1960, **23,** 360–371.

Maddi, S. Motivational aspects of creativity. *Journal of Personality,* 1965, **33,** 330–347.

Maron, M., & Kuhns, J. On relevance, probabilistic indexing and information retrieval. *Journal of the Association for Computing Machinery,* July, 1960, **7,** 216–224.

Marrazzi, M. Messengers of the nervous system. *Scientific American,* Feb. 1957, **196**(2), 87–94.

Marsh, S., & Perrin, F. An experimental study of the rating scale technique. *Journal of Abnormal and Social Psychology,* 1925, **19,** 383–399.

McClelland, D., & Atkinson, J. The projective expression of needs. I. The effect of different intensities of the hunger drive on perception. *Journal of Psychology,* 1948, **25,** 205–222.

McDonald, F. *Educational psychology.* (2nd ed.) Belmont, Calif.: Wadsworth, 1965.

McQuitty, L., *et al.* An approach to isolating dimensions of job success. *Journal of Applied Psychology,* 1954, **38,** 227–232.

Mefferd, R., Moran, J., & Kimble, J. Methodological considerations in the quest for a physical basis of schizophrenia. *Journal of Nervous and Mental Diseases,* 1960, **131,** 354–357.

Metfessel, N., & Sax, G. Systematic biases in the keying of correct responses on certain standardized tests. *Educational and Psychological Measurement,* 1958, **18,** 787–790.

Meyers, Russell. Personal communication, 1962.

Miles, M. (Ed.) *Innovation in education.* New York: Bureau of Publications, Teachers College, Columbia University, 1964.

Mill, J. S. *A system of logic.* New York: Harper and Brothers, 1874.

Miron, M., & Osgood, C. Language behavior: the multivariate structure of qualification. In R. Cattell (Ed.), *Handbook of Multivariate Experimental Psychology,* 1966, Chapter 27, 790–819. Chicago: Rand McNally.

Moreno, J. *Who Shall Survive.* New York: Beacon House, 1953.

Moreno, J., et al. (Eds.) *The sociometry reader.* Glencoe, Ill.: Free Press, 1960.

Morison, E. *A case study of innovation.* Alhambra, Calif.: C. F. Brown and Company, 1950.

Morris, J. *Principles of scientific and technical writing.* New York: McGraw-Hill, 1966.

Mosier, C. Symposium: The need and means of cross-validation. I. Problems and designs of cross-validation. *Educational and Psychological Measurement,* 1951, **11,** 5–11.

Mosteller, F., & Wallace, D. *Inference and disputed authorship: The Federalist.* Reading, Mass.: Addison-Wesley, 1964.

Murphy, G. (Ed.) *Human nature and enduring peace.* Third Yearbook of the Society for the Psychological Study of Social Issues. Boston: Houghton Mifflin, 1945.

Mursell, J. *Psychological testing.* New York: David McKay, 1947.

Nagel, E., Suppes, P., & Tarski, A. (Eds.) *Logic, methodology, and philosophy of science.* Stanford: Stanford University Press, 1962.

National Science Foundation. Characteristics of scientific journals, 1949–1959, *Report 64-20.* Washington, D.C.: Office of Science Information Service, 1964.

Naylor, T. *Computer simulation techniques.* New York: John Wiley, 1966.

Nehnevajsa, J. Soziometrische Analyse von Gruppen, Part II. *Kolner Zeitschrift für Soziologie,* 1955, **7,** 119–140.

Nehnevajsa, J. Sociometry: decade of growth. In J. Moreno, et al., *The sociometry reader,* Part IV. Glencoe, Ill.: Free Press, 1960.

Newell, A., & Simon, H. GPS—a program that simulates human problem-solving in *Proceedings of a conference on learning automata.* Munich, Germany: Oldenbourg, 1961.

Nosanchuk, T. A comparison of several sociometric partitioning techniques. *Sociometry,* 1963, **26,** 112–124.

Oppenheimer, R. Analogy in science. *American Psychologist,* 1956, **11,** 127–135.

Osgood, C. The nature and measurement of meaning. *Psychological Bulletin,* 1952, **49,** 197–237.

Osgood, C., Suci, G., & Tannenbaum, P. *The measurement of meaning.* Urbana, Ill.: University of Illinois Press, 1957.

Oswald, V. The automatic extraction and display of the content of documents. *Interim Report, PRC-R-91,* March 15, 1959, Contract AF30(602)-1748.

Parten, Mildred. *Surveys, polls, and samples.* New York: Harper and Brothers, 1950.

Pearson, K. Regression, heredity, and panmixia. *Philosophical Transactions of the Royal Society of London,* 1895, 187A, 253–318.

Perrin, P. *Writer's guide and index to English.* (3rd ed., rev.) Chicago: Scott, Foresman, 1959.

Perry, J., Kent, A., & Berry, M. *Machine literature searching.* New York: Interscience, 1956.

Platt, J. Strong inference. *Science,* 1964, **146,** 347–352.

Proctor, C., & Loomis, C. Analysis of sociometric data. In M. Jahoda, M. Deutsch, & S. Cook, *Research methods in social relations,* Part 2: Selected techniques. New York: Dryden Press, 1951.

Psychometric Society, Rules for preparation of manuscripts for Psychometrika. *Psychometrika,* 1967, **32,** 113–114.

Reisman, S. (Ed.) *A style manual for technical writers and editors.* New York: Macmillan, 1962.

Riffenburgh, R. A method of sociometric identification on the basis of multiple measurement. *Sociometry,* 1966, **29,** 280–290.

Riley, M., Riley, J., & Toby, J. (Eds.) *Sociological studies in scale analysis,* New Brunswick, N.J.: Rutgers University Press, 1954.

Roethlisberger, F., & Dixon, W. *Management and the worker.* Cambridge, Mass.: Harvard University Press, 1940.

Rogers, Anna. *Graphic charts handbook.* Washington, D.C.: Public Affairs Press, 1961.

Rorer, L. The great response style myth. *Psychological Bulletin,* 1965, **63,** 129–156.

Rosenthal, R. *Experimenter effect in behavioral research.* New York: Appleton-Century-Crofts, 1966.

Royce, J. A synthesis of experimental designs in program research. *Journal of General Psychology,* 1960, **43,** 295–303.

Rozeboom, W. Mediation variables in scientific theory. *Psychological Review,* 1956, **63,** 249–264.

Ruch, F. *Psychology and life.* (3rd ed.) Chicago: Scott, Foresman, 1948.

Ruebhausen, O., & Brim, O. Privacy and behavioral research. *American Psychologist,* 1966, **21,** 423–437.

Sackman, H. *Computers, system science, and evolving society.* New York: Wiley, 1967.

Savage, T. *The preparation of auto-abstracts on the IBM 704 data processing system.* Yorktown Heights, New York: International Business Machine Corporation, 1958.

Schaie, K. A general model for the study of developmental problems. *Psychological Bulletin,* 1965, **64,** 92–107.

Schmeckebier, L., & Eastin, R. *Government publications and their use.* Second edition. Washington, D.C.: Brookings Institute, 1961.

Schmid, C. *Handbook of graphic presentation.* New York: Ronald, 1954.

Schutz, R., & Baker, R. The experimental analysis of behavior in educational research. *Psychology in the Schools,* July, 1968. (In press)

Selltiz, C., Jahoda, M., Deutsch, M., & Cook, S. *Research methods in social relations.* Revised one-volume edition. New York: Holt, Rinehart and Winston, 1959.

Senders, V. *Measurement and statistics.* New York: Oxford University Press, 1958.

Sheldon, W., & Stevens, S. *The varieties of temperament.* New York: Harper and Brothers, 1942.

Sidman, M. *Tactics of scientific research.* New York: Basic Books, Inc., 1960.

Sidman, M. *Operant techniques.* Chapter 6 in A. Bachrach (Ed.), *Experimental foundations of clinical psychology.* New York: Basic Books, Inc., 1962.

Simon, H., & Newell, A. Models: their uses and limitations, pp. 66–83. In L. White (Ed.), *The state of the social sciences.* Chicago: University of Chicago Press, 1956.

Skinner, B. "Superstition" in the pigeon. *Journal of Experimental Psychology,* 1948, **38**, 168–172.

Skinner, B. The science of learning and the art of teaching. *Harvard Educational Review,* 1954, **24**, 86–97.

Skinner, B. A case history in scientific method. *American Psychologist,* 1956, **11**, 221–233.

Skinner, B. Why we need teaching machines. *Harvard Educational Review,* 1961, **31**, 377–398.

Spear, M. *Charting statistics.* New York: McGraw-Hill, 1952.

Steinzor, B. The development and evaluation of a measure of social interaction. *Human Relations,* 1949, **2**, 103–122.

Stephenson, W. The inverted factor technique. *British Journal of Psychology,* 1936, **26**, 349–361.

Stephenson, W. *The study of behavior: Q-technique and its methodology.* Chicago: University of Chicago Press, 1953.

Stern, G., Stein, M., & Bloom, B. *Methods in personality assessment.* Glencoe, Ill.: Free Press, 1956.

Stevens, N. The moral obligation to be intelligible. *Scientific Monthly,* 1950, **70**, 111–115.

Stiles, H. The association factors in information retrieval. *Journal of the Association for Computing Machinery,* 1961, **8**, 271–279.

Stouffer, S., *et al. Measurement and prediction.* Studies in Social Psychology in World War II. Vol. IV. Princeton, N.J.: Princeton University Press, 1950.

Symonds, P. On the loss of reliability in ratings due to coarseness of the scale. *Journal of Experimental Psychology,* 1924, **7**, 456–461.

Tasman, P. Indexing the Dead Sea scrolls by literary data processing methods. *International Business Machines,* New York: World Trade Corporation, 1958.

Taylor, D., Berry, P., & Block, C. Does group participation when using brainstorming facilitate or inhibit creative thinking? *Technical Report No. 1,*

NR150-166, Department of Industrial Administration and Department of Psychology, Yale University, 1957.

Thorndike, R. *Personnel selection test and measurement techniques.* New York: Wiley, 1949.

Thornton, G. The effect upon judgments of personality traits of varying a single factor in a photograph. *Journal of Social Psychology,* 1943, **18,** 127–148.

Thornton, G. The effect of wearing glasses upon judgments of personality traits of persons seen briefly. *Journal of Applied Psychology,* 1944, **28,** 203–207.

Thurstone, L. A law of comparative judgment. *Psychological Review,* 1927, **34,** 273–286.

Thurstone, L. *Multiple factor analysis.* Chicago: University of Chicago Press, 1947.

Thurstone, L., & Chave, E. *The measurement of attitude.* Chicago: University of Chicago Press, 1929.

Torgerson, W. *Theory and methods of scaling.* New York: Wiley, 1958.

Treloar, A. *Biometric analysis: an introduction.* Minneapolis, Minn.: Burgess Publishing Company, 1951.

Tryon, R. *Cluster analysis.* Berkeley, Calif.: University of California Press, 1939.

Turner, J. Money still isn't everything. *Science,* 1959, **30,** 533.

Turner, M. *Philosophy and the science of behavior.* New York: Appleton-Century-Crofts, 1967.

Underwood, B. Verbal learning in the educative processes. *Harvard Educational Review,* 1959, **29,** 107–117.

United States Government Printing Office. *Style manual.* (Rev. ed.) Washington, D.C.: USGPO, 1967.

Vickery, B. The structure of semantic coding: a review. *American Documentation,* 1959, **10.**

Wald, A. *Statistical decision functions.* New York: Wiley, 1950.

Walker, E. A second look at education. *School and society,* 1960, **88,** 44–48.

Walker, H. M., & Durost, W. N. *Statistical tales: their structure and use.* New York: Bureau of Publications, Teachers College, Columbia University, 1936.

Wallace, D. A case for and against mail questionnaires. *Public Opinion Quarterly,* 1954, **18,** 40–52.

Wallach, M., & Kogan, N. A new look at the creativity-intelligence distinction. *Journal of Personality,* 1965, **33,** 348–369.

Webb, E., Campbell, D., Schwartz, R., & Sechrest, L. *Unobtrusive measures: non-reactive research in the social sciences.* Chicago: Rand McNally, 1966.

Webster, H. Correcting personality scales for response sets or suppression effects. *Psychological Bulletin,* 1958, **55,** 62–64.

Wiener, B. *Statistical principles in experimental design.* New York: McGraw-Hill, 1962.

Wilks, S. Sample criteria for testing equality of means, equality of variances and equality of covariances in a normal multivariate distribution. *The Annals of Mathematical Statistics,* 1946, **17,** 257–281.

Williamson, S. How to write like a social scientist. *Saturday Review of Literature,* 1947, **30**(40), 17, 27–28.

Winer, N. *The human use of human beings: cybernetics and society.* Boston: Houghton Mifflin, 1960.

Withall, J. The development of a technique for the measurement of social emotional climate in the classroom. *Journal of Experimental Education,* 1949, **17,** 347–361.

Wolfe, D. *Factor analysis to 1940.* Psychometric Monographs, No. 3. University of Chicago Press, 1940.

Wollins, L. Responsibility for raw data. *American Psychologist,* 1962, **17,** 657–658.

Young, Pauline. *Scientific social surveys and research.* Englewood Cliffs, N.J.: Prentice-Hall, 1956.

Name Index

Subject Index

Abative scores, 278n
Ability, 268–69
Abstracting, automatic, 136–38
Abstracts, 150–51
Achievement, 268–69
Action research, 34, 71, 76, 405–6
Activity analysis, 65
Age scores, 277–78
Agreement, method of, 94
Alienation, coefficient of, 303–4
American Educational Research Association, 139
American Educational Research Journal, 154
American Library Association (ALA), 131, 132
American Library Association Glossary of Terms, 145n
American Psychological Association
  Committee on Ethics, 312
  Committee on Psychological Tests, 310
  Council of Editors, 398
  literature classification system, 135
  Publication Manual, 398
  and standardization of writing, 139
American Sociological Review, The, 398
American Sociological Society, 139
Analogy. *See* models

Annual Review of Physiology, 149
Annual Review of Psychology, 149
Anonymity of subjects, 409–10
A priori tests, 254
Aptitude, 268–69
Arithmetical mean, 191, 203–4
Armed Services Technical Information Agency (ASTIA), 139
Artificial intelligence, 133
Association
  definition of, 184
  graphic representation of, 215–17
  kinds of, 215–16
  statistical measures of, 184, 215–22
  testing for, 239–46
Association of Research Libraries, 139
Atlases, 155, 157
Atomic Energy Commission (AEC), 139
Authority, method of, 9
Average, 203
Average deviation, 206–7
Avoidance, 58

Barnum (P. T.) effect, 88–89
Base line manipulation, 57
Base rate of error, 306
Basic research, 409
Bayesian statistical inference, 43, 259–261